Ideas for Development

Robert Chambers

London • Sterling, VA

First published by Earthscan in the UK and USA in 2005

ISBN: 1-84407-088-3 paperback
      1-84407-087-5 hardback

Typesetting by JS Typesetting Ltd, Porthcawl, Mid Glamorgan
Printed and bound in the UK by Bath Press, Bath
Cover design by Susanne Harris

For a full list of publications please contact:

Earthscan
8–12 Camden High Street
London, NW1 0JH, UK
Tel: +44 (0)20 7387 8558
Fax: +44 (0)20 7387 8998
Email: earthinfo@earthscan.co.uk
Web: **www.earthscan.co.uk**

22883 Quicksilver Drive, Sterling, VA 20166-2012, USA

Earthscan is an imprint of James & James (Science Publishers) Ltd and publishes in association with the International Institute for Environment and Development

A catalogue record for this book is available from the British Library

Library of Congress Cataloging-in-Publication Data has been applied for

Printed on elemental chlorine-free paper

Contents

List of Figures, Tables and Boxes

Figures

Tables

Boxes

Preface

The idea for this book came from Jonathan Sinclair Wilson. It was to be a selection of things I had written. So I chose writings on themes in development which I thought had been neglected or poorly understood. Putting these into a book would, I imagined, be quick and straightforward. How wrong can you be? I soon found that I had to reflect and comment in the light of what had happened since the time of writing, and then think about the future.

I enjoyed that. But the more I wrote, and read, and sought advice, the more there was to think through and try to say. Much had changed and was continuing to change. It was, and remains, a struggle to keep up with the work of colleagues and with new experiences and insights in different parts of the world. Continuities there were, to be sure; and I was surprised, alarmed even, that I did not disagree more with what I had written earlier. But there were many new nuances, angles and twists, new ways of doing things, new words and concepts, and new priorities perceived. The earlier writings became points of departure. And review and reflection led to new questions and directions.

* * *

For all the fun of reading, reflecting and writing, I cannot separate this book from its context. I am so angry at what has been done, and continues to be done, in our world. It is hard to believe that the nightmare is real. We seem trapped in grotesquely unjust systems, more and more dominated by power, greed, delusion, denial, ignorance and stupidity, fuelled by symmetries of terrorism and fundamentalisms. For some Christians, especially in the US, this takes the form of a perversion in which the Sermon on the Mount and the Parable of the Good Samaritan have no place. The refusal of the US government to ratify the Kyoto Protocol or the International Court of Justice, its flouting of the United Nations in supporting Israel against Palestine, its illegal invasion of Iraq in which the UK joined, its arrogance as selfish and brutal world bully, when it could and should be an inspiring and responsible leader – these actions would be pathetic were they not so profoundly tragic. For many who like me have been born British, that 'our' government should have gone along with some of this in spite of our protests is a matter for fury and shame. And throughout we must distinguish people from their governments.

For some, the concerns of this book may seem a diversion from overarching issues like these. The reader may ask: 'why do you not deal with agricultural subsidies in the US and EU, armaments, climate change, corporate exploitation, corruption, currency speculation, the decimation of fish stocks, the destruction of forests, disarmament, the drugs trade, electoral systems in the US and the UK, the funding of political parties. . .?' – and this only gets as far as 'f' in an alphabetical listing. 'And why have you not focused more on poverty, exploitation and abuses of human rights? And why have you not dealt with solutions – Kyoto, fair trade, social audits, the Tobin tax, a tax on aviation fuels, a stronger United Nations, corporate accountability, more democratic voting systems in the United States and Britain. . .?'

There are three reasons. First, no book can be about everything. Second, it makes sense for me to write on the subjects about which I am less ignorant. And third, and this is the nub, all these big issues have to be and can be confronted at the personal level: it is through people behaving differently and taking action that they can be tackled and solutions sought, agreed and implemented. And in this, all of us, whatever the defeats and frustrations, have agency and the ability to act and change the world.[1]

So *Ideas for Development* is not directly about politics, trade, debt, international relations, governance, agricultural subsidies in the North, or the latest acronyms like PRSPs and MDGs. But indirectly it is about all of these, through the personal and collective agency that can act on them by people taking action. If development is good change, agency and power are the key to development. This applies to those with more power and wealth: they can choose the gains of living better by acting responsibly on our Earth and empowering those who are weaker and poorer. It applies too to those who are weaker and poorer: they can combine collectively in old and new ways to resist and reverse bad trends, and to struggle for a fairer, safer, more humane and more fulfilling world for themselves and for us all.

As people we are now, as never before, all in this together – all of us human beings, wildly different though our circumstances are – young men caged and tormented in Guantanamo Bay, corporate fat cats complacent in capital cities, child soldiers in African conflicts, middle class children of the OECD, skinny people scouring for scraps and obese people stuffed sick, those who see evil and those who see good, those who hate and those who love, fundamentalists and ecumenicals, believers and sceptics – a kaleidoscope of people, cultures, languages, faiths and beliefs. . . We see all these differences, but they are overwhelmed by what we have in common – our global habitat, our miraculous genes, our brains, the mystery of consciousness, our ability to reflect on ourselves, and our potential for selfishness and greed to be overturned by generosity and altruism.

* * *

As a title, *Ideas for Development* has two meanings: ideas which could be used in thinking about and taking action in development; and, more modestly, ideas that may themselves have scope to be developed. The analysis is meant to contribute to practical theory, to understandings that help in action. It is part of the struggle of trying to see how to do better in the processes we call development.

The puzzles, questions and suggestions are addressed to all of us who are in some sense development professionals. It does not have conventional boundaries. It is a typical fond and often delusional hope of an author that a book will be relevant and useful for many people in different places. In this case, let me dare to cast the net wide and include practitioners, academics, teachers and students in all professions and disciplines concerned with development in its varied aspects. Not least among these are those who work in lending and donor agencies, in governments, and in national and international NGOs, both in programme, finance and human resources departments, and in headquarters and the field. Many of the themes concern us all.

Let me alert the reader to the structure. Part 1 of each chapter is something I wrote in, and for, an earlier context. Part 2 then reflects on what has happened since, and present ideas for the future. The abstracts in italics at the head of each part can give a quick overview of the book as a whole. The subheadings and index are meant to make it easy to trace topics across chapters. The glossary is a guide to the meanings that I try to be consistent in giving to some words, and both the glossary and the references are meant to make it easier for readers to find out more.

Let me warn the reader about some of the biases and limitations inherent in the book. My practical field experience in development has been largely limited to eastern Africa and South Asia. The examples on which I draw are mainly from sub-Saharan Africa and Asia, with some from the Caribbean, and rather few from Latin America. A further weakness is that I am vulnerable to optimism and enthusiasm, and often tend to see what looks good, promising and consensual rather than nastiness and conflict. My tendency, increasing I fear with age, to assert without evidence may be especially dangerous in our world of accelerating change. And for all the horrors and injustices of war, poverty, power and greed, I cannot resist seeking ways to make what we do not just fulfilling but fun.

★ ★ ★

Writing has made me see old things in new lights. It has also been an experience of exploration and discovery. Writing, reflecting and rewriting have been stimulated and informed by ongoing and evolving discussions and debates. Many of the ideas originate from others. In the course of all this, the following three threads or themes have emerged.

The first is 'words and practical concepts'. Commitment, continuity and irreversibility (Chapter 1) and administrative capacity (Chapter 2) are argued to be underperceived, underused and undervalued in decision-making and action. Congruence, power and relationships are seen as part of a new agenda in development (Chapter 7).

The second thread or theme is 'institutional change'. The potential here is for good change through devising and changing procedures and adopting principles (Chapter 3), participation at all levels and with innumerable creative applications

(Chapter 4), and better understanding of issues and actions in scaling up (Chapter 5).

The third theme is 'agency and reflexivity'. Agency implies that individuals can make a difference, whoever and wherever they are (except perhaps those in solitary confinement). Reflexivity refers to critical self-awareness of one's predispositions, relationships and interactions in the formation of knowledge. We can reflect on ourselves, our mindsets, beliefs and values. Our attitudes and behaviour (Chapter 6) are basic to development and yet still largely overlooked. Responsible well-being (Chapter 7) can be augmented by good use of agency, and reflection on the effects of our actions and non-actions, especially on the part of those with power and wealth.

The ideas here are directions not destinations. Some may lead to false trails. Let me hope that some at least will serve as provocations, signposts or springboards leading to action, reflection, learning and good change. In development, we will always live in flux. We will always need to learn and unlearn in order to do better. We will always travel and never arrive. Ideas for development will always be creatures of their time and context. For all their limitations, let me dare to hope that, in however small a way, some of the ideas in this book will help to take us further.

Robert Chambers
June 2004

Notes

1   This short, simple and adequate definition of agency is from VeneKlasen and Miller (2002, p55), which on the same page also gives an excellent description of different forms of power (power over, with, to, and within).

Acknowledgements

To Publishers

For permission to reproduce all or part of the earlier works I am grateful to Routledge and Kegan Paul, the *International Development Review* (now *Development*), Weltforumverlag, the Scandinavian Institute of African Studies and Kumarian Press, IDS Sussex, *PLA (Participatory Learning and Action) Notes, Social Change* (New Delhi), and *World Development*. The publications and dates were:

Chapter 1 Final section of Chapter 12 'Some practical implications', in *Settlement Schemes in Tropical Africa: A Study of Organisations and Development* (Routledge and Kegan Paul, London, 1969, pp257–262), and final section of Chapter M 'The Perkerra irrigation scheme: A contrasting case', in *Mwea: An Irrigated Rice Settlement in Kenya, 1973* (edited jointly with Jon Moris, Weltforumverlag, Munchen, 1973, pp361–364).

Chapter 2 Reproduced from 'Executive capacity as a scarce resource', *International Development Review* (June, 1969, pp 5–8), republished as *Communication Series 42* (IDS, Sussex, February, 1970). (The journal continues as *Development*, published by Palgrave Macmillan for the Society for International Development. See www.sidint.org/development.)

Chapter 3 Précised and edited extracts from Chapter 1 'Points of departure and directions', in *Managing Rural Development: Ideas and Experience from East Africa* (Scandinavian Institute of African Studies, Uppsala, 1974, pp12–34; reprinted by Kumarian Press, New Hartford, Connecticut, 1985).

Chapter 4 Précised and edited extracts from Chapter 4 'Managing local participation: rhetoric and reality', in *Managing Rural Development* (op cit, pp84–113).

Chapter 5 'Making the best of going to scale', *PLA Notes* (24, 1995, pp57–61).

Chapter 6 'Behaviour and attitudes: a missing link in agricultural science', in V. L. Chopra, R. B. Singh and Anupam Varma (eds) *Crop Productivity and Sustainability: Shaping the Future* (Proceedings of the Second International Crop Science

Congress, Oxford and IBH Publications, New Delhi and Calcutta, 1998, pp809–818), republished in *Social Change* (Delhi) (vol 28, nos 2 and 3, June–September, 1998, pp108–121).

Chapter 7 'Editorial. Responsible wellbeing: A personal agenda for development', *World Development* (vol 25, no 11, 1997, pp1743–1754).

In précising and editing the two sections which draw on *Managing Rural Development* I have cut out tedious supporting evidence and tried to be faithful to the original while making it easier to follow. With the Chapter 7 editorial, references that were 'forthcoming' have been given in their later published form. Elsewhere I have almost always left the original text unchanged. This shows up in the jarring male-biased syntax from the 1960s and 1970s, which reminds us of how far we had to come in gender awareness.

In two cases I have changed the original words. The first is in the 1969 article which is the basis for Chapter 2. The term *executive capacity* had a brief life but gave way to *administrative capacity*, which I have substituted. The second is in Chapter 5 on scaling up. After much searching and hesitation, I have changed *benign virus* to *meme*. Several people objected that viruses could not be benign. So I toyed with *benign gene* and *yeast* but both these misled by implying organisms. Then at a late stage I discovered Richard Dawkins' *meme*. This useful word, meaning an idea, habit, skill, story or any kind of behaviour that is copied from person to person by imitation, expresses what I want to mean. But some may still prefer *benign virus* as a more familiar metaphor.

To People

For valuable comments on the whole book I am grateful to Alan Fowler, Jethro Pettit, Jules Pretty and Ian Scoones. To Ian I owe a special thanks for detailed suggestions on individual chapters and for a critique that led to major revisions. Across all the chapters, Philip Middleton gave capable support in searching for sources and checking and commenting on detail. Others who have been generous with helpful comments, suggestions and contributions include Fiona Chambers, Jenny Chambers, Andrea Cornwall, Rosalind Eyben, John Gaventa, Leslie Groves, Rosemary McGee, Lyla Mehta, Sammy Musyoki, Celestine Nyamu, Kath Pasteur, Garett Pratt, Patta Scott-Villiers, Daniel Were and Farhana Yamin.

For quick and efficient work I wish to thank Laura Cornwell for scanning text and Shereen Karmali for preparing it for publication. Jethro Pettit gave good advice and support throughout. Jane Stevens, as ever, contributed in many helpful ways in dealing with the text and managing the process through to publication. I also thank all those at Earthscan who accommodated my wishes, dealt patiently with detail and contributed good ideas.

A good deal comes from learning with and from ActionAid (now ActionAid International). I am grateful to many in that family for sharing experience, and for the stimulation and challenge of keeping up with a fast-moving, committed and innovative INGO. My thanks go to all, and not least over the years to David Archer, Rosalind David, Sam Joseph, Robin LeMaitre, Antonella Mancini, Harsh Mander, Charles Owusu, Salil Shetty, Ramesh Singh, Koy Thomson and Karen Twining, all of them thinkers and actors who combine courage and creativity with radical realism.

From Leslie Groves and Rachel Hinton and the contributors to their volume *Inclusive Aid* (Earthscan, 2004) have come many thoughts and ideas, not all of the sources of which are acknowledged in the text.

Much in writing a book depends on people and places. I owe so much to my colleagues in the Participation Group and others in IDS who have helped to change the feel and culture of the institute as a place to work; to Gauriben and Bhavnaben, local leaders of SEWA in Gujarat, for the inspiration of their lives, and to Reema Nanavaty and Praful Patel for much learnt from them; to people casually encountered in the north-west of Scotland whose friendliness restored my faith in human nature in the face of bad things done by many of the powerful in our world; and above all to Jenny Chambers for ideas, tolerance, and the music of violin and piano while I was writing.

I thank all of the above, and apologize to and thank all others whom I have not managed to name. They have contributed insights, ideas and 'Aha!'s. They have saved me from mistakes. Still, some of them may not agree with all I have written and, as ever, responsibility for views expressed and for errors of fact and judgement that remain is mine and mine alone.

And finally, I cannot resist naming the places where I had the good fortune to be when writing this preface: Gairloch in Wester Ross, Scotland; Kingston near Lewes in England; and Yabello in southern Ethiopia.

Robert Chambers
June 2004

List of Acronyms, Abbreviations and Organizations and Addresses

AAA	Aashray Adhikar Abhiyan, U55/B Lane 4, Shakarpur, Delhi 110092, India Tel: 91 (0) 11 202 2440 or 492 2455 Email: righttoshelter@hotmail.com; homeless@vsnl.net www.indev.nic.in/delhishomeless
ABC	attitude and behaviour change
ActionAid	The Gambia
ActionAid, India	C-88 South Extension – II, New Delhi 110 049, India Tel: 91 11 516 40571 Email: aaindia@actionaidindia.org www.actionaidindia.org/index.html
ActionAid, UK	ActionAid, Hamlyn House, MacDonald Road, Archway, London N19 5PG, UK Tel: 44 (0) 20 7561 7561 Fax: 44 (0) 20 7272 0899 Email: mail@actionaid.org.uk www.actionaid.org
AI	appreciative inquiry
ALPS	Accountability, Learning and Planning System (ActionAid)
APMSS	Andhra Pradesh Mahila Samatha Society (India), Plot No 39, Aravinda Nagar Colony, Donalguda, Hyderabad 500029, India Tel: 91 40 763 0057
APNSD	Association for the Promotion of North–South Dialogue Kaiser-Friedrich-Strasse, 53113 Bonn, Germany Tel: 49 (0) 228 103 337 Fax: 49 (0) 228 24 39 532 Email: edp@exposure-nsd.de www.exposure-nsd.de
BMZ	Bundesministerium für wirtschaftliche Zusammenarbeit und Entwicklung, Friedrich-Ebert-Allee 40, 53113 Bonn, Germany Tel: 49 (0) 228 535 3000
Bretton Woods Project	The Bretton Woods Project, Hamlyn House, MacDonald Road, Archway, London N19 5PG, UK www.brettonwoodsproject.org
CARE	151 Ellis Street, Atlanta, Georgia 30303, US Tel: 1 (0)404 681 2552 Fax: 1 (0) 404 589 2651 E-mail: info@care.org www.care.org

CBO   community-based organization
CD   community development
CDR   complex, diverse and risk prone (applied to farming)
CDRA   Community Development Resource Association (Cape
                        Town), PO Box 221 Woodstock 7915, South Africa Tel:
                        27(0) 21 462 3902 Fax: 27(0) 21 462 3918 Email:
                        info@cdra.org.za www.cdra.org.za
CDS   Centre for Development Studies, University of Swansea,
                        Singleton Park, Swansea SA2 8PP, Wales, UK Tel: 44
                        (0)1792 295 332 Fax: 44 (0)1792 295682 Email:
                        h.lewis@swansea.ac.uk www.swan.ac.uk/cds
CGIAR   Consultative Group for International Agricultural
                        Research (comprises a consortium of donors, secretariat
                        and the International Agricultural Research Centres)
CLTS   community-led total sanitation
COP   control-oriented, or control-over, procedure, principle or
                        process
Council for Social   Sangha Rachana, 53 Lodi Estate, New Delhi 110003,
Development   India
CSO   civil society organization
CTA   Technical Centre for Agricultural and Rural
                        Cooperation, Postbus 380, Wageningen, The Netherlands
                        Tel: 31 (0) 317 467100 Fax: 31 (0) 317 460067 Email:
                        cta@cta.int www.cta.int
DAC   Development Assistance Committee
Danida   Royal Danish Ministry of Foreign Affairs, 2, Asiatisk
                        Plads, DK-1448 Copenhagen, Denmark Tel: 45 33 92 00
                        00 Email: um@um.dk www.um.dk
DELTA   Development Education and Leadership Teams in
                        Action
DFID   Department for International Development, 1 Palace
                        Street, London SW1E 5HE, UK Tel: 0845 300 4100
                        (local call rate from within the UK) or 44 1355 84 3132
                        (from outside the UK) Fax: 44 (0) 1355 84 3632
                        Email: enquiry@DFID.gov.uk www.DFID.gov.uk
DSC   Development Support Centre, Nr Government
                        Tubewell, Bopal, Ahmedabad 380 058, India Tel: 91 (0)
                        2717 235994, 235995, 235998 Fax: 91 (0) 2717)
                        235997 Email: dsc@satyam.net.in
Earthscan   Earthscan, 8–12 Camden High Street, London, NW1
                        0JH, UK Tel: 44 (0)20 7387 8558 Fax: 44 (0)20 7387
                        8998 Email: earthinfo@earthscan.co.uk www.earthscan.
                        co.uk
EDP   Exposure and Dialogue Programme
EU   European Union
FAO   United Nations Food and Agriculture Organization

FCO	Foreign and Commonwealth Office of the UK government
FPR	farmer participatory research
FFS	Farmer Field School (facilitated series of meetings of farmers in which they learn from their own experiments and observations)
FTP	*Forests, Trees and People* Newsletter, FTP Network, SLU Kontakt, Swedish University of Agricultural Sciences, Box 7034, 750 07 Uppsala, Sweden Tel: 46(0)18 672 001 Fax: 46(0)18 671980 Email: ftpp.network@kontakt.slu.se www.trees.slu.se
FOE	Friends of the Earth, 26–28 Underwood Street, London N1 7JQ, UK Tel: 44 (0) 20 7490 1555 Fax: 44 (0) 20 7490 0881 Email: info@foe.co.uk www.foe.co.uk
FPR	farmer participatory research
Greenpeace, UK	Greenpeace, Canonbury Villas, London N1 2PN, UK Tel: 44 (0)20 7865 8100 Fax: 44 (0)20 7865 8200 Email info@uk.greenpeace.org www.greenpeace.org.uk/
GDP	gross domestic product
GIS	geographic information systems
GM	genetically modified
GRIP	Grassroots Immersion Programme (World Bank)
GTZ	Deutsche Gesellschaft für Technische Zusammenarbeit, Gmbh, Postfach 5180, D-65726 Eschborn, Germany Tel: 49 (0)6196 79 0 1709 Fax: 49 (0) 6196 70 6109
HelpAge International	PO Box 32832, London N1 9ZN, UK Tel: 44 (0)20 728 7778 Fax: 44 (0)20 7713 7993 Email: hai@helpage.org www.helpage.org
IBRFP	Indo-British Rain-fed Farming Project
IDRC	International Development Research Centre, PO Box 8500, Ottawa, Ontario K1G 3H9, Canada Tel: 1 (0)613 236-6163 Fax: 1 (0) 613 563-2476 Email: info@idrc.ca www.idrc.ca
IDS	Institute of Development Studies, University of Sussex, Brighton BN1 9RE, UK Tel: 44 (0)1273 606261 Fax: 44 (0)1273 621202 www.ids.ac.uk; bookshop website: www.ids.ac.uk/ids/bookshop/index.html; participation group website: www.ids.ac.uk/ids/particip/
IFAD	International Fund for Agricultural Development, Via del Serafico, 107, 00142, Rome, Italy Tel: 39 0654591 Email ifad@ifad.org www.ifad.org/
IFIs	international financial institutions (notably, the World Bank, IMF, Asian Development Bank, African Development Bank and Inter-American Development Bank)

IFPRI	International Food Policy Research Institute, 2033 K Street NW, Washington, DC 20006-1002, US Tel: 1 (0) 202 862 5600 www.ifpri.org
IH/AA	International HIV/AIDS Alliance, Queensberry House, 104–106 Queen's Road, Brighton BN1 3XF, UK Tel: 44 (0)1273 718 900 Fax: 44 (0)1273 718 901 Email: mail@aidsalliance.org www.aidsalliance.org
IIED	International Institute for Environment and Development, 3 Endsleigh Street, London WC14 0DD, UK Tel: 44 (0) 20 7388 2117 Fax: 44 (0) 20 7388 2826 Email: info@iied.org www.iied.org
IIMA	Indian Institute of Management Vastrapur, Ahmedabad, India
IIRR	International Institute of Rural Reconstruction Y. C. James Yen Centre, Silang, Cavite, the Philippines Tel 63 (0) 46 414 2417 Fax 63 (0) 46 414 2420 Email publications@iirr.org www.iirr.org/
IISD	International Institute for Sustainable Development, 161 Portage Street East, Winnipeg R3B OY4, Canada Tel: 1 204 958 7700 Fax: 1 204 958-7710 Email: info@iisd.ca www.iisd.org/
ILAC	Institutional Learning and Change (network of initiatives in the International Agricultural Research Centres)
ILEIA	Centre for Information on Low External Input and Sustainable Agriculture, PO Box 64, 3830 AB Leusden, The Netherlands Tel: 31(0)33 432 60 11 Fax: 31(0)33 495 17 79 Email: ileia@ileia.nl www.ileia.org
ILO	International Labour Organization
IMF	International Monetary Fund
INGO	international non-governmental organization
INTRAC	International NGO Training and Research Centre, PO Box 563, Oxford OX2 6RZ, UK Tel: 44 (0) 1865 201851 Fax: 44(0)1865 201852 Email: info@intrac.org www.intrac.org/
IPGRI	International Plant Genetic Resources, Institute Via dei Tre Denari 472/a 00057, Maccarese, Rome, Italy Tel: 39 06 61181 Fax: 39 06 61979 Email: ipgri@cgiar.org www.ipgri.cgiar.org
IPM	Integrated Pest Management
IRC	International Water and Sanitation Centre, PO Box 2869, 2601 CW Delft, The Netherlands Tel: 31 (0) 15 291 2939 Fax: 31 (0) 15 219 0955 Email: general@irc.nl www.irc.nl
ISNAR	International Service for National Agricultural Research Now (2004), IFPRI-ISNAR Programme, PO Box 5689, Addis Ababa, Ethiopia. Tel: 251 (0)1 463215 Fax: 251

	(0) 1 461252 Email: ifpri-AddisAbaba@cgair.org www.ifpri.org
IT Publications	ITDG Publishing, Bourton Hall, Bourton-on-Dunsmore, Rugby CV23 9QZ, UK Tel: +44 (0) 1926 634 400 Fax: +44 (0) 1926 634 406
IWMI	International Water Management Institute, PO Box 2075, Colombo, Sri Lanka Tel: 94 (0)1 787404 Fax: 94 (0)1 786854 Email iwmi@cgiar.org www.iwmi.cgiar. org
JFM	Joint Forest Management (India)
LAST	lowers as teachers
LEAT	Lawyers' Environmental Action Team, Kings Palace Hotel Building, Sikukuu Street, Kariakoo Area, PO Box 12605, Dar es Salaam, Tanzania
LFA	logframe (or logical framework) analysis
Lokayan	13 Alipur Road, Exchange Building, Civil Lines, Delhi 110 054, India
MA	Millennium Ecosystem Assessment
MDBS	multi-donor budget support (Ghana)
MDG	Millennium Development Goal
MKSS	Mazdoor Kisan Shakti Sanghatan (Movement for the Empowerment of Peasants and Workers, Rajasthan)
M&E	monitoring and evaluation
MP	member of parliament
MRDP	Mountain Rural Development Programme (Vietnam)
MYRADA	No 2 Service Road, Domlur Layout, Bangalore 560 071, Karnataka, India Tel: 91 (0) 80 535 3166 Fax: 91-80-5350982 Email: myrada@vsnl.com www.myrada.org
NEF	New Economics Foundation, 3 Jonathan Street, London, SE11 5NH, UK Tel: 44(0)20 7820 6300 Fax: 44(0)20 7820 6301 Email info@neweconomics.org www.neweconomics.org
NEPAN	Nepal Participatory Action Network, PO Box 13791, New Baneshwor, Kathmandu, Nepal Tel: 977 01 478 1955 Fax: 977 01 478 0959 Email: nepan@mos.com.np www.nepan.org.np
NESA	New Entity for Social Action, 93/2 Charles Campbell Road, Cox Town, Bangalore 560 005, India Tel/fax: 91 (0) 80 2548 3642/7654/5134 Email: nesa@vsnl.com
NGO	non-governmental organization
NIB	National Irrigation Board (Nairobi, Kenya)
NNGO	national non-governmental organization
NNP	non-negotiable principle
NOVIB	NOVIB – Oxfam Netherlands, Postbus 30919, 2500 GX Den Haag, The Netherlands Tel: 31 70 3421777 www.novib.nl/en/
NRM	natural resource management

NWDP	National Watershed Development Programme (India)
OBA	obligation-based approach
ODI	Overseas Development Institute, 111 Westminster Bridge Road, London SE1 7JD, UK Tel: 44(0)20 7922 0300 Fax: 44(0)20 7922 0399 Email odi@odi.org.uk www.odi.org.uk
OECD	Organisation for Economic Co-operation and Development, rue Andre Pascal, 75775 Paris Cedex 16, France Email: webmaster@oecd.org www.oecd.org
OHCHR	Office of the High Commissioner for Human Rights, United Nations Office at Geneva, 1211 Geneva 10, Switzerland InfoDesk@ohchr.org for general enquiries www.ohchr.org/english/
Oxfam GB	274 Banbury Road, Oxford OX2 7DZ, UK Tel: 44 (0) 870 333 2700 Fax: 44 (0) 1865 312600 Email: enquiries@oxfam.org.uk www.oxfam.org.uk/
PALS	Participatory Action Learning System
PAR	power and relationship
PCI	Pastoralists' Communication Initiative, PO Box 20768, addis Ababa 1000, Ethiopia Tel: 251 1444 196 Email: globalpastoralistgathering@yahoo.co.uk
PEP	participation- or people-empowering procedure, principle or process
PIA	programme implementing agency (India National Watershed Development Programme)
PIM	Participatory Irrigation Management (India)
PIM	Programming and Implementation Management system
PLA Notes	'The world's leading informal journal on participatory approaches and methods': a publication of the IIED, which began as *RRA Notes* (1988) for issues 1–21, continued as *PLA Notes* in issues 22–49, and is now *Participatory Learning and Action* for issues 50 onwards. Available in hard copy or on CD-ROM from the IIED. New issues free of charge (as of 2004) to non-OECD organizations and individuals. Write to *PLA Notes* Subscriptions, Earthprint Limited, Orders Department, PO Box 119, Stevenage SG1 4TP, UK. Email iied@earthprint.com www.planotes.org/
PLA	participatory learning and action (term designed to be more inclusive of participatory methodologies than implied by the term PRA on its own)
PM	participatory methodology
PM&E	participatory monitoring and evaluation
Population Council/ Horizons Program	4301 Connecticut Avenue NW, Washington, DC 20008, US Tel: 1 (0) 202 237 9400 Email: horizons@pcdc.org www.popcouncil.org/horizons

PPA   participatory poverty assessment

PRA   participatory rural appraisal (occasionally participatory rapid appraisal, and now increasingly participatory reflection and action)

PRA/PLA   a compromise term for PRA and other somewhat similar participatory methodologies, especially as included in the publication *PLA Notes*

PRAM   participatory rights assessment methodology

PRAXIS   Institute for Participatory Practices, C – 75, South Extension Part II, New Delhi – 100 049, India Tel/Fax: 91 (0) 11 5164 2348 2 Pataliputra Colony, Patna 800 013, India Tel/Fax: 91 (0) 612 262 027 www.praxisindia.org/

PRRP   participatory review and reflection process (in ActionAid's ALPS)

PRSP   poverty reduction strategy paper

PSIA   poverty and social impact analysis

PTD   participatory technology development

PUA   participatory urban appraisal

QEH   Queen Elizabeth House, 21 St Giles, Oxford OX1 3LA, UK Tel 44 (0) 1865 273600 Fax 44 (0) 1865 273607 Email: library@qeh.ox.ac.uk www.qeh.ox.ac.uk/

RBA   rights-based approach

RCPLA   resource centre for participatory learning and action

REFLECT   Regenerated Freirian Literacy through Empowering Community Techniques Email: reflect-action@yahoo.co.uk www.reflect-action.org

RIPS   Rural Integrated Project Support Programme (Tanzania)

RRA   rapid rural appraisal

SACOSAN   South Asia Conference on Sanitation

SAP   structural adjustment programme

SDC   Swiss agency for Development and Cooperation, Freiburgstrasse 130 CH-3003, Bern, Switzerland Tel: 41 31 323 2795 Fax: 41 31 324 1695 www.deza.admin.ch

SEWA   Self-employed Women's Association, Krishna Bhuvan, opp. Sakar-II, Town Hall Road, Ahmedabad 380 006, India Tel: 91 (0) 79 6577115/6580414 Fax: 91 (0)79 658 7708 Email: mail@sewa.org www.sewa.org

Sida   Swedish International Development Cooperation Agency (formerly SIDA), SE-105 25 Stockholm, Sweden Tel: 46 8 698 500 00 Email info@sida.se www.sida.se

SOSOTEC   self-organizing systems on the edge of chaos

SRDP   Special Rural Development Programme (Kenya)

SSC   Statistical Services Centre, University of Reading, Harry Pitt Building, Whiteknights Road, PO Box 240, Reading

	RG6 6FN, UK Tel: 44 (0) 118 378 8025 Fax: 44 (0) 118 975 3169 Email: statistics@lists.reading.ac.uk www.rdg.ac.uk/ssc/
Sustain	Alliance for Better Food and Farming, 94 White Lion Street, London N1 9PF, UK Tel: 44 (0) 20 7837 1228. Fax: 44 (0) 20 7837 1141 Email: sustain@sustainweb.org www.sustainweb.org/
SWAp	sector-wide approach (where funders support the development of a sector)
TNC	transnational corporation
TOT	transfer of technology
UN	United Nations
UNDP	United Nations Development Programme, 1 United Nations Plaza, New York 10017, US Fax: 1 212 906 5364 www.undp.org/
UNHCR	United Nations High Commissioner for Refugees
UNICEF	United Nations International Children Emergency Fund
UNRFSD	United Nations Research Institute in Social Development
UPPAP	Uganda Participatory Poverty Assessment Process
USAID	United States Agency for International Development
VERC	Village Education Resource Centre, Anandapur, Savar, Dhaka, Bangladesh Tel: 880 771 0412 Email: verc@bangla.net
VIKSAT	Vikram Sarabhai Centre for Development Interaction, Nehru Foundation for Development, Thaltej Tekra, Ahmedabad 380 054, Gujarat, India Tel: 91 (0) 79 2685 6220 Fax: 91 (0) 79 2685 2360 Email mail@viksat.org www.viksat.org
VIP	very important person
VIP	Village Immersion Programme
VSO	Voluntary Service Overseas 317 Putney Bridge Road London SW15 2PN, UK Tel: 44 (0) 20 8780 7200 Fax: 44 (0) 20 8780 7300 Email: enquiry@vso.org.uk www.vso.org.uk/
WCD	World Commission on Dams
WCED	World Commission on Environment and Development
WDR	World Development Report
World Bank	1818 H Street NW, Washington, DC 20433, US Tel: 1 (0) 202 473-1000 Fax: 1 (0) 202 477-6391 www.worldbank.org
WDT	watershed development team
World Neighbours	4127 NW 122nd Street, Oklahoma City, Oklahoma 73120-8869, US Tel: 1405 752 9700 Fax: 1 405 752 9393 Email: info@wn.org www.wn.org

WRI   World Resources Institute, 10 G Street, NE (Suite 800),
                       Washington, DC 20002 USA Tel: 1 202 729 7600 Email:
                       swilson@wri.org for general enquiries www.wri.org/
ZOPP   Ziel-Orienterte Projekt Planung

Glossary

Words mean different things to different people. To make what is being said clearer to myself and to the reader, here are some meanings. They are not necessarily what the words *ought* to mean, only what I have tried to be consistent in using them to mean.

Agency: Refers to individual people, and the ability to act and change the world.

Aid agency: An organization that provides development support from outside a country, whether multilateral, bilateral or international non-governmental organization (INGO), and whether funder, lender, donor, provider of technical assistance or service, or engaged in advocacy.

Congruence: The quality of corresponding, fitting together, being mutually consistent, agreeing in nature. It is used to describe relations between some or all of personal orientation and behaviour, organizational cultures, procedures, relationships, professed values and professional norms. From the Latin *congruere*: to meet together, agree.

Diffuse: To spread or cause to spread in many directions. See also disseminate, replicate, scale up and spread.

Disseminate: To scatter or spread, as with sowing seeds. See also diffuse, replicate, scale up and spread.

Donor: An organization that provides grants for development. Donors are typically bilateral government aid agencies and INGOs.

Farmer Field School: A facilitated series of meetings of farmers in which they learn from their own experiments and observations.

Funder: A provider of funds, whether grants or loans.

Institutional:	Refers to formal and informal rules, regulations, norms, incentives and regularities of practice.
Integrated Pest Management:	Participatory methodology for groups of farmers to observe, monitor, map, experiment, analyse, plan and act collectively to use mainly biological controls for crop pests.
Irreversibility:	The quality of being impossible or difficult to restore or return to a former condition (Alcamo et al, 2003, p212).
Joint Forest Management:	Programme in India intended to promote participatory management of the forest resource jointly between local communities and the forest department.
Lender:	An organization that provides loans for development. Typically, these are multilateral banks such as the World Bank, the IMF, the Asia Development Bank and so on.
Livelihood:	A means of living, and the capabilities, assets and activities required.
Logframe (or logical framework) analysis:	System of planning adopted and for the time being still required by a number of lender and donor agencies.
Lowers:	People who, in a specific context, are subordinate or inferior to uppers. A person can be a lower in one context and an upper in another. Compare uppers.
Meme:	An idea, habit, skill, story or any kind of behaviour that is copied from person to person by imitation (Dawkins, 1976, cited in Blackmore, 2003, p22). In this book, memes are often part of a methodology, but can spread independently, as for example 'ask them' from PRA.
Method:	A way of doing something.
Methodology:	A system of methods and principles.
Non-negotiable:	A principle or practice about which an organization or individual is not willing to compromise.
Paradigm:	A pattern of mutually consistent and supporting concepts, values, methods, behaviours and relationships.

Participatory irrigation management:	Used to describe programmes in which various degrees of control of water distribution, maintenance and funds are handed over to or vested in groups or communities of irrigators.
Participatory rural appraisal:	(Occasionally participatory rapid appraisal, and now increasingly participatory reflection and action.) A family of approaches, behaviours and methods for enabling people to conduct their own appraisal, analysis, planning, action, monitoring and evaluation, which often includes activities in small groups and showing things visually; also applied to urban, organizational and other contexts, and described by some as a philosophy.
Party numbers:	Numbers derived from the use of participatory approaches and methods.
Power and relationships:	Words used to describe partnership, empowerment, ownership, participation, accountability and transparency.
Procedure:	A way of acting or progressing in a course of action, typically with a sequence of actions. Procedures belong to the category of rules only when they are authoritatively required.
Programme:	A general initiative with broad funding, often in a sector and involving the budget of a sectoral ministry, implemented at national or sub-national level, and without the local boundaries of many projects.
Project:	A bounded and focused initiative with dedicated funding. A project may be multi-sectoral in content and limited to a local area, or it may be an initiative on a specific topic.
Rapid rural appraisal:	Family of methods and approaches to enable outsiders to learn quickly and efficiently about rural realities.
Reflexivity:	Refers to critical reflection and self-awareness concerning knowledge and action. This includes the part that our predispositions, relationships and interactions play in the formation, framing and representation of knowledge, the reasons why we act as we do, and the effects of our actions and non-actions (see also Eyben, 2003a, p21).
Replicate:	To make a copy of or to be spread as copies (see also diffuse, disseminate, scale up and spread).
Rule:	An authoritative regulation or required procedure. Authoritative regulations (e.g. many laws) are rules but are not, or only in part, procedures. Compare procedure.

Scale out: To spread from one application or activity to another or to increase the types of participation (after Gaventa, 1998, p155).

Scale up: To spread through increasing the scale of an organization or programme and the quantity of participation – for example, the number of participants or of places where it takes place (after Gaventa, 1998, p155).

Spread: To extend or cause to extend over a wider space and/or to other individuals, groups, communities, organizations and/or other levels and/or contexts. Spread is used to include diffuse, disseminate, replicate and scale up, as well as scale out, scale down (in its sense of spreading downwards), and scale down and out.

Uppers: People who in a context are dominant or superior to lowers. A person can be an upper in one context and a lower in another. Compare lowers.

1

Words and Ideas: Commitment, Continuity and Irreversibility

All words are pegs to hang ideas on (Henry Ward Beecher, 1887).

Part 1 presents writing on settlement schemes in tropical Africa from the late 1960s and early 1970s. Part 2 reviews subsequent developments with settlement schemes, and then explores and develops wider contemporary meanings, relevance and applications for three words and ideas from the earlier experience: commitment, continuity and irreversibility.

Part 1: Learning from Experience

In the 1950s and 1960s, settlement schemes were conspicuous in tropical Africa. Many of them were politically committing and effectively irreversible. Once settlers had been introduced they were difficult to abandon. Schemes considered failures became robust dependent survivors. Many arguments could be mustered to justify continuing support, although this was often at high financial cost to governments. The Perkerra Irrigation Scheme in Kenya was one such project which by almost any criteria should never have been started, and once started, not continued. It performed disastrously but became increasingly difficult to abandon. In project appraisal, the political irreversibility of commitment is a neglected aspect of risk, and varies by type of project.

Introduction: Settlement schemes in tropical Africa (2004)

In the Sub-Saharan Africa of decolonization and early national independence, much prominence was given to agricultural settlement schemes. They seemed to promise win-win solutions to political demands, perceived pressures of population, and the need to produce more from the land. With many origins, taking many forms, having high political priority, and being bounded and visible, they were attractive to researchers. I was one of those who succumbed to the temptations they presented. I started my research on the fragile and vulnerable Perkerra Irrigation Settlement in Kenya, and then concentrated on its stronger sibling, Mwea. The Mwea Irrigation Settlement had several advantages. It was by most criteria more successful; it had a stable water supply and in irrigated rice a reliable crop and a protected market; it was better organized; it had a high profile and was frequently visited, being a convenient distance from Nairobi for VIPs;[1] and, for the indolent PhD student it had the advantage of being well documented, with time series tables which could (I hasten to add, with due acknowledgement) be transposed easily to make a thesis look good, at least to any examiner too pressed for time to look deeply. Many researchers were attracted to Mwea, and the managers were so interested and articulate that we were able to combine to produce a book with 13 chapters and 529 pages (Chambers and Moris, 1973).[2]

In parallel, numerous studies of settlement schemes were undertaken in other countries, especially Sudan, Zimbabwe (Southern Rhodesia as it was), Zambia (Northern Rhodesia as it was), Tanzania, Uganda, Nigeria and Ghana. These provided a wonderful collection for comparisons. Much of what was learnt is now of mainly historical interest. However, analysis at the time pointed to three neglected angles or themes which were important then and remain important and still relatively neglected: commitment, continuity and irreversibility. The two extracts of studies from this period, which follow, raise practical questions not only about projects, but also about policies and programmes promoted and pursued by lenders, donors and Governments in the 2000s.

Conclusions from *Settlement Schemes in Tropical Africa* (1969)

Risks and irreversibility of commitment[3]

A neglected aspect of evaluation, which has far wider application than merely to settlement schemes, concerns the relationship between risks and irreversibility of commitment.

Settlement schemes, especially those that are more complex in system and costly in capital, are high-risk undertakings. They share with non-settlement approaches to agricultural development the uncertainties of innovations, weather, pests and markets, and the disruptions of rapid turnovers in senior staff. In addition, however, they have to face other serious risks and difficulties which do not have to be borne in non-settlement situations. The land on which settlement takes place may be available for settlement for the simple reason that it is marginal or unsuitable for cultivation. The locations of many settlement schemes, often with poor communications and far from the services of urban centres, raise costs and the difficulties of management. There is a danger that both organizational and productive effectiveness will be restrained by the inbuilt incompatibilities of complex schemes, by the cancelling out of managerial and settler efforts, in the games of enforcing and beating the system. Moreover, adaptations of schemes to ensure the continued presence and participation of settlers may have to be made through increased payouts or through services which at best, reduce revenue to government and, at worst, add to a loss. In addition, where government withdrawal is intended, there is a high risk that it will take longer than expected. At the point at which implementation of a settlement scheme or programme is considered, all these factors, all of them implying economic risks, should be weighed.

But these risks do not present the complete picture. Wherever a government starts a programme or project the actual risks are compounded by the extent to which the commitment to maintain the programme or project is irreversible. The process of commitment can be lengthy, subtle and insidious. It begins with an opportunity and a vision. These may arise from a disturbance in the relationships of men[4] and land, or the perception of unoccupied land: the Mwea [in Kenya], inviting development after the Kenya Land Commission's recommendations; the bush of South Busoga [in Uganda] after its evacuation in the first decade of this century; the narrow strip of uncultivated land on the edge of the Rift Valley at Upper Kitete [in Tanzania]; the cleared bush of Kongwa, Urambo and Nachingwea after the Groundnut Scheme fiasco [in Tanzania]. Or the opportunity may be provided by a resettlement operation which presents a captive population which can be directed into a new agricultural system: the displacement of Halfawis by the Aswan Dam, [in Sudan] was exploited through resettlement on the controlled irrigation scheme at Khasm-el-Girba; and the evacuees from the Volta Lake were thought to provide 'a unique opportunity to wean an appreciable proportion of Ghana's farmers from the wasteful, fragmented, and shifting system of agriculture to a settled and improved pattern of farming'.[5]

The opportunity attracts and nourishes the idea of a scheme. In such conditions a personal commitment can develop in a man of vision like Simon Alvord in Rhodesia or Chief Akin Deko in Nigeria. Funds are obtained for surveys: the surveys that are carried out are themselves committing. Where their findings are marginal, as was the United Nations Special Fund survey of the proposed Tana Irrigation Project in Kenya,[6] further investigations are called for. It becomes increasingly difficult to turn back. Once funds have been made available for a substantive scheme, the successive activities of planning, construction, settlement and production draw after them deeper and deeper personal, departmental and political commitments. The establishment of settlers sets a seal on commitment at a higher level, making abandonment extremely difficult and the use of protective political arguments extremely easy. The full repertoire of defences to ensure scheme or programme survival can now be brought into play. Moreover, officials and politicians in circumstances such as these may regard government funds as fair game, as an ecological feature to be exploited much as a river might be tapped for irrigation water. The risks involved in the original initiation of a project are now more obvious: risks not merely that it would fail, but that having failed it would survive as a parasite that could not be shaken off or killed.

The issues involved in a decision to terminate a scheme are, of course, not simple. Those responsible for the decisions may not even agree about whether the amount of money already sunk in a project is a relevant consideration. Attitudes and ideas are sufficiently confused and contradictory for irrational elements to have free play. It is extremely difficult, for example, to see the large quantities of fine onions grown on the Perkerra Scheme in Kenya, and to compare the green irrigated fields with the surrounding desert, and at the same time to sustain a conviction that the Scheme should be abandoned. Running water through channels and onto dry land, growing abundant crops where there was only bare soil and barren bush before, and enabling people to enjoy a level of prosperity they have never previously known, appear inherently and incontrovertibly good. It is Isaiah's vision:

> *The wilderness and the solitary place shall be glad for them; and the desert shall rejoice, and blossom as the rose (The Bible).*

To suggest closure seems ignoble and destructive, an affront to the aspirations and achievements of the human spirit. If a neutral visitor can have this feeling, it may be expected all the more in those whose lives and work are bound up in a scheme. Yet the power of this emotion multiplies the risks of starting projects of this sort through making it exceptionally difficult to close them down however uneconomic they may prove.

There is, indeed, a strain of Utopianism in most complex settlement schemes. Often there is an idealized view of the human situation that settlement will create. In colonial times this was often the stabilized African, fixed and controlled on a piece of land. Since independence, it has varied: in West Africa it has been an urban farmer; in Kenya, a sturdy yeoman; in Tanzania, a co-operative worker. Another Utopian aspect is the frequency with which stresses and breakdowns are not anticipated: as Apthorpe (1966, p23) has pointed out, provision is often lacking either for failure of the social system or for mechanical repairs. Again, it is very common for the targets for land preparation, settlement, production and withdrawal to be wildly optimistic and for achievements to fall far short of them. These features are partly explicable in terms of the self-delusion of men who are transported by a vision. When an ideal is pursued by a whole community, as in some communal economy schemes, it may make a scheme feasible through the sacrifices the participants are prepared to accept; but when the vision is only in the mind of the initiator, as it has been with most complex settlement schemes, the effects are often a sequence of unrealistic estimates, uneconomic measures and personal commitments which comprise part of the risks of the project.

Resisting temptation[7]

Since all these disadvantages have applied in the past they can be expected to continue to apply in the future, and should be taken into account in assessing proposals for settlement schemes and similar agricultural projects. It is not enough to carry out evaluations[8] which consider only those economic factors which can be quantified; it is necessary also to include administrative factors and the probable motivations and behaviour of the actors involved. Allowance has to be made, for example, for the expected patterns of settler and managerial behaviour, for departmentalism, for staff discontinuities and for the inbuilt incompatibilities of scheme systems. Moreover, comparisons with alternative approaches to agricultural development should take into account the high opportunity costs of trained staff and the expected ease or difficulty of abandoning a project or programme if it proves uneconomic. When all this is done the case against high capital and complex settlement schemes becomes stronger than when only conventional cost-benefit criteria are used. While this does not mean that such schemes should be ruled out altogether, it does mean that they should be approached with greater care and understanding.

Where a settlement scheme is unavoidable, and where there is a choice of type to be adopted, there is much to be said on organizational grounds for the simplest type of scheme that is compatible with the circumstances of settlement. The simpler approaches are relatively undemanding of scarce administrative and technical capacity, and engage it for shorter periods. They involve relatively low risk and low commitment. Moreover, schemes with individual holdings exploit the drives of property ownership and individual incentive which can make productive the labour which is the most abundant unused resource in much of the third world. The simpler schemes also require intermediate levels of organization corresponding with the intermediate technology which may also be appropriate. If the beginning is ambitious, a complex organization may collapse and find equilibrium at a lower level; but if the beginning is modest, a more complex technology and organization can grow up organically and gradually. For example, the tractors appearing on Chesa in Rhodesia and on the Kenya Million-Acre Schemes as a result of settler initiative represent a self-sustaining upward movement in which productivity may increase without heavy government investment or commitment. If such developments are to be possible, it is important that advisory and technical services be available when needed, and even more important that the system of land tenure adopted should allow for future flexibility in farm size. Given such flexibility, it is usually safer and sounder to develop piecemeal from an existing base, whether this is farmers already on their land or settlers, already on a scheme, than to attempt radical transformation in one long step.

Settlement schemes, particularly those which are complex in system, will remain temptations. Because of their creative possibilities, they will continue to find energetic and enthusiastic sponsors. Because of their visibility, clear boundaries, organizational coherence, and Utopian overtones, they will no doubt continue to attract successive colonization – by administrators who negotiate their emergence, constructors who build them, agriculturalists who manage them, settlers who populate them, and in their wake foreign aid personnel and research students[9] in various capacities – all of whom will find satisfaction in occupying a bounded and identifiable territory. What is vital is not that such schemes should be avoided on principle, but that those who act in these situations should appreciate what is happening. It is especially important that those who make development decisions should understand themselves well enough to be able to compensate in their acts of judgment for the strong pull of the psychological attractions of such schemes, and should be able to see clearly the risks they entail and the benefits that might accrue from alternative uses of the resources involved. Exceptional restraint and imagination are needed among politicians and civil servants if the lure of the big scheme is to be neutralized so that a balanced and realistic assessment can be made. Perhaps it is fortunate that so many African politicians and civil servants possess and farm their own land. While this may be distraction it may also satisfy desires for property and territory, so that they are less prone than their expatriate predecessors to seek such satisfaction through their work. It may in the long term enable them to take more balanced views of policy and to appreciate more fully the alternatives that exist. Certainly it is important to recognize that the choices are neither clearcut nor easy. It is not enough, as was done in Kenya before independence (Government of Kenya, 1962, p1), to quote Gulliver's report of the views of the King of Brobdignag:

> *And he gave it for his opinion, that whoever could make two ears of corn or two blades of grass to grow upon a spot of ground where only one grew before, would deserve better of mankind, and do more essential service to his country than the whole race of politicians put together (Swift, 1726, Chapter 7).*

For the issues are less simple: they include whether, with the same resources, many more ears of corn, or many more blades of grass, might not be grown in other ways or in other places; and whether those politicians and civil servants who make major policy decisions have the freedom, the insight and the courage to choose those other ways or places, however unspectacular they may be.

Learning from project pathology: The case of Perkerra[10]

Introduction (2004)

The Perkerra Irrigation Scheme in Kenya was launched precipitously in 1952 during the Mau Mau Emergency. It was known that there had been a proposal for irrigation on the Perkerra river, but the 1936 exploratory report could not be found. Detainees were placed in camps on the site and employed on road building and preparing works and fields for irrigation. From the start, capital and recurrent costs were high and revenue negligible. Tenants were settled but many left. Areas irrigated consistently fell far short of those targeted. Agricultural and marketing problems were intractable. In 1959 with just over 100 settler families, it was decided to close the scheme down. The decision was then reversed and changed to running on a care and maintenance basis for three years. By 1962 closure had become more difficult. The scheme was instead expanded to try to make it less of a recurrent burden on government. By 1967, with over 500 settler families, commitment had become even harder to reverse, and the scheme continued, with cross-subsidies from an economically successful sister scheme in another Province, the Mwea Irrigation Settlement.

Lessons from Perkerra (1973)

Many lessons could be culled from the Perkerra experience. Only some of the more obvious and important will be mentioned here.

In the first place, the high costs and risks of hasty development with inadequate surveys are abundantly clear. To embark upon a major irrigation project with little knowledge of river flows and with what limited knowledge there is indicating unreliability; without any assurance that a cash crop can be grown and marketed;

without experience of tenants' performance; and without any pilot project – these are to court disaster. Moreover, one effect of such ignorance is to encourage over-investment in unprofitable directions which have then to be abandoned: the 430 acres of basin irrigation which were overrun by nutgrass, and the extensive cultivation, before adequate trials had been carried out, of tomatoes, groundnuts and even onions. When, as has occurred at Perkerra, most of the experimental work is carried out not on a research station but with tenants on their plots the risks of failure are multiplied by the dangers of tenant dissatisfaction, of loss of confidence in the management, of absenteeism, and ultimately of permanent departure from the scheme.

Second, when a complex project requiring a favourable coincidence of several interdependent factors begins to run into trouble, difficulties tend to compound one another. On Perkerra, lack of water has sometimes limited the acreage that can be irrigated, in turn limiting returns to tenants and revenue to the Scheme, increasing the dependence of the Scheme on subsidy and aggravating the problems of tenant management. Unstable onion prices have affected tenant and staff morale as well as revenue. Evictions and other disciplinary measures to secure effective tenant performance may be partly self-defeating by reducing the tenants' sense of security on a scheme and encouraging them to spend more time and energy on their off-scheme activities. Such chain reactions as these make heavy demands both on managerial skill and patience and on the financial resources of a parent organization. Where a scheme has, like Perkerra, a generally unfavourable physical environment and narrow technical limits of tolerance, able management may reduce or cushion some of these reactions but is unlikely always to overcome them. In these circumstances, financial support of various forms becomes the variable that is easiest to manipulate, with the result that a scheme is maintained but at a heavy cost to the rest of the economy.

A third lesson emerges from the process of creeping commitment to the Scheme, starting with the first ideas of replacing the indigenous irrigation which had been destroyed [by a flood in 1919], leading to preliminary surveys and then to a situation in which the idea of irrigation was at large and ready to be seized on whenever an opportunity presented itself. There was never any meeting or moment at which a decision to implement the Scheme was clearly taken. Even the siting of the camp at Marigat was only partly associated with the possibility of irrigation. But the very presence and use of the labour; the posting in of staff; the allocation of funds; the physical developments such as building the camp, construction of the weir, and land preparation; the deepening enthusiasms of individual officials and the increasing involvement of departmental interests; the visits of VIPs to inspect progress; the selection, induction and management of tenants; the growing and marketing of crops – all these in multiple ways progressively secured the Scheme as a permanent entity and strengthened its capacity to survive. It became increasingly difficult to close it down. To abandon the Scheme would have meant to accept failure, to write off heavy government expenditure, and to have to resettle tenants, transfer staff, and save a number of faces. It was always easier and involved less immediate acceptance of responsibility to allow the Scheme to continue. The chance in 1962 when the tenants could have been resettled in the former European highlands was allowed to slip, and by 1968, with some 500 tenants to varying degrees dependent on the Scheme, closure had become politically and humanly difficult even to contemplate.

A fourth observation is that the true costs of a project like Perkerra may usually be greater than their apparent costs. To evaluate any scheme is, of course, a complex operation with several quantifiable and many unquantifiable factors to be taken into account; and, to be sure, even with Perkerra there have been hidden benefits – learning on the part of the tenants, including their introduction to a cash economy; experience gained by government officials; investment of incomes generated by the scheme; indirect government revenue; and seasonal employment, among others. But schemes which are heavily committing in terms of capital expenditure, departmental and individual involvement, and political interest and support tend to receive a perverse protection: the levels of external support and of tolerance in evaluation vary inversely with their economic performance. Except in stringent economic evaluations, 'success' for a scheme like Perkerra is defined in less exacting terms than for an economically more viable scheme such as Mwea. Protective standards of assessment and hidden subsidies are easily combined to give a false impression of favourable economic performance. Moreover, a scheme such as Perkerra has to be evaluated not just in isolation but in terms of benefits foregone from alternative uses of the resources involved – especially capital, managerial competence and effort, and labour. Had the sum of over £500,000 and the human resources invested in Perkerra by 1968 been used in other ways, the results might have been substantial benefits instead of continuing indefinite liabilities.

These four lessons – the costs and risks of haste and ignorance; the compounding of problems in complex projects; the irreversibility of the creep of commitment; and the high true costs of poor projects – combine in a criterion applicable to choices in agricultural development. The Perkerra Irrigation Scheme, with its requirement from the start of complex and continuing organization involving government support, can be contrasted as a policy with the implications of an incident in the history of the Scheme. In1961 the Manager noted that 'A tenant was given a sample of Taboran maize seed which ripened about four weeks earlier than the local variety and yielded at a rate of 11 bags per acre. The tenant concerned was besieged by others wanting seed to plant.' This was, of course, an event on an irrigation scheme, but the implications are wider and apply to non-irrigated agriculture. The contrast here is between on the one hand a major project like Perkerra which requires ongoing government involvement, and on the other programmes like the introduction of a new seed variety which can be one-shot efforts. In a major project the risks and liabilities are shouldered by government: if the project succeeds, government is obliged to continue to service and manage it; if it fails, it may prove politically and administratively impossible to abandon it. In the one-shot programme, however, the risks and liabilities are accepted by the individual farmers: if the innovation succeeds, it is propagated without further government intervention; if it fails, it is quickly and easily abandoned by the farmers without additional cost or administration for government.

There are, of course, a great many other considerations which bear on policy choices; but capital and administrative capacity are typically scarce resources to be used sparingly; and in choosing between alternative approaches to agricultural development there is a case, other things being equal, for preferring those which are cheap, simple, administration sparing and easy to withdraw from to those which are expensive, complex, administration intensive and committing.

It is not enough merely to be aware of these considerations; there must also be a climate and machinery in government to make sure that they are taken into account. In British colonial government in East Africa in the 1950s there was a relative absence of economic criteria in official thinking and a readiness to support the initiative of officers at the local level when they promoted projects. There was sympathetic backing in the Kenya central government for the vision and enthusiasm of the civil servants at provincial and district level who energetically launched the Perkerra Irrigation Scheme. Entrepreneurial capacity of the sort which they demonstrated is certainly an asset to a government, but as the Perkerra story shows it can be dangerous unless it is controlled. What is needed is a powerful and perceptive presence in governments which, while not stifling local initiatives, ensures that schemes as unpromising as Perkerra are never begun; for it is far easier to prevent a bad project than, once it has been started, to close it down.

Part 2: Developments, Concepts and Discourse (2004)

The legacy of Perkerra and its need for subsidies has continued into the 21st century. After the 1960s agricultural settlement projects became less favoured in most parts of the world. Big dams and other projects were increasingly recognized to have high human costs in the many who were displaced, dispossessed and inadequately compensated. Champions within the World Bank and internationally networking activists made lenders, donors and, to a lesser degree, governments, more aware of human costs and more reluctant to fund dams and other projects which displaced people.

Commitment to projects and continuity of aid agency and developing country government staff, created conditions for innovation, learning and changes in practices and policies. In the 1990s, as aid agencies and governments shifted their priorities to programmes and policy, there were human and ethical costs as projects were abandoned. With the new priority to influence policy so continuity, partnerships, relationships, understanding and trust became and remain more important than ever.

Irreversibility is neglected in conventional economics compared to risk and uncertainty. The Precautionary Principle in environmental and other decision-making recognizes irreversibility, but it remains underdeveloped as a practical concept. Far more attention should be paid to human activities like quarrying and mining, which are controllable but have effects that are irreversible.

Commitment, continuity and irreversibility are Cinderella words and concepts, which merit more analysis and prominence in development discourse and practice.

Agricultural settlement in decline: Twists in the tale

After the 1960s, agricultural settlement schemes became less common and less conspicuous. In Africa, their problems and costs, the less land available and political factors combined to reduce their popularity and prevalence. In Zimbabwe, although earlier settlements had been quite successful, the greed and intransigence of the later political leadership prevented an orderly programme that might have served equity and peace by transferring land from European to African farmers, as had been achieved during the 1960s in Kenya. More generally, the withdrawal of the state from administered development such as settlement schemes has been so widespread and so comprehensive that we find ourselves now, in the 21st century, looking back on the 1960s as another world.

Legacies of earlier irreversibility have, though, lingered on, with twists in their tails and tales. The Perkerra Irrigation Scheme has survived. For a long time it was probably still a costly recurrent liability.[11] Reportedly its performance improved somewhat in the 1990s with diversification of crops, and contracts from the Kenya Seed Company for growing hybrid maize seed. A research station was established at Perkerra, jointly under Horticulture Research International and the Kenya Agricultural Research Institute. The irrigated area remained low. Papaya and maize were grown on 350 hectares out of the 2350 hectares designated for irrigation. Perkerra was reported to perform relatively well compared with other irrigation schemes such as Hola, West Kano and Bunyala, which were 'virtually dead' (Akumu, 2002). But the vulnerability and financial dependence of the scheme continued.[12] In December 2002, floods in the Perkerra River destroyed the weir and 259 houses. 'The embankment of the water reservoir which used to flow through the canal to the scheme, and which was built way back in 1954, collapsed under pressure from the waters' (Njeru, 2003). So the history of vulnerability to flash river flows, which in 1919 broke the sill of rock on which the Njemps built their brushwood weir for irrigation, was repeated in 2002. For reconstruction the NIB (National Irrigation Board) was to put in US$20,000[13] and the United Nations Development Fund Kenya, US$100,000.[14] It remains to reflect on the relative ease and low cost of closure in 1959 and for a few following years when there was the option of resettlement in the (as they were) 'White Highlands', and then on the continuing costs of rehabilitating and maintaining the Scheme. For each generation of government officers, and for local politicians, the easier course was always to keep it going. Moreover, commitment can hardly have been diminished by the Scheme's location in the constituency of Daniel arap Moi, the long-time powerful President of Kenya. The opportunity cost of the funds devoted annually to maintaining the project must have been high, indeed.

The history of the rice-growing Mwea Irrigation Settlement is a contrast. From its inception, it was economically more viable. But, increasingly, during the 1990s farmers' incomes were hit by dues deducted by the management, heavy charges for milling and marketing, and competition from cheap rice imports with liberalization. The centralized administration, seen in earlier days as a strength of the Mwea scheme (Giglioli, 1973; Veen, 1973), gave scope for much resented corruption. Cross-subsidization also took place from Mwea to Perkerra and other schemes. In 1998, farmers rebelled and took over the management, milling and marketing. The next year two young men were shot dead in a confrontation with police (Kenya Human Rights Commission, 2000). In 2003, negotiations were in progress to establish a new relationship between the Mwea settlers and the NIB. Interestingly, the very continuity of the draconian rules and centralized organization of the scheme can be seen as a factor leading to the Mwea rebellion, and its end, for a time, as an administered scheme. The lack of democracy, accountability and transparency, earlier thought to be a strength, had become a liability.

Worldwide, administered agricultural settlement schemes became rare during the 1980s and 1990s. There were fewer resources, less land and the state was in retreat. In India, large- and medium-scale irrigation did not settle farmers, but supplied water to farmers on the land that they already farmed. In Israel, the idealistic and communal organization of the *kibbutzim* eventually came to an end. Elsewhere, the state disengaged where it could from responsibilities to settlers.

Some exceptions to these trends do, though, stand out, ranging from the tightly administered to the near chaotic. For example, on Palestinian land, the closely protected, notoriously illegal Israeli settlements were precisely intended to be irreversible forms of appropriation and colonization, excluding Palestinians from their land. In Sri Lanka, in a humane but closely administered tradition, the Mahaweli Development Authority continued to settle families on newly irrigated land and to provide a high level of special services. In Southern Africa, there were limited programmes of buying out large European farmers and settling African smallholders. In Ethiopia, despite the bad record of earlier population transfer and resettlement, the early 2000s saw renewed attempts to resettle people from the highlands to the lowlands. At the chaotic extreme, in Zimbabwe, self-settlement of self-designated freedom fighters took place on commercial farms from 2001 onwards, carried out by force and with disastrous economic consequences.[15] In their different extreme ways, the Israeli and Zimbabwean governments pursued or permitted settlement with gross disrespect for human rights and legality.

As for refugees, in 2003 there were, in the world, some 20 million persons identified by the UNHCR (United Nations High Commissioner for Refugees) as 'people of concern' (UNHCR, 2003). Of these, 12 million were refugees. The remainder included internally displaced persons, stateless persons, asylum seekers and returnees. Refugees were concentrated especially in Africa, Thailand, Iran and Pakistan. Earlier, during the 1970s and 1980s, hundreds of thousands of refugees had been established on agricultural settlements, notably in Tanzania at Mpanda and Ulyankulu. But during the early 21st century, almost all refugees were either dispersed among host populations or held and supported in camps. New agricultural small farming settlement projects for refugees and displaced people followed the global trend and had become rare.

'Oustees', rights and ease of exit

The retreat from agricultural settlement during the 1970s and 1980s was paralleled by neglect by governments of responsibilities for people displaced by dams, roads and other infrastructure projects. In 1994 and subsequently, those displaced were estimated to number worldwide about 10 million a year (World Bank, 1994a; Mehta, 2002a). With dams, the word 'oustee' came to be used. Earlier, during the 1960s, Nuba and others who lost homes and livelihoods to Lake Nasser, created by the Aswan Dam in Sudan, were given the option of resettlement on the new irrigation project of Khasm-el-Girba; and some 80,000-odd people displaced by the Volta Dam in Ghana were offered resettlement in new communities, which a majority of them took up (Chambers, 1970). But no such responsibilities were similarly discharged in India on any scale, despite the building of many dams and the displacement of hundreds of thousands of marginal and politically impotent poor people. Over four decades in India, 20 million people were displaced by development programmes and forced into involuntary resettlement. Seventy-five per cent of them were without 'rehabilitation', and the vast majority were impoverished by the process (Cernea, 1997). Michael Cernea and his colleagues at the World Bank, and Thayer Scudder and others outside it, showed how damaging displacement was to lives and livelihoods, how widely ignored were the rights and interests of those displaced and how much more numerous they often were than was acknowledged in project documents. As a vigorous and committed group, they were instrumental in drawing up and gaining agreement for the World Bank's policy on involuntary resettlement, issued in 1980. This major step forward was influential both inside and outside lending and donor agencies, though less so with governments. At the same time, internationally networking activists made lenders, donors and, to a lesser degree, governments, more aware of the human costs of dams and other projects that displaced people and more cautious about funding them (Brown and Fox, 2001). Evaluation and research have improved understanding of involuntary resettlement and of what could and should be done (e.g. Cernea 1997, 1999; Picciotto et al, 2001). The World Bank code, international networking and lobbying by civil society, the new human rights agenda, and predictable protests and adverse publicity have increasingly combined to discourage lenders and donors from supporting big projects that displace many people.

The Sardar Sarovar Dam in India, and the Narmada River project of which it was a part, is a case in point. It developed into a high-profile saga with dramatic civil disobedience. The Indian Central and State Governments failed to meet World Bank requirements for compensation and resettlement of the people who were to be displaced. When a distinguished international panel laid bare misinformation and abuse (Morse and Berger, 1992), the World Bank withdrew its support. The Indian Government pressed ahead on its own, facing a long and high-profile campaign of protest led by Medha Patkar and supported by the novelist and activist Arundhati Roy (Roy, 2002).

Other withdrawals of international aid followed for other dams. The UK government backed off from supporting the Pergau Dam in Malaysia when the World Development Movement brought a case against it and a UK court ruled that it was illegal. In 2001, in the face of strong criticism, it also withdrew support from the Ilisu Dam in Turkey, which would have displaced a large Kurdish population and inundated historical sites. Meanwhile, the World Commission on

Dams (WCD, 2000; Imhof et al, 2002) set new standards for inclusiveness and consultation, having among its members both Medha Patkar, who as an activist had been on hunger strikes in protest against the Narmada project, and Goran Lindahl, the Chief Executive of one of the world's largest engineering firms (Dubash et al, 2001, p1). The WCD's remarkable consensus report presents a new policy framework that gives prominence to the rights of people adversely affected by dams (WCD, 2000, p240ff).

In this new climate, international funders, though less so governments (as India's Narmada and China's Three Gorges projects illustrate) have become more circumspect in keeping open options for exit from such projects. With the earlier settlement schemes in Africa, irreversibility of commitment was linked to political and moral responsibility to those who had been settled. After a phase of neglect, such obligations are now again more extensively recognized and accepted. Commitments have become more public and open to scrutiny, more frequently debated and less firm. High-profile opposition has made it easier for funders to withdraw support. The irreversibility found in earlier projects is now less common because of greater awareness of the consequences of displacement and the opposition that new projects provoke.

Commitment, continuity and creativity

Changes in commitment can be understood in the context of the well-recognized changes in development policies and practices of both national governments and aid agencies.

To summarize these in broad brush terms, during the 1950s and 1960s, infrastructure projects were prominent – for example, industrial plants, harbours, roads, railways, telecommunications, airports and irrigation projects. The 1970s became a heyday for area-based initiatives, including Integrated Rural Development Projects promoted and supported by the World Bank (World Bank, 1988). These did not have settlers, only small farmers or pastoralists already on the land; so when many failed, as they did especially in Africa, they were easier to abandon. Unlike Perkerra, they passed into history on the ground, leaving a legacy of disillusion, debts and staff housing. In aid policies during the 1980s and 1990s, structural adjustment programmes became prominent, required by lenders for the repayment of debts. And the 1990s were marked by shifts towards sector programmes and direct budget support, debt relief, good governance, participation and human rights policies proclaimed as pro-poor. As the new century came in, lenders and donors were abandoning field projects and focusing on policy.

Some big projects, though, if well surveyed, fairly administered and then irreversibly implemented, are needed and justified. I was probably wrong, on an ILO mission to Sri Lanka in 1978, to muster arguments against the Accelerated Mahaweli Development Project to increase hydropower and irrigation and to brand it Sri Lanka's *Concorde*.[16] And who now would wish to argue that it would have been better not to have built the Volta Dam or the Aswan Dam? Some big projects are right. Some are not. And much depends upon how well and fairly they are undertaken.

All of this may be quite well accepted. Perhaps less explored is the changing significance of dimensions of commitment and continuity and their implications for practice. In what follows, much of the focus is on aid agencies, and their priorities, activities and relations with governments; but much also applies to governments themselves. Let us follow the historical sequence and start with projects.

Commitment and continuity with projects

For exploring the relevance of irreversibility and commitment, especially with projects, insights come from Albert Hirschman's classic *Development Projects Observed* (Hirschman, 1967). From a study of 11 World Bank-supported projects, all of which had serious problems, Hirschman put forward his hypothesis of the 'Hiding Hand'. This was the principle that those proposing and planning projects habitually underestimate the difficulties that will be encountered, but that this may be just as well, since they also habitually underestimate the creativity that can be mustered to overcome them. With hindsight, the Perkerra experience suggests that Hirschman may himself have made an underestimate – of the costs of 'creativity', for these can include recurrent costs of staff, subsidies and protection, additional infrastructure and the pre-emption of scarce administrative capacity (see Chapter 2). Still, in Hirschman's view, too little commitment and too easy withdrawal could mean premature abandonment before there was time to learn and improve. This, he argued, was a weakness of agricultural projects, which were easier to abandon than, say, electric power or railways. Irreversibility, in his view, could be an asset because of the creativity it stimulated and the learning to which it gave rise.

Hirschman's thesis about commitment, continuity, learning and creativity is borne out by the RIPS (Rural Integrated Project Support) Programme in Lindi and Mtwara Regions in Tanzania (Freling, 1998; Groves, 2004). Finland supported a programme there for some 20 years, much of it installing water supplies. By all accounts, these were a substantial failure. Accepting failure and abandoning the project would have been easy to justify. But the Tanzanian Government and the Finns did not give up. They hung in and tried again. There was then a continuity of involvement and commitment of key individuals on both the Finnish and the Tanzanian sides, which fostered a good spirit of long-term trust, understanding and partnership.[17] In 1993, an Indian trainer, Kamal Kar, introduced participatory rural appraisal (PRA) through a series of workshops (Johansson, 2000). Participatory approaches gained strong support from the two Regional Commissioners, Colonel Nsa Kaisi and Colonel Anatoli Tarimo (and, subsequently, his successor A.Y. Mgumia). Implications for institutionalization and bureaucratic change were recognized (Kar, Adkins and Lundstrom, 1998; Swantz, 1998). The programme was transformed. Innovations multiplied (Freling, 1998). To take but one example, participatory media were developed (de Waal, 2000) through a village radio network and through participatory video. These enabled people to make claims and supported mediation between competing or conflicting stakeholders. Participatory video was used in reforming a fish market, forcing officials to use the correct procedures and leading to the person who was 'eating' the tax collected being transferred elsewhere (Nyamachumbe, 2000). It also played a key part in the turbulent process of ending the dynamiting of coral to catch fish (Swantz, Ndedya and Masaiganah, 2001). Another innovation was to introduce PRA with participatory planning and action in most of the communities in the two regions. The results of this community-level participation were so successful that, through a sequence of national workshops, it influenced Tanzania-wide policy. Results included a permanent secretaries' two-day retreat on participation (MRALG, 1999) and a later one for regional administrative secretaries. Throughout the 1990s, the donor agency and the Tanzania government were co-learners and co-beneficiaries. Had they given up after the earlier 20 years of failure, the positive lessons from pioneering participation would never have been learnt and national policies and practices would not have been influenced.

The Sida-supported Mountain Rural Development Programme in Vietnam is another striking illustration (see Chapter 5). Sida had a long-standing relationship with Vietnam as the only Western donor who hung in with support through the 1960s and 1970s. A sequence of projects, initially a pulp mill, then for forestry and farm forestry, and subsequently rural development, involved long continuities of staff and relationships. Edwin Shanks and Bui Dinh Toai noted in a paper they wrote for a conference in 2000 that their combined experience was 16 years, having worked on the project since 1993 and 1991, respectively. They also observed that 'due to the relative stability of staffing structures in Viet Nam, many of our colleagues still working on the programme at province and district levels were also involved from the very beginning' (Shanks and Toai, 2000, p23). It is difficult to imagine that the slow, patient and successful introduction and co-evolution of participatory approaches to government agencies in that project could possibly have been achieved without this continuity and sustained commitment.

With aid agencies shifting to sector support and policy influence, development projects were being abandoned during the early 2000s. In Uganda, between one financial year and the next, DFID's (the UK Department for International Development's) ratio of project-to-programme funds shifted with astonishing abruptness from 5:2 to 2:5, without a significant change in total.[18] Ironically, this was at a time when, in my view, lenders, donors and governments were getting better at learning from projects. But as and when these were terminated, governments and aid agencies lost the precious opportunities they had had for innovation and co-learning. With one project in Tanzania, local-level staff had devoted years to project preparation and negotiation only to find that they had been led up the garden path and there would be no project (Groves, 2004). With another in Brazil, after relationships with NGOs (non-governmental organizations) and communities had been built up over three years, people's time and energy had been invested, and enthusiasm and expectations had been raised, a decision was taken in DFID to withdraw, leading to much anger, anguish and disillusion. The hidden costs of such abandonment can be incalculable. Local people who have engaged in participatory planning and have been led to expect support are left in the lurch and reconfirmed in their resentment and cynicism about government. Field staff are seen to have misled their clients; they are made to look foolish, if not duplicitous, and are furious, embittered and de-motivated. Decent and perceptive aid agency staff, too, are demoralized, embarrassed and ashamed, but do not have to face the people on the ground. Centrally isolated office-bound policy-makers in northern capital cities may be blithely or wilfully[19] unaware of the distant damage they have done. All too often, abandoning projects was unethical and anti-poor.

With experience from western India comes David Mosse's (2003 and in press) fascinating, perceptive and subtle analysis of the IBRFP (Indo-British Rain-fed Farming Project with which he was closely involved until 1998, and which he revisited and reviewed three years later in 2001. Despite his early criticisms, and despite managerially exacting contradictions in the project, he shows that much had been achieved, not least through participatory seed breeding and selection. This was a core project innovation that challenged the prevailing regulatory frameworks and bureaucratic practice of Indian agricultural research (Witcombe et al, 1996), with huge implications for policy and practice. The project had also 'brought a version of "development" more meaningful than any previous to Bhil tribal communities excluded from even the most basic state services' (ibid, p24). However, by 2001 it had fallen from favour in DFID and was threatened with closure, not because it was failing but because projects had become unfashionable. As Mosse (2003) puts it:

> *Project practice seemed to me unchanged – meaningful engagements between staff and villagers still produced important local benefits even under conditions of severe drought. But a fundamental change had occurred, not in the project but in donor policy. . . DFID's India programme had become reorganized around the funding of state-wide government programmes, sectoral reform and donor–government partnerships. Unable to articulate this policy, the IBRFP project began to lose its support and, consequently, its reality. It bore new policy labels of exclusion: 'enclave project', 'niche project', 'replicable model', 'parallel [to the state] structure', 'sectoral, downstream, micro-managed project'. IBRFP had suddenly become the flared trousers[20] of the DFID wardrobe.*

In abandoning projects, lenders and donors have succumbed to a tragic pathology. Notwithstanding the common view of colonialism, I found, in the late colonial settlement projects that I studied in Africa, a strong commitment of local-level administrators to 'their' projects and to the settlers. Administrators on the ground were face to face with the realities. To varying degrees, subsequent political representation also provided commitment and support to local projects. It is only now, with lenders, donors and policy-makers interacting and influencing one another more and more, insulated in their capital city cocoons, that projects can more easily be abandoned. RIPS in Tanzania, the project in Brazil, and IBRFP in India all provoke sad reflection on the costs of abandoning projects: staff demoralized, people disillusioned, government discredited, 'money down the drain', benefits to the poor foregone, and opportunities lost for ground-truthing, learning, innovation and capacity-building. In our brave new 21st century of aid, for many poor people, projects have not proved irreversible enough.

Commitment and continuity with policy

This view gains new relevance with the dominant development aid policies of the new century. There are signs of a new consistency in two domains: in rhetoric, extolling partnership, country ownership and policies that are pro-poor; and in targets, with the international and now MDGs (Millennium Development Goals) set for achievement by 2015. Sector programmes may, perhaps, not demand as much long-term commitment as projects. But whether for projects or for sector support, inconstancy is a feature of much aid. In this, agencies differ. USAID, for example, stands out for its short-term swings of policy and vocabulary, and its relative unreliability.[21] Overall, the shift from projects to sector programmes and policy influence may have meant a move for aid agencies from the grounded, bounded and stable to the more nebulous, permeable and inconstant.

With projects, failures were harder to hide. There were reasons to hang in there and try to make them work. With sector support, failures by lenders, donors and governments may, perhaps, tend to be less embarrassingly conspicuous and responsibility less attributable. More actors are involved. The scale is wider. The impacts are further away. So responsibility and accountability are more diffuse. Both political risk and institutional commitment have diminished. In consequence, it may be easier to exit and to deny responsibility. The new dangers implied may not be well recognized by lenders, donors and recipients. The dangers include, as Albert Hirschman might note were he to revisit the aid scene, that less long-term commitment and less continuity mean less creativity and less learning.

Personal continuity, motivation and effectiveness

With the shift of emphasis in aid from projects to sector programmes and policy influence, and with the language of partnership and ownership, so relationships and continuity have become ever more important (Eyben, 2004a; Groves and Hinton, 2004). Good relationships are fostered by continuity of aid agency staff in country and in post. Continuity also provides incentives and opportunities for vital learning. How can a foreigner be engaged in sensible policy dialogue without knowing and understanding a country?

A crucial aspect of continuity is people staying in the same post, place or sector, gaining experience and developing good working relationships. Quite exceptionally for an Indian Administrative Service officer, Syed Hashim Ali was left in charge of irrigation command area development in Andhra Pradesh for seven years, from 1974 to 1981. Through this continuity and his personal commitment, much learning took place and he was able to make and oversee major shifts and improvements in policy and practice. Continuity in linking field experience with policy can also be important. E. G. Giglioli's experience as manager of the Mwea Irrigation Settlement was crucial to the insights and authority that he later brought to the establishment and management of the National Irrigation Board in Kenya (Chambers and Moris, 1973).

Partnerships in the Philippines and in Uganda show how continuity and long-standing relationships can be the foundation for major changes. Over some ten years in the Philippines, Benjamin Bagadion of the National Irrigation

Administration and Frances Korten of the Ford Foundation worked together with a stable network of colleagues. During this time they were instrumental in gradually transforming much irrigation policy and practice (Bagadion and Korten, 1989). In Uganda, the UPPAP (Uganda Participatory Poverty Assessment Process) was promoted and supported by an alliance of champions in both donor and recipient organizations working closely together over a number of years (Yates and Okello, 2002, pp90, 93; Kakande, 2004). It continues as an innovative programme that has given poor people's priorities policy clout and has also influenced PPAs (participatory poverty assessments) in other countries (see Chapter 4). In my judgement, neither the Philippine irrigation reforms nor UPPAP could have occurred without the relationships, trust and shared purpose, which could evolve because the main actors remained for some years in their posts and organizations. Without that continuity, the loss would have been not just national, to the Philippines or to Uganda: irrigation management in the Philippines has probably been more influential worldwide than in any other country, and UPPAP experience has influenced many other PPAs. The loss would have been international, to many countries, and to our understanding of how to do better in development.

Expected and actual continuity in post has profound effects on motivation, behaviour and learning, whether in government, INGOs (international non-governmental organizations) or aid organizations. Over time relationships can go beyond mutual respect and collegiality and flower into friendship.[22] Three conditions that help are long journeys together by car or train, mild hardships in the field and a shared vision. Continuity in post and relationships rise in some places and decline in others. In INGOs, in some countries, there is an impression that staff are switching organizations with greater frequency, treating them as stepping stones more than as places in which to stay and work for a matter of years. But those who do hang in gain types of experience denied to those who hop about. World Neighbours, one of the most innovative INGOs, has staff members with over 20 years' service. In recruiting it looks for people whose careers have shown 'stick-to-itiveness' – that is, who have stuck to the same job or organization for a substantial time (Jethro Pettit, pers comm).

The behaviour of those who expect short spells is predictable. If foreigners, they lack incentives to learn a local language or to take pains to understand local people and conditions, or to take a long view. If energetic and committed, they are liable to be tempted to go for actions with quick effects, neglecting those that need longer-term negotiation and support. For aid agency staff, 'It is difficult to learn and to assume a long-term vision in a local donor community. Each individual is operating in a short time frame related to average residence of three years in any country and she wants to see herself as having "made a difference"' (Eyben, 2003, p28). In their haste, staff make mistakes from avoidable ignorance. Not having to stay long enough to deal with intractable problems, they do not have to muster Albert Hirschman's creativity in overcoming them. Moving on soon, they are not there when the chicken comes home to roost. There is little incentive to develop more than superficial relationships, and as Rosalind Eyben has argued and shown, relationships matter for supporting change in favour of poor people (Eyben, 2004a).

Opportunities to learn and change are missed. These are among the costs of staff moves in the restructurings endemic, if not epidemic, in some aid agencies. Uncertainty and transfers impede other changes. In ActionAid in the UK, the introduction of the new radical ALPS (Accountability, Learning and Planning System) (see Chapter 3, 'Liberation by letting go') became increasingly difficult when 'staff were coming and going at all levels' as part of a massive restructuring process (David and Mancini, 2004, pp17–18). Individual and organizational learning are hampered. Lack of continuity means that by the time lessons can be learnt from what works and what does not, and how mistakes can be mitigated, staff have moved on. After reviewing the history of a donor-supported development programme in Kenya, Samuel Musyoki (2003, p166) concluded: 'The staff turnover in bilateral programmes is very high and there is a tendency of the new management to erase history and create a new knowledge base.' Just as the benefits of continuity are habitually underestimated, so too are the costs of premature transfers. A successful incumbent in almost any responsible post, whether in a government, national NGO or aid agency, tends to achieve more in a third year than in the first two together, and again more in a fourth year than a third, by which time much has been learnt, and relationships and understandings have had time to mature. Diminishing returns set in, if at all, after five or six years or more.

The importance of continuity is also indicated in the reactions of developing country nationals, whether in governments or NGOs, to foreign staff, and whether this is at local or central levels. They resent the short time that those in aid agencies spend in one place. No sooner have they got to know and developed a working relationship with one person than they leave, another takes over and they have to start all over again. Relationships are fractured and understandings are undermined. In the words (October 2003) of a developing country national about USAID 'When we negotiated there was a very good person. Then the boss changed and was very bureaucratic and she left.' Such discontinuities occur with nationals working in INGOs as well as with foreigners. ActionAid's community development workers in The Gambia 'have, on average, been moved every one or two years, with the attendant need to familiarize themselves with a new area, to build trust and sometimes even to learn a new language before they could start to perform to a reasonable standard' (Howes, 2002, p114). When some ActionAid staff in India were concerned that their local NGO partners would resent their relatively high salaries, they were surprised that there was no objection as long as they stayed in the same place for a decent length of time. Then they could get to know one another and develop mutual understanding. Salaries were unimportant compared with continuity and longer-term relationships (Amar Jyoti, pers comm).

In sum, the costs of lack of staff continuity are unseen, unaccounted for, incalculable and often unnecessary. At the same time, continuity is not a simple thing, always to be maximized. From the point of view of a foreign agency, a danger is perceived of out-posted staff 'going native', becoming personally, professionally and emotionally too close and too attached to a country and people. When staff fail it can be right to transfer them. When they move they learn new things. But with the focus of aid on policy, it matters more than ever for aid agency staff to understand local conditions.[23] The costs of lack of continuity, always high, have risen further. Only three years in a post looks too low. The proximate costs of early transfers are relationships broken, trust undermined, demotivation and learning foregone. The wider effects are bad for poor people through errors of judgement and what is then done and not done.

Responsible commitment and continuity can, then, be seen to matter now more than ever. They are a moral imperative where poor people have been led to invest their time and energy in expectation of support. They are a practical condition for constructive relationships, trust and learning. Understanding and optimizing commitment, continuity and their synergies should be high on the agenda for development in the 21st century.

Irreversibility

When a word lodges in the mind, it surfaces in different contexts. So it has been for me with 'irreversibility' since writing my thesis.[24] What began with seeing how commitment to settlement schemes could be irreversible, as with Perkerra, led to thinking of and seeing irreversibility in other domains, including economic decision-making and environmental change.

To sharpen the issues, consider extreme and tragic forms of irreversibility. Perhaps the best known is the extinction of species. A world without the tiger, white rhinoceros or panda would be profoundly diminished. Nor is this a question of only such iconic species, but of a great range that are endangered. The irreversibility and uncertain risks of GM (genetically modified) crops are another case. Less recognized is the destruction of rocks. A stark tragedy is the destruction through quarrying of rocks near Delhi and in and near Hyderabad.[25] These were formed billions of years ago and have weathered over geological time. Apart from intrinsic worth, they have (or had before being destroyed) cultural, aesthetic, ecological, recreational and spiritual value to us humans, giving experiences of place and beauty, sustaining a diversity of life, and providing for the recreation and fulfilment of rock-climbing. Their destruction is utterly irrevocable. Trees that are cut can be replanted. Even soil that erodes can be replaced. But with rocks, restoration is not an option. Once blasted and removed, they are gone. Forever. With a dreadful finality.

Reflecting on these biological and physical examples, if we are to assure options and resources for future generations, irreversibility simply has to be a key concept embedded in our thinking and informing our decisions and actions and non-actions. It is then striking that it is not significant in mainstream economic thinking. Much attention is paid to *risk* – 'the probability or probability distribution of an event or the product of the magnitude of an event and the probability of its occurrence' (Alcamo et al, 2003, p214) and *uncertainty*, the condition of not being known or predictable, where the probability distribution is not known (Devereux, 2001, p508), and each has a considerable literature. But *irreversibility* is less well developed and less frequently mentioned as a concept. Two standard economics textbooks – *Economics* (Begg, Fischer and Dornbusch, 2003) and *Economic Development* (Todaro and Smith, 2003) – include risk in their glossaries; but neither mentions irreversibility.

Not only is irreversibility little considered, but conventional economic practice systematically undervalues it. First, discounting gives low or negligible present values to distant future benefits or costs (Chambers and Conway, 1992, pp18–19). Present value has, however, often been taken as a basis for decisions. To correct this, Zhao and Zilberman (1999) have proposed a new concept of irreversibility cost, and point out that discounting may encourage a pattern of developing now and restoring later. This applies, for example, with the high costs of decommissioning nuclear power stations, which in present value terms were very low at the time of deciding to build them. Irreversibility traps a project or society into having to pay such costs.

Second, substitutability is invoked, with the idea that technological development will find substitutes for resources or services that are depleted, damaged or destroyed. In this view, depletion and degradation of ecological capital are not irreversible in the sense that they can largely be overcome by the accumulation of knowledge and of manufactured and human capital.[26] However, even if technological substitutes exist or are found, their cost is typically high, limiting access to those who are more affluent and putting them beyond the reach of communities and people who are less well off.

Third, non-renewable natural capital resources, like rocks, minerals, oil or gas, are not normally given intrinsic value in economic assessments. When they are irreversibly exploited they appear in themselves costless. To be sure, there are the costs of land, licences and royalties, and of extraction, processing and bringing into use; and sometimes costs are attributed to loss of amenity and physical and ecological damage. But non-renewable natural resources are not given an inherent capital value. So they come out on the wrong side of the ledger as benefits when, unless recycled, they are more strictly costs in the form of irreversible losses.

Fourth, the cultural, aesthetic, ecological, recreational and spiritual values threatened or diminished by irreversible 'development' cannot be measured in money; yet they are deep elements in the quality of human life and experience. Attempts to measure some of them in cash equivalents appear crude. What is the dollar value of being able to watch a bird or climb a rock, now and for future generations? Some may justify giving these a cash value as a short-term expedient in order to talk to hard-core economists in their own terms. In my view, responsible imagination and reflection on stewardship of the heritage of countless future generations will always be better and should carry more weight.

The effects of these biases and neglect are pervasive. Take even the report of the World Commission on Dams (WCD, 2000). Though a remarkable achievement and *tour de force*, it does not give irreversibility as much prominence as the concept would seem to merit. For irreversibility applies both to structures and their impacts and to decision processes. Despite siltation, earthquakes and other hazards, dam structures and their immediate impacts are large and irreversible. As for decision-making, the central values that run through the report are equity, efficiency, participatory decision-making, sustainability and accountability. Irreversibility is mainly addressed indirectly, by presenting five key decision points in planning and project development. Although the last of its seven criticisms of cost–benefit analysis is ignoring 'the effect of uncertainty and irreversibility of investment', the report does not make irreversibility a central issue (WCD, 2000, ppxxiii, 181, 263).

Over the past decade, and offsetting such biases and neglect, some economists have given more attention to irreversibility and related concepts. Faucheux and Froger (1995), for example, examine decision-making in the conditions of uncertainty, irreversibility and complexity, which they say characterize most environmental problems. Zhao and Zilberman (1999) distinguish between technical irreversibility, when technologies to mitigate negative impacts do not exist, and economic irreversibility, when 'it is not optimal to restore the development even though technologies exist to do so' (ibid, p560). This is because of the level of what they call irreversibility costs or restoration costs. Faucheux and Hue (2001) in their article 'From irreversibility to participation: Towards a participatory foresight for the governance of collective environmental risks' move the discussion into the social realm, stressing the need for vigilance and describing experiments with forms of participatory 'social foresights' – which articulate 'demand' as signalled in the views of citizens. These include public inquiries, citizens' panels, citizens' juries, consensus meetings and mediation.

Issues around irreversibility became clearer in 2002 in discussions about concepts for the MA (Millennium Ecosystem Assessment). The MA is an ambitious project to understand better the relationships between ecosystems, ecosystem services and human well-being. Members of the multidisciplinary group of 51 authors met four times to evolve the conceptual framework[27] published as *Ecosystems and Human Well-being: A framework for assessment* (Alcamo et al, 2003). This defines concepts relevant to this discussion (ibid, pp208–216). *Irreversibility* is 'the quality of being impossible or difficult to restore, or return to, a former condition'. Reversibility is related to *resilience* – 'the capacity of a system to tolerate impacts of drivers without irreversible change in its outputs or structure'. *Thresholds* are 'a point or level at which new properties emerge in an ecological, economic or other system, invalidating predictions based on mathematical relationships that apply at lower levels. . . Thresholds at which irreversible changes occur are especially of concern to decision-makers.'

In the MA's conceptual framework, values are seen to bear heavily on decision-making where thresholds and irreversibility are or may be involved. In the process of evolving the framework, values were much debated, both as *intrinsic* – the value of someone or something in and for itself, irrespective of its utility for someone else, and as *ecosystem services* to human well-being, classified as provisioning, regulation and cultural. Cultural values were recognized as spiritual and religious, recreation and ecotourism, aesthetic, inspirational, education, sense of place and cultural heritage (Alcamo et al, 2003, p5).

A recurrent theme was keeping options open for future generations. For this, *option value* was defined as:

> . . . the value of preserving the option to use services in the future either by oneself (option value) or by others or heirs (bequest value). Quasi-option value represents the value of avoiding irreversible decisions until new information reveals whether certain ecosystem services have values society is not currently aware of (ibid, p213)

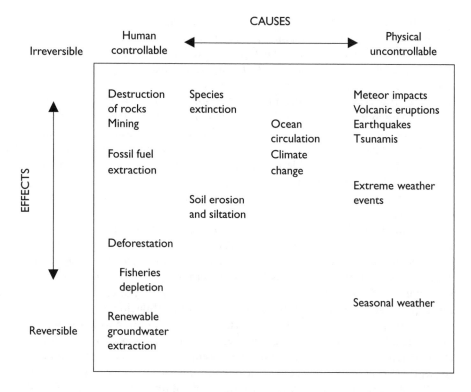

Figure 1.1 *Clusters of environmental change by types of cause and irreversibility*

Source: developed in discussions with Christopher Chambers and Jenny Chambers

The precautionary principle, embodied as Article 15 of the *Rio Declaration* (United Nations, 1992, p3; see also Harremoës et al, 2002) applies here. This is the management concept stating that in cases:

> . . . *where there are threats of serious or irreversible damage, lack of full scientific certainty shall not be used as a reason for postponing cost-effective measures to prevent environmental degradation.*

Despite all of this, and the way it underlies much of the precautionary principle, irreversibility remains an underdeveloped concept.[28] Further steps are needed to distinguish types, degrees and sequences of reversibility and irreversibility. One approach is to classify changes as clusters according to two dimensions: causes, polarized between primarily human and totally physical; and adverse effects, polarized between reversible and irreversible (as in Figure 1.1). In the north-east of the figure are irreversible large-scale events beyond our control, most of the effects of which are irreversible – earthquakes, meteor impacts and volcanic eruptions. In the east are tsunamis and extreme weather events such as tornadoes, hurricanes, floods and droughts that are uncontrollable, but where there is more scope for mitigating adverse effects. In the south-east is seasonal weather, uncontrollable but often with reversible adverse effects. In the south-west is renewable groundwater extraction, and above it deforestation and fisheries depletion, which are less reversible, at least in the shorter term.[29] While these are all vitally important, and so often demand urgent and sustained intervention, it is the remaining areas that merit the closest and most intense attention: the north-west with mining, oil and gas extraction, quarrying and species extinction – controllable but irreversible; and the north and centre with climate and ocean circulation change, and soil erosion and siltation. These are areas where human agency is a major cause and adverse effects are irreversible in the medium and long term or forever. It is in these areas that long-term future options are closed off through human action, and that the precautionary principle applies, and should be made to apply, with most force.

To take the rocks example, the short-term gain from blasting the rocks near Delhi or Hyderabad for building contributes to current livelihoods and GDP (gross domestic product), but is at the cost of cultural, aesthetic, recreational and spiritual experiences of future generations *forever*. And these generations, let us hope, will be billions of people over thousands, if not millions, of years. To destroy such rocks manifests an extreme of blinkered and myopic philistinism.

As articulated, the precautionary principle does not fit, and is too weak for this context. There is no lack of certainty. And the term *cost-effective* leads us astray for two reasons: first, we are concerned with incommensurable values not susceptible to economic calculus; and second, discounting overvalues the clear short-term economic gains and ignores millennia of future benefits. To offset this weakness, much depends upon social and ecological responsibility, access to information, the exercise of imagination, and commitment to the democratic representation of future generations who, we must hope, will dramatically outnumber us, giving their interests a very high weighting.

Any broader formulation of the precautionary principle risks a comprehensiveness that could be used to support a conservationism that would discriminate against today's poor people. Nothing that follows should undermine the moral and practical case for participatory conservation (see, for example, Ghimire and Pimbert, 1997). The concern has to be a balance of the social and environmental, of values and actions, and of the present and future. Each of us might wish to think through and elaborate our own version of a revised precautionary principle. Here is mine:

> *In the interests of poor people, future generations and the planet, where there are threats or certainty of serious or irreversible environmental damage or loss, neither lack of full scientific knowledge nor short-term economic gain shall be used as a reason for postponing preventive action that is socially and ecologically responsible. The more irreversible the damage or loss, the greater the urgency and the higher the cost justified to prevent it.*

This formulation is a provocation for reflection, not final words, and surely for debate. Not least, there are questions of what is damage and what is social and ecological responsibility. There will also always be trade-offs. But this at least can be concluded: irreversibility is a practical concept; it needs more analysis and elaboration; and it should have more weight in decisions and actions. In understanding and applying it, the key is, perhaps, to struggle, and to struggle in every context and in every generation, and to act in ways which are responsible, socially and ecologically, both for the present and the future.

Cinderella concepts and criteria

In the contexts reviewed above – of settlement schemes and other bounded projects, of staff motivation and performance, and of the environment – ideas of *commitment*, *continuity* and *irreversibility* manifest themselves in different forms, with different implications. What stands out in common is that they have been relatively neglected as concepts and as criteria for weighing choices, for deciding what to do and for evaluation. As the restless search for novelty in development impels us to learn and use new words, concepts and criteria, old ones are buried and forgotten. This is the more so with these three since at no time have they enjoyed much popularity in development. They have been marginalized even more by the new prominence of the words which refer to power and relationships: empowerment, ownership, partnership, participation, accountability and transparency. Commitment, continuity and irreversibility have become more than ever Cinderellas, unrecognized and overlooked.[30] Yet, as I have argued, they are fundamental to good development practice.

Most surprising is the neglect of continuity of staff in post. It is easy to measure, which makes it odd that it is so rarely done. Part of the explanation may be that it is so often determined by personnel or human resource departments that are out of touch with field realities, or by central people in senior posts, or by politicians, or by combinations of these. One transfer can generate a chain of other transfers, multiplying its costs. The bad effects of one transfer can then be immense, though unseen, unmeasured and unrecognized. Too long in a post can also be bad, with loss of freshness and excitement; and there is a positive side to transfers – they can give a new clean start, re-energize and broaden experience. But all too often time in post is too short.

The neglect of commitment is less surprising. It is more abstract and not amenable to measurement. It is to be optimized, not maximized. Its dimensions are diverse: they can be personal – with commitment to, for example, an ideal, a cause or a relationship; or organizational – with commitment to a programme, project, a group of people or a mission; or political – with commitment to a programme or policy. Commitment is also contextual, evolutionary and difficult to forecast.

As for irreversibility, in economics it has been overshadowed by preoccupations with risk, uncertainty and sustainability. It has not been incorporated significantly into economic analysis. It is difficult to quantify and it confronts and contradicts conclusions that come from discounting. Nor is it always bad: as with continuity, more of it can be better or worse, depending upon the case. If factors like these explain why it has been such a marginal concept, the case is strengthened for offsetting them, developing it further as a concept and giving it more prominence.

Questions of commitment, continuity and irreversibility are relevant to much decision-making and action. The issues they raise differ by context. It is tempting, then, to dismiss them as too vague and variable to be of much use. But there is a paradox here. For the very diversity of their meanings makes them versatile in their applications. The lesson is not to pass them by, but to define and apply them, context by context. They should be part of any checklist of criteria for review in formulating policies, making decisions and taking action. They deserve to be brought out of the shadows into the light closer to centre stage. Given more weight in development, and applied again and again, they should prevent or reduce damage from errors and, at the same time, ensure that more good things are done.

Notes

1   Mwea was so frequently visited by VIPs, researchers, school parties, women's groups, government officials and others that the Manager told me he spent 45 per cent of his time on public relations. This led to the recruitment of a Deputy Manager for whom this was his major work.

2   The recent history of Mwea has been turbulent. During the late 1990s, farmers increasingly protested against the National Irrigation Board's corrupt management and high service charges. In January 1999, two young men were killed by police in a demonstration. The farmers took over the scheme to run it themselves (Kenya Human Rights Commission, 2000). This evidently failed, and in January 2003, negotiations between the farmers' co-operative and the National Irrigation Board led to the formation of a committee to oversee the Scheme (*Daily Nation*, 27 and 29 January 2003).

3   This section is from Chambers (1969, pp257–262). A few details of evidence have been edited out, together with a paragraph on Perkerra.

4   I struggled with my wish to change 'men' to 'people'; but have left the male-biased word, which was in the original. It situates the piece historically. This was before the gender-awareness revolution. That said, Jon Moris and Jane Hanger, the authors of the much-cited and influential Chapter H, 'Women and the household economy', in the Mwea collection (Chambers and Moris, 1973, pp209–244) deserve credit for showing how markedly settlement conditions made things worse for women, leading, for example, to a high rate of divorce.

5   Nicholas, in *Volta Resettlement Symposium Papers* p. 86, subsequently edited and republished in Chambers 1970.

6   Interim report of a United Nations Special Fund survey of the lower Tana Basin in Kenya, as reported in *East African Standard* (Nairobi), 17 November 1965, and *Daily Nation* (Nairobi), 17 November 1965. Despite a long sequence of adverse appraisals, the project (named Bura) was eventually implemented and must rank as one of the economically most disastrous settlement projects ever.

7   The heading in the original text was 'Concluding'.

8   The word now would be appraisals. Evaluations are ex post, appraisal ex ante, but this distinction was not yet a convention in the late 1960s.

9   *Mea culpa.*

10   This section is taken from the final pages of Chapter M 'The Perkerra Irrigation Scheme: A contrasting case', in Chambers and Moris (1973, pp 344–364). I would like to thank the past and present officials of the Kenya government who have helped me with the research for this case study. I am especially indebted to E. G. Giglioli, J. G. Stemf, S. G. Sandford and R. E. Wainwright for comments on an earlier version. Responsibility for what is written here is, however, entirely mine and should not be attributed to any other person or to any organization.

11   Attempts to obtain accounts or details of how Perkerra was financed have not been successful. There are reasons to infer that the cross-subsidization through the National Irrigation Board using surpluses from the more viable Mwea Irrigation Settlement continued until 1998, when the Mwea farmers rebelled; but I have been unable to substantiate this with direct, authoritative or numerical information.

12   According to one report, which remains unconfirmed, the Perkerra staff went unpaid for six months when the Mwea settlers rebelled and cross-subsidization of Perkerra from Mwea ended.

13   This equates to 1.5 million Kenyan shillings.

14   *Daily Nation*, 21 March 2003, www.nationmedia.com. This may have subsumed the earlier US$20,000 pledged by the National Irrigation Board.

15   This is not to justify the gross inequalities of landholdings in Zimbabwe. The government, however, chose not to take up aided programmes of settlement of the sort that had been so successful in Kenya. There were numerous reports of how farm labourers suffered and lost when land was seized.

16   In October 2003, *Concorde* had its historic last flight. The Mahaweli project is still alive, extensive and, to the best of my knowledge, well.

17   A contributory factor reflecting continuity of relationships may have been that the Tanzanian President was a Finnophile. The only place in Tanzania with a sauna bath was, and to the best of my knowledge remains, Mtwara. Though its construction provoked a divisive ideological debate among Finnish expatriates, it could hardly have been a political liability when it was patronized, as it was, by the President.

18   Statistics for DFID aid to Uganda compiled by Lister and Nyamagusira (2003) from www.DFID.gov.uk/sid for 1999/2001 and 2000/2001, respectively, give project aid dropping from UK£41.467 million to UK£17.686 million, and programme aid rising from UK£17 million to UK£45 million. The possibility must be recognized that part of this dramatic contrast may have been the result of a change in accounting.

19   To be wilfully unaware is to decide not to know or not to take steps to know, when it is apparent that there is something discordant to understand. Most people do this from time to time. I certainly do.

20   Hanging in and patience can bridge gaps until fashions come back in again. My grandmother's long skirts were for long a legacy of the past, but became *avant garde* fashion when hemlines dropped again, and casual observation suggests that, in 2003, for some young women at least, flared trousers have

come back. Those aided projects that survive may in due course find themselves part of a wave of the future.

21   USAID's lack of long-term commitment and tendency to lurch from one priority and language to another is a commonplace development experience, has done much hidden damage and deserves a special study. An example is its policies towards family planning. In Jordan, for example, support to a project was withheld after field preparations had begun. 'In such situations, with expectations raised at the local level, organizational credibility is diminished, and time and energy must be spent to regain the trust of partners in the field' (bint Talal 2003, p190).

22   I owe the word friendship to Norman Uphoff, who frequently stresses it in Gal Oya (Uphoff, 1992), and to Elmer Ferrer at the Community-based Coastal Resources Management Festival, held at Subic Bay in the Philippines in June 2003, who eloquently stressed how friendship had been fostered by people from different backgrounds and organizations staying together for a long time, working with a common cause.

23   Rosalind Eyben (pers comm) has pointed out that: 'Interestingly, the FCO [Foreign and Commonwealth Office of the UK government] now has "anchors", so although someone is only posted for three to four years at any time to a particular country, they do go back again later on and possibly for a third time, as well, during their career. Diplomats appreciate the importance of local knowledge much more than do aid staff.'

24   While courting my wife Jenny, I was in Bihar when she had an excellent job offer that would have put us in different continents for two years. Forced to communicate by cable with few words, I pleaded with her to 'minimize irreversibility commitment'. To my great good fortune, though not necessarily hers, it worked.

25   I write this with passion, anguish and guilt. One of the biggest, most selfish errors of my life was to spend many of the Sundays during three and a half years living in New Delhi rock-climbing on endangered rocks at Damdama and Dhauj, instead of devoting my time to saving them and their environments for future generations. The finest rocks are still, but precariously, intact at the time of writing (2004); but at Dhauj outlying rocks have been mindlessly quarried and destroyed forever. In Hyderabad a vigorous Society to Save Rocks has done great work; but to my knowledge there is no equivalent in Delhi, or, indeed, in any other city in the world.

26   For a discussion of substitutability and well-being, see Alcamo et al (2003, pp79–81).

27   I was lucky to be involved both in drafting the chapter on human well-being and in plenary discussions across the whole range of subjects. This was one of the most stimulating and mind-opening experiences of my life.

28   I will be grateful to anyone who can contradict or qualify the assertion that irreversibility remains underdeveloped as a concept.

29   Caution is needed here in distinguishing cases. Some groundwater can be renewed in an almost linear manner. However, restoration to a former condition implies a reversibility that is not characteristic of ecological systems.

Depletion, as through over-fishing, may take an ecosystem below a threshold of resilience, so that 'recovery' is very slow or follows a pathway to a different species composition and community structure. In Newfoundland fishery, the failure of cod to recover quickly is an illustration of this (David Schoeman, pers comm).

30 The Cinderella analogy works as a metaphor for exclusion by those with power and influence. Her ugly sisters did this to Cinderella. Ugly in this sense myself, I was responsible for excluding 'continuity of staff in their posts' from the prescriptions of an IDS (Institute of Development Studies) policy briefing paper on power, procedures and relationships (Chambers, Pettit and Scott-Villiers, 2001), as I recollect murmuring that continuity was 'old hat'.

2

Aid and Administrative Capacity

. . .meeting multiple donor requirements employs a significant proportion of developing countries' administrative capacity (OECD, 2003, p3)

This chapter considers the costs of demands on the time and energy of staff of governments receiving aid and of the aid agencies providing it, and the implications of treating administrative capacity in aided countries as a scarce resource. Part 1 is an article published in 1969. Part 2 outlines some salient implications for aid agency and government policy and practice in the 21st century.

Part 1: Administrative Capacity as a Scarce Resource: A Challenge on Aid and Development[1] (1969)

In development activity, administrative capacity – the capability of getting things done – though often limiting and relatively inelastic, is neglected in project and programme appraisals. There are technical, organizational and diplomatic reasons for this neglect. The practical implications of treating administrative capacity as a scarce resource are:

- *checking consistency between demands on administration, including the effects of new demands on staff in drawing them away from other activities;*
- *restraining demands for information, the true costs of which in staff time are often very high;*
- *weighing indirect administrative costs, including the costs of coordination and the costs of taking staff away from other organizations; and*
- *preferring policies that are administration sparing, and avoiding those that are administration intensive and administration persistent.*

Unless administrative capacity is weighed as a scarce resource in development decision-making, some policies will delay or inhibit, rather than promote development.

The literature of development is well-seasoned with references to public administration as a bottleneck.[2] Delays, inefficiencies, shortages of properly prepared projects, inadequate or inaccurate information, failures to draw down funds allocated for public-sector expenditure – these are often remarked upon and blamed for disappointing performance. Those involved tend to assume that there is something wrong that needs to be corrected, and the positive approaches of manpower planning, training, administrative reforms and technical assistance are invoked and brought to bear. The bias of advice and policy is constructive: the administrative machine must be made able to do whatever it is thought desirable that it should do. Obviously, this is a necessary attitude, even though, with the partial exception of technical assistance, the process typically takes a long time.

There is, however, another neglected approach which could supplement these traditional measures. If the administrative capacity – the capability of getting things done – of the government bureaucracies of poorer countries is a severe constraint on development, then there would seem to be an *a priori* case for treating it as a scarce resource and subjecting it to the attitudes implicit in the techniques – rationing, testing for consistency of use, unit costing, shadow-pricing and so forth – employed with other scarce resources; in short, a case for being careful and sparing in its use.

This seems so obvious that it has to be asked why this approach receives so little attention. There appear to be three particularly potent reasons. The first is technical. Administrative capacity is difficult to measure. To be sure, trained manpower can be counted; but bureaucratic performance is related not just to stocks of manpower but also to organizational, motivational, social and economic variables which are difficult to quantify. In so far as planners are committed to mathematical procedures they are liable to be drawn away from giving due weight to unquantifiable factors, administrative capacity among them.

The second reason concerns the politics of organizations. Neither a donor agency nor a recipient organization has a direct interest in considering administrative capacity as a limited resource from the recipient's national point of view. Their immediate interests are narrower – the success of the projects or programmes they are promoting, evaluated largely in isolation from the total national environment. Together, the donor agency and the recipient ministry or department may contrive to attract scarce able administrators to their projects and programmes without weighing the indirect costs of removing them from other posts, or the greater benefits that might derive from their deployment elsewhere. To consider a rational allocation of able men would, in these circumstances, be to reduce the chances of project or programme success and therefore to undermine the donor, recipient and project organizations.

The third reason is diplomatic. A donor may fear that to draw attention to limited administrative capacity would give offence, and be taken as implying that the recipient country lacks the ability to handle its affairs; and for a recipient to refer to it might be regarded as damaging to national pride.

These technical, organizational and diplomatic factors, while going some way towards explaining why administrative capacity has been neglected as a scarce resource, also serve as a warning. Since they can be expected to continue to operate in the future, it is all the more important that this subject should be explored and the policy implications stated. What follows is based partly on the insights of others,[3] but is still at an elementary level of analysis. The approach used is to assume first, that for the time being administrative capacity is a fairly inelastic scarce resource and second, that the universe of account should be the national economy of a less developed country and not just a particular project or programme. With these two premises, four complementary prescriptive points can be made.

Checking consistency between demands on administration

It is easy to assume that if demands on personnel and organizations are increased, so their output will increase. But for each individual and organization, output is finite, and beyond a certain pressure output may drop through a combination of overwork and demoralization. The imposition of an extra task on a person or organization may, thus, often lead to a failure to perform other tasks. In such a case, the cost of losses through failure to perform those other tasks is part of the true cost of the performance of the new task.

This may be illustrated by an example from Tanzania. Following a successful pilot project in one part of a region, the agricultural extension staff throughout the whole region were to have been concentrated on a campaign to persuade farmers to plant their cotton early. On the basis of the pilot programme, considerable increases in production-mad farmer incomes were anticipated. Before this could occur, however, tractors arrived as part of an aid project and the extension staff were diverted full time to mechanization. The early planting programme had consequently to be abandoned. The mechanization project, costed on its own, turned out to be of doubtful value; but when the loss of additional production from foregoing the early planting campaign was added, the tractors could be seen to have had a strongly adverse effect on economic development. Had the administrative implications of the tractors been considered at the time of aid negotiation, they might never have been accepted, with a net gain in production for Tanzania.

The moral is that before policies are adopted they should be tested for consistency between the demands they make on administration. Part of the preliminary evaluation of a project or programme should, thus, include an assessment of its effects on the administration of other projects and programmes. Unfortunately, the immediate interests of donor and recipient organizations are usually in the success of a project or programme regardless of the damage it may inflict on existing ones. In the present state of the art, it would be surprising, though laudable, if in feasibility studies, project evaluations and even national economic planning, adequate precautions were taken to avoid administrative inconsistency. Yet, particularly with increasing aid to agriculture, and with each agency trying to promote its own policies, there is a danger of a succession of programmes imposing heavy and incompatible loads on staff.

Restraining demands for information

Aid donors and planners commonly place a heavy burden on administration through demands for information. Donors need data to be able to convince critics at home that their aid is being well applied, and planners are professionally hamstrung without statistics. Regarded in isolation, and without considering the full implications, a good case can often be made out for more detailed surveys and more elaborate compilations of information before a project is considered and approved, and then later for frequent reports on its progress. Feasibility surveys and performance returns have such obvious payoffs – in establishing project viability, in alerting staff to considerations they might otherwise have missed, in contributing to the personal development of officials, in maintaining efficiency, and so on – that they can appear to be automatically beneficial.

But, of course, it is notorious that information is not costless. In the central governments of developing countries, senior civil servants are often subject to many important competing demands on their time. When a visiting mission requests information for a survey of the economy, the invisible but real cost to the country in terms of activities not performed by the civil servants who have to provide the information may be very high. As Papanek (1968, pp4–7) has forcefully pointed out, the desirability of bilateral aid is diminishing as a result of increasing controls over aid expenditure by donors stemming from the need to satisfy domestic critics of aid. Followed along the chain of causation, the true cost to a recipient of a hostile question about aid in a donor's legislature may be substantial if the result is a demand for stricter and more detailed returns.

Similarly, for the field administrations of developing countries, the true costs of requests for information may be very high. It may take a planner only five minutes to draft a circular asking for crop acreage figures; but it may take many thousands of man-hours to provide them. In one case in Tanzania, had the agricultural field staff been put onto providing for the planners all the information they required, they would have had scarcely any time for their other more directly productive activities. One may wonder, too, at the costs, in terms of alternative activities foregone, of such an enterprise as the World Indicative Plan for Agriculture compiled by FAO (United Nations Food and Agriculture Organization) on the basis of information requested from the already overburdened administrations of the countries of the developing world. The costs of information can, indeed, go beyond the simple diversion of staff from other activities: the demoralization of agricultural extension staff so often found in the poorer countries can be attributed partly to the flood of instructions and poorly articulated demands for information which flow out successively from capital cities.

The moral is that donors, planners and civil servants in the less developed countries should all be self-critical before they ask for facts. It is an old gibe that planners are prepared to cost anything but planning itself; but neither their activities nor those of aid donors deserve immunity from stringent evaluation. Before they request information they should ask themselves these questions: first, whether the information already exists (for instance, has another aid agency recently compiled information on the state of the economy?); second, whether the information is likely to be accurate enough to be usable; third, whether, once collected, it will in fact be used (self-deception on this point being particularly easy); and fourth, whether from the point of view of the poorer country's national development the expected benefits from the information justify the costs of obtaining it, and particularly the costs in terms of the loss of the benefits of alternative staff activities.

Weighing indirect administrative costs

Most projects have indirect costs of an administrative nature. They frequently make demands on existing government organizations which provide them with subsidized services. Perhaps more important, they require coordination with existing organizations, entailing correspondence and meetings with officials who are often already overburdened. Indeed, there is a seductive danger of a cult of meetings which coordinate without deciding and which, in the meantime, consume much time and energy. Coordination, like planning, sounds like a self-evident good; but like planning, it has high administrative costs. It may sometimes be cheaper to accept some of the mistakes which follow from less coordinated but more timely and vigorous action.

There may also be high costs arising from the transfer of staff to new projects. Often such costs are reckoned in terms of direct financial expenditure on salaries, allowances and so forth; but there is an obvious and strong case for shadow-pricing to take account of their opportunity costs in terms of benefits foregone from the alternative activities they might have carried out. This is especially crucial in agriculture, where middle-grade staff are often diverted from the less visible activities of agricultural administration in an extension service to more visible activities, usually in site-bound projects such as settlement schemes, state farms and irrigation undertakings. If these projects were costed in terms of production foregone from not deploying the staff elsewhere in other ways, and in terms of the disruption caused by their translation from other organizations, then they might emerge as much less favourable investments than they are usually allowed to appear.

These arguments bear on Albert Hirschman's thesis of the Hiding Hand,[4] according to which habitual underestimation of the difficulties of a project is offset by habitual underestimation of the creativity which can be mustered to overcome them. Looked at closely much of this creativity may be revealed as quite simply diversion of administrative resources from other parts of the national economy and administration. Creativity sounds, but is not, costless. Its costs, however, tend to be concealed or ignored because both for the aid agency and for the local project organization the universe of account is the project and not the national economy. The forms taken by creativity in practice include not only hidden subsidies and fiscal protection but also increased demands on government departments and poaching of staff from other organizations, which may consequently be critically weakened. The result may be that the aid agency can show that the project has been a success when considered, as it tends to be, in isolation and by conventional cost-benefit criteria. But the receiving country as a whole may be a net loser. Only rarely can projects which emerge as 'successful' after overcoming major difficulties have been as beneficial as they are allowed to appear.

The moral is that the indirect administrative costs of projects and programmes, including the likelihood of having to meet the costs of 'creativity', should be taken into account in pre-investment evaluations.

Preferring administration-sparing policies

There are wide variations between the administrative demands of different approaches to development, particularly in agriculture. If, for instance, a new seed variety is self-propagating and does not require intermittent renewal or additional inputs, its dissemination has low and temporary requirements in administration: once farmers are growing it they will sell it to other farmers and it will spread itself without further official intervention.[5] Not only are administrative demands low, they are also temporary, releasing staff for other tasks later. In contrast, approaches which involve the introduction of officially administered cultivation systems – tractor hire services, co-operative production farming, state farms or controlled irrigation systems, for instance – tend to make heavy demands on administration which also tend to persist. Often the commitment of government to providing services and controls is virtually irreversible. Not only are risks compounded by this irreversibility, since abandonment is difficult, but decisions about future deployment of personnel are pre-empted, reducing flexibility in future policy-making.

The question of the relative administration-intensiveness and administration-persistence of different types of project and programme deserves much more careful and perceptive analysis than can be attempted here. For instance, it is important to ask whether the policies which are most attractive to donors and recipients may not often be those which make relatively high and lasting demands on administration. Certainly the preference of donors for projects which involve capital goods and the preference of recipients for projects which are bounded, visible and easy to exhibit and inspect, may exert a bias towards a requirement for high-level manpower and persisting administration. Similarly, the capital content of more dispersed programmes may exert a bias towards heavier and more lasting administrative demands. In agriculture, for example, rural credit or the introduction of tractor services may particularly intensive and persistent administrative requirements which are the easier to ignore because of the effort of imagination required to regard the time and energy of the junior staff who would have to carry them out as a scarce resource.

These questions must remain open, and invite research. But whether or not there is, in aid, a bias away from policies which make low and temporary demands towards those with high and lasting demands, the main point stands. Where administrative capacity is scarce, preference should be given, other things being equal, to policies which are administration-sparing, both in the intensity and in the persistence of their requirements.

Now that the Pearson Commission[6] on international aid is taking a fresh hard look at policies and performance to date, it would be timely for these four complementary points to be examined in much more detail than has been done here. It is all too easy to call for more research, and research on public administration in the poorer countries itself makes demands on administrative resources and is therefore subject to these very same criteria. But if the burden of the argument presented above is sound, then a very high priority for research should be the comparative administrative demands of different development projects and programmes.

This is particularly urgent because of the enthusiastic attention being paid to agriculture and the rural sector, with the World Bank, other multilateral agencies and national donor organizations all attempting to step up assistance to rural development. For rural development is by its nature biased towards the use of the normal field administrative and technical services of a government, and these may have particularly inelastic administrative capacity. It is relatively easy, as the World Bank often does, to insist on the setting up of a semi-autonomous agency to operate a project, and then to apply influence and assistance to ensure that it operates fairly efficiently. It is far harder to assess or influence the position in a dispersed network of field agencies. To the visiting expert or the senior government official, neither of whom may have time or inclination to stray far from the capital city except perhaps to visit one or two specially favoured projects or areas, the agricultural extension workers at the bottom of the agricultural hierarchy may be dim and remote persons whose lives and problems it is difficult or uncongenial to imagine. But a choice between, say, a campaign for timely planting on the one hand, and a long-term agricultural credit programme on the other, may have huge implications for the work and effectiveness of junior staff. In the former case, they may be involved only in one-shot explanation and persuasion; in the latter, they may be tied for many years to an administration-intensive programme which will not only cast them in the roles of policemen and debt-collectors but also absorb a high proportion, if not all, of their time, pre-empting the possibility of introducing other programmes for as long as the credit programme continues.

It is to be hoped that the Pearson Commission and other bodies examining aid and development policies will pay close attention to administrative capacity as a scarce resource. If it is not adequately weighed in development choices, then some aid policies will continue to be dysfunctional, serving to delay or inhibit rather than promote development. It would be wrong, however, to gloss over the difficulties of applying the four principles advocated above, for they imply that evaluations of aid projects and programmes should often be less favourable than they are, and this may be sensed as a threat to both donor and recipient organizations. Moreover, in so far as choosing less administration-intensive and less administration-persistent policies may mean abjuring more prestigious and visible technologically advanced and capital-using policies, it will require considerable self-restraint on the part of all concerned. But if administrative capacity is not treated as a relatively inelastic scarce resource, and if at the same time the volume of official aid is stepped up, it has to be asked whether there is not a danger of sharply diminishing – indeed of negative – returns to much of the increased effort.

Part 2: Rethinking Policies and Practices in Aid (2004)

As the bloated state of the 1960s and 1970s slimmed in many developing countries to the indebted and even anorexic state of the 1980s and 1990s, relative scarcity shifted from administrative capacity to other resources, especially finance. In parallel, though, new demands on staff time and energy came from a proliferation and fragmentation of aid, especially for smaller and poorer developing countries. Transaction costs were involved in servicing aid agency missions, negotiations, meetings, workshops, policy dialogues, and reporting and providing information. Corruption also took time and effort. Now, in the 2000s, with fewer field projects and the focus on sector aid and policy, aid agency staff are increasingly trapped in capital cities. The limited administrative capacity of lenders and donors is now also a constraint. So, too, for governments and civil society organizations is HIV/AIDS, where it is prevalent. Solutions can be sought in reducing lender and donor demands, appropriate levels of staffing, and shifting from capacity-building to capacity development. Intentionally or not, lenders and donors maintain their dominance through heavy and ever-changing demands on governments' capacities. It is, above all, through changes in behaviour to reduce demands, open spaces for responsible action and level power relations that administrative capacity can be most effectively enhanced.

From past to present

Since the section above was written over three decades ago, much has changed. The male-biased syntax, the frequent reference to planners, and the use of the concepts and language of cost–benefit analysis are marks of the 1960s. At that time, economic planning had a high profile. It helped to use the language and concepts of economics, not just for their inherent utility, but as a means of influencing the economist planners[7] who were powerful in high-profile planning ministries and departments. The term *scarce resource* carried with it a simplistic implication of a quantifiable entity to which the techniques and thought processes of economics could be applied. Seeing administrative capacity as scarce was also relevant where administrations were in transition from colonial to post-colonial conditions, with older expatriates leaving and younger nationals taking over and facing new pressures and demands, and with the development state in the heyday of its growth. Aid agencies providing technical assistance demanded counterpart staff from the host country, intended as a long-term contribution to what is now called capacity-building or capacity development, but in the short term making staff shortages worse. Then, when a new function was thought of, the common reflex was either to expand an existing organization or create a new one. Parastatals proliferated. In many countries of what was called the Third World, there were recently established separate departments and organizations for co-operatives, community development and settlement and resettlement, and, above all, departments, commissions or ministries for economic planning and development.[8]

During and after the 1960s, many countries in the South had their first, and then second, and then third and subsequent five-year plans, and in some, for example India, these continue as a tradition. Administrative capacity in government was scarce partly because the state was trying to do so much. Rural development illustrates this point. The latter 1960s and the 1970s were a high tide for investments in rural and agricultural development through special projects. In sub-Saharan Africa, foreign technical assistance was often brought in. In India, three-fourths of the expenditure on the 12 Districts of the Intensive Agricultural Districts Programme was for added district staff and district services, intended to accelerate agricultural development through increased administrative capacity. (An authoritative evaluation, however, found it probable that the actions could have been completed in less time, at a lower cost, and with equal quality using other institutions and methods; see Brown, 1971, p99). Elsewhere, geographically bounded integrated rural development projects were promoted with enthusiasm, notably in Africa where most of them were costly failures (World Bank, 1988). But these were the days before debt had begun to bite. It is sobering, saddening and a little bewildering to look back and recognize the relative abundance of finance at the time and the widespread belief in a future in which state-administered projects would play a major, if not *the* major, part in economic and social development.

The subsequent story is well known. International loans were not only available but were pushed on countries during the 1970s by multilateral lenders and, following their lead and on a larger scale, by private-sector banks. The short-sightedness of incurring debt to pay for capital and recurrent expenditures would be more difficult to understand had it not continued into the 21st century. Its persistence, when the long-term effects are so bad, demands explanation. The reasons have not changed. One is the practice of discounting future costs, which then appear trivial in the present, but are anything but trivial when they have to be met. Another is alliances of short-term interests. These are drivers within organizations, especially the World Bank and the regional development banks whose survival depends upon lending. The status, careers and livelihoods of their staff are enhanced by the scale of the loans they make. And they are similarly part of the motivation of those in borrowing countries whose short-term political and career prospects (and, where corrupt, income) are improved variously by the prestige, patronage and plunder provided by large loans. And all actors can blithely bequeath repayment to the next generation, by which time they will have retired or moved on in other ways.

During the 1960s and 1970s, many projects had high costs, not just financially but also in drawing off capable staff from line departments. At the same time, overfed with loans and grants, the state grew fat. To describe it as bulimic may be a touch whimsical; but binges there certainly were. Then the zenith of direct government action passed. The debts began to be called in. Profligate spending was overtaken by austerity. Especially in Latin America and Africa, the slimming demanded by structural adjustment programmes was traumatic. The state, once force fed and obese, was starved and shrank to become skinny – one might almost say, anorexic.

During the 1970s and 1980s, resources other than administrative capacity became scarcer. In many countries (but not India, which is an exception to many of these generalizations), recurrent budgets were slashed. Staff salaries were inflexible; but travel budgets could be, and were, cut again and again down to ridiculous levels. Field staff found themselves marooned. In Zambia in the early 1980s, when I asked if I would find a district agricultural officer in his office I was told: 'You won't find him anywhere else.' Then, more and more, as structural adjustment programmes came in, further heavy cuts were imposed. Especially in sub-Saharan Africa, the capacity to do things was constrained less by staff or their capabilities, which had grown, and more by lack of other resources – paper, textbooks, drugs, fuel, vehicles, bicycles, allowances and even pay – and linked with these, demoralization.[9]

In the 1990s and now the 2000s, the patterns have changed again.[10] Lenders and donors have reduced their support for projects and shifted into support for sectoral programmes, providing direct budget support (known in Ghana as multi-donor budget support, or MDBS) and influencing policy. The rationale for reducing projects was that they were supply driven by aid agencies, and not owned by governments, performed patchily and were often linked to tied aid.

A distinction has to be made between middle-income and low-income countries. Very large countries such as India and China, and middle-income countries that did not receive much aid, might still welcome aided projects as a risk-free means of experimenting and learning (Eyben, Lister et al, 2004); but in smaller and poorer countries they distorted national budgets. So 'enlightened' aid agencies led the shift away from projects. Now, to a degree that during the 1960s would have been vilified as gross neo-colonialism, in many small and low-income countries – especially in sub-Saharan Africa – lenders and donors not only fund much government expenditure (over 50 per cent in Uganda; Lister and Nyamugasira, 2003, p5), but also call many of the policy shots. The focus is more and more on poverty. The MDGs (Millennium Development Goals) for poverty reduction by 2015 have become the rallying cry and are embraced as orthodox objectives. In addition to SWAps (sector-wide approaches), the weight of lenders' and donors' influence is brought to bear on issues variously concerned with gender equality, sustainable livelihoods, decentralization, capacity-building, good governance and human rights.[11]

In heavily aided countries, these changes have forced lenders and donors together. When they were dealing more with field projects, their attention and the demands they made were more scattered. Now focused on sectors and policy, they concentrate on officials in capital cities. This has brought new demands on administrative capacity, putting it, once more high, on the agenda.

Proliferation and fragmentation

A study 'Aid Proliferation: How responsible are the donors?' (Acharya, de Lima and Moore, 2004) has analysed what the authors identify as a major trend making increasing demands on administrative capacity. This is the proliferation and fragmentation of bilateral aid (the study does not include multilaterals). The years of analysis are 1999, 2000 and 2001.

Proliferation relates to the number of countries aided by a donor and the number of disbursements, described as aid events. An astonishing finding is that over the three years the 22 bilateral donors aided an average of 107 countries each, 72 of them with aid events of over US$500,000. *Fragmentation* refers to the number of donors to a recipient country and the number of aid events in it. During 2000, the average number of bilateral donors per recipient was found to be 14 (n = 22) and of bilateral and multilaterals together, 26 (n = 53).

Excluding the special case of the US, the study finds that the donors who proliferate most are generally those with the most altruistic and progressive aid programmes – Germany, Canada, The Netherlands, Switzerland, Norway, Belgium and Sweden. 'Relatively unconstrained by historical, cultural or geo-strategic considerations that might otherwise lead them to concentrate their assistance, they have extended their aid programs widely to the poorer and more "deserving" nations. The net result of these good intentions has been a serious exacerbation of aid proliferation, and the problems to which it, in turn, gives rise' (ibid, 2004). The authors conclude:

> *The very high degree of* fragmentation *experienced by some aid recipients is directly attributable to the fact that they receive aid from aid donors especially guilty of* proliferation. *If the worst* proliferators *would mend their ways, with each concentrating their aid more on fewer recipients, there would be substantial immediate impacts on the recipients suffering the worse fragmentation.*

At the margin, the net effects of proliferation may then be negative. An extra lender or donor may, in other words, diminish development and make things worse for poor people. For this to show up, evaluations would have to include the opportunity costs of the extra demands on administrative capacity. Such evaluations are both difficult and improbable. Lenders and donors prefer to omit unquantifiable externalities of this sort, and limit themselves to more direct effects, or even indirect effects such as improvements to the MDGs. The self-negating irony of proliferation can be illustrated from Malawi, where at one time there were seven separate projects 'strengthening' the Ministry of Finance (Edwards, 1999, p132, citing Ademoloku et al, 1997).

Transaction costs

The main problem to which proliferation and fragmentation give rise is the transaction costs for recipient countries making demands on their administrative capacity. This is marked in some of the poorest countries. At one time there were 405 aided projects in the Mozambique Ministry of Health alone. In the early 1990s in Tanzania, there were 40 'donors'[12] and more than 2000 projects. More recently, Tanzanian government officials have had to prepare about 2000 reports of different kinds. At one time during the 1980s Burkina Faso was receiving visiting missions at the rate of almost one a day (Carl Widstrand, pers comm). By the turn of the century in Tanzania the figure had risen to three times higher, with more than 1000 aid delegations each year (World Bank, 2003, p193; WDR, 2003, Chapter 11, cited in Acharya, de Lima and Moore, 2004).

As a result of these changes the burden on officials in capital cities has increased. The multiplicity of lenders (the World Bank, the IMF and the regional banks) and donors (multilateral, bilateral and INGOs), as well as their consultants and contractors, make many demands, including:

- *Visitors*: arrangements have to be made for short-term visitors. These can take up much time. Many of them require meetings, a programme, logistical support and negotiations.
- *Reports and information*: there are imperious requirements for World Bank assessments. For each country the World Bank has five core reports – poverty

assessments; country economic memoranda or development policy reviews; public expenditure reviews; country financial accountability assessments; and country procurement assessment reviews. In addition, there are 16 sector or issue reports that are done only in selected countries (Wilks and Lefrançois, 2002, p13). Different donors often have different requirements, multiplying the reporting work required. As I have discovered, it only takes one donor (in this case DFID) among several to require a logframe for it to be obligatory to follow its evaluation and reporting requirements, even if the other donors to the same project consider them unnecessary.

- *Negotiations*: multiplying aid agencies multiplies interactions and negotiations, often involving different ministries or levels within a ministry; and each lender or donor has its own style of negotiation.
- *Policy dialogue* concerning sectoral and direct budget support, drawing on the various assessments, complicates the policy process for officials of recipient governments.
- *Workshops*: these have proliferated, at times to epidemic levels, in and near capital cities. They are convened in the name of consultation, participation, partnership, experience sharing, establishing networks, capacity-building, and discussions of policy. On one day in Accra in 2003 I became aware of four concurrent workshops, and these may have been only the visible tip of the iceberg.[13] Just as projects and coordination earlier drew off or absorbed administrative capacity, so now workshops, whatever their benefits, have hidden costs in work not done because of preparation and absence.

A further and hidden dimension is corruption. Where this is extensive, much time and concentrated effort on the part of officials may be demanded by political liaisons and negotiations and by parallel accounting. These fill a box of invisible size that has often, it would seem, grown bigger. Corrupt transactions would also seem likely to take priority over other, more legitimate, development activities.

Lenders and donors have recognized transaction costs. Part of the rationale for shifting from projects to SWAps and direct budget support was to coordinate aid agency actions so that they spoke with one voice, and to reduce administrative demands.[14] However, it is no new insight that coordination has its own costs. The OECD's (Organisation for Economic Co-operation and Development's) two-year study *Harmonising Donor Practices for Effective Aid Delivery* recognized the significant proportion of developing countries' administrative capacity employed by aid agencies' demands. It conducted a survey 'to identify donor practices that placed the highest burdens on partner countries in terms of ownership, aid transaction costs and aid effectiveness' (OECD, 2003, p13). Many donor representatives in Tanzania:

> *. . . expressed their concern about increasing transaction costs on their side in connection with the development and monitoring of SWAps and similar coordinated aid arrangements (while at the same time appreciating the higher levels of transparency, information-sharing and, therefore, potential quality of their support). It is clear that those developments, if followed in any detail, require*

> *an intensive participation from the local donor community. Likewise, the*
> *Ministry of Finance and other central ministries will find that the pressure on*
> *them will increase (ibid, p116).*

Compensating benefits were recognized, and in an ideal SWAp/budget support arrangement there would be devolution from head office, fewer visiting missions, and a much reduced workload on tedious administration for all. However, for the ingredients of this happy condition it is not the present but the future tense that is used.

Perhaps the jury is out on whether, where and in what ways the shift of balance from projects to programme and policy support has increased or decreased demands on administrative capacities. The pattern is likely to be mixed. But it remains relevant to ask how often a mission visit,[15] a policy dialogue meeting, a demand for information, a reporting requirement or a workshop is assessed in terms of the opportunity cost of the time and energy of those involved.[16]

These demands also affect NGOs, especially INGOs, but in varied ways. As NGOs have increasingly become involved in advocacy and policy influence, so they have been drawn into meetings and workshops – for example, discussing PRSPs (poverty reduction strategy papers). More serious, perhaps, have been the requirements for proposal writing and reporting. As NGOs have derived more of their support from lenders and donors, so more of their time has been taken up in these activities. Different funders for the same project require different reporting formats. Competitive bidding for contracts exacerbates costs, enhances the power of lenders and donors as supplicant bidders struggle to find out what is wanted and what will succeed, and demoralizes and diminishes the effectiveness (through the opportunity cost of their time) of all who take part. In the words of someone in an Irish NGO:

> *The flow of money lasts for a very short time, so what we need to do is present*
> *proposals to donors to get the money. . . To get information, to fulfil the donor*
> *requirements is actually what takes our energy. By the time you have your*
> *USAID proposal put in, in the right format in 40 pages, you are brain dead*
> *(cited in Corcoran-Tindill, 2002, p72).*

The opportunity costs of staff time vary. Taking the time of those who are influential and committed to their work can have very high costs, indeed. On the other hand, there are some who, had they not been writing a report, would have been reading the newspaper, dealing with private business or simply absent. My experience has been that many government officials, and almost all staff in NGOs, want to do a good job, and are committed to making the world a better place. When such people are overloaded and diverted by visiting missions, negotiations, reporting, workshops, policy dialogue and corruption, it is at the cost of the poor and of the good changes we call development.

The capital trap

One effect of these trends is widely reported[17] to be less travel outside the capital city. Many pulls and restraints deter lender, donor, INGO and government staff from local travel. Many commitments and activities trap them in capitals. Like iron filings to a magnet they are drawn in and held in place. The image of a black hole is extreme; but there is a strong and seductive inward- and upward-looking tendency to orient away from the peripheries and poor people, and towards power and sources of funds. Where decisions and staff have been decentralized to a country office, there may be more internal meetings to attend. Where decisions remain centralized in the home headquarters, there may be more visiting missions to meet and manage – for example, local travel may be deterred, prevented or cancelled by important visitors from headquarters. NGOs – funded, as they increasingly are, by lenders and donors – suffer knock-on effects. In an Asian capital, a bilateral official funding half an education programme demanded, at short notice, that two of the INGO staff involved should be in the capital for the week when someone was coming from Washington. To its credit, the INGO did not even reply. Most lamentably, local travel outside the capital city may be discouraged and even forbidden.[18]

Readers will judge for themselves whether it is a caricature to see a spectre of government, lender, donor and NGO staff in capital cities; meeting one another in workshops and at round tables; negotiating; influencing one another; writing and receiving reports and failing to find the time to read them; demanding and constructing logframes; meeting visitors; imposing conditions that entail weeks of work by others; organizing and going to workshops; participating in consultations and dialogues concerning IPRSPs (interim poverty reduction strategy papers), PRSPs, PSIAs (poverty and social impact analyses) and whatever other new processes and procedures have been introduced; and keeping up to date with the latest policy directives from head offices in Washington, New York, London, Brussels, Stockholm, Rome, Paris, Tokyo and so on. They do all this hoping to influence the World Bank, the government and other partners in ways that will make life better for poor people and improve the chances of achieving the MDGs.

In this scenario, younger staff in donor agencies believe that they will promote their careers best by involving themselves in the big policy issues, not by going to the field. 'The field' in their organization, in any case, refers to the country where they find themselves, not the towns, villages and homesteads outside the capital. From the perspective of their headquarters, their offices in the capital are 'in the field' and they are gaining 'field experience' there. These younger staff have heard of the biases of rural development tourism, and use this as an excuse for not visiting rural areas.[19] Nor have their agencies any field projects left for them to visit, and which might, through their staff, give them some 'ground-truthing' about rural realities. The more they stay in the capital, the more they may privately fear the exposure, uncertainty and, perhaps, discomfort of going out. In any case, they might not be rewarded or recognized for doing so. Better by far to learn to write well-phrased memos, to speak well in meetings, to keep on good terms with headquarters by spending the budget and to impose logframes on 'partners' and evaluate performance against them – in short, to conform to the norms of behaviour that are seen to be rewarded.

Readers will judge to what degree this is fair or a caricature. Conditions, values, norms and practices vary between aid agencies, countries, individuals and institutional cultures. But if and where this picture is true, it is deeply troubling. For how on earth can aid agency staff engage well in policy discussions about poverty unless they have a sense of the realities of poor people in the country where they work?

Whose capacity is scarcer? Twists in the tale

In the development discourse of earlier decades, *absorptive capacity* was a common phrase. It referred to the capacity of a country and its administration to take in and spend funds for development. Lack of absorptive capacity was frequently seen as a problem, especially for lenders with large loans (though, paradoxically, it may have helped by delaying and reducing the slide into debt). It varied by country, sector and type of project or programme. In South Asia, it was less of a constraint than in sub-Saharan Africa. Delays in negotiation, preparation and spending were described as 'slippage'. A World Bank staffer told me that there were informal rules of thumb for different countries for the months or years of slippage to be expected at different stages in the life cycle of a project. Eighteen months overall was quite common. The mindset was that of blaming the victim. It was a deficiency of the borrower or receiver, not of the lender or donor when there was slippage.

This can be turned on its head. Responsibility for delays could equally have been attributed to the many procedural hoops and conditionalities imposed by the lenders and donors, the limited number of aid agency staff and the many pressures they were under. Their own rules, regulations and lack of staff limited and still limit their capacity to disburse. In the words of a well-informed observer:

> At a minimum, donor staff must follow many non-negotiable administrative procedures that consume weeks of their time, such as entering financial data properly in tracking systems, filing project documents carefully, and reviewing monitoring and evaluation reports. Donor staff are deluged with policy statements from their own organizations on cross-cutting issues to be incorporated into every project design, from gender concerns, to addressing HIV/AIDS, to environmental concerns, to addressing human rights issues. Donor organizations then measure performance of their staff in ways that create additional pressures. For example, meeting disbursement targets is a key measure of performance for donor staff. They are expected to achieve quick and quantifiable results, which often take precedence over process results. A constant focus on reducing overheads means time spent negotiating decisions is seen as a cost to be reduced, rather than a necessary or developmental process (Garett Pratt, pers comm).

Throughout most if not all of the development decades, there has been pressure to reduce administrative overheads, often principally construed as numbers of staff and staff costs.

In consequence, the administrative capacity of aid agencies has been a growing constraint. In some INGOs, as well as in lender and donor agencies, the struggle has been to spend more and, of course, better, but with fewer staff.[20] The issues are not simple, as more staff may mean more time spent in meetings and other internal interactions such as emails; and fewer staff can mean more ownership and autonomy for the recipient government. All the same, many of the best actions are staff intensive, involving relationships and learning. For overall effectiveness in spending a budget, especially when the intention is to reduce poverty, it has to be asked again and again whether more would be achieved with more staff. Increasing budgets and, at the same time, reducing the staff who manage them can be a cruel absurdity.

In response, lender and donor staff have been driven to search for ways to spend more money faster. Short postings accentuate the incentive to achieve something in the short run in ways that are sparing in staff time. Field projects and capital expenditures tend to have long gestation periods and slippage, with slow disbursements, and to be staff intensive. Recurrent expenditures on salaries and supplies are more reliable ways of spending quickly and might be supposed to place fewer demands on recipient countries. But to what extent sector-wide approaches meet the need for administration-sparing disbursements through such recurrent expenditures is open to question: pooling funds for the agricultural sector in Mozambique had 'huge costs' and took more than seven years of negotiations to reach implementation, 'as well as an enormous amount of expertise and resources on both sides to manage the process' (Pavignani and Hauck, 2002, p17, cited in Acharya, de Lima and Moore, 2004). Direct budget support would seem simpler, if more risky, with potential for lower additional demands per dollar transferred on the administrative capacity of both funder and funded than either projects or SWAps.

These are, though, in part speculations. There is a research agenda here to evaluate projects, programmes and budget support, evaluating not only their more obvious costs and benefits, but also the demands placed on the administrative capacity of recipients and funders alike, and their transaction and opportunity costs.

Administrative capacity and HIV/AIDS

A new factor in some countries is HIV/AIDS. Its impact has been most acute in sub-Saharan Africa, especially Southern Africa, but trends in South Asia and elsewhere are ominous. In most African countries, HIV/AIDS has been responsible for an insidiously creeping erosion of administrative capacity. Most obviously this has been through the sickness and death of staff in organizations, whether government, private or civil society. In Malawi, for example, it was estimated in 1998 that by 2005 40 per cent of teachers, nurses, doctors and military personnel would have died from AIDS (World Bank, 1998, cited in James and Mullins, 2002).[21] Less obviously, other factors interact to reduce performance: among these are staff worrying about and caring for sick relatives and orphans, time off for funerals, declining team work, stress and lower performance when the extra work of others is taken on, costs of recruiting and training replacements and demoralization.[22] In addition, there is the administration intensity of meeting the financial costs, and of revising and managing staff health and welfare policies.

In African and other countries badly afflicted by the HIV/AIDS pandemic, the wheel has come full circle. The arguments of the 1960s and 1970s about administrative capacity as a scarce resource apply again and with tragic force. The situation is even worse, as with HIV/AIDS it costs more to achieve less. In the slide from capacity-building to capacity maintenance, to the rearguard action of minimizing capacity loss, organizations face extra costs such as sickness benefits, continuing to pay sick staff who cannot work, recruiting, training and inducting their replacements, and providing anti-retroviral therapy. At the same time, as staff and their experience are lost, programmes suffer. James and Mullins (2002) point out that aid agencies limit their support to insisting that partners mainstream HIV/AIDS into their programmes, ignoring the fact that the disease means that it will cost their partners more to have less impact. Yet, they 'are blithely demanding the reverse: more impact for less money. Unless remedial action is taken . . . NGOs in sub-Saharan Africa will follow the same trajectory as the disease; they will get sicker and less effective until they finally die, with donors standing [at] a comfortable distance blaming them for their own irresponsible behaviour' (ibid, p17). In such conditions, the arguments for making sparing administrative demands are stronger than ever, including rethinking costings, reporting requirements and relationships.

Managing staff and reducing demands

The direct approach to reducing poverty, achieving the MDGs and disbursing funds has been sector-wide and direct budget support, meaning that funds are channelled direct to governments. The case for these is unproven. In Ghana, MDBS (multi-donor budget support) was described to me by an aid official in 2003 as 'untested, an experiment on a huge scale'. The approach is vulnerable to corruption, can generate a dependent addiction and may prove politically and practically committing and difficult to withdraw from. To the extent that they reduce disbursement blockages, sector-wide and MDBS approaches are also in danger of diverting attention from the practical implications of treating administrative capacity as a scarce resource.

Three such implications stand out. The first concerns staff transfers, management and recruitment: allowing and encouraging staff to stay longer in post (see Chapter 1, pp17–20); increasing their numbers; and changing their composition. The issues are not simple, and for every general prescription exceptions and objections can be found. The clearest case is for aid agency staff, especially but not only expatriates, spending more of their time out of the capital city, learning the realities and experience of poor people, appreciating national and local cultures, and developing relationships of trust with their national counterparts. The case is also strong for increasing numbers of staff to improve the quality of aid and for strong representation of national staff in lender and donor country offices.

The second is to reduce proliferation and fragmentation. This means that bilateral donors would reduce the number of countries aided, and countries aided would follow India's lead in reducing the number of donors.[23] The more aid agencies there are, the higher are the transaction costs of coordination and the longer it takes. Conversely, the fewer there are, the lower the costs and the shorter the time required.

The third is to reduce demands on national administrations and other organizations. The agenda is not new and includes:

- Introduce procedural reforms, reducing and lightening the hoops and requirements. This includes working to reduce the degree of controls and the burdens of reporting by substituting trust, good relationships and reflection and review (see Chapter 3).
- Agree with other aid agencies to standardize *minimum* requirements, especially reporting, so that recipients do not have to write separate reports.
- Optimize, not maximize, negotiations, workshops and other demands on recipient governments and staff, bearing in mind transaction and opportunity costs.

Guidelines on *Harmonising Donor Practices for Effective Aid Delivery*, published by the OECD (2003) as a reference document, result from two years' work by a DAC (development assistance committee) Task Force on Donor[24] Practices. Perhaps for the first time (and, if so, a bit late), these confront the problem of demands on administrative capacity. The analysis and recommendations apply both to lenders and donors, and to recipient ('partner' or 'host') governments. The core problem is seen to result from the combination of three factors: partner countries' institutional capacity and policies; aid agencies' requirements and policies; and the lack of fit between these. The recommended good practices include simplifying and harmonizing aid agency procedures, reducing unnecessary duplication, synchronizing budget cycles, converging on the host government's procedures, and capacity-building. The difficulty is implementing the good practices. Donor proliferation aggravates the problems. A needs assessment survey in 11 partner countries found that 'Most of the people who advocated greater harmonization felt that there was insufficient political will in the donor community to achieve this' (ibid, p118). Despite the rhetoric, aid agencies set up separate systems in Uganda (ibid, pp104–105). And even if procedures are harmonized, they may be added to each other and end up more complex and demanding, not less.

The guidelines recognize many of the issues. What should be done has been made clearer – but it will be difficult because it requires many aid agency staff to work differently and to confront the cultures, procedures and narrow views and interests of their agencies. Perhaps there are some champions and heroes here in the making, if they can avoid being prematurely transferred.

Words and concepts

In parallel with these changes, language, concepts, thinking and action related to administrative capacity have evolved and continue to evolve. During the major decolonizations of the 1960s and for the following decade, the view in development aid was that skills and experience were needed, especially in African countries. When IDS in Sussex was set up in 1966, *courses* for *training* were in vogue and training was a major part of its purpose. Soon, both words declined in development speak, though like five-year plans, they survived robustly in India. For many years, IDS then conducted five-week *study seminars*. The words course and training were less often heard (except, notably, for staff training in electronic skills).[25] Attitudes, language and activity have shifted, over almost 40 years, from courses to workshops, from instructing to facilitating, and from teaching to sharing experience.

From the 1980s onwards the term *capacity-building* began to be used. For some it was simply a synonym for training, as in 'I have been sent on a capacity-building course'. David Korten (1984, p177) lamented the way pressures for immediate results measured by goods and services delivered drove out attention to 'building the capacity' of local institutions and for local problem-solving. During the 1990s, capacity-building was used as an inclusive term for sustainably enhancing the competence and problem-solving capabilities of people and institutions. Deborah Eade, in her book *Capacity-Building:An Approach to People-centred Development* (1997), also gave the term a broad meaning, as an approach to development, not something separate from it. It went far beyond investing in people to investing in organizations and in networks, and supporting capacities that were intellectual, organizational, social, political, cultural, material, practical or financial (Eade, 1997, pp23–49).

During the 1990s, a transition of usage began from capacity-*building*, with its connotations of design, construction, structure, materials and a builder, to capacity *development*, with its associations of adaptation, evolution, growth, good change and facilitation. In the late 1990s, a website, www.capacity.org, was set up and entitled 'a gateway on capacity development'. Under the leadership of Doug Horton, ISNAR (International Service for National Agricultural Research) conducted an action-learning initiative on *Evaluating Capacity Development* (Horton et al, 2003). This extended the concept and practice to embrace the use of participatory evaluation as a direct means for capacity development in research and development organizations. The aim of capacity development is to improve an organization's potential performance – its ability to apply its skills and resources to accomplish its goals and satisfy the expectations of its stakeholders. This encompasses both an organization's capacities to carry out its day-to-day activities and its capacities to learn and change. In seeing how this works out in practice, and to avoid thinking in terms of a uni-linear process, Dindo Campilan (2002, p84) introduced the concept of *contribution* in place of impact. A capacity development programme then can make a contribution to the capacity development of individuals and organizations, which, in turn, makes a contribution to their work performance, which ultimately contributes to changes among those who are meant to benefit.

Administrative capacity, agency and power

To think of administrative capacity as a scarce resource, as I did originally, remains useful in forcing reflection on the transaction and opportunity costs of actions demanded by and within aid agencies. But its use can be simplistic. Administrative capacity is not a commodity, nor a quantity to be measured whether in numbers of staff, or their salaries, or in other ways. Many other variables make it elastic. To enhance it can be a matter of numbers of staff, to be sure, but also of capacity development and institutional learning and change. A crucial capacity in all of this is awareness of the other – reflection on and recognition of the realities of others in other organizations, and of the procedures and cultures of those organizations. This means that both funders and recipients examine the demands they make on one another, and the costs and opportunity costs of their being met. This applies more forcefully to funders since they are usually the dominant partners. It means also creating and protecting commitment and continuities in post (see Chapter 1), adopting empowering organizational procedures, cultures and trust (see Chapter 3) and obtaining political support. It means avoiding and moderating the multifarious distractions of corruption. Most of all, perhaps, it is a question of personal qualities and motivation, commitment, energy and integrity (see Chapters 6 and 7).

So much here depends upon individual agency and awareness. Many of the good things that have happened in development can be traced to individual champions and their alliances.[26] One appealing strategy for those in aid agencies and governments who seek to get more done, and done better is to find and support such people, try to ensure that they stay in posts where they can innovate and influence, and help them to form alliances and networks through which they can express their energy and creativity.

This strategy is, though, vulnerable: champions can be marginalized, penalized, undermined and transferred. It can also divert attention from the bigger question of responsibility and power in aid relationships. Reflection on these almost inevitably starts with the organization which exercises most power in determining the development agenda – the World Bank. A consistent finding, overwhelming in all regions and in virtually all countries, from a survey of 2600 'opinion-formers in 48 countries' was that the World Bank forced its agenda on developing countries (Princeton Survey Associates, 2002).[27] Against this perceived reality, which by association includes other lenders and donors who coordinate with the Bank, the rhetoric of ownership and partnership is not short on hypocrisy. At the same time as it proclaims country ownership, and stresses how the country must be in the driving seat, the World Bank maintains its power over countries and their policies. It sustains its dominant position, in part, through its prestige, competitive culture and staff. Its prestige attracts staff of exceptional intelligence, competence, energy and ambition, whose capacities are then honed and enhanced by a culture and incentives that reward dominant behaviour. They then continually introduce new procedures, mechanisms and requirements and their acronyms. So, we have a progressive accumulation[28] of CASs (country assistance strategies); CDFs (comprehensive development frameworks); CPRGSs (comprehensive poverty reduction and growth strategies); IPRSPs (interim poverty reduction strategy papers); ISPs (institutional strategy papers); MTEFs (medium-term expenditure frameworks); NDSs (national development strategies); NPESs (national poverty eradication strategies); PAFs (poverty action funds); PAPs (participation action plans); PEAPs (poverty eradication action plans); PERs (public expenditure reviews); PETSs (public expenditure tracking studies); PPAs (participatory poverty assessments); PRGFs (poverty reduction and growth facilities); PRSs (poverty reduction strategies); PRSCs (poverty reduction strategy credits); PRSPs (poverty reduction strategy papers); PRSP-PRs (poverty reduction strategy paper progress reports); PSIAs (poverty and social impact analyses); PSRs (poverty status reports); PTFs (poverty task forces); SAPs (structural adjustment programmes); SAPRIs (structural adjustment participatory review initiatives); SWAps (sector-wide approaches); TSPs (target strategy papers); and the like, and by the time this is read, no doubt some more. Taken individually, the rationale for each can be understood. Collectively, they mystify anyone who is unfamiliar with them.[29] Following each hard on the heels of others, they reinforce and sustain the dominance of the World Bank and its staff: they disempower and subordinate national staff by absorbing their time and energy in lives spent learning to dance to new tunes from Washington, DC, and who then have no time or space to compose their own. In this perspective, the dominance of the World Bank is a confidence trick, with influence far beyond anything justified by the scale or importance of its lending programme or patronage. As Charles Abugre has asked:

> . . . *if the PRS process were a government-led process, why would the [World] Bank and Fund send numerous missions to the country to develop the PRS? Why would the Bank develop a 1000-page sourcebook to tell developing country groups how to create a PRS (Abugre, 2000, cited in Wilks and Lefrançois, 2002, p11)?*

As a mischievous verse has it, the World Bank and its followers are saying to recipient countries:

> *One proviso you must meet,*
> *You sit in the driver's seat*
> *But don't you ever dare reveal*
> *Whose hands you know are on the wheel.*

The passengers are, moreover, swung around and disoriented by the way the hands repeatedly jerk the wheel.

Unequal relations and power over governments and other recipients are maintained by lenders and donors through the ever-changing demands they make on administrative capacity. If they are serious about ownership and nationals sitting in the driving seat, funders have to recognize how their demands disempower. They have to learn to behave differently. This means working for reciprocities, for combinations of restraint, respect and trust on their part, complemented by proactive autonomy, responsibility and trustworthiness on the part of recipients. The aim has to be to open up more spaces for individual action in bureaucracies

– of aid agencies and recipients alike. This requires sensitivity and will on the part of the stronger – those actors who, in a context, are uppers (lenders, donors, seniors, etc.) – to limit their demands and controls. It also requires guts, solidarity and responsibility on the part of the weaker – those actors who in a context are lowers (borrowers, receiving governments, juniors, etc.) – to resist, to negotiate, to earn trust by using responsibly the spaces they gain, and to show themselves and others what they can achieve. If the uppers and lowers can combine with less control, lower transaction costs, and more trust and trustworthiness, more will be done and it will be done better. It is through a synergy of reducing demands, levelling power relations and taking responsible action that administrative capacity can most effectively be enhanced.

Notes

1   Originally published with the title 'Executive capacity as a scarce resource: A challenge on aid and development policies' (Chambers, 1969, pp5–8). The term executive capacity never caught on, so I have substituted the more familiar administrative capacity.
2   For an authoritative exposition, see Waterston (1965).
3   Particularly Gray (1966); Hunter (1967); Belshaw (1968); and Papanek (1968). The term 'executive capacity' has been borrowed from the writings of C. S. Gray.
4   As elaborated by Albert Hirschman (1967) in *Development Projects Observed*. Hirschman also describes concealed benefits from projects, and these should, of course, also be taken into account.
5   Some new seed varieties require renewal and additional inputs, and therefore become administration intensive and administration persistent (Raghavan, 1967). The implication is that seed breeders should select varieties that will be relatively administration sparing.
6   The Pearson Commission was set up during the late 1960s under the chairmanship of Lester Pearson, the former Canadian prime minister, to review development assistance.
7   For a recent example, see Chapter 7 for the various 'capitals' that contribute to a sustainable livelihood. Social capital, a rather amoebic concept, flowing here and there, has made it easier for non-economist social scientists to talk to economists about social dimensions of importance, which would otherwise have been more overlooked.
8   The costs of these new organizations included the huge investment of time and energy in battling with other departments and struggling to survive and to gain resources. See 'Creating new organizations for rural development' (Chambers, 1971).
9   A remarkable exception was the commitment shown by teachers and other professionals in Uganda during the 1980s when hyperinflation had made their salaries almost worthless – to the point where two months of a secondary school head teacher's salary were needed to buy a bicycle tyre. While they

survived largely through farming, teachers were still working as teachers and were proud of the results they were achieving (Whyte, 1987).

10   I am grateful to Rosalind Eyben for personal communications and her writings, which have contributed to this chapter and saved me from a number of errors. This does not mean she necessarily agrees with the views expressed, which are my responsibility alone.

11   At this point the reader, who is playing development bingo, (also known as *tombola* and *housey-housey*) may be crying 'development'.

12   The usage 'donor' is the one adopted by the WDRs (World Development Reports). For reasons that are readily interpreted as public relations, the WDRs do not distinguish lenders (who put countries in debt, like the IFIs (international financial institutions) from donors who make grants. For an analysis of this usage in the 2000/2001 World Development Report, *Poverty and Development,* see Chambers (2001).

13   I have been told that at one time some officials in Tanzania could expect to attend at least one workshop a month, for which they could receive allowances equivalent to a month's salary. Lenders and donors, having at first competed in a free market by paying more and more in *per diems* to attract officials to their workshops, then tried to form, as it were, a cartel and to fix prices.

14   When I sat in on a lender/donor meeting with the Ministry of Finance in Tanzania, the lenders and donors spoke with many voices. This seemed to empower the Tanzanians, who could divide and rule. The main administrative burden seemed to fall on the aid agencies, who were left with homework to do. This was, though, just a snapshot and may not have been typical.

15   There is a seasonal dimension here. In 1979 the Select Committee on Overseas Development of the UK House of Commons wanted to make its annual visit to India. The best time to go to India was February, cold in the UK and pleasantly warm but not too hot in India. The Indian Government requested a delay as this was a busy time near the end of their financial year. The committee did not budge, and was courteously if inconveniently received. This timing was no new thing. As the verse has it:

> *The international experts' flights*
> *Have their own seasons. Winter nights*
> *In London, Washington and Rome*
> *Are what drive them in flocks from home.*

16   A rare exception is the ALPS (Accountability, Learning and Planning System) of ActionAid, introduced in 2001 (ActionAid, 2000, 2001a; Scott-Villiers, 2002; and see pp69–72). This was intended to reduce time writing reports, with more attention to learning and changing through participatory review and reflection processes.

17   The decline in travel outside capital cities by aid agency staff has not, to my knowledge, been systematically researched and documented. But in private conversations it has been so repeatedly mentioned by staff in different agencies that it can be asserted with some confidence.

18   This is phrased cautiously because it is so wilfully blinkered to forbid aid agency staff to travel, unless there are strong security reasons, that it is not easy to believe that this has really happened. I have been told, however, that in two countries without serious security problems, staff of one bilateral donor have been instructed not to leave the capital city. I just hope these anecdotes are unfounded.

19   Having written about the biases of rural development tourism (Chambers, 1983, pp10–23), I find this so sad. The point of stressing the biases was to be aware and to offset them. There are many ways of doing this (see, for example, Hirschmann, 2003). And even if they are not offset, it is better to go than not to go.

20   The most extreme form of this pathology that I have encountered was with Bandaid. A strong anti-bureaucratic ideology demanded that staff costs should be minimal. Reliance on volunteers went some way to offsetting this bias; but I do not doubt that the Bandaid money dedicated to development projects would have been better spent with a larger staff.

21   High and quotable figures like these for projected deaths of teachers from AIDS in Southern Africa have been challenged by research, which finds them exaggerated (Paul Bennell, pers comm). This is a contested area with deeply held views.

22   For a fuller account of the many costs and disruptions caused by the HIV/ AIDS pandemic, see James and Mullins (2002) who consider these for NGOs in Malawi.

23   In 2003, India terminated its aid relationship with several donors. Given India's size, its ability to handle donors and the quality of some of the bilateral programmes, this was a questionable decision from the standpoint of poor people. In smaller countries the case for reducing numbers of donors will be much stronger.

24   In the usage of the report, 'donor' includes 'lender'.

25   The right-wing think tank, the Adam Smith Institute, has no such linguistic inhibitions and unashamedly describes short seminars for senior officials as 'courses'.

26   See, for example, Leonard (1991), Roe (1993) and Chambers and Pettit (2004).

27   To give a more balanced view, it has to be noted that it was reported that, overall, respondents took a generally favourable view of the World Bank's influence on their countries.

28   These are listed in alphabetical, not chronological order; most, if not all, originate from the World Bank. Daunting though it is, the list is based only on an I-CARP (interim comprehensive acronym review process).

29   For example, from a recent donor's action plan 'PSIA should be an integrated part of the PRS process and linked into the PRSC/PRGF'.

3

Procedures, Principles and Power

The check always is on whether organizational systems and procedures support or hinder the two primary processes: direct contact in the field and learning towards improved practice and strategy (CDRA, 2000, p16).

. . . transparency is a non-negotiable in the development relationship (CDRA, 2001, p21).

We can only respond to the questions raised if you can promise that you will not victimise us by cancelling our project (community-based organization member during an ActionAid Kenya Participatory Review and Reflection Process, 2001, cited in David and Mancini, 2004, p19).

Part 1 of this chapter comes from *Managing Rural Development*, published in 1974, and draws lessons from experience in Eastern Africa, especially the Kenya Government's Special Rural Development Programme. Part 2 considers the relevance of this experience for the 21st century, and analyses how procedures, principles and processes can change power relations and make space for creative local diversity.

Part 1: Recalling Lessons from the Past (1974)

Points of departure and directions [from Managing Rural Development 1974]

Managing rural development was considered from an Eastern African perspective in 1973. Despite the priority of rural development, government administration had not performed well in supporting it. Area-bound projects, sectoral programmes, and local development planning all had disappointing records. Four diagnoses were common but misleading: a shortage of high-level manpower; poor attitudes among public servants; lack of integration and coordination; and government organizational structure. Direct measures to deal with these missed a key prescription, to improve management procedures. These had a part to play in shifts of focus from urban to rural, from planning to implementation, from capital to recurrent expenditure, and from hierarchical authoritarian administration to more decentralized and democratic management of field staff.

The context[1]

A 2004 precis of pp12–22

Managing Rural Development: Ideas and experience from East Africa (1974) presented and analysed evidence and experience from Kenya, notably the Special Rural Development Programme, and also from Botswana, Tanzania, Uganda, and Zambia. It began by outlining the priority of rural development. This was based on population, with the vast majority not just of people but of the poorest people living in rural areas; on concern about drift to the towns; on the invisible presence in rural areas of most of the very poor people (with migration it was often the widows, the deserted wives, the old, the feeble and the very young who remained behind); and on economic arguments. In addition to fiscal devices, a major, perhaps the major, means of government intervention to promote rural development and welfare was through government administration in such fields as education, health, roads and communications, water supplies, co-operatives and marketing, credit, agricultural research and extension, forestry, family planning, nutrition and community development.

The three main rural development initiatives had a mixed record. Multi-sector bounded-site projects were visible, and much visited, researched and written about, but were centralized, sensitive to quality and continuity of management, and often failed. Sectoral programmes were less visible but had more potential with their large field staffs and budgets, but were criticized for failures to spend the funds allocated to them, for poor performance by field staff, and for lack of coordination. Area management in which departments at the local level combined in development committees, in spending decentralized block grants and in making and implementing plans for particular areas, had at best a mixed record: development committees were vulnerable to becoming large talking shops; and block grants sometimes galvanized activity but were not always well used.

Managing Rural Development (1974) continues

The most disappointing experience has been development plans for particular areas. The common outcome of plan formulation without implementation has taken three main forms. The first is *disaggregation of national targets* to local levels as an incentive to staff, but where the staff were not involved in setting the targets, the targets were often unrealistic, and the attempt an outright failure. The second is preparation of long *shopping lists* of projects, justified by the needs for 'participation' in planning, compiled with enthusiasm and in considerable detail by local-level staff and sent in to Ministries of Planning for incorporation in the national plan. This occurred as a preliminary to the second plans of Kenya, Tanzania and Zambia, but in each case the large stacks of local proposals were regarded with despair by central economists and largely ignored in the formulation of the national plan. The third form of planning without implementation has been *data collection without practicable action proposals*, typically carried out by high powered teams from the centre who leave behind a so-called 'plan' for an area which joins the other unused and unusable documents on the shelves of government offices. The outcomes of these various failures are not just that nothing happens; they involve costs in the time of government staff, in government expenditure, and most seriously of all, in the disillusion of local level staff who become realistically cynical about any further attempt at area planning.

Area planning with implementation has been rare. The most important example is probably the Special Rural Development Programme (SRDP) in Kenya... The SRDP demonstrated, as did the earlier experiences with target disaggregation, shopping lists, and data plans, the extreme difficulties of area planning without decentralization. It went further and exposed many of the problems of implementation, particularly the delays in fund releases which so often hold up and sometimes destroy projects in the field. It also showed, despite able management at the centre and good inter-ministerial cooperation, that the main bottleneck in rural development in Kenya was in Nairobi, just as in Zambia it was in Lusaka, and in Tanzania it was in Dar es Salaam.

Taken as a whole, the experience with government-administered initiatives in rural development in the countries of Eastern Africa up until the early 1970s fell far short of what had been needed and hoped for. The enthusiasm for multisector bounded-site projects which followed independence waned as their multiple difficulties, their limited impact, and sometimes the dominance of foreigners in their management became evident. Instead, attention turned to sectoral programmes and area management and to the more complex and intractable problems of mobilizing the huge government field administrations for more effective action in those rural areas where the vast majority of the population lived. It became more important than ever to analyse past shortcomings and to see how they might be surmounted in the future.

Four diagnoses and a missing prescription

Four diagnoses were popular in the 1960s. All had some validity. But each could generate misleading recommendations for remedial action because of a vital missing prescription.

The first diagnosis was shortage of high-level manpower. This was indeed a serious constraint in all the countries of Eastern Africa in the 1960s, and it remains serious in some, such as Botswana, in the early 1970s. De-Europeanizing and Africanizing an administration, undertaking additional functions including defence, foreign affairs and closer management of the economy, creating and staffing parastatals, Africanizing the private sector – from the time of independence onwards these tasks created a demand for high-level manpower which far exceeded the supply. The manpower planning of the 1960s had a crucial part to play in mitigating the crisis and in identifying ways in which it could be overcome. Too often, however, 'a lack of high-level manpower' was used as an excuse for poor performance and for failing to probe into its causes, and as a polite expression to cover up culpable inefficiency and corruption. It was a convenient explanation: it placed blame correctly on the failure of the colonial administration to develop education and training faster, and it suited the economists who dominated planning ministries since it was something they could do. But by the early 1970s in most of the countries of Eastern Africa the great majority of field staff were qualified nationals, many with substantial experience. The issue had become much less one of numbers of trained staff, and much more one of performance and output on the job.

The second diagnosis has been that field staff are poorly motivated, lack entrepreneurial attitudes, drink too much, work too little, and spend too much time on their private interests. Again, it is a convenient explanation for those in the capital. But much of the poor performance of field staff can be attributed to a work situation in which they are reacting rationally to a situation in which it is not clear what is expected of them but in which it *is* clear that the exercise of initiative in development matters is at least as likely to be penalized as deviant behaviour as rewarded for being good work. At its most pathological the field staff member's work life is liable to consist of sudden transfers (leading to acute problems of family separation and continuity in children's education), of sudden changes in those staff immediately senior to him, of a flow of mutually incompatible instructions and programmes from headquarters, overlaying and eventually burying one another, with demands for information which is never used or for plans which are never acted on (or if acted on, are not implemented while he is still in the post), and high powered flying visits by senior officers in which snap decisions are taken and instructions issued on the basis of patently inadequate information. Periods of being ignored alternate with periods of intense but superficial evaluation. With better projects to implement, better and more consistent supervision, greater continuity of service in one place, more involvement in planning their own work, and evaluation and rewards by results, in short, if management were better, it seems fair to suggest that their performance would improve sharply.

A third misleading diagnosis is a lack of integration and coordination. 'Integrated' rural development became very popular in international circles in the latter 1960s. The origins of this usage would make a fascinating subject for research. One of the sources was the peculiar and pressing need for specialized agencies of the United Nations to reduce rivalry and to work better together. 'Integrated' development meant development in which several UN agencies collaborated, or were meant to collaborate. Much loose thought and many vacuous statements were permitted, encouraged and made temporarily respectable by the vogue of integration. It is perhaps a little unfair to chastise the authors of UN documents, since desperate mental gymnastics may be needed in order to achieve the compromises which make their issue possible at all; but a quotation from the UN publication *Integrated Approach to Rural Development in Africa* will illustrate the obscure generality which sometimes resulted:

> . . . *the concept of the 'integrated' approach in the context of rural development means an 'integral' approach in the sense that it is a highly structural and systematic exercise in which all components in the system of development can be*

understood as important and appreciated for the part which they play individually and collectively. In this sense, the concept differs from the 'harmonization' of plans and the 'cooperation' of various agencies. It also has significance for the coordination of rural development plans (UN, 1971, p42).

Whatever meaning statements like this may have they scarcely help in trying to see how to get things done.

Equally, the word 'coordination' provides a handy means for avoiding responsibility for clear proposals. It is perhaps for this reason that it is much favoured by visiting missions who are able to conceal their ignorance of how an administrative system works or what might be done about it by identifying 'a need for better coordination'. Indeed, a further research project of interest would be to test the hypothesis that the value of reports varies inversely with the frequency with which the word 'coordination' is used. Moreover, by using 'integrated' and 'coordinated' more or less synonymously and in alternate sentences, long sections of prose can be given an appearance of saying something while in fact saying very little indeed.

When the activities to which they refer are looked at in detail 'integration' and 'coordination' can be seen to have heavy costs as well as benefits. The integrated approach to rural development is liable to mean a simultaneous implementation of many different programmes in the same area. But if rural development is seen as a sequence, then programmes themselves should follow sequences. Further, an attack on many fronts in one area may involve a wasteful and inequitable concentration of resources. Integration and coordination are too easily regarded as automatic benefits. If integration and coordination are good, the thinking goes, then maximum integration and maximum coordination are best of all. But unless interaction between officials is regarded as an end in itself, this is patently untrue. Coordination can have high costs in staff time spent in meetings and in dealing with paperwork. With maximum coordination staff time would be completely taken up in meetings and arrangements and the output would be nil. Coordination and integration should in fact be optimized, not maximized. Unconnected projects are best implemented in an unconnected fashion. And even when projects are connected, the costs as well as the benefits or whatever procedures are proposed for relating them together have to be weighed in assessing whether they would better continue independently.

These two words have done grave disservice by allowing vague thinking and by discouraging identification in detail of certain important relationships and potential benefits. The processes of rural development may be helped through organizing the activities of government and other agencies so that they complement one another, do not duplicate one another, do not compete for the same resources, and use scarce resources sparingly. In some rural development programmes and projects more than others, it may be worthwhile to arrange collaboration between agencies, joint planning of programmes, programming the sequence and timing of activities, sharing transport, addressing the same meetings, and so on. For example, projects for women's groups, including vegetable growing, nutrition, health, family planning, and home economics may involve several departments: there may be substantial benefits from joint planning of the work to avoiding overlapping and to avoid confusing or overloading the groups. Sequences of extension work may also be planned. But making proposals in this sort of detail is often uncongenial and difficult for consultants, advisers and civil servants. It is tempting and easy to take refuge in statements like 'there should be better co-ordination between departments X and Y in order to achieve an integrated approach to Z', instead of thinking the problem through and saying something like 'a meeting should be held at the end of each month, chaired by A, attended by B and C, at which joint work programmes should be drawn up', specifying the detail of the procedure.

A fourth common diagnosis is that something is wrong with the structure of government. Recommendations can then take several forms. One is the setting up of new organizations, usually parastatals. While there may be good reasons for such action, the costs are likely to be high in new overheads, in staff transfers, in prolonging reliance on foreign personnel whether in the new organizations or in the organizations from which local staff are transferred, and in the energies devoted to creating the organization, overcoming its teething troubles, and establishing its position in the community of other organizations. But weighing against recognition of these costs is the ease with which a new organization can be recommended by a commission, committee, or adviser, and its attractiveness to civil servants for whom it often provides an opportunity for advancement. Another recommendation is that ministerial responsibilities should be realigned, with the transfer of departments (Community Development and Water Affairs being favourites) from one ministry to another. When the dust has settled, however, the staff of the department are usually to be found sitting at the same desks in the same offices doing the same work. The appearance of change on paper is not matched by a change in working realities. Yet another line of recommendation is for internal reorganization of departments, ministries, or government as a whole. This is more difficult to devise and more difficult to effect. The Tanzanian and Zambia decentralizations are examples of this approach. They demonstrate the detailed and imaginative thinking that is required, and the steady will that is needed for implementation. There can be little doubt that reforms like these can be amply justified and well worth the effort they require. But they too have costs. There is always a danger that they and other structural changes will divert attention from the less dramatic but sometimes more important task of making function more effectively those structures which already exist.

The analysis of these four diagnoses points to a missing prescription: improving management procedures. For high level manpower and other staff in field situations, management procedures provide a point of entry for trying to improve performance through modifying the rules and practices which prevail in their working environments. Whatever integration and coordination are desirable can be promoted through careful procedural design; and procedures present an opportunity to improve the operation of existing government organizations as an alternative or complement to major structural change.

In practice, however, management procedures receive much less notice and care than they deserve. To academics they are often an unopened book and believed to be a very dull and unacademic one at that. To short-term consultants they are unattractive because procedural recommendations involve hard work and require a detailed understanding of the administrative system. To lower-level staff they are often empty rituals performed to placate their superiors. To senior government servants embroiled in day-to-day affairs they are just one extra burden, and are thought out under pressure, embodied in circulars, and then introduced on a national scale without either pretesting or subsequent evaluation. But the principles of experimental testing which apply to pilot projects should also apply to procedures. That this so rarely happens is one reason why the detailed rules and conventions by which government agencies in rural areas operate are so often crude and inappropriate, and why the better design of management procedures presents a key point of leverage for improving performance.

Shifts of focus

Further analysis of the experience with rural development plans, programmes and projects builds up a case for a series of shifts of focus and priority, with implications for future resource allocations, particularly of high-level manpower. There are four main thrusts.

First, urban bias is insidious and pervasive. All too often middle-ranking civil servants in field postings intrigue and apply for transfers to the capital city. Those already in the capital only rarely make major field visits. Technical officers give *de facto* priority to urban projects to the neglect of rural. The financial allocations for towns are spent, while those for rural areas remain unspent. Rural development has to fight against a silent conspiracy of centripetal forces which amass human and material resources in the towns and cities. The main reasons are not far to seek. The most obvious is perhaps the educational systems which have oriented aspirations towards white collar jobs and the bright lights of the city. But for middle-ranking civil servants there is much more to it than that. They perceive, usually correctly, that status and chances of promotion vary inversely with distance from the capital: those working in central ministries have the best chances, while those who have disgraced themselves are sent to 'penal' posts at the periphery. For technical officers such as water engineers, architects, roads engineers and electrical engineers, work in a city or town is likely to be more complex, more satisfying and better professional experience than work in villages. Once installed in a central house and office, staff find it difficult to go out to rural areas even if they want to, and easy to stay if they do not. The round of official and domestic engagements, unexpected crises, sudden demands from the minister for a brief, and the number of people who may have to be consulted before a rural visit can be made, combine to chain the civil servant, often a happy prisoner, to his desk. But the application of financial and material resources requires personnel, and money is often spent where staff happen to reside. A major implication, understood in Tanzania and Zambia, is that, in order effectively to shift priorities to rural development, staff have themselves to be moved out into the rural areas.

Second, in rural development there has often been a failure to plan planning and plan management, both in headquarters and in the field. In practice, planners have concentrated on planning and budgeting to the neglect of other activities: on plan formulation perhaps because of its intellectual attraction, its susceptibility to mathematical treatment, its insulation from the details of administration, and its position at the beginning of the sequence of activities; and on budgeting partly because of its undeniable priority and intractable deadlines. In line with these biases, planning literature has been preoccupied with plan formulation, presented as sets of procedures, with less detailed attention paid to implementation, presented as sets of problems. At both national and local levels, resources and effort have been devoted to data collection, plan formulation and plan writing, while programming, implementation, monitoring and evaluation have been relatively ignored. The common result – plan formulation without implementation – constitutes a form of mismanagement and misallocation of resources.

Third, central planners, field administrators and politicians have been preoccupied with capital and development expenditure and with capital projects to the relative neglect of recurrent expenditure and of programmes which are implemented through existing field organizations. This preoccupation appears to have several origins. Donor agencies are biased towards financial aid tied to capital inputs. Economists can more easily carry out their professional activities with capital projects than with recurrent expenditure for which the data may be poor or non-existent. Field administrators find visible capital projects more satisfying, more creative, and easier to present as tangible evidence of development activity, than dispersed field programmes. Politicians, most particularly, need to be able to demonstrate achievements which their constituents will identify with their leadership. At the extreme, donor agencies (most notably the World Bank) may insist on the formation of a special agency to handle a programme or major project rather than working through and improving existing organizations.

From a national point of view, however, very large recurrent resources in the form of trained staff and operating expenses are already committed in the field. For some countries, the iceberg analogy is apposite: the visible tip represents the development projects which attract attention and analysis, while the larger recurrent commitments remain hidden and largely unanalysed below. In both Kenya and Zambia reported recurrent expenditure in 1973/1974 was almost exactly twice capital expenditure.

By way of illustration, in 1973/1974 the Department of Technical Services in the Kenya Government's Ministry of Agriculture had a staff of nearly 14,000, of whom some 6,300 were junior and senior staff, of whom in turn over 3,000 were agricultural assistants, animal health assistants and animal husbandry assistants. For personal emoluments alone, the estimate was for 38 per cent of the Ministry's estimated recurrent expenditure (Republic of Kenya, 1972, pp1, 37, 40). Such heavy allocations as these are committed more or less automatically year by year and without more than marginal choices at a planning level. In planning activities, recurrent resources have thus been relatively neglected and there is a strong case for subjecting recurrent allocations and their use to more stringent appraisal, evaluation and management.

One factor in the lack of attention to recurrent resource allocation and management is what Moris (1972, p115) calls the 'centrist ideology' of planning and administration, the system of beliefs and attitudes which holds that initiative and control do and should reside primarily in the capital city, and outside the capital city higher rather than lower in the hierarchy. A corollary of this view is the belief that field staff are generally rather incompetent and idle, a belief which is unlikely to foster the exercise of the discretion and responsibility required from them if they are to perform well. Without a management system which allows, encourages and rewards the exercise of initiative and the performance of good work, it is scarcely surprising that field staff have often appeared to those in the centre to justify adverse comment. The centrist ideology in fact sustains the conditions which justify it. Over-centralization prevents the exercise of initiative at the lower levels, good performance passes unnoticed, and field staff come fatalistically to accept as a fact of life the flow of instructions and plans from above in the formulation of which they have not played any part and for the implementation of which they do not expect to receive any credit. The authoritarian style of the internal administration of some departments is in sharp conflict with accepted management practices, but preserved by low visibility and the lack of management advisory services in governments. There are, of course, incompetent, poorly trained, and just plain lazy staff. But on the basis of the SRDP experience and many subjective impressions it appears that most field staff have far greater capability for managing their work than most of their superior officers assume. An imaginative management approach to the operation of field agencies might mobilize and exploit the great potential at present cramped and constrained by outdated administrative outlooks and practices.

The four main shifts implied by these analyses – from urban bias to rural; from plan formulation and budgeting to programming, implementation and monitoring; from capital projects to recurrent resource management; and from hierarchical, authoritarian administration to more decentralised and democratic management of field staff – combine with the earlier argument for more attention to procedures to make a case for improving the operation of existing government organizations. For this, specialists in such fields as management, organization and methods, and organizational behaviour, should be recruited and trained, perhaps with a compensating decrease in numbers of economist planners; and that in those countries which have not effectively decentralised, there may be good reasons for posting more high-level staff to the field and giving them more responsibility.

Clusters of procedures

The dangers of isolated partial reforms are notorious (Molander, 1972), but these dangers may apply at least as much to management training without procedural reform as to procedural reform without management training. The thrust of the argument is that procedures provide a neglected key point of entry.

It has proved useful to think in terms of six clusters of procedures, each of which is susceptible to largely independent experimental treatment. These are:

Programming and implementation;
Field staff management;
Local participation;
Evaluation;

Rural research and development
Plan formulation.

The sequence in which these are listed is deliberate. A more logical order might start with plan formulation, leading into programming and implementation. But it has been precisely the logic of starting with plan formulation that has generated the stacks of unimplemented and unimplementable plans which moulder, fade and feed termites on the shelves of offices throughout Eastern Africa. A book which began logically with plan formulation would be in grave danger of repeating the experience and never fighting free from the innumerable considerations, qualifications and ramifications of plan-making. Instead of being about managing rural development, it would be about planning techniques which, if followed, might well impede rural development. Listing the clusters of activities in this unconventional order is part of a deliberate attempt to maintain a balance, as well as to divert some attention and resources from the fashionable activities of evaluation, research and plan formulation to the more difficult and less developed activities of programming, implementation, the management of field staff, and local participation. For all too often the neglect or mishandling of these latter activities have been serious hindrances. And their importance can be expected to increase as governments struggle to give priority to rural development and as they come closer to grips with the obstinate and persistent impediments to getting things done in rural areas.

Part 2: Procedures and Principles to Empower (2004)

Experiments with management procedures were a major focus in the early 1970s' SRDP (Special Rural Development Programme) in Kenya. Somewhat mechanistic and time-intensive, they did not take root. Lessons can be learnt from the SRDP about tendencies: for procedures to accumulate, being easier to introduce than abolish; for reporting and coordination to have costs; for 'lowers' to refrain from criticizing procedures required by 'uppers'; and for procedures to be instruments of power, control and upward accountability. Though thought of as empowering downwards, the SRDP procedures made exacting demands, and were experienced as instruments of upward accountability.

In the 1990s and early 2000s management procedures again became a focus of attention. Logical framework analysis (LFA) shared upward accountability and other characteristics with the SRDP procedures. The significance of power and relationships in development was increasingly recognized, together with how these are influenced by rules and procedures. LFA and targets required by many funding agencies asserted control, hierarchy and upward accountability. This contrasts with the practices of organizations that have empowered poor people. Examples illustrate how power relations can be reversed in three ways: by minimum rules which empower; by affirming non-negotiable principles, which put poor people first; and by downward accountability. To achieve downward accountability and to counter external top-down 'magnetic' requirements of governments and funding agencies demands congruence of behaviour, commitment and organizational culture.

The challenge is to use procedures and rules to reverse and balance relationships of power, with decentralized and democratic diversity. What is done and how it is done are then largely determined by local people, especially those who are poorer. The true tests of empowering procedures and rules are the diversity of the good things that are done, and whether the poor and marginalized gain.

Reflections on the SRDP experience

Managing Rural Development (Chambers, 1974), from which these extracts come, was based on Eastern African experience in the late 1960s and early 1970s. Much of this derived from the SRDP in Kenya. Working from the IDS at the University of Nairobi, I was responsible for setting up its evaluation. The SRDP was designed to evolve and test innovative approaches in six divisions (sub-districts), each of which had a Kenya Government Area Coordinator for the programme. The programme was energetically and ably promoted from within the Ministry of Economic Planning and Development[2] and was enthusiastically supported by donors. Despite, or perhaps partly because of this, it gradually lost political support and after a number of years faded away. My own contribution was, at best, mixed. With what I now recognize as political naivety and insensitivity, I sought to set up an evaluation organization with impatient haste. Its generous resources were resented by others and I did not manage it well. *Managing Rural Development* was written precisely because I withdrew from trying to handle the programme's evaluation and, instead, reflected on the experience and evaluated the evaluation. It may not be a new irony that a failed manager finds the time and has the negative experience to write a book on management.

The book is a startling reminder of how different were the mindsets, practices and policies of the early 1970s. My male-biased and gender-insensitive usage was normal and unquestioned, as with 'manpower' planning: and any suggestion that 'the African farmer' was mainly a 'she' would have been met with incomprehension. Planning was high profile compared with implementation: the SRDP's attempt to shift the balance towards implementation faced, and was weakened by, criticism from academic and consultant economists still trapped in neo-Fabian intellectualizing (and there was no shortage of technical assistance economists in ministries of planning). Specially managed projects were the vogue: the SRDP had 'special' in its title, and was unusual in being inserted into the government bureaucracy; the norm, pushed by the World Bank with its integrated rural development projects, was to establish new separate organizations, making the state fatter, a policy which, as part of one of its cyclical U-turns,[3] the Bank was later to recognize as disastrous (World Bank, 1988). Instead of setting up new organizations, state and parastatal organizations were then to be variously slimmed, disbanded and privatized. Thirty years later, it is another world that we look back on.

Procedures were among the innovations of the SRDP. Some of these originated within government. Others came from the evaluators, including Deryke Belshaw and myself. Ideas and relationships were consciously drawn from engineering systems analysis.[4] The PIM (Programming and Implementation Management) system included an annual programming exercise and annual phasing forms, a monthly management meeting and a monthly management report.[5] Bar charts were to be used in planning and also for monitoring progress against plans and targets. They were intended to help the Area Coordinators in their coordinating, monitoring and catalysing roles, and to improve implementation.

The adoption and 'success' of the procedures was limited and temporary. It is easy to see, now, that they were too mechanistic and time consuming. They had, moreover, been designed centrally, with little participation of those who were to use them. From the experience, some general lessons can be drawn:

- *In hierarchies those 'below' may not speak up against irksome and counterproductive innovations when these come 'from above'.* On one occasion I found myself having to try to persuade Area Coordinators to collect and send monthly reports on information that had been listed centrally as useful and needed. They said little, but their non-verbal resentment was eloquent. The system went ahead on paper but never worked; and if it had worked, I do not believe the data would have been either of much use or much used. This negative experience led to the recommendation in *Managing Rural Development* (pp158–159) that procedures should be evolved with those who were to use them in a participatory manner and in conjunction with pilot testing.

- *It is easier to introduce new procedures than to abolish old.* The SRDP management was unable to release the Area Coordinators from the normal reporting and accounting requirements of government. In consequence, they had a double load. As in this case, procedures are often additive: new ones are required but old ones are not abolished. This can lead to absurd overloads. In North Arcot district in India in the 1970s, a deputy agricultural officer in a block was required to submit 316 reports in a year (Chambers and Wickremanayake, 1977, p163). Even when procedures are formally stated to be no longer required, they may continue. When ActionAid introduced its ALPS (Account-ability, Learning and Planning System) in 2000 (see below), country annual reports were no longer required; but many Country Directors continued to produce them.[6] More generally, to abolish a required procedure entails taking responsibility for the consequences.[7] Prudent bureaucrats prefer to play safe. They are reluctant to take part in the execution of habitual procedures. Instead, they connive at their gradual demise from neglect, overload and irrelevance.

- *Reporting, coordination and management systems take time and can demoralize.* Area coordinators were frustrated and irritated by the amount of time they had to spend on reporting and in coordination with government departments. The costs of seeking and providing information and of turf wars were high, and reduced the time and energy for the programme itself. With hindsight, the heavy procedural requirements of the SRDP can be seen as a burden, which, in the longer term, did not help it to survive. The normal tendencies in such conditions are well known. An organization becomes less efficient and effective. Those required to report, slowly and subtly sabotage and resist. This takes many forms, covert and overt. Reports are fabricated; or they are routinized and become repetitive and largely meaningless; or they are delivered late and, eventually, not at all. The less accurate and useful the reports are, the lower the morale of the staff, the less effective the organization and, eventually, the greater its vulnerability.

- *Adding procedures can weaken, not strengthen, an organization*. If they are taken seriously, additional procedural requirements can lead to a creeping sclerosis. At the extreme, new management systems can lead to what, for the Canadian public service, was described as 'saturation psychosis' (Laframboise, 1971) and protests on the lines of 'I can either do your management system, or I can do my job, but I can't do both.' This may be a growing problem for the World Bank. It has striven to accommodate pressures from two opposite directions – the US Government and US-based NGOs. It has sought to do this by introducing more and more 'operational directives' (Wade, 2001). These have made life increasingly difficult for staff and World Bank loans less attractive to borrowers who are faced with more and more hoops to jump through. In consequence, borrowing countries have shifted increasingly to the private sector for loans with less hassle and lower transaction costs. One can speculate that resulting shrinkage of the lending programme could eventually threaten the long-term viability of the Bank.

Procedures and power: COPs and PEPs

In the first decade of the new century these lessons still apply. We have also moved on in seeing more clearly that procedures are linked with power and relationships, and that acknowledging power and working on relationships are central issues in doing better in development (Eyben, 2004b; Groves and Hinton, 2004). Procedures are then levers for change and can have either positive or negative effects. They can be assessed in terms of the values and realities intended by the six power-and-relationship words that are now so widely used: partnership, empowerment, ownership, participation, accountability and transparency. In particular, the questions can (and, I would argue, should) be asked: who is empowered and motivated? And who is disempowered and de-motivated?

Procedures can be classified in terms of their purposes and effects on the distribution of power. There are two polar extremes. Those who introduce new acronyms often deserve public vilification, the more so when they have criticized others for theirs (see Chapter 2). So, I may suffer for suggesting that we have COPs (control-oriented procedures), and PEPs (people-empowering procedures). COPs are devised for top-down control, and reinforce hierarchy and the power of those who are central and superior. PEPs are devised for bottom-up empowerment, and enhance local autonomy and the power of those who are peripheral and subordinate. Power, and its exercise and effects, are also channelled and mediated by principles and processes. The second Ps of COP and PEP can therefore stand for any of the three Ps, separately or together: procedure, principle or process. In practice, some procedures, principles and processes do, in their intention and effects, both control and empower at the same time. But treating them as polar opposites serves to illuminate issues about power.

COPs are the normal or default mode. They are popular with the powerful and can be spread top down as requirements. Many of the conditions set by lenders and donors are COPs. The example considered here is logframe analysis. PEPs, to date, have been so rare as to be abnormal. The example considered here is ALPS – ActionAid's Accountability, Learning and Planning System.

Contrasting cases

Illogical control: The logframe

Some of the procedures of the SRDP were reportedly taken up by consultants in the US who changed a few details, added some bits of colour coding, and remembered to invoice generously for the service. However, the suggestion that some of the origins of LFA (logical framework analysis) were in the SRDP system is probably unfounded.[8] More likely, it drew on some business practices of the 1960s, such as Management by Objectives, and came into use in development in the 1970s at the time when business was abandoning the sort of approach it represented.

LFA has been widely required by donor agencies.[9] With antecedents in management practices applied to projects and infrastructure, it embodies a linear logic associated with things (such as constructing a bridge) rather than people (such as capacity development, institutional learning and change, or influencing a policy). It goes with simple and controllable causation and conditions. Its many incarnations (including Ziel-Orienterte Projekt Planung, or ZOPP) entail what has been called vertical and horizontal logic. The vertical logic is from variously named objectives, goals, and purposes, followed by outputs and activities (or inputs); and the horizontal logic includes objectively verifiable indicators and means of verification. Assumptions are also listed. In preparing a logframe, all these are to be agreed and presented in a 4 × 4 matrix. LFA has given rise to a small army of consultants who train others in the technique, and then help them to carry it out. In the early 2000s, it has been widely challenged and more and more frequently resisted; but it is not clear whether its popularity with lenders and donors has yet passed its peak.[10]

There are two main sets of problems with the logframe: the logic and the practice. On the *logic*, there is no dispute about the benefits of basic planning. To think through objectives (goals, purposes), activities and outputs, as in the vertical logic, is sensible. Nothing that follows denies the value of preliminary thinking through what one hopes to achieve, by doing what, with what causal linkages, and with what resources and timing. This applies even in highly unpredictable processes involving people or policy influence. It is also sound practice periodically in any process to revisit objectives, what has been done and with what effects; to reflect on the experience and the lessons; and to change course and modify what one is trying to achieve. Learning and changing are key, with flexible adaptation. In contrast, the content of a logframe is set. The problems include:

- *Misfit*: the frame is rigid and does not fit unpredictable, uncontrollable multi-causal processes and relationships involving people and policies. In the words of a bilateral donor staff member: 'When you get into broader objectives and partnership it is almost impossible to follow the logic through.'

- *Complex causality*: causal linkages are more complex than allowed by the horizontal logic (for example, multiple causality can invalidate objectively verifiable indicators).
- *The counterfactual*: what would have happened anyway is not assessed (for example, things can be better, when without the activities they would have been even better, appears positive, but is actually negative; or things can be worse, when without the activities they would have been even worse, appears negative, but is actually positive).
- *Reductionism*: in classical ZOPP (GTZ, 1988), the stakeholders were to brainstorm until they agreed on one single core problem.[11] In real life, there are many problems, they differ for different people and in different places, and they change.
- *Missing much that matters*: some of the most significant factors can be overlooked, especially in evaluation. These may concern politics, transfers, relationships and institutional, personal and diplomatically unmentionable dimensions from which much could be learnt.

On the *practice*, LFA has for many been experienced as a disempowering imposition, reinforcing unequal power relations, control and exclusion. It has been disliked and resented by those subjected to it (see, for example, Johansson, 1995; Dohad, 1995, pers comm, cited in Chambers, 1997a, pp43–44; Edington, 2001; Marsden, 2004; Win, 2004). Often expatriates have dominated. The language has usually been English.[12] Typically, meetings have been in offices or hotels. They have tended to be exclusive: they have hardly ever included poor people, and if they have it seems unlikely they could participate at all freely or fully. The frame and the process are often accepted as a necessary evil. A staff member of an INGO (international non-governmental organization) may have spoken for many when she said: 'We would fill in those boxes because it's the only way to get the cash – and then never look at them again' and another: 'I grinned and beared it [sic]. I knew we had to do it to get our grant.' When the contents of a frame are negotiated and agreed, the funder – the stronger party – then disappears; the recipient – the weaker party – is left with a blueprint. Once completed, the logframe has been ignored by those who dare. For many who dare not, it has been experienced as rigid, constraining and frustrating, when what is needed is flexibility to change goals and activities according to changing conditions, problems and opportunities. Reporting becomes an agonizing nightmare, when what is being done is more responsible and better than what is in the frame; but the donor does not know and has not been around to discuss it. And there is the impending doom of the external 'purpose-to-outcome' evaluation and the dilemmas of risky transparency or dangerous dissembling.

LFA is, however, robustly sustainable. It is buffered against learning and change. Power relations insulate its advocates and facilitators from being told or learning. No matter that it is so often felt as oppressive. The power relations that it reinforces inhibit frank feedback. When I asked an INGO informant whether she had told the consultant facilitator what a bad experience it had been, she replied: 'No. I felt badly for her. She was just doing what her terms of reference told her to do.'

The upward accountability of the logframe comes, then, at a cost of rigidity, resentment, frustration and anxiety. The common experience is loss of transparency, trust and learning, which impedes, prevents and undermines the partnership, empowerment, ownership and participation that are extolled by lenders and donors in their rhetoric. Substantial and amicable debate has not, to date, resolved sharply different views of LFA: a workshop entitled 'ZOPP marries PRA?' (Forster, 1996) was stimulating and fun, but frustratingly fell short of consummation. Whatever the benefits of LFA, it is often in spite of it, or contrary to what is in it, that good things are done. A colleague describing a successful innovative programme which reversed power relations told me that its logical framework had been 'completely and absolutely evaded'. But not all on the receiving end have her courage and confidence. Logframes reinforce top-down power relations and accountability. For those in aid agencies who wish to make the rhetoric of development real by reversing power relations, the logframe is illogical, an own goal, scored by looking and kicking in the wrong direction.

Liberation by letting go: ALPS and PRRPs

The ALPS of the INGO ActionAid,[13] and most notably its PRRPs (participatory review and reflection processes), were designed to turn centralizing and upward accountability tendencies on their head.

If the logframe is part of the still dominant top-down COP culture, ALPS represents a nascent PEP counterculture. It was devised after years of failed attempts to reduce onerous reporting requirements (for a 'selective history', see Scott-Villiers, 2002). Some estimated that staff were spending three months each year writing and rewriting reports, with much effort polishing their prose. Many for whom it was their second or third language felt they would be judged on the quality of their English. The reports were of little use anyway. A succession of new systems devised in a participatory manner ended up making much the same demands as before. Throughout the organization there was palpable frustration. In these conditions, the leaner, simpler and more radical system of ALPS came almost *ex cathedra* from a group of six international staff who brainstormed for five days in Harare. Paradoxically, for an organization which prided itself on participatory approaches, the ALPS system was then endorsed centrally and disseminated in a centre-outwards manner to ActionAid teams in some 30 countries. The term 'roll-out' was even used. Sent out with central authority, it was designed to empower at all lower levels. Some of the contrasts between the LFA and ALPS are presented in Table 3.1.

With ALPS, teams, together with their partners, were encouraged to explore and devise their own processes. Reporting could be in new formats – by video, in local or national languages or in other forms. A key part was a series of annual PRRPs (IA Exchanges, 2002) at all levels (including the level of international directors), with multiple stakeholders, involving variously poor people, communities, partner organizations, ActionAid staff and ActionAid's donors. Downward accountability was stressed, with transparency of budgets between all levels. There was no one formula. Diversity was encouraged as an efficient way of learning, with exchanges of experience within areas and countries. The guide *Notes to Accompany ALPS* carried at the head of each page:

> *Health Warning: ideas and options only'.*

Apart from the requirement for PRRPs at all levels and in all parts of the organization, and together with poor people and partners, the essence of ALPS was in principles more than procedures (see Box 3.1).

Box 3.1 The principles of ALPS

ActionAid's main accountability 'is to the poor and marginalized women, men, boys and girls and our partners with whom we, and they, work'.

- commitment to gender equity;
- application to the whole organization at all levels;
- information to be relevant and useful to the people who produce it;
- information providers to receive feedback;
- learning rather than writing long reports;
- financial expenditure to be related to programme quality;
- critical reflection: learning not only from successes but also failures.

Source: summarised from ActionAid (2000, p3).

The early experience with ALPS was fascinating. Some staff continued to prepare reports that had been abolished, saying that they needed them for various audiences. India produced a draft manual, which included a quite rigorous and demanding contribution from the finance and audit side. Nepal and Bangladesh followed with their manuals. However, effects of the first rounds in some places were radical and dramatic. Staff, partners and community members, required to have annual PRRPs in accordance with ActionAid's principles, had to work out for themselves how to do them. The inventiveness demanded led to many innovations (ActionAid, 2002).

ActionAid Uganda stands out for transformations in which PRRPs were one element. This had much to do with Country Director Meenu Vadera and two consultants, Tina Wallace and Alan Kaplan, who worked at intervals over two years (Kaplan, 2003; Vadera, 2003; Wallace, 2003). In the reports from PRRPs there was:

> . . . a striking degree of self-questioning and openness about difficult development issues. . . Staff were no longer simply counting their activities and reporting on these, but digging into what they were doing, questioning why and how much their work was appreciated, understood or seen as relevant by those they were working with. This was a huge shift in thinking and analysis from two years earlier (Wallace, 2003, p20).

Table 3.1 *Contrasting paradigms: LFA and ALPS*

	LFA	ALPS
Origins	1950s and 1960s engineering and management, including Management by Objectives	Frustration with failures to reduce reporting Search for means for downward accountability
Goals	Set with targets	Evolving
Non-negotiables	4 × 4 matrix and logic	Principles and PRRPs
Procedure/process	Formal Predetermined sequence Standardized	Informal Invented and interactive Diverse
Key activities	Planning, M and E	Reflecting, sharing, learning
Quality assurance and characteristic monitoring process	Objectively verifiable indicators Output to purpose review	Sharing and judgement in 360-degree annual PRRP meetings
Main language	Dominant external language	Local language
Accountability and transparency sought	Upwards to funder	Downwards at each level, as well as sideways and upwards
Reporting	Written, upwards	Various, 360 degree
Ownership	Those who drew up logframe – mainly funders	All stakeholders – mainly those who take part
Transparency	Upwards	360 degree
Power relations	Funder dominated; recipients often resent	Intended to empower, with funder avoiding dominance
Intelligibility, local	Lower	Higher

Sources: David Korten and Jethro Pettit are among the several people whose ideas have contributed to this table

But this came briefly under threat. There were external pressures from donors for 'business as usual' (David and Mancini, 2004, p17). In consequence:

> . . . *ActionAid in London sent out a monitoring framework in the form of a log-frame for presenting achievements and progress against* Fighting Poverty Together. *The framework was to be used for . . . compiling an Annual Global Progress report on ActionAid's work. The lack of clarity surrounding its purpose led to staff in Uganda believing that they now had to use the framework for reporting. . . The staff had to be encouraged to hold to their process and stay true to their way of analysing their work, and not fall back on listing their activities and achievements in a matrix, which appeared to threaten the new project of reflective development thinking (ibid, p17).*

Among African countries, two complied and reported in the matrix form, 11 did not refuse but did not comply, and only Uganda refused explicitly. The eventual (readable, self-critical, insightful and credible) Annual Global Progress report (ActionAid, 2002) contained more from Uganda than from any other country!

Any table of contrasts between LFA and ALPS (as in Table 3.1) can make everything on the LFA side look 'bad' and everything on the ALPS side 'good'. Nothing is ever so simple. If LFA were modified or replaced, more strengths could be expected on that side. As ALPS works itself through over the years, weaknesses may become more evident. That said, these two procedures belong to different paradigms. LFA is a control-oriented COP and ALPS is an empowering PEP. LFA has formalized top-down controls that demoralize and threaten participatory approaches. ALPS has opened up ways of transforming behaviour and relationships in ways that make partnership, participation and empowerment more real (see, for example, ActionAid, 2002; Scott-Villiers, 2002; Wallace, 2003; David and Mancini, 2004; Owusu, 2004).

Reversing relations of power

Chapter 2 concludes that 'it is through a synergy of reducing demands, levelling power relations and taking responsible action that administrative capacity can most effectively be enhanced'. But power relations are, to a degree, unavoidable and necessary. The key is to recognize and acknowledge them, and then to manage and moderate them well. The bottom line is whether they benefit and empower those who are poor, weak and marginalized. This implies uppers empowering lowers between all levels. To do this, they must individually relinquish degrees of control themselves. The implications for personal behaviour and attitudes will be considered in Chapter 6. Here the focus remains on procedures, principles and process.

Relationships, and the actions that affect and flow from them, have become a new focus of attention in development (Eyben, 2003, 2004a; Groves and Hinton, 2004; Marsden, 2004; Pasteur and Scott-Villiers, 2004). A major emergent theme, elaborated and illustrated in *Inclusive Aid* (Groves and Hinton, 2004) is that to make development effectively pro-poor requires investing in relationships. The conventional view has been that aid instruments and policy influence are the means to achieve pro-poor change. In fact, the instruments and the influence are mediated and their quality and effectiveness determined by relationships. To make the much-abused rhetoric of development real then requires a radical change of mindset and behaviour to place relationships centre stage.

In the SRDP, LFA and ALPS, procedures, processes and principles were consciously designed and chosen. The question raised is to what extent, and how, they can be designed and chosen to change power relations, relationships and organizations.

Before investing in relationships there is a prior question of whether they are needed, and if so, by whom. In aid, donors and lenders may need to be able to give and lend; but potential recipients may not need to receive or borrow. A first step is to establish whether the 'lower', the potential recipient or borrower, does, indeed, have a need. VSO (Voluntary Service Overseas) (the main volunteer organization based in the UK)[14] has pioneered and spread a day-long workshop process to answer this question. A VSO staff member facilitates a potential partner organization that might wish to host a volunteer to develop its vision and review its resources, capabilities and needs (Norma Burnett, pers comm). Sometimes it emerges that a volunteer is not needed at all. The process empowers the potential partner and improves the prospects that volunteers who are placed will, in fact, be useful. For VSO, the challenge is to recognize and reward staff for placing fewer volunteers because they facilitate this process well. It would be an impressive indication of pro-poor commitment if other aid agencies regularly rewarded staff who found that loans and grants were *not* needed. I cannot recollect any such case.[15]

The next question is to what extent relationships will be control oriented or empowering. The contrasts, as we have seen, are paradigmatic. With a control orientation, specifying outputs and indicators is a common feature. With an empowerment orientation, the focus is more on discussion, negotiation and agreements on principles, process and directions, with these subject to review, reflection, learning and adaptation. Recent experience points to three approaches which can empower:

1 minimum rules;
2 non-negotiable principles or 'uncompromisables'; and
3 downward accountability.

Empowerment through minimum rules

Empowerment means transforming the normal bureaucratic reflexes to standardize, simplify and control in a dominating top-down mode to provide instead conditions for local diversity, complexity and autonomy.

The computer science of complexity provides relevant insights (Resnick, 1994; Waldrop, 1994). Minimal simple rules have been found to give rise to complex and diverse behaviour, such as random objects on a screen coming together and behaving like a flock of birds. Such behaviour could never have occurred through detailed top-down orders. It takes place in the area known as 'edge of chaos', which lies between the rigidity of over-specification and the chaos of no rules at all.

Emergent self-organizing systems with human organizations and behaviour require enabling minimum rules and commitment on the part of the actors.[16] In participatory workshops, SOSOTEC (self-organizing systems on the edge of chaos) need only a simple basic frame, as with Open Space, in which minimal rules enable groups to form around whatever topics they wish (Chambers, 2002, pp123–128). MYRADA, an NGO in South India, has catalysed thousands of women's self-help savings groups insisting on only two things: transparent and accurate accounting; and democratizing the leadership through rotation, calling those with responsibilities not presidents or secretaries, but representatives. In the Rwanda government's participatory poverty assessment process, cellules (communities) that present plans according to basic guidelines are eligible to receive US$1000 (Sam Joseph, pers comm). With community-led total sanitation (CLTS) (VERC, 2002; Kar, 2003; and pp109) in Bangladesh, Cambodia, India and other countries, earlier designs, standards and regulations for latrines are dispensed with. The minimum conditions are no subsidy and good facilitation. The common outcome is community initiatives which achieve total sanitation with the creativity of many different local latrine designs.

Empowering minimum controls such as these run counter to normal professional, bureaucratic and philanthropic reflexes. They are the exception, not the norm, and are vulnerable to the pervasive pattern of disablement through professional standards, regulation and over-provision. In many languages there are phrases for 'not too much, and not too little, but just right'. Unfortunately, those with power almost always go for 'too much', making rules and imposing controls that inhibit and demotivate, dampen creativity and discourage diversity. It requires imagination, confidence and courage to abstain from doing too much, and to see and establish only those minimal rules that enable and empower.

Non-negotiable principles

Principles can be expressed as values, objectives or behaviours. And these can be presented as non-negotiable. If both parties in a relationship start by reflecting on and stating their NNP (non-negotiable principles), they may discover incompatibilities that prevent them from working together, or they may gain from mutual learning and find ground and objectives in common. If their non-negotiables are shared or mutually respected, there is less need, and it may well be harmful, to try to plan in detail. Targets can be replaced by trust.

Mahila Samatha's non-negotiable principles

Non-negotiables and reversed power relations are illustrated by the inspiring example of the APMSS (Andhra Pradesh Mahila Samatha Society).[17] This is an NGO, supported and protected by an influential board of trustees known for their outspoken commitment, some of them former government officials (Korten, 1990, p4; Biggs and Neame, 1995). The society's objectives include 'to create circumstances so that women have a better understanding of their predicament

---

Box 3.2 Non-negotiables of Mahila Samatha

From early in its life, Mahila Samatha adopted these principles, to be kept in mind during all stages, and which are not open to negotiation:

- The initial phase where women are consolidating their independent time and space is not be to hurried or short-circuited.
- Women in a village determine the form, nature, content and timing of all activities in the village.
- The role of project functionaries, officials and other agencies is facilitative and not directive.
- Planning, decision-making and evaluation processes at all levels are accountable to the collective of village women.
- Education is understood as a process which enables women to question, conceptualize, seek answers, act, reflect upon their actions and raise new questions. It is not to be confused with mere literacy.
- The educational process and methodology must be based on respect for women's existing knowledge, experience and skill.

Source: APMSS (1994)

---

and move from a state of abject disempowerment towards a situation in which they can determine their own lives and, hence, influence the environment' (APMSS, circa 1998). To achieve its objectives, the society 'seeks guidance not from targets, but from certain inviolable principles' (APMSS, 1994, p2) (see Box 3.2).

It is worth noting the nature and level of these non-negotiable principles. They are neither macro-principles at the level of 'love thy neighbour as thyself', nor micro-principles at the level of 'identify the single most important problem'. They are, rather, meso-principles special to the organization and its philosophy. They indicate attitudes and guide behaviour without saying in detail what should be done. They both express and reinforce a culture of commitment.

With its non-negotiable principles the society has been funded by the Indian Government, substantially with Dutch aid. This has been without a logframe, and without specification of outputs or targets. The non-negotiables have empowered the women, the staff and the organization. Perhaps because of the confidence and trust created by the non-negotiables, the Dutch are perceived as 'the most non-interfering donor'. This is efficient, leaving staff free from the distractions of multiple funders (travel, negotiations, visitors, report-writing and the like) and able to devote more of their time and energy, which they do in full measure, to the substance of their work. The relationship with the donor is congruent with the relationships with poor women. The non-negotiable principles are polar and paradigmatic opposites of targets. Targets are incompatible with participatory actions in which poor women determine the pace.

Principles of engagement: The Pastoralists' Communication Initiative

The PCI (Pastoralists' Communication Initiative) is an NGO, working especially in Ethiopia, which seeks to enable pastoralists in East Africa to amplify their voice. It is remarkable for the extent to which it holds off from being prescriptive. Its principles of engagement are:

- PCI is independent of any of the involved actors.
- It acts as a mediator between different stakeholders.
- It enables advocacy rather than advocating for specific policies.
- It advocates only for a more inclusive policy process for pastoralists.
- It respects the institutions and individuals with which it works, especially the Government of Ethiopia.
- It recognizes the need for continuous learning with the various actors (Patta Scott-Villiers, pers comm).

The mode of operation is to convene, catalyse, facilitate, mediate and support. Unlike most advocacy NGOs, it does not advocate policies except at the level of a more inclusive policy process for pastoralists. It is pastoralists and their representatives who themselves decide what they want and what they want to advocate for.

Downward accountability

Downward accountability is a well-established phrase. Its spatial metaphor is universally understood, as is that of upward accountability. Some object that it puts 'them', the poor, down and us, the non-poor, up. Reverse accountability has been suggested as an alternative, to emphasize reorienting the flow of accountability, reporting and decision-making towards community institutions (Shah and Shah, 1995, p184). Primary accountability is another – accountability to the primary stakeholders, those who are poor, vulnerable, deprived and powerless. Primary accountability resonates with and reinforces the pro-poor development sought by funders, sponsors and taxpayers and their representatives, to whom there is secondary accountability. Primary accountability to poor people then serves to fulfil secondary accountability.[18]

Writing over a decade ago in 1992, Chris Roche observed that in developing local accountability 'Nobody has the answers.' He called for 'bolder, more experimental steps . . . to permit a real devolution of power' (Roche, 1992, p188). Since then, accountability, especially that of NGOs, has been an issue in development literature,[19] notably in the 1995 volume *Beyond the Magic Bullet: NGO Performance and Accountability in the Post-Cold War World* edited by Michael Edwards and David Hulme. There has been much innovation: new procedures, mechanisms or means for primary or downward accountability have been developed and spread. These go beyond accountability to citizens through elections. Some notable developments have been:

- Participatory monitoring and evaluation (PM&E), in which local people monitor and evaluate programmes (Estrella et al, 2000). Parmesh Shah and Meera

Kaul Shah (1995) describe reciprocal accountability in the path-breaking work of AKRSP (The Aga Khan Rural Support Programme, India) in which village institutions evaluated AKRSP. The 15 criteria brainstormed by members of village institutions included management style, transparency in decision-making, sensitivity of staff, ability to influence government, and participation of village representatives in key policy decisions of AKRSP. An accessible evolving methodology is the PALS (Participatory Action Learning System) (Mayoux, 2003a, 2003b, 2003c), which uses diagramming as part of an empowering approach to monitoring, evaluation and impact assessment.

- Transparency and information initiatives (Norton and Elson, 2002, pp40–42) – for example, the long campaign of the Mazdoor Kisan Shakti Sangathan (MKSS, or Movement for the Empowerment of Peasants and Workers) in Rajasthan for the right to see and have copies of documents and hold government to account, and the broader right to information movement in India (Jenkins and Goetz, 1999; Goetz and Jenkins, 2001; Mander, 2004, pp267–303).
- Participatory budgeting (Norton and Elson, 2002, pp42–43), in which citizens take part in open, public assemblies to decide which investments are most important and then in expenditure monitoring, as pioneered in Porto Alegre and spread elsewhere in Brazil and internationally (Schneider and Goldfrank, 2002).
- Report cards (Paul, 2002), where surveys compile citizens' experiences of the performance of government agencies and publish these in quantified form.
- Citizen's juries (Coote, 1997; Pimbert and Wakeford, 2002; *PLA Notes*, 2003), in which ordinary people hear expert evidence on issues and form their own judgements, which are then disseminated.
- Social audits, developed by the New Economics Foundation in the UK, which seek to enable all stakeholders in an organization to monitor the organization's performance. Michael Edwards (1999, pp210, 218) suggests that this is a simple thing that all development agencies they could do in the short term.

ActionAid's experience is also illuminating. In the *Notes to Accompany ALPS* (ActionAid, 2001a, p10), the first major section is on downward accountability. It opens:

> *Central to the spirit of* Fighting poverty together *is our accountability to the poor and marginalised women, men, boys and girls with whom we work. Alps encourages this by promoting greater participation and transparency in all our work. . . . At present most lines of accountability move upwards. The real challenge for ActionAid is to make accountability work downwards. Being accountable to our partners and poor and marginalised groups will require us to examine our current practices.*

The questions raised and confronted include how to involve poor and marginalized groups in decision-making, in influencing the behaviour of ActionAid and its partners, in recruitment and performance appraisal of staff, and in monitoring and evaluation. A central block and challenge has been transparency and sharing information about budgets and actual spending, and doing this in forms that make sense and can be understood. Some experiences were:

- At a workshop in Bangalore, ActionAid's five local NGO partners were invited to a two-day workshop with outside facilitators to evaluate ActionAid. Making the ActionAid budget transparent cleared the air and set an example for partners to follow, in turn, sharing their budgets with communities (Bhattar-charjee, 2001).
- In Kenya, after meetings in which he participated with communities, the ActionAid finance officer said that he would restructure the accounting system so that it would break down intelligibly for partners and communities (Kimana, 2001).
- On the sensitive issue of their higher salaries, some ActionAid staff were embarrassed to tell their partners what they were paid. When they did, the reaction was on the lines of: 'We don't mind as long as your work shows you deserve it', making their salaries less a source of resentment and more an incentive (Amar Jyoti, pers comm).

These examples indicate how the challenge of primary or downward accountability is more than just procedures and transparency. In Alan Fowler's words (1997, p183), incorporating bottom-up, community-based accountability is a very difficult reversal for NGOs and the aid system because 'it is not just a question of applying new techniques and procedures, but of reversing many aspects of organizational culture which lie at the heart of assumptions and behaviour'. To achieve and sustain downward accountability is personally challenging. The necessary changes of mindset and behaviour may need constant reaffirmation and renewal. It helps that those who achieve degrees of downward transparency and accountability usually find it a good experience. Disempowering oneself in order to empower others might be supposed to traumatize and frustrate. The common experience is, to the contrary, better relationships and personal fulfilment.

Continual challenges

Development organizations which struggle to combine minimum empowering controls, non-negotiable principles and degrees of downward accountability do so with difficulty. They face challenges and threats that are internal and external: internally the challenge is to create and sustain common commitment and a congruent culture; externally it is to fight off threats from powerful funders and professionals whose attitudes, behaviours, values, procedures and demands are discordant and undermining.

Common commitment and congruent culture[20]

Common commitment of individuals and a congruent culture of organizations vitally depend upon each other. ActionAid's *Fighting Poverty Together* (ActionAid,

1999) illustrates the point. This is a passionate document inspired by outrage. It is combines vision, values and realism. In itself that might not seem unusual for an international NGO. It was unusual, though, for the prolonged participatory process involving staff, in all the countries where ActionAid was active, in reflecting, expressing and sharing their views and values. The outcome (see Box 3.3) was a radical and practical core statement of which staff were proud and to which they frequently referred.

Box 3.3 ActionAid's vision, mission and values

Vision

ActionAid's vision is a world without poverty in which every person can exercise their right to a life of dignity.

Mission

ActionAid's mission is to work with poor and marginalized people to eradicate poverty by overcoming the injustice and inequity that cause it.

Values

ActionAid lives by the following values:

- *Mutual respect*, recognizing the innate dignity and worth of all people and the value of diversity;
- *Equity and justice*, requiring us to work to ensure that everyone – irrespective of sex, age, race, colour, class and religion – has equal opportunity for expressing and utilizing their potential;
- *Honesty and transparency*, requiring us to be accountable for the effectiveness of our actions and open in our judgements and communications with others;
- *Solidarity* with poor and marginalized people, so that our only bias will be a commitment to the interests of the poor and powerless;
- *Courage of conviction*, requiring us to be creative and radical, without fear of failure, in pursuit of the highest possible impact on the causes of poverty;
- *Humility*, recognizing that we are part of a bigger alliance against poverty and requiring our presentation and behaviour to be modest.

Source: ActionAid (1999, p3)

With *Fighting Poverty Together*, and as ActionAid shifted from service delivery to rights-based approaches, some staff left while others joined because they shared the values of the organization. The process and the content of *Fighting Poverty Together* contributed to a common commitment and organizational culture. One result has been the trust needed to support the decentralized discretion and creative

diversity of ALPS; recognition of distinctiveness was expressed in the use within
ActionAid of the adjectives 'ALPSian' and 'non-ALPSian'.

A feature of inspiring organizations is the congruence of commitment, culture
and practice *at all levels*. The participatory review and reflection processes (PRRP)
of ALPS have been practised by the international directors, as well as by partners
with communities. Another striking example is the SEWA (Self-employed Women's
Organization) in India. This trade union of self-employed women has over half a
million members. Yet despite its size, its culture is pervasive and manifests in the
same way in different contexts. Whether a meeting is poor women in a village or
senior managers in Ahmedabad, it starts in the same way, sitting on the ground,
praying and singing the same songs of solidarity.[21] There is an understood,
expected, shared culture of egalitarian sisterhood whoever is in the meeting and
wherever the meeting takes place.

For its part, Mahila Samatha recognized the importance of congruence when
it added this to its non-negotiable principles:

> *Every intervention and interaction occurring in the project must be a microcosm
> of the larger process of change – i.e. the environment of learning; respect and
> equality; time and space; room for individual uniqueness and variation must be
> experienced in every component of the project (APMSS, pers comm).*

One means of maintaining and strengthening commitment and congruence is
through recruitment, acculturation and appraisal. Organizations that are successful
in this mode have staff or members with strong shared commitments. For example:

- In self-help savings groups, solidarity is essential. In the Working Women's
  Forum in Tamil Nadu, group leaders have themselves selected their members.
- SEWA pays much attention to staff selection and induction, and assuring
  common commitment to codes. It goes to special lengths to orient and induct
  new staff members. They may be middle class in origin and unfamiliar with
  the realities of poor women. For new recruits there is a process of EDPs
  (Exposure and Dialogue Programmes) in which they spend days with a poor
  host woman member of SEWA, sharing her life and tasks, and learning and
  writing up her life history. This is followed by in-depth reflection (SEWA
  Academy and APNSD, 2002).
- After some years of experience Mahila Samatha added to its non-negotiables:
  'A participatory selection process is followed to ensure that the project
  functionaries at all levels are committed to working among poor women and
  that they are free of caste/community prejudices.'
- Poor people can be involved in recruitment and appraisal of front-line staff.
  In ActionAid 'where possible, poor and marginalized members of the community and partners are directly involved in recruiting and appraising members
  of front-line staff, of both partners and ActionAid' (ActionAid, 2000, p5).
- ActionAid encourages 360-degree staff appraisal throughout the organization,
  including for the Chief Executive. This means appraisal and feedback on
  performance by those who are lower, as well as higher and peers.

Practices of recruitment, acculturation and appraisal like these serve to sustain, strengthen and renew commitment and culture, with evolving interactions and congruence between the personal and the institutional. This matters all the more because external threats can be so strong.

Fighting magnetic fields

Internal congruence of practices and relationships is not enough. Advice from the experience of the AKRSP in India puts it succinctly:

> *Do not use participatory methods for bottom-up accountability if you are not prepared to change your own decision-making processes and accountability structures,* particularly towards other stakeholders who are used to having top-down accountability *[emphasis added] (Shah and Shah, 1995, cited in Fowler, 1997, p182).*

This is easier said than done. If part of fighting poverty is fighting for downward accountability, it is also fighting top-down magnetic fields of other people and organizations. It is as though there are magnets pulling and orienting hierarchically, North–South, upwards and downwards in individuals, in organizations and in society. Individuals, organizations and groups who seek to balance, level or reverse relationships of power are vulnerable to the pull of these interlocking forces.

Threats can penetrate through people whose personal and professional orientation, mindset and behaviour are top-down and dominating. Their sabotage of participatory processes may be innocent and unaware. In one ALPS participatory review and reflection, top-down relationships were reasserted and reinforced simply by a student with a questionnaire-type checklist demanding information from partners (Gareth Pratt, pers comm). The PRRPs of ALPS are vulnerable to routinization and manuals. Whole organizations can also be 're-magnetized'. Participatory cultures and relationships introduced and nurtured by one head of an organization can be annulled by a successor with control-oriented centralizing reflexes.

Transaction costs are another threat, especially when funders have norms and requirements that conflict with principles and values. Demands and conditions imposed or created by funders mean time, effort and stress – for example, the disabling frustrations of the procedures (such as LFA) and the requirements for targets, reports and evaluations that judge without learning. Then there are the distractions and distortions when visits by staff of funding agencies are in an inspection mode, and disempower and demoralize those who receive them. Sticking to principles can also take time and effort. ActionAid's principles in *Fighting Poverty Together* may have helped towards the first Programme Partnership Agreement in which DFID provided uncommitted funding to an INGO. But this was after a year of negotiation and over 20 drafts of the agreement. Discussions were 'long and circuitous' and, at times, tense. 'What occurred with DFID occurs practically every time we seek donor funding' (David and Mancini, 2004, p17). There have to be questions whether costs of resistance and negotiation exceed the benefits of the funds.

On the other hand, good non-negotiables and a good record can disarm magnets and reverse power relations. Where funded organizations stick to their principles and perform well, two factors can turn things on their head. First, non-negotiables can reverse power all the way up the system – for example, the Mahila Samatha principle that women in a village determine the form, nature, content and timing of all activities in the village means that would-be funders cannot demand targets by set times. Second, funding agencies need to spend money and to spend it well. They have competed to support both Mahila Samatha and the PCI (Pastoralists' Communication Initiative). Mahila Samatha's failed suitors include DFID and the World Bank in the person of its President, who to his credit is said to have threatened a sit-in if his offer of assistance was turned down. Being in a strong negotiating position reduces demands on time and administrative capacity, which can then be devoted to getting on with the job and doing even better. While poverty remains high on the development agenda, people and organizations who empower those who are poor, weak, vulnerable and marginalized should be able to negotiate from positions of strength, needing funders less than funders need them: for they can help make the funders' pro-poor rhetoric real.

The challenge, then, becomes not raising funds but avoiding funding and engagements which subvert principles. In late 2002, Mahila Samatha was, albeit with great caution, moving towards collaboration with a UNDP/Government of Andhra Pradesh programme that had targets. Mahila Samatha recognized the dangers and was determined not to compromise its principles. If this succeeded, UNDP and the Andhra Pradesh Government would have to abandon their targets. In the almost inevitable tug-of-war the stakes were high, for it would be a breakthrough to establish in a UNDP and government programme; and such a bridgehead might then expand a target-free zone.

At the personal level, the big magnets have subversive weapons. Flattery, ego and career prospects are insidious threats. My ego has been flattered by the World Bank:[22] I have felt pleased to have been recognized and invited to workshops and to be able, on return to the IDS, to let slip that I had been there, whom I had met and what they had said. I may be unusually vain and vulnerable in this respect. But I have noticed the pride with which officials in India mention that they are working on World Bank or other internationally funded programmes, and put this on their visiting cards. Officials who work and negotiate 'successfully' with the World Bank in various countries can end up in Washington.[23] Engagement with power may be the right thing to do. But feeling flattered is bad if it means failing to stick to principles or accepting damaging conditions. We need many people with the guts to reject such pulls and pressures; and those who hold out and succeed are to be celebrated and admired.

Conclusion

So the journey that began with the management procedures of the SRDP (Special Rural Development Programme), devised top-down with an engineering mindset, has led through error and experience to another set of prescriptions: reversals of power through minimum controls, non-negotiable principles and downward accountability, and congruence of behaviour, commitment and organizational culture. Looking back, my earlier beliefs and actions appear naive. Yet, at the time, the SRDP procedures seemed to be opening up a neglected and promising frontier. Could the journey have been faster? In 30 years' time, if this book survives and anyone reads it, will they marvel again at the naive optimism of what I have written now? I dare say.

Still, the broadening stream that runs through this chapter may endure: the recognition and use of procedures and rules, and then principles, as levers and supports for good change. There may always be a struggle to achieve a balance and synergy between rules and routines that are essential and those flexible and continuously creative processes that are so much a part of doing well. There will always be a bottom line of minimum requirements for auditing and financial reporting necessary for honest and transparent accounting. But almost always, more control and more information than are needed are demanded by those above, orienting accountability upwards, de-motivating lowers and diverting them from better things that they have to do. The lessons from the experiences of SRDP, LFA, ALPS, APMSS and PCI are to explore and agree non-negotiables, principles and processes between partners; to maintain only minimum controls; to invent and use processes that make space for reflection, learning and better performance; to strive for responsive downward accountability; and throughout to foster transparency and trust.

Procedures, rules and principles can, then, be used to reverse and balance relationships of power. The questions are to what extent the less powerful in each relationship can determine what is done and how it is done; and whether this can apply throughout the system so that those who are weakest will gain. Reversals of power in relationships, between all levels, can make space for decentralized and democratic diversity. If procedures, rules and principles empower well, it will show in the diversity of the good things that are done and in who benefits.

Notes

1   This section is taken from *Managing Rural Development: Ideas and Experience from East Africa* (Chambers, 1974).

2   See Roe (1993) for an account of the key role of James Leach in the SRDP. The word donor is strictly correct. No lenders supported the programme. An attempt to interest the World Bank was unsuccessful.

3   The periodicity of the World Bank's policy reversals and radical changes deserves scholarly study, not least to identify whether the intervals show (as I suspect they do) some regularity. Any reader who can direct me to such a study will earn my gratitude.

4   We were influenced by Earl Kulp's formidable and intimidating volume *Rural Development Planning: Systems Analysis and Working Method* (1970).

5   The details of the PIM system are described in tedious detail in *Managing Rural Development* (Chambers, 1974). For a contemporary evaluation, see Chabala et al (1973), and for context into which it was introduced, David Leonard's (1973) *Rural Administration in Kenya*.

6 Country directors argued, with some grounds, that they needed annual reports for a wider audience than just ActionAid itself.

7 The capacity of pointless procedures to survive can astonish and delight. From the early 1980s until early in the 2000s, passengers arriving in India on an international flight and transferring to another international flight that would take them somewhere else in India had first to enter India through Indian customs, and then, before boarding the internal flight, to have a second customs inspection. This required a declaration that the passenger had no imported zip fasteners. It was inadvisable, however, to declare to the customs officials any such items on one's clothing.

8 The two systems were probably developed in parallel, with the logframe starting a little earlier. The original version of the logframe matrix stems from the work for USAID during 1969–1970 of Leon Rosenberg, first at Fry Associates and then at Practical Concepts Associated (Solem, 1987, cited in Gasper, 1997, p6), while the SRDP Programme Implementation Management (PIM) system was evolved and introduced, starting in 1970.

9 For authoritative and balanced reviews of the history, strengths and weaknesses of the logical framework, see Cracknell (2000, pp101–121) and Gasper (1997, 2000), and for an insightful discussion CDRA (2001).

10 Edington wrote in 2001: 'Most donors have in the past few years dropped the requirement of logframes'; but there is another view that their use is still spreading – for example, in aid programmes of the European Union.

11 Insisting that there should be a single core problem reinforces the power of donors and facilitators:

> *By requiring their partners to ZOPP*
> *Donors rule, with their talkers on top.*
> *That one problem is core*
> *For those absent and poor*
> *Is agreed when thought comes to a stop.*

12 Marsden (2004) records that the switch of a foreign adviser in Nepal from speaking in English to Nepali 'radically changed the dynamics. The silence of hierarchy was broken and competence was suddenly reversed as the adviser sought help and clarification as she tried to express herself in Nepali.'

13 The Participation Group at the IDS Sussex was invited to provide a team, led by Patta Scott-Villiers and including Garett Pratt, Andrea Cornwall and, to a lesser degree, myself, to accompany ALPS in India, Kenya, Ethiopia, The Gambia and Brazil. These summary remarks draw on this collective activity and on insights from Rosalind David, Antonella Mancini, Charles Owusu and others of ActionAid's Impact Assessment Unit. The ALPS (ActionAid, 2000) and *Notes to Accompany ALPS* (ActionAid, 2001a) are on the ActionAid website at www.actionaid.org/resources/pdfs/alps.pdf and www.actionaid.org/resources/pdfs/alps_notes.pdf, respectively. See also www.ids.ac.uk/ids/particip for other related materials. For critical reviews, see ActionAid (2002), Scott-Villiers (2004), who gives a perceptive and critical historical account, and Owusu (2004) and David and Mancini (2004) for

ActionAid insiders' insights and reflections. As ever, responsibility for views expressed is mine and mine alone.

14   VSO being 'based in the UK' is phrased with deliberate care, since volunteers are also recruited in Canada, Kenya and the Philippines.

15   There must be cases. I shall be indebted to any reader who can give me examples.

16   I have elaborated the points in this paragraph in more detail in 'Public management: Towards a radical agenda' in Minogue et al (1998, pp118–120) and in Chambers (1977, p199–201).

17   For information about APMSS, I am indebted to personal communications from Y. Padmavathy and other staff and to a series of annual reports.

18   For the term 'responsive accountability' I am grateful to Karen Brown in a brainstorming with Antonella Mancini. Responsive accountability has much to recommend it, implicitly recognizing top-down power relations, the need for 'lowers' (poor and marginalized people) to analyse their situation and priorities, and then for 'uppers' to respond.

19   For further discussion of NGOs' accountability, see Shah and Shah (1995) for the significant innovations of AKRSP (India), Fowler (1997, pp59–60, 180–183) for an analytical overview and Holmes (1998) for a review of participatory mechanisms for increasing downward accountability.

20   I am intrigued that I have resisted using the word ideology to describe common commitment. I think the reason is that it carries some heavy baggage. The *Collins English Dictionary*, Millennium Edition (Collins, 1998), gives the first meaning of ideology as 'a body of ideas that reflects the beliefs and interests of a nation, political system, etc., and underlies political action'. I associate ideology with dogmatism, intolerance and arrogance, in contrast with the value-based open-mindedness, tolerance and humility being discussed here.

21   The mind boggles at the thought of meetings in DFID starting with 'God Save the Queen'; but it was moving to experience a workshop with New Zealand Aid in Wellington that began with a Maori welcome, prayer and song.

22   For a fuller confession, see 'Power, knowledge and policy influence: Reflections on an experience' in Brock and McGee (2002, p160).

23   I do not intend this, nor would it be fair, as a generalized slur. It is an empirical statement. There is a perfectly legitimate argument that by joining the World Bank, individuals are putting themselves in a position to have major influence to make the world a better place. [In typing this I found I had written bitter. The letter 'i' is nowhere near 'e' on the typewriter. My unconscious may have been anticipating the next sentence.] There is also a legitimate argument that the World Bank does so much harm, and is so much a self-sustaining system, that it is better to stay away and work from outside.

4

Participation: Review, Reflections and Future

All good things that exist are the fruits of originality' (John Stuart Mill, 1859, Liberty Chapter 2)

Part 1 of this chapter, from *Managing Rural Development* reviews lessons from the rhetoric and realities of participation in Eastern Africa in the early 1970s. Part 2 describes and analyses aspects of PRA and participatory approaches in the 1990s and up to 2004, and points to promising developments and transformative potentials for the future.

Part 1: Participation: Rhetoric and Reality (1974)

Local participation as defined in Eastern Africa in the early 1970s was both top-down through development committees and block grants, and bottom-up in the form of innumerable self-help projects. Self-help projects were not centrally planned, and were often intended by local people as pre-emptive bids for government support and services. Problems included the duplication of buildings and structures put up by rival groups, excess demand for government resources, and school buildings and health clinics which could not be serviced. Contrary to the common view, local participation was often inequitable because of compulsory labour, contributions in kind exacted by force, regressive levels of contributions, and the capture of benefits by local leaders and elites.

Managing local participation: Rhetoric and reality (extracts from Chapter 4 of *Managing Rural Development*, 1974)[1]

> *The Plan is a people's plan. It was designed and formulated by the people for their own development (Introduction to the Zambian Second National Development Plan 1972–1976; Republic of Zambia, 1971, pv)*

There is a plan being drawn up now for this area. As soon as it is out, we will let
you know what you are expected to do. (A Locational Agricultural Assistant in
a public meeting in Migori Division, Kenya; reported by Oyugi, 1973, p7)

Rhetoric has important political functions and relies on the loose use of words
with ideological overtones. There is some justification for the vague use by political
leaders of phrases like 'self reliance', 'participatory democracy', and 'local participation' in order to secure support and action; but there is less justification for the
imprecise use of these terms by academics and civil servants since for them such
usage may cover up bad or lazy thinking. For the purposes of analysis and
prescription it is best first to clarify the senses in which phrases are used and then
to appraise the relationship between those senses and the reality. When this is
done a wide gap may be found. This chapter seeks to clarify some of the issues
involved and to suggest means . . . whereby the gap between rhetoric and reality
might be narrowed. It draws heavily on comparative experience with 'local
participation' in the countries of Eastern Africa.

Local participation can conveniently be analysed in three ways:

1   Who participates: those who participate may be government staff at the local
    level, the local inhabitants of an area or a combination of these two.
2   What institutions are involved. In Eastern Africa, over the past decade these
    have included local government authorities, development committees, com-
    munity development committees, self-help groups, public meetings and local
    interest groups such as churches, women's groups and political parties.
3   The objectives and functions of participation. The values ascribed to it in its
    various forms include:
    •   making known local wishes;
    •   generating developmental ideas;
    •   providing local knowledge;
    •   testing proposals for feasibility and improving them;
    •   increasing the capability of communities to handle their affairs and to
        control and exploit their environment;
    •   demonstrating support for a regime;
    •   doing what government requires to be done;
    •   extracting, developing and investing local resources (labour, finance,
        managerial skills, etc);
    •   promoting desirable relationships between people, especially through
        cooperative work.

Local participation can be analysed in terms of two streams of initiatives, communication and resources: those which are top down, originating in government
headquarters and penetrating towards and into the rural areas; and those which
are bottom up, originating among the people in the rural areas and directed upwards into the government machine . . . the two most notable and important top-
down initiatives in Eastern Africa have been development committees and block
grants; and the most important bottom-up initiatives have been self-help projects.[2]

Top down: Development committees and block grants

Development committees

In the mid 1960s the participation of local level staff and political leaders in discussing local development matters was widely sought through the formation of development committees at provincial/ regional and district levels. In their early composition, style and operation they fell into two groups: large political forums and smaller caucuses of civil servants. At best, meetings were dominated by a strong chairman; at worst, they echoed with hollow rhetoric.

Block grants

The most widespread and obvious developmental task that has been given to development committees has been responsibility for managing block grants for development purposes. A most important lesson to be gleaned concerns the right balance between the sums involved, the discretion devolved, the level to which devolution takes place, and the capability that exists at that level. Large sums distort existing programmes and are liable to bias actual resource distribution to favour the better off areas where the capacity to spend is better developed. Too little discretion encourages evasion and bending the rules at the local level, while too much encourages corruption. Devolution too far down the hierarchy leads to problems of control and reconciling proposals, while devolution only to provincial/ regional level may encourage a bias towards only the larger and more prestigious projects. The capability among government field staff effectively to handle block votes is, however, probably far greater than the cautious accountants of central treasuries are inclined to recognize; and in the absence of resources and discretion, much of that capability lies unexploited, a dormant national resource. In mobilizing that capability, careful use of block grants is a valuable and proven means.

Increases in authority and discretion for government staff at local levels is sometimes confused with participation by the people; but it is by no means the same thing. Development committees and block grants at regional/provincial and district level increase participation by staff and often by certain of the locally based elite. The extent of participation by the people associated with or resulting from the top-down approach represented by development committees and block grants depends partly on development committee composition but much more on the procedures which govern their operation, the resources of which they dispose, the strength and nature of popular demands, and the local institutions and interest groups through which they are articulated.

Bottom-up: Self-help and demands

It may be quite generally the case, elsewhere as in Kenya, that the failures of local government and the weakness of the party in representing and giving meaning to local aspirations have coincided with the growth and vigour of self help groups. Lacking any other effective and reliable means of getting what they want, clans, churches and other groupings have identified themselves, organized, worked and competed for government and other external resources. The latest development in Kenya, where the urban elite, at high cost to themselves in money and time, have been promoting Institutes of Technology (Godfrey and Mutiso, 1973) appears to represent the most advanced manifestation of this 'unofficial' competition for resources, prestige and legitimacy, but now on a wider regional and ethnic instead of a narrower clan or religious basis. Like the earlier self help projects in which secondary schools and health centres were put up all over the country, often without staffing or other recurrent resources, these latest institutes conflict with rational planning by some strictly economic criteria. But like the earlier schools and health centres, they are likely to be built for they represent the sublimation of powerful drives which, if frustrated, might find other outlets which would threaten political stability.

The vigour, nature and geographical density of self help projects varies between countries, within countries, and in any one area over time. There are places where a community development effort is needed to help people to see what they need; there are other places where an explosion of enthusiasm has created a chaotic proliferation of projects. There are situations (as in parts of Kenya in 1973) in which self help groups wish to hide, to avoid political or administrative support which might distort or unreasonably expand their projects (Almy and Mbithi, 1972). At the other pole, there are self help groups with extremely dependent attitudes which have formed themselves only as a device for securing resources. There are also sharp contrasts between countries: Zambia has been cursed with ample government resources which have stunted local self help by making it rational for people not to help themselves but to petition for help; Kenya, at the other extreme, may be exceptional in the extraordinary energy and diversity of the Harambee movement, with its roots in the long struggle for independence (Anderson, 1971) and its highly competitive local character.

Self help presents major opportunities for development. The extractionist view that it enables the exploitation of resources which would otherwise lie dormant, that it saves government funds, that it makes use of under-utilized labour, that it releases pressure on overextended government agencies is valid as far as it goes. But self help also has other values. It can increase the competence and confidence of a group and its members in handling their affairs. The example of the so-called *mabati* groups of women in Kenya indicates how one success can lead on to another: for having begun by working together to raise funds to put iron (*mabati*) roofs on their members' houses, they moved on to buying grade cattle, fencing dips, building better kitchens, and demanding the services of community development, health, veterinary and home economics staff. Again, where a capital asset is put up, schools being the most common example, continuing management is much more likely to be successful where there is a group and personal commitment through past contributions and sacrifices made. There is also a political gain in the sense of change and achievement which flows from self help. A major value, in Kenya at least, has been the barrage of demands directed by self help groups to civil servants, particularly in community development (Edward, 1969) which, although sometimes distracting, keeps them on their toes. In ways such as these in most countries of Eastern Africa, self help initiatives have made major contributions to national development.

The management of self help projects, seen primarily from a top-down government point of view, has, however, presented huge problems, a nightmare for planners, a headache for administrators, and a wobbly plinth for politicians. These problems can be considered under four headings: control and planning; authoritarianism; implementation; and operation and maintenance.

First, control and planning problems have received the most attention, being the most monumentally conspicuous. Self help groups often form to construct buildings designed for the provision of services. The long term objective is usually that the government should provide the service to the local community – most notably schools and health services in the 1960s. But the resources required government funds, contributions from the elite, and most important of all, high level approval for staffing and recurrent expenditure are scarce and difficult to secure. For these scarce resources, the clans, religious groups, clusters of population and other interest groups which take part in self help compete with one another. The main focus of the competition is the construction of a building. This lends itself to self help activity through contributions in labour and in kind and through the visibility of achievement; but at least as important, the building constitutes a powerful bid in the competition. As Holmquist (1970, p222) has well said, self help projects are pre-emptive. If there can be only one health centre in a locality, the group that constructs the first and best building for it may stand the best chance of securing it for their sublocality. The strategy is risky but understandable.

The results are, however, often unfortunate. Examples are legion and well known: two dips built by rival clans within a few yards of one another; two secondary schools, one empty, the other with only a few pupils, a mile or two apart; shells of buildings which have never been completed, or if completed, never used; poorly staffed schools; dispensaries in low priority areas while higher priority areas lack health facilities; and technical considerations ignored, as in the classic case in Kisii District in Kenya where technical rationality in a dips programme required a steady spread of dips to expand the frontier of a disease free zone but where the self help groups were scattered and moved at different speeds (Holmquist, 1970). The outcomes have been not only unsystematic development, heavy strains on government resources and often disillusion at the local level, but also more positively the expression of popular wants which political parties, local authorities and civil servants were unable or unwilling to carry. The gradual legitimation of Harambee secondary schools in Kenya and their progressive incorporation into the official educational system is an example of a powerful grassroots movement forcing the government's hand, of the tail wagging the dog.

A second problem is the authoritarian style of much of the mobilization for self help, at least in Kenya. In several respects administrative officers are political leaders and concerned with their legitimacy and acceptance by the people. Lacking other meaningful developmental roles, they have devoted attention to stimulating and supporting self help, but they have naturally brought to this task the style and techniques of other aspects of their work. There is a tendency for communication in *barazas*[3] to be one way, from the District Officer or the Chief to the people (Nyangira, 1970). Moreover, so-called voluntary contributions of labour may cover a wide range of practices, from forced labour with a legally enforceable penalty for default, to work in a group voluntarily joined without pressure. Whenever there is administrative pressure for labour turnouts, then the forced nature is likely to be more pronounced. It is, however, in contributions of cash or kind that the totalitarian character of some self help is most noticeable. Administrative officers, chiefs and subchiefs transfer easily the style and methods for collecting tax to collecting for self help. Nyangira (1970, p10) reports that those who refused to contribute to a Harambee Secondary School in Western Kenya had one sheep or goat per head of household confiscated and auctioned, the proceeds going towards the project. An administrative reflex has been applied to self help, and this is by no means entirely bad; but it does change the view of self help from a pure spontaneous voluntary movement to a semi-compulsory form of quasi local government, in which contributions are exacted like any other tax, but with the advantage over conventional local authorities that the relation between contribution given and service received is clearer to the person taxed.

Third, there has been a wide range of problems in implementation. Where bids have been made for official resources, there have often been unconscionable delays: the request is sent upwards and sometimes lost forever in a bureaucratic maze; or returned after many months with requests for additional information; or accepted, but only after long enough has passed for local enthusiasm to have waned. (A notable exception was the handling of self help fund requests in Botswana in 1972, with quick decisions made by a central committee which met every two weeks.) In other cases, the procedures to be followed and the path to be traced by a request are not known and time is wasted in chasing up blind alleys. Where official support is given, there may then be problems of phasing inputs. The cement arrives but sets in the rains because all able bodied people are out planting their farms and cannot afford time for labour. A pipeline laying crew arrives but the trenches for the waterpipe have not been dug, or not dug deeply enough. Technicians have their programmes to follow, and the local people also have theirs – critically important where subsistence cultivation is concerned; and these two often do not mesh. Or technical advice is not sought, or sought too late, or provided too late, or not provided at all. There may be inter-departmental problems in the official agencies: community development staff at loggerheads with the Administration, a common condition based on mutual jealousy; or a technical department – water affairs, or veterinary services – wishing to employ direct labour to get a job done quickly, while community development and the administration prefer to mobilize the people to work. Or again, a certain level of local contribution in cash may be required and may be delayed, holding up and even disrupting a programme of work for officials. Some of these problems may sometimes be difficult to avoid; but many of them, on close inspection, relate to communication, perception and understanding between individuals and groups and should be remediable.

A fourth and neglected set of problems concerns the operation of completed projects. This is liable to be dismissed as a function of good initial control and planning: if the health centre had been 'properly planned' then there would have been adequate staff and drugs to operate it. But in practice it is often not so simple. The group which built the dip did not realize that they would have to employ a dip attendant, would have to raise funds for the dip poison, would have to maintain the fence and would have to ensure the water supply. The group that built the school ignored the need for teachers' houses, the rising standards demanded by teachers, the need for a water supply, and so on. But perhaps it is right that these needs are not always clearly perceived in the early stages. They then later call forth the 'creativity' of Hirschman's principle of the Hiding Hand (1967), according to which it is often only because people do not foresee difficulties that they launch out on projects and become committed to them; but faced later with unforeseen problems, they find they have a greater capacity or creativity for overcoming them than they thought. Whether such creativity is mustered depends critically on the degree of self reliance of the self help group. If it has been featherbedded with excessive outside help, it will be less likely effectively to manage the operation of the completed project than if it has made most of the initial effort itself.

[Principles and measures proposed to tackle these problems (Managing Rural Development, pp105–106) included programming resource allocations; joint programming by government staff and self-help groups; devolution and decision-making lower down the hierarchy in government in order to reduce delays and difficulties; and the use of programming bar charts. Some other suggestions were: effective two-way communication and progress reporting between self-help groups and government.]

Almy and Mbithi (1972) have good suggestions and point out the dangers of non-discussion and non-representation through the medium of meetings of leaders, senior representatives and the higher-level development committees. They write, of Kenya:

> *The sub chief's* baraza *has usually been a forum for earnest discussion of plans and rectification of complaints, but the chief's* baraza *is usually addressed only by recognized local leaders and at the Divisional/District levels the only local participation is to sit in the hot sun and clap when visiting dignitaries have finished lecturing in a strange language (Almy and Mbithi, p1972, p69).*

It is, perhaps, only at the very low levels that the full and open meeting is effective; and higher up there has to be resort to representation or selection of leaders and discussion in committee. The moral would seem to be that government staff should try to penetrate down to the level at which such general meetings can be effective, and that above that level there should be a hierarchy of development committees including local opinion leaders and staff.

Administrative control and mediation

Preventing bad self help (bad siting, duplication, no staff, no funds, no recurrent resources, etc) is likely to be an untidy and incomplete operation where self help is vigorous, but a good upwards information system through community development or other staff, and good downwards communication of policies and guidelines may go a long way in discouraging poor initiatives. But the essence of self help is that people identify a need for themselves and try to satisfy it; and launching out secretly on a 'bad' project, or allowing several projects to go ahead, in the expectation that there will be a better chance of at least one of them being supported, is often rational behaviour on the part of would be client groups or their leaders. As with other aspects of participation, we are concerned with establishing and maintaining balances in shifting situations according to conflicting criteria, especially 'rational' planning against popular demand. The optimal situation will always be suboptimal from a planning point of view alone.

Avoiding top-down collection targetry

The most damaging forms of extra legal expropriation of property and extortion of funds that have taken place in the name of self help have resulted from collection targets set at provincial or district level and then disaggregated down to chiefs and even subchiefs, with deadlines for delivery, reaching such unreasonable lengths that a subchief might resign over the issue, as in one case when the collection demanded was in a poor area suffering from drought in order to support a new service in a richer area. People, or at worst local leaders, should set their own collection targets, if targets there are to be. Administrative staff may perhaps reasonably be judged by their tax collections; they should not be judged by the extent to which they collect centrally determined sums of self-help contributions.

Participation and equity

The way in which words are used in the rhetoric of self reliance and participation encourages the idea that increased participation will mean a more democratic, egalitarian and equitable society. The idea that the participation advocated in plans and policy speeches reaches and benefits all the people is important for the reassurance of political leaders. There is just enough truth in this belief to sustain it; and it is reinforced by the highly selective experience of political leaders who are usually shown the best of everything, and who usually see that best on its best behaviour. But very often, and far more often than either political leaders or civil servants perceive or wish to perceive, participation means more influence and resources to those who are already influential and better off, while those who are less influential and less well off benefit much less, or do not benefit, or actually lose.

There are many ways in which 'participation' accentuates inequity. Greater local participation in planning tends to widen regional inequalities. It favours those areas which are better able to produce plans and to implement them: the early experience with the Regional Development Fund in Tanzania was that the more prosperous regions (with the more competent staff, better infrastructure, better services) were more effective in spending the fund, while some of the remoter and more backward regions lagged and returned large sums unspent.

Participation in planning is also likely to mean plans drawn up either by civil servants or by civil servants together with a few members of the local elite. Participation in development committees can mean that those who are already well off approve projects and programmes which favour and support those who are already well off. Participation in self help labour can mean that the women, already overworked, turn out while the men find excuses. Participation through 'voluntary' contributions can mean an income regressive flat rate tax which hits the poorest hardest; and failure to pay, as with contributions to some of Kenya's institutes of technology, may be penalized through the denial of public services, health treatment, the right to buy a bicycle licence, and so on until a receipt for a minimum contribution can be shown. Participation in the local management of economic activities is even more inequitable. The privileges secured by the richer and more influential members of marketing cooperatives in Eastern Africa and elsewhere have been widely exposed (Widstrand, 1970, 1972; Worsley, 1971; Apthorpe, 1972, p81; Saul, 1973). In pastoral societies measures for communal management of grazing and water resources have almost invariably benefited the larger stock owners to the detriment of the smaller men: dam committees set up in Botswana to manage new dams charged a flat rate to all users, regardless of whether they brought hundreds of stock to water, or only one or two, in effect excluding the poorer people from the club; similarly when Council boreholes, which charged on a pro rata basis for numbers of stock watered, were handed over to local syndicate management, rates were changed to a flat rate for each stock owner regardless of the number of stock he watered. Again, it is notorious that land reform programmes, necessarily (short of a revolutionary situation) working through local committees, are captured by local elites who benefit more than the programme intends. In sum, all too often participation proclaimed on the platform becomes appropriation and privilege when translated into action in the field.

This should scarcely be surprising, except to those who, for ideological reasons or because they are simple minded, or more commonly from a combination of these causes, reify 'the people' and 'participation' and push them beyond the reach of empirical analysis. The tendency for local elites to capture projects and programmes and use them for their own benefit should indeed be recognized as a fact of life. Moreover, there are benefits as well as costs in this. Leaders are often leaders because they have ability, and projects may be better managed through their participation. Leaders, especially where there is an active political party, may seek support and legitimacy and so have an incentive to spread the benefits of projects to more rather than fewer people. A conflict between the aims of good leadership and management on the one hand, and of distribution and equity on the other, is, however, likely to be a persistent feature which will remain difficult to overcome. Moreover, there are such variations between conditions in different, areas that generalized prescriptions for participation and equity are more shaky and dangerous than in other more uniform contexts such as field staff management. All the same, six measures to mitigate the inequity which flows from participation and to improve its equity effects can be proposed.

First, in allocating support between alternative self help projects, *preference should be given to those to which all have access*, or to which a wider rather than narrower band of the population will have access. A scale of desirability can be drawn up according to this criterion, with at one pole those projects which benefit all members of the community more or less equally – the village well, the health post (if treatment is free), the social hall, moving through those which benefit all but some much more than others – the access road, the nursery school, the primary school, the cooperative store, to those which only benefit a minority of the community or a few individuals who are already better off – the secondary school with high fees, the cash crop processing plant when only a few can grow the cash crop, the institute of technology to which only a few will be able to send their children.

Second, *contributions to projects should be related to economic status*, the richer paying more and the poorer paying less, and limited to those who are expected to benefit from the service resulting. There are conflicting considerations here. It may be very important for a person's self-respect that he contribute equally with his richer neighbour; and unless carefully handled, the identification of a 'poor' group which contributes nothing or contributes less, may be humiliating and resented. If levels of contribution are permissive, then each potential contributor can make his own decision. At one extreme there is little justification for the confiscation of a poor widow's hen to help pay for a secondary school that she will never be able to send her children to. On the other hand, if some degree of persuasive pressure is not exerted, there will be those in the community who could contribute but refuse to do so even though they will use the service later. President Nyerere faced this dilemma and after at first opposing compulsion came to the view that indolent members of a community should be made to work and contribute. 'From each according to his means, to each according to his need' may be an unattainable ideal, but the first half at least is close enough within range in most East African rural communities to justify a determined attempt to achieve it.

Third, *policies for participation, should be related to the stage of development reached.* Typically different regions within the same country are at different stages.[4] In the first stage, as in Turkana or West Pokot in Kenya, the major tasks are finding and using leaders who will help to get development moving through education, infrastructure, opening up markets and movement into the cash economy; self-help may be impossible and the formation of interest groups premature. In the second stage, as found in much of the Coast Province of Kenya and many of the areas which are marginal for arable agriculture, leaders are still important in decision making; in setting an example, and in adopting innovations, but increasingly a shift of official extension can be directed towards leaders and groups together. Self help is active, but follows the tendency for the first projects to benefit all or almost all the community, while later and later projects benefit fewer and fewer. In the third stage, as found in the more highly developed high potential smallholding areas of Kenya such as Nyeri and Kisii, interest groups form themselves spontaneously and the progressive farmers can rely more and more on specialized commercial services. It is at this stage that a special effort is justified, to leap over the leaders and the elite groups who can look after themselves, the cooperative committee of prosperous farmers, the groups (Maendeleo ya Wanawake) of their wives and the wives of civil servants, in order to reach, rouse and help the people who have been left out. This can be done through the reorientation of extension services, through encouraging the expansion of membership of existing groups such as the *mabati* women of Tetu in Kenya, through individual extension contacts, and through concentrating attention on those groups which have wider non-elite memberships. In this stage, community development should be less concerned with conventional self help projects, which will have shown their usual trend towards serving the better off members of the community (as for example with dips and secondary schools) and official liaison with which can be handled by technical officers. Community development workers should, rather, be concentrating on welfare extension programmes which have a reasonable chance of adoption and success among the less well-off members of the community, such as nutrition, vegetable growing, home economics, health and family planning. In this third stage, community development workers often find themselves overtaken by events and initiatives and left standing; but they can, by redirecting their attention to these less privileged groups, again find a useful role.

Fourth, especially *in these highly developed third stage areas, a radical reorientation of staff activities is required.* Moris (1972) has shown how central directives can be distorted in the course of application in the field, and their original objectives subverted. To reduce such tendencies carefully devised procedures and careful supervision can help. But if staff are to behave very differently, shifting their attention and services away from local elites to local non-elites, they must themselves be convinced that this is right; and they are unlikely to be convinced that this is right merely through the issue of circulars and orders. The SRDP in Kenya showed the potential of a participatory approach to inter-departmental action. Seminars held over periods ranging from three days to three weeks, in which departmental staff heads came together and together thought through problems with some outside assistance, showed that at both divisional and district levels this sort of open participation could yield ideas, consensus and commitment. As so often, the imagination, intelligence and diligence of field staff proved to be far greater than many imbued with the centrist ideology would have supposed. In any reorientation towards equity programmes, a think tank open ended seminar approach is a powerful, perhaps essential, means of securing strong commitment on the part of staff.

Fifth, a major if surprising obstacle is *the invisibility of poverty to field staff.* This can be tackled through preparatory work for the seminars mentioned above. It was through acting as enumerators in a random sample survey of farmers that the SRDP field staff in Vihiga came to perceive the poorer people. To replicate such a survey on any scale might be difficult; but before attending any seminar, staff could be quickly trained to carry out their own small surveys of one or two areas. Various rules of thumb for selecting respondents could be suggested; but in any case it could be a requirement that at the start of the seminar each participant should describe in detail the circumstances of a number of the poorest people in the area where he worked and put forward his suggestions for how they could be helped.

Sixth, as with other aspects of managing rural development, the *design, testing and modification of procedures is critical.* Oddly, university research in Eastern Africa, with a few notable exceptions including those quoted in this chapter, has neglected the detailed dynamics of local participation. In its earlier stages, the experimental opportunities of the SRDP were not being exploited to explore this vital area; yet such exploration, with experimental testing, is surely a very high priority, especially given the likelihood that equity will be a major preoccupation of the 1970s.

Finally, this concluding section will itself be little better than rhetoric, and far from reality, unless there is a very determined *political will* to reach the poorer people. Fine phrases in development plans do not feed children; nor does public oratory. In the early 1970s an oversimplified impression is that Tanzania and Botswana have the political will and are building the machinery to implement it; that Kenya has the machinery in the form of an efficient civil service, but not the will; and that Zambia may still be having difficulty in creating both the will and the machinery. These judgements may be harsh. But they are needed to emphasize that the end which is sought, a more equitable rural society, is very difficult to achieve; that trying to achieve it is kicking against the pricks; and that the non-revolutionary course towards it requires sustained effort, a high level of management in the rural areas, and above all a credible and consistent political will.

Part 2: Applications, Potentials and Transformations (2004)

Since the early 1970s much has changed. Looking back, some expectations from the SRDP were unrealistic. Since then different streams of participation have come together and new ones, including PRA/PLA, have evolved and spread almost explosively, with many methods and innumerable applications and results. Some practice has been excellent. Much, at least in these early years, has been bad, and justly criticized, not least by practitioners. Diverse views and forms of participation are reflected in different definitions and 'ladders' of participation but in all of them power is an element.

For the future, there are many applications of participatory methodologies. PRA/ PLA can enable sensitive subjects to be aired, analysed and tackled, as it has already with sexual and reproductive health, violence and abuses, and defecation. Poor people's realities and priorities can be expressed, and policy influenced, through participatory poverty assessments. Participatory approaches and methods can explore issues concerning human rights. They can also generate numbers as alternatives or complements to questionnaires. The scope for better development practice through levelling and reversing power relations is immense. In good participatory practice, innovation is a way of being. The overarching challenge is through participation to enable those who are most marginalized, powerless and poor to achieve a better life for themselves.

Looking back

Looking back, the conditions, approaches and outlook in Eastern Africa in the late 1960s and early 1970s were strikingly different from those of the early 21st century.

In the earlier period, in sub-Saharan Africa, many conditions were better. The outlook was optimistic. Neither I, nor any but the most dire pessimists, could have dreamt of the downturns that were to come. In Eastern African, 30 years later, it is appalling to see how much has changed for the worse. In the 1960s and early 1970s, the future was bright. There was nowhere to go but up. Now, in the 2000s, among the countries considered, in no case except Botswana is the state as well provided with resources as it was (though, offsetting this, Botswana has the highest reported incidence of HIV/AIDS of any country in the world). Elsewhere, from the 1980s onwards, governments and district administrations were more and more starved of funds, materials and machinery. Under these conditions, unless it was in the constituency of an influential politician, it would have been laughable for a community to follow the strategy of the 1960s and early 1970s and to muster self-help to build a school, clinic or dip, hoping that the utility would then be equipped and staffed. As school enrolments fell, clinics lacked drugs, dips went unserviced and roads deteriorated the losing struggle in many places was to slow the rate of decline, to stave off collapse and to retain some sort of service from infrastructure that already existed.

There are continuities, though, in mindsets and practices. These have remained top down in their deep structures despite programmes of decentralization. The extent to which in *Managing Rural Development* I depicted participation as part of administration, involving officials and politicians as participants, as well as bottom up, coming from local people, reflected my own orientation as a former administrator and trainer of administrators in the Kenya Government. That top-down mindset and orientation, and the behaviours and attitudes that go with them, remain alive and well in many development bureaucracies. Decentralization through district committees, district planning and block grants recurs, as with current and recent decentralizations in Ghana, Kenya and Uganda. It is noteworthy how little is known or remembered from earlier experiences, and how little historical depth (except, perhaps, in the memories of local leaders in an area) there is in understandings of the principles, procedures, potentials and pitfalls of these forms of decentralization.

There are also striking differences. Language has changed. In the 1970s we did not use many of the words that are current today. 'Equity' and 'poverty' were there. But of the six power-and-relationship words now in common use, the only one I have found in what I wrote is 'participation': there is no trace of 'empowerment', 'ownership', 'partnership', 'accountability' or 'transparency'. These concepts and priorities had not yet been articulated. As for the self-help groups, they were part of what we now call CBOs (community-based organizations). The terms NGO and civil society were not in use. The future was still seen to lie primarily with government. And it was to university and government that we looked for innovation in participatory approaches and methods when, in the event, it was people working in NGOs who were to be the main innovators. Yet, what we now call spontaneous participation was there under our noses. The self-help groups were appraising, planning, implementing, monitoring and evaluating all the time, largely inventing their methods for themselves. And we had little idea how they were doing it and no idea of learning from them.[5] The biggest difference, though, was that during the 1970s many of the methods and approaches that we have today had not evolved. It is like looking back on the Jurassic or Cretaceous periods before there were mammals. PRA, AI (appreciative inquiry), Planning for Real, Participatory Technology Development, participatory monitoring and evaluation, and numerous others (see, for example, Lewis and Walker, 1998) simply did not exist.

With hindsight I can see that, in the SRDP work, I was unrealistic in two ways. The first was expecting university staff to engage in and be good at developing participatory procedures. Of the six clusters of procedures identified (see Chapter 3, 'Clusters of procedures'), what were called 'local participation procedures' ended up as a poor relation. I sought to pass the buck by inviting university staff to develop them. But sustained engagement was required in the field. At the time, university staff had not only normal commitments to teaching, but were also in rapid transition. Generally, too, work with communities is liable to generate fewer publishable papers than more conventional research. Universities did, however, play a part later in pioneering RRA (rapid rural appraisal), a methodology for learning more and faster, and that was seen as contributing directly to research: it was the University of Khon Kaen in Thailand that convened an international conference on RRA in 1985 and published the proceedings (KKU, 1987). But later, in the 1990s, universities were with few exceptions[6] slow to learn about the spread and potential of PRA, let alone to adopt and promote it. But with PRA, requiring as it did deeper and longer engagement, and raising more ethical questions, university departments were little in the action, and innovation and dissemination were largely led by NGOs. Before the early 2000s, it was exceptional for a university to offer modules on PRA or on participatory methodologies more broadly.

A second unrealistic hope was to call for political will to reach (note 'reach', not 'empower') the poorer people. In a review of *Managing Rural Development*, Manfred Bienefeld pointed out that I ended five of the six chapters with such an appeal. A call for political will is often a hope that powerful people will work against their perceived material and power interests. That can happen; but to make it happen (see Chapters 6 and 7) is problematical, to say the least. And a common condition for it to happen well and on a wide scale is organized demand from poor people themselves.

Streams of participation

Participation through the development decades (the 1950s onwards) has had many streams, with flows separating and merging, and new springs coming in.[7] Participation in Africa during the 1970s owed much to the idea and experience of community development. Paulo Freire (1970) and the Latin American movement of popular education (Kane, 2001) were widely influential in many countries and contexts. In the US, the civil rights movement, Miles Horton's work with trade unions, John Gaventa's work with marginalized and exploited poor communities in the Appalachians (Gaventa, 1980) and that of the Highlander Research and Education Center all drew upon and amplified the Freirian tradition (Bell et al, 1990). UNRISD (United Nations Research Institute for Social Development) made participation a theme in the 1970s and 1980s. Peter Oakley's advocacy and writing on participation were influential (see, for example, Oakley and Marsden, 1984; Oakley, 1991). A UN (United Nations) inter-agency Panel on People's Participation was set up in 1982. Milton Esman, Norman Uphoff and others at Cornell University published the excellent *Rural Development Participation Review* from 1979 to 1982 until USAID, with sadly characteristic myopia and abruptness,[8] withdrew its support.

These were but some of the many institutions, individuals and publications contributing to participation, and to a new stream that began to emerge in the late 1980s.[9] This was known initially as PRA (participatory rural appraisal).[10] Then, from the mid 1990s onwards, PRA was increasingly relabelled and, together with other traditions, was known as PLA (participatory learning and action), or sometimes PRA/PLA. PRA drew on several sources, including popular education and the teachings and practice of Paulo Freire, social anthropology, farming systems research, Training for Transformation (Hope and Timmel, 1984), agro-ecosystem analysis (Conway, 1985), and RRA (rapid rural appraisal) (KKU, 1987), among others. And PRA methods and approaches, especially participatory visuals on the ground or on paper, such as social mapping, seasonal diagramming and matrix scoring, which evolved and spread during the 1990s, were adopted, adapted and further developed in other methodologies with other labels. Activities and processes called PRA were simply one part of what participation had been and remains: a braided stream of ever-mingling methods, approaches and traditions.

With PRA, what had begun in parallel in East Africa and India, and then exploded in India, spread to many countries, to all continents except perhaps Antarctica and from the South to the North. Aid agencies demanded participation in their projects, often specifying PRA. It evolved in many forms and included and involved many activities, domains and sorts of people. It spread in many directions – for example:

- from appraisal and analysis to planning, action and participatory monitoring and evaluation (PM&E);
- from rural to urban (with participatory urban appraisal, or PUA);
- from 'community' participation to participation by groups by gender, age, wealth, poverty and occupation, and including children (e.g. Johnson et al, 1998) and old people (e.g. HelpAge International, 2002);
- from a few sectors to many;
- from action to participatory research;
- from action to policy influence;
- from field applications to applications in organizations;
- from NGOs to government departments, aid agencies, consultants, universities and the private sector;
- from a few countries to many, and from countries in the South to countries in the North (*PLA Notes*, 2000);[11]
- from practice to theory (asking: why does it work?);
- from methods to professional, institutional, behavioural and personal change.

There are many other approaches, methodologies and traditions, among them popular education, participatory action research, PTD (Participatory Technology Development), AI (Appreciative Inquiry), Planning for Real, and popular theatre.[12] *Participation Works!*, a publication of the New Economics Foundation (Lewis and Walker, 1998), describes 21 techniques for community participation, while Guijt and Veldhuizen (1998, p3) list 33 participatory methodologies used in agricultural research and extension. Much experience has been gained with participatory learning and action in NRM (natural resource management) (Probst and Hagmann et al, 2003). For all the diversity of names and methodologies, they rarely represent separate, bounded flows. Sharing, intermingling, borrowing and adapting prevail. Mono-methodology fundamentalists stuck in ruts do exist, mainly in big programmes that have quickly gone to scale (see Chapter 5). But for many (and, I sense, more and more) practitioners and trainers there is a delight in eclectic opportunism, seeking, borrowing, adopting, adapting and inventing different and new things to do and ways of doing them.

Participation in various forms has always been widespread. But it was only in the 1990s that it entered almost every field development activity and became a preoccupation on a global scale, preached about and promoted by lenders, donors, INGOs and governments alike.[13] By the turn of the century, the words *participatory* and *participation* were embedded in development speak. There was an explosion of activities described as participatory, taking many forms. More and more colleges, training institutes and universities[14] began to recognize, learn about, teach, and allow and encourage their students to use participatory approaches and methods. When university teaching and research methods catch up, it is time to acknowledge that something has truly entered the mainstream. In the early years of the 21st century, participation, in name if not in reality, is now part of almost every development activity.

Methods and applications

The 1990s also witnessed an explosion of creativity and innovation with what have become known as PRA methods.[15] Typically, these use visuals and tangibles, done by local people themselves, often in small groups. Some of the best-known and most widely adopted were mapping (see, for example, Alcorn, 2000), diagramming, ranking and scoring. A flood of insights and surprises followed, not least concerning people's unsuspected capabilities, the recognition that 'they can do it'. 'Ordinary' people, and especially those marginalized and looked down on by others, showed far greater ability to describe, present, diagram and analyse their realities than most professionals had believed.

Applications of activities described as PRA and PLA multiplied.[16] Applications of participatory methodologies in which PRA methods and approaches were prominent evolved in fields such as community planning and action, project appraisal, agriculture, natural resources management, health, poverty, and gender and livelihoods, and spread to literacy and empowerment with REFLECT (Regenerated Freirian Literacy through Empowering Community Techniques),[17] education, training, water and sanitation, and many forms and topics of research – for example, on social capital (Fraser et al, 2003a, 2003b). Further developments included applications in participatory monitoring and evaluation (Guijt, 1998; Guijt and Gaventa, 1998; Estrella et al, 2000; Bayer and Waters-Bayer, 2002; Guijt, forthcoming) and in local government linked with issues of citizenship and human rights (VeneKlasen with Miller 2002).

Quality and critiques

Quality and ethics became grave concerns for many practitioners, especially regarding PRA.[18] The power and popularity of the methods, and their visibility, contributed to their rapid adoption during the 1990s and to the even more rapid adoption of the PRA label. Lenders, donors and governments alike sought to go instantly to scale. Consultants and trainers unqualified either in experience or in behaviour and attitudes put themselves forward to meet an exponential demand.

Among many issues, one that stood out as vital from the start was who participates, where, when, with whom and with what equality. Who is excluded from participation, or marginalized in it, whether by gender, age, poverty, social group, religion, occupation, disability or other similar dimension, has been a persistent concern. Analysis by groups has many strengths, and groups do not have to be homogeneous to be democratic. But diverse groups can be dominated by some, while others stay silent or are bullied into consensus. Gender and participation is a major area here.[19] In some early cases of going to scale, women were notably neglected. As PRA spread fast there was bad practice in excluding those who were variously female, weak, poor and busy, contrasting with the good practices of empowering the powerless.

So, it was right that participation, participatory methodologies, in general, and PRA/PLA, in particular, provoked critiques. Around the turn of the century publications on participation and PRA proliferated. In 1998 NEPAN (the Nepal Participatory Action Network) began publishing its journal *Participation*. Other journals had special issues – for example, *Social Change* (New Delhi) on Participatory Pathways (Balakrishnan, 1998) and the *Canadian Journal of Development Studies* on participatory development (Cowie, 2000). Two books put PRA under a critical lens: *Participation: The New Tyranny?* (Cooke and Kothari, 2001), with a more academic orientation, and *Participation in Practice: Case Studies from The Gambia* (Brown et al, 2002), drawing on extensive field research. Ilan Kapoor (2002) argued that PRA was insufficiently theorized and politicized. David Mosse, a long-term constructive and perceptive critic of participation, reviewed the history of a project in India with which he had been involved in an article 'The making and marketing of participatory development' (Mosse, 2003). IIED, which had played a major part internationally in the evolution and spread of PRA, conducted a critical self-review, *Participatory Approaches to Research and Development in IIED: Learning from Experience* (Kanji and Greenwood, 2001). The Participation Group at IDS Sussex published a series of critical working papers,[20] convened a reflective review workshop of some 50 practitioners and in the Pathways to Participation project, together with colleagues in many countries, reviewed experiences with PRA (Cornwall and Pratt, 2003). Outcomes of the project were summarized in 12 pages, with a front page headed: 'Defying definition: A diversity of meanings and practices' (Participation Group, IDS, 2002).

Some of the most perceptive critics were practitioners themselves. Some made mistakes, learnt the lessons, corrected their practices and were exploring new approaches, methods and applications by the time academics caught up and noticed what was happening. Some of the more academic critics implied that their own deficient practice or that which they had observed was inherent in PRA – for example, assuming that PRA activities were normally large public affairs, with all their well-known shortcomings. At the same time, they were liable to miss the built-in bias against women because it is usually harder for women than men to find the blocks of time needed for the diagramming and discussion that is often part of a PRA process.[21] To try to offset this, it is good practice to 'ask them': to ask women what time and place would be best for them, and then to fit in with their preferences (in South Asia, the best time for meetings, quite often, is an hour or two after dark), however inconvenient it may be for the outsider. Perhaps some academic critics missed this because they did not have personal experience to draw upon.

That said, the challenges and opportunities are immense. The big question of how to go to scale with participation without sacrificing quality is considered in Chapter 5.

Definitions, types, ladders and limitations

Definitions of participation vary. Strikingly, definitions whose origins have given them some authority have been concerned with power. The UNRISD research programme on popular participation in the late 1970s defined it as:

> . . . *the organized efforts to increase control over resources and regulative institutions in given social situations on the part of groups and movements hitherto excluded from such control (Pearse and Stiefel, 1979).*[22]

In 1994, the World Bank defined participatory development as:

> . . . *a process through which stakeholders influence and share control over development initiatives and the decisions and resources which affect them (World Bank, 1994, pi).*

Reportedly, this was a negotiated definition, the word 'primary' before 'stakeholder', referring to poor people, being deleted after protests by non- OECD governments that it would constitute political interference in their internal affairs.

For DFID in its remarkable manifesto on human rights, participation is:

> . . . *enabling people to realise their rights to participate in, and access information relating to, the decision-making processes which affect their lives (DFID, 2000).*

This is seen to be linked to democratic institutions and organizations of the poor to represent their interests. The three cross-cutting principles of a rights perpective are presented as particpation, as above, inclusion based on values of equality and non-discrimination, and obligations, strengthening accountability of institutions to protect and promote rights.

Participation has no final meaning. It is not a rock. It is mobile and malleable, an amoeba, a sculptor's clay, a plasticine shaped as it passes from hand to hand. And perhaps it is right that this should be so, and that each generation, each group, each person, should puzzle out what they think it should mean and how they can best give it expression. And while the definitions above are set in a field development context, much of the discussion of participation applies to human relationships in other contexts – the organization, the workplace, the family, the social group, the meeting.

In any case, whatever the definition, participation has types and degrees. Peter Oakley (1991, pp8–10) distinguished participation in projects as contribution, as organization and as empowering. Types of participation are often characterized as ladders. The first ladder was probably that of Sherry Arnstein (1969), with eight rungs. Since then there have been many others (see Table 4.1). Some have highly autonomous participation at the top, and some have it at the bottom. The ladder can be drawn with steps up and people climbing (e.g. Samaranayake, 2001, p52), or it can be simply a list with explanations. One put forward by Bhatnagar and Williams (1992, pp178–179) for the World Bank to apply to its operations stresses participation by disadvantaged people. It has four levels or degrees:

1 *Information-sharing*: people are informed in order to facilitate collective individual action.
2 *Consultation*: people are consulted and interact with an agency, which can then take account of their feedback.
3 *Decision-making*: people have a decision-making role, which may be theirs exclusively, or joint with others, on specific issues of a policy or project.
4 *Initiating action*: people are proactive and able to take the initiative.

Some ladders have clear dimensions along which the categories are spread out. Arnstein's original ladder shows different ways in which an organization can involve participants. Others mix several polarizations or characteristics, as with roles and relationships, outsiders' and local people's actions, and ownership (see Table 4.2).

In 2002, with Ethiopian MPs representing pastoralists, the ladder was concerned with relationships and activities of MPs with their constituents, as follows:

- COMMAND
- INFORM
- CONSULT
- REPRESENT
- EMPOWER.[24]

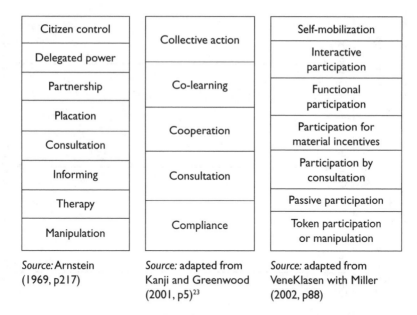

Figure 4.1 *Three ladders of citizen participation*

Ladders can thus be devised to fit particular contexts and needs. There is no one right or final ladder. Participatory definition is a good practice. Individuals or groups can be invited to invent their own.

Ladders unpack participation and show that the same word can be used for different activities and relationships. They can also show how much participation is about power. This can reduce pretence and hypocrisy and improve practice. The danger is, though, that it will be considered sufficient to use a ladder and make practices more rather than less participatory. This misses two points.

First, higher on a ladder (that is, being more participatory) is not necessarily better. Participation for material incentives may look a second best; but is not necessarily so: providing communities in Rwanda with food for the three days of a participatory assessment could be seen as material inducements, or as sensible and decent behaviour, making it easier for people to take part and not worry about how to feed themselves. This is more than material incentives in any crude sense; rather it is ethical reciprocity. Sequences, too, can make sense – for example, starting by informing, then consulting, and then enabling decision-making.

Second, equity is important: who gains and who loses. The 'spontaneous' self-help in Kenya during the 1960s and early 1970s was at the top of the ladders – citizen control, collective action and self-mobilization. But it was gender blind. As we have seen, it could involve poor women working or paying to benefit men and those who were better off. It could mean the confiscation of a poor widow's hen. Certainly, there are positive values of self-respect in making a contribution, and in community social solidarity. But this should not conceal how fine words about self-mobilization can mean forced labour and unfair taxation for the poorer and weaker, often women. So, citizen control can mean manipulation; collective action

Table 4.1 *A participation ladder with roles and relationships*

	Outsiders' objectives	Roles/Relationships Outsiders'	Roles/Relationships Local people's	Actions Outsiders	Actions Local People	Ownership
TOTALITARIAN	State political	Dictator	Slave	Command	Comply	Outsiders'
NOMINAL	Cosmetic legitimization	Manipulator	Puppet			
EXTRACTIVE	Obtain local knowledge for better planning	Research/planner	Informant			
INDUCED	Gain action through material incentives	Employer	Worker			
CONSULTATIVE/ INSTRUMENTAL	Improve effectiveness and efficiency	Rational economizer	Collaborator			
PARTNERSHIP	Share responsibility	Co-equal partner	Co-equal partner			
TRANSFORMATIVE	Facilitate sustainable development by local people	Facilitator/ catalyst	Analyst/actor/ agent			
SELF-MOBILIZING	Support spontaneous action	Supporter	Owner/controller	Support	Initiate	Local people's

Sources: Draws from several sources, including the versions of Andrea Cornwall (pers comm) and Pretty (1994, 1995b), and those in Table 4.1

can mean compliance; and empowerment can mean licence to gender discrimination and petty tyranny. Participation can concentrate power and benefits in the hands of men and of local elites. Ladders of participation are not enough. They need to be qualified by ladders of equity. And these may require authoritative, non-participatory interventions to ensure that those who are poor and weak gain and do not lose.

Streams with promise

Thematic potentials

There are many domains where the participatory processes and visuals associated with PRA, and with other methodologies, hold promise for the future. In my view, eight have exceptional potential:

1 *Participatory monitoring and evaluation*: across many domains and activities, PM&E (Estrella et al, 2000) can empower and inform local people, and help them to improve their practice and hold others to account. Visual records, whether as diaries or displayed in public, can be powerful instruments. The significant shift to be sought here is from one-off evaluation by external specialists for impact assessment and upward accountability, to continuous monitoring by participants for learning and change.

2 *Formal education*: PRA diagramming in primary and secondary education, as a means of empowering children and democratizing decision-making (Cox and Robinson-Pant, 2003), and as a life skill for representing and analysing complex realities and relationships. At the individual level, one medium for this is computer programmes for analytical diagrams.

3 *Psychotherapy*: this involves PRA diagramming in psychotherapy where a patient can use a diagram she has drawn to better understand the causes of distress and how to respond (Fiona Chambers, pers comm), as well as visualization as part of REFLECT processes for those suffering from trauma (AduGyamfi, 2003).

4 *Total institutions*: PRA processes can enhance the lives of the 'lowers' and liberate the 'uppers', who are confined by their roles, in total institutions[25] (Goffman, 1961), such as mental hospitals, prisons, boarding schools, monasteries, nunneries, some brothels, old people's homes and ships.

5 *Management processes*: this can involve participatory diagramming, including card writing and sorting, for drawing up meeting or workshop agendas and for decision-making – for example, in committee meetings, planning workshops and appointments boards, especially for seeking convergence and consensus.

6 *Conflict management and resolution*: in participatory diagramming for conflict resolution, agreed visuals promote mutual awareness and provide a basis for negotiation (see, for example, Conway et al, 1989). Going further, the use of geographic information systems (GIS) and participatory three-dimensional modelling has proved effective in providing a visual basis for negotiations over indeterminate and disputed boundaries between community areas in the Philippines (Rambaldi et al, 2002).

7   *Social audit in corporations*: applications here include employees' participatory analysis of their conditions of work. A pioneering example is an independent participatory assessment in a factory and neighbouring communities in Turkey for Levi Strauss (Sarah Clancy, pers comm).

8   *Rights, citizenship and deliberative democracy*: the scope here is to explore not just participatory approaches, but also the use of visuals in appraisal and analysis, in advocacy, in facilitating awareness of rights and in claiming them. Participatory maps of fishing areas and corals have empowered fisher folk in the Philippines to claim rights and protect resources. New democratic spaces have been opened up (Cornwall and Coelho, 2004). Applications include participatory foresight (Faucheux and Hue, 2001), policy focus groups, citizens' juries (Coote, 1997; Pimbert and Wakeford, 2002; *PLA Notes*, 2003), participatory budgeting (Schneider and Goldfrank, 2002) and report cards (Paul, 2002).

Lifting lids and liberating

Participatory approaches can lift the lids from domains that are unpleasant, hidden, private or dangerous. One of the finest contributions of sensitive participatory research has been to open up understanding and action in areas of human deprivation and suffering which have been either ignored or regarded as too difficult or threatening. Through PRA and participation, people have uncovered the hidden, exposed the unseen, shown the unsaid, spoken the unspeakable, and done the undoable. They have found they can escape from the inescapable.

Let three inspiring examples illustrate.

The first is aspects of *sexual and reproductive behaviour and well-being*. These have been explored, analysed and documented as never before by *Realizing Rights: Transforming Approaches to Sexual and Reproductive Well-being* Cornwall and Welbourn (2002). The lives and realities of those who are marginalized, despised, excluded and ignored have been brought out into the light. Sex workers, for example, come to life as people like other people, for whom respect, security and good relations matter as much, if not more, than they do for others (see Chapter 6). Participatory approaches to HIV/AIDS, especially through the group processes known as Stepping Stones (Welbourne, 1995, 2002) have brought what was hidden or unspoken into the open, with frank talk about sex and death, concern for sensitive behaviour and relationships, acceptance of HIV-positive women and men, and counselling and care for the sick and dying. Participatory approaches and methods have also been developed for HIV/AIDS work with drug users (International HIV/AIDS Alliance, 2003).

The second is *violence, physical insecurity and social abuses*. Participatory studies of violence in Jamaica, Guatemala and Colombia[26] have broken new ground, revealing wide differences between the beliefs of policy-makers and the realities experienced by ordinary people. Small arms and their impact have been studied in Asia (Banerjee and Muggah, 2002). Participatory mapping has been used in mine clearance (Simon Conway, pers comm). In Peru, participatory time lines, matrices and maps were used in Ayacucho as part of the *Colectivo Yuyarisu* ('We remember') process of theTruth Commission (Comision de laVerdad y Justicia). Using these methods, over 100 groups recollected and reconstructed human rights violations that had taken place in the era of political violence of 1980–1994 (Francke, 2003, and pers comm). In many contexts, domestic abuse and violence against women has been brought out into the open. An early example was an all-women's PRA activity inTamil Nadu in 1990 (Sheelu Francis and John Devavaram, pers comm), in which women mapped households and marked with a yellow circle those where the husband was a drunkard. A later example, in 2000, was analysis and presentation of perceived prevalence and trends of domestic violence against women, carried out by groups in over 200 communities in 23 countries (Narayan et al, 2000, pp119–131; see also Sutherland and Sakala, 2002, for Zambia).

Participatory monitoring of abuses may be a potent instrument for change. New Entity for Social Action (NESA), an NGO inTamil Nadu working 'to secure life with dignity among Dalit, Adivasi and other vulnerable communities' has evolved, tested and introduced into 2500 villages an Internal Learning System in which people keep visual diaries (non-literate women and men can do this). In these diaries, they score degrees of abuse (from 1 to 5) every six months. Aspects of life monitored include husbands drinking, domestic violence, Dalits having to drink out of separate glasses, Dalits being made to carry dead bodies or dead animals, and whether a girl can select her life partner (Vimalathan, Nagasundari and Noponen, pers comm). The diaries are aggregated to give an indication of social change.

The third inspiring example is *open defecation,* widespread in South and South-East Asia and a major source of sickness and mortality. It is also associated with gross gender discrimination in that, unlike men, women are compelled by custom to go unseen, which without latrines means only before dawn or after nightfall.[27] For long the solution sought has been the subsidized construction of latrines. With very few exceptions, this has benefited only a minority, while all continue to lose from fouling and infection caused by the continuing open defecation of others. In 2000, Kamal Kar, working in Bangladesh with theVillage Education Resource Centre (VERC) and supported by the international NGO WaterAid, evolved a PRA approach of community appraisal, analysis and action that tackles the problem, substituting self-respect for subsidy (VERC, 2002;WSPSA, 2002; Kar, 2003). Community members make defecation maps, walk transects, inspect the defecation areas, confront the reality, draw flow diagrams, calculate the cartloads of shit produced and the amounts ingested, and are encouraged to take action on their own.There is no hardware subsidy.There are no required engineers' latrine designs. The process is facilitated, not administered. The results of this community-led total sanitation (CLTS) have been dramatic, with total sanitation proudly achieved in numerous rural communities in Bangladesh, and with promising starts elsewhere. In late 2004, the nascent movement was reported to have achieved total coverage in well over 2000 communities in Bangladesh and was being promoted and spread in Maharashtra and other states in India, and in Cambodia and Mongolia.There were starts and bridgeheads too in Indonesia, Nepal, Uganda and Zambia. Graffiti in one totally sanitized village in Maharashtra read: 'Daughters from our village are not married to villages where open defecation is practised.' In rural South Asia, where open defecation is widespread, the scale of the potential gains in health, reduced mortality and well-being for millions of women, children and men is so vast that it is difficult fully to appreciate.[28]

Sexual and reproductive health, violence and abuses, and defecation are but three areas that have opened up. In each case, what we witness are beginnings. We have to ask how these three inspiring and liberating developments have come about. Interpretations may be many. The three developments differ, but each exhibits a combination of:

- courageous, committed, imaginative and sensitive facilitation;
- group visual sharing, activities and synergies;
- confronting and attacking the poverty and ill health of poor and marginalized people;
  and, most strikingly,
- the empowerment of women.

This last stands out. Repeatedly, in context after context, in culture after culture, participatory approaches have enhanced the well-being of women and, at the same time, through better relationships, those of men. In my view, there is no other near-universal domain of human life, except, perhaps, how we bring up children, with greater potential for gains in quality of experience and being than transforming gender relations. For this to occur, participation is central.

The question stares one in the face: beyond these three domains, what other hidden or forbidden areas are there waiting to be opened up? I have suggested total institutions above – but what about human trafficking; child abuse; other issues linked with human rights; street gangs; drugs; corruption; and interest rates and value chains?

If there are limits to such liberations, they are not yet in sight.

Participation, policy and practice: PPAs and PRAMs

PPAs (participatory poverty assessments),[29] designed to enable poor people to analyse and express their realities and priorities and to influence policy, have used a variety of methodologies. The application of PRA approaches and methods was piloted in Ghana in 1993 and 1994 (Dogbe, 1998). Other countries followed, including Zambia, South Africa, Mozambique and Bangladesh, and by 2004 many PPAs in this tradition had been conducted nationally and at sub-national levels in Africa, Asia and Latin America. In their first generation these PPAs were mainly one-off events. They gave significant insights on aspects of poverty, such as seasonality of deprivation and vulnerability, physical isolation as a key factor in access to services and markets, the decline of traditional safety nets, and hunger and dietary inadequacy as a distinct dimension of deprivation (Booth, Holland et al, 1998, p8). These PPAs were embodied in reports; any follow-up had mostly only a limited impact on policy (see, for example, Agyarko, 1997, for Ghana).

A second generation of PPAs was concerned more with creating new relationships and understandings within policy and budgetary processes at different levels. The UPPAP (Uganda Participatory Poverty Assessment Process) (Bird and Kakande, 2001; Yates and Okello, 2002; Kakande, 2004) is a much cited exemplar of this second generation. It was planned to extend over three years, but was continued beyond that. A key feature was that it was managed from within the Ministry of Planning and Economic Development. It involved both government and NGOs, and both central and district levels, and was designed to enhance capacity for participatory policy research and poverty monitoring. On a second round, it deepened understandings of poverty concerning, for example, different categories of poor people, the causes of poverty (highlighting ill health and limited access to land) and the increasingly overburdened life of women (Richard Ssewakiranga, pers comm). The UK Poverty Programme visited Uganda and is seeking to apply some of the UPPAP approach in the UK.[30]

An emerging third generation of PPAs aims to stimulate collective action at the community level, facilitate personal and institutional commitment and change, and involve government officials more fully in the processes. The Rwanda PPA, as of 2004, is designed to foster *ubudehe* – traditional collective action and community-level action – to enhance local problem-solving abilities, to deepen understanding of poverty (especially of the poorest), to involve officials, and to be integrated within the budgetary process (Republic of Rwanda, 2001a, 2001b; McGee with Levene and Hughes, 2002, pp59–65; Sam Joseph, pers comm). It seeks to enable local people, as consumers of policy, to influence policy and, at the same time, to take action at the community level.

The quality, depth and continuity of processes described as PPAs range from one-off, quite shallow, participatory research by an NGO or research institute, leading to a slim report, to deeper, longer multi-institutional processes as undertaken in Uganda and Rwanda. Where short processes, such as the PRSPs (poverty reduction strategy papers), are introduced, CSOs (civil society organizations) have not been able to engage fully and their involvement has usually been limited to being consulted, often in a rushed and unsatisfactory manner (McGee with Levene and Hughes, 2002; Stewart and Wang, 2003). A major lesson is the need, if policy and practice are to be influenced, for a PPA process to be an integral part of government. CSOs have shown that they have a part to play, not least in training facilitators and in continuing engagement in policy dialogue.

Participatory rights assessments using PRAMs (participatory rights assessment methodologies) (CDS et al, 2002) have much in common with PPAs. Human rights and rights-based approaches in development gained momentum and prominence during the late 1990s, and were elaborated by DFID in *Realising Human Rights for Poor People* (DFID, 2000), which identified the three underlying principles of participation, inclusion and obligation. Participatory rights assessments seek to involve poor and marginalized people in appraisal and analysis, as in PPAs, and to promote the realization of human rights. With pilot activities in Malawi, Peru, Romania and Zambia, they are (as of 2004) in an early stage of development. Use of PRA methods has been proposed, with an intention of linking participation and institutional change. If it could be spread, the Internal Learning System of NESA (see the earlier section on 'Lifting lids and liberating', pp108–110) could not only monitor changes in the realization of human rights, but also have direct effects.

Some of the frontiers for innovation and learning now are:

- Evolving and diversifying third-generation PPAs.
- Introducing PPAs to OECD countries; methodologies are now well known. Following pioneering work inspired and influenced by experience in the South (e.g. Sellers, 1995; Cornwall, 1997; Johnson and Webster, 2000), participatory poverty research in the UK has exploded (for a review, see Bennett with Roberts, 2004), but appears less widespread in other OECD countries.
- Involving policy-makers and policy-shapers in PPA processes so that they experience them directly and personally, and have opportunities to hear and learn from poor people. Participatory poverty research by donor agency (SDC) staff in Tanzania suggests that this is feasible (Jupp et al, 2003, Jupp, 2004).
- Conducting research to understand how PPAs, PRAMs and approaches such NESA's Internal Learning System can be spread and more effectively feed into and influence processes of policy-making, implementation and actual change (McGee, 2002)

Participatory numbers

Participatory numbers (sometimes 'party numbers') is short for 'numbers from participatory approaches and methods'. It is a common belief that participatory methodologies produce only qualitative data, while questionnaire surveys or scientific measurement are required for numbers and statistics. Innumerable examples demonstrate this dichotomy to be false. There are many ways in which participatory methodologies can generate numbers.[31]

Mainly since the early 1990s, a quiet tide of innovation has developed a rich range of participatory ways by which local people themselves produce numbers, most of them using visible and tangible methods. These have variously entailed counting, calculating, measuring, estimating, valuing, ranking and scoring, and combinations of these. The best-known methods are social and census mapping. There is also now much experience with aggregation from focus groups. The methods provide a common meeting ground for professionals since they are independent of any discipline.

There is, here, a little-recognized opportunity for replacing many questionnaires and conventional sources of official statistics. Some questionnaires will always be needed. But examples have multiplied where visual and tangible participatory methods have not only generated numbers similar to those from questionnaires, and similarly amenable to statistical analysis, but have also proved to be more accurate. One example is the national census in Malawi. When calibrated against a participatory census mapping with cross-checking in 54 carefully sampled communities, this pointed to a rural population of 11.5 million, against the census figure of 8.5 million, an undercount of some 35 per cent (Barahona and Levy, 2003). Another is health statistics in the Philippines. When these were aggregated from volunteer *barangay* (village-level) health workers' records, they contradicted those of the Department of Health's Field Health Surveillance and Information Centre, and came to be accepted as more accurate (Nierras, 2002).

Participatory numbers have proved difficult to legitimize and spread. Some professionals seem unable or unwilling to recognize how questionnaires could be replaced, complemented or calibrated by more accurate participatory methods. These, moreover, promise the best of both worlds by generating qualitative as well as quantitative insights. Nor have the pioneers, whether NGO staff or professional statisticians, usually at first seen the significance of what they have done. Soon, surely, such approaches and methods will be more widely accepted.

Questions remain concerning:

- *ethical issues* of taking people's time and of raising expectations that will not be fulfilled; the code of conduct for party numbers sponsors, trainers and practitioners will give guidance (Holland, in preparation);
- *quality assurance* in developing methods, conducting training and assuring ethical and effective facilitation, and the application, where appropriate, of statistical principles;
- *aid agency restraint* in not demanding too much too fast, and, in particular, allowing enough time and resources, in each context, for evolving and piloting a methodology for each case, for facilitator recruitment and for training;
- *writing and sharing*, supported by research to evaluate and calibrate different approaches and methods for participatory numbers, and to explore their strengths, weaknesses and limits, especially compared with questionnaires.

Transformations

Power relations

Power is a latecomer to the development agenda. Participation is about power relations. It is about much else, as well; but power relations are pervasive: they are always there, and they affect the quality of process and experience.

Transforming Power (ActionAid, 2001b) is the synthesis of a workshop held in Bangladesh in 2001. Since the workshop was billed as the ActionAid Participatory Methodologies Forum, most of the 40-odd participants, including myself, went expecting to share experiences with participatory methodologies. In the event, we never did that. Instead, we found ourselves engaged with power and power relations. We observed and reflected critically on how we were behaving and relating to one another. One group monitored this and reported back daily. The planning team of eight individuals was itself a workshop within a workshop, and at the end presented diagrams to show its own internal power dynamics and conflicts. At times I felt frustrated, at times threatened, and often inhibited. I came out finally recognizing more of my own power (white, male, educated, older, with English as my native language, a trustee of ActionAid, etc) and my tendency to dominate. The experience was traumatic because I did not want to see myself as I was. It was inhibiting because I felt I had to hold back and not speak when I wanted to, sometimes when I was bursting with something to say. Three years later, after prolonged convalescence, I recognize the experience as seminal. I have come to see more than ever the central significance of power and power relations in development practice. As one participant put it: 'Only with a deep awareness of power at all times and at all levels can we use participatory processes effectively.'

The stream for the future is to develop and spread good ways of understanding and managing power relations. 'Good' is critical. To be good, such methodologies should enable people to:

- Acknowledge their own power. 'If we deny our power, it does not go away. We must recognize it if we are to transform it positively.'
- Be aware of how they (often habitually) disempower others.
- Learn to use power to empower those with less power.
- Avoid being harmfully inhibited by the learning.

It is possible to be too participatory. There are times for leadership, for decisiveness and even for dominance, especially in crisis. Nevertheless, the scope for better development practice through levelling and reversing power relations is immense. This applies in all hierarchies. And the bottom line is empowering those who are marginalized, powerless and poor.

Innovation as a way of being

A more obvious heading might have been '*participation* as a way of being'. For some, that may be right. For some, participation is more of an end than a means, something of an ideology. For myself, it is only by chance that I have stumbled on participation. For me, it deserves a place among other words and ideals, recognizing that too much of it can become a tyranny, as in 'You will participate'; 'You did not participate'; 'Where were you?'; 'What were you doing?'; 'Why are you not participating?' Participation can result from social pressures. It can take excessive time. It can be tedious, as well as exhilarating. It has to involve other people, and too much of it can negate the basic human right, for those who wish, to spend time on their own. Participation has wonderful power and potential. But it is not the whole of life. It is something to optimize, not maximize.

Participation is always something new. It is continuously improvised and invented through interactions and relationships. Past experience and known methods and approaches contribute; but if made routine and repeated like rote, they become rigid, wooden and disempowering. Good participation is co-produced, a collective improvisation. Irene Guijt's striking phrase 'seeking surprise' (Guijt, forthcoming) expresses the intention of exploration, excitement and learning. As Heraclitus famously said: 'You cannot step twice into the same river, for other waters are continually flowing on'.[32] The river may be channelled between banks; but the currents, eddies, whirlpools and flows are constantly changing and never repeated. Different every time, participation is, of its nature, always innovative.

Innovation as a way of being is saying something different from participation as a way of being. Participatory or not, in a sense we innovate all the time. Every moment we are doing something new: every moment, every situation, every encounter is unique. It has never happened before and will never happen again;

and we respond and, at the same time, influence and fashion what happens. Innovation is a way of being because it is part of welcoming and enjoying uncertainty. Good participatory processes are unpredictable. So those who facilitate them must be at ease with not knowing what will happen and then able and willing to help it happen. They may channel processes and use controls, but lightly. The spirit of this is captured in Salil Shetty's (2000) introduction to the ALPS (Accountability, Learning and Planning System) when he describes 'fostering a culture where staff and partners do not have the comfort of relying on rules and procedures, but have to use their own initiative to achieve our common mission'. Innovation, initiative, taking responsibility and participation go together. Trying new ways of doing things, exploring new relationships, improvising and inventing with others – these are all part of good participation.

For the future

The lessons from the past are positive: to continue to evolve and improve participatory practices; and to make innovation and learning a way of life. The flip side of bad practice is the opportunity to do better. So much remains to be learnt, discovered and achieved. The conclusion to draw from experience is not to give up and look for something else. It is, instead, to engage; to commit; to persist (exploring, inventing, taking risks, learning by doing and often failing forwards); to deepen and intensify self-critical reflection on practice, learning from experience and critiques; and to seek congruence through internalizing participation personally, professionally and institutionally and at all levels. It is to accept participation as an enduring opportunity to form good relationships and to confront and transform over-centralized power. Thus, above all, it is to meet the overarching challenge: to enable and empower those who are marginalized, powerless and poor to gain for themselves the better life that is their right.

Notes

1 This section is taken from Chapter 4 of *Managing Rural Development: Ideas and Experience from East Africa* (Chambers, 1974).
2 For more detail on block grants and development committees in Botswana, Kenya, Tanzania, Uganda and Zambia, see Chambers (1974, pp88–100).
3 Swahili: public meeting typically called by an official or other authority.
4 For a useful three-stage analysis of rural development, see Hunter (1970, pp26–28).
5 To say that 'we' had little idea is unfair to those who worked in community development, a low-status department in the government hierarchy. Community development had for years encouraged and supported self-help. But during the 1960s, self-help took off on its own and was completely 'out of control'. That it did so must, in part, be seen as a success for the earlier work of the department.

6   A major exception was Clark University in the US. Richard Ford, together with colleagues in the National Environment Secretariat in Nairobi, developed a system of community action plans during the late 1980s, starting a PRA tradition continued by Francis Lelo and others at Egerton University in Kenya (PID and NES, 1989; NES, 1990). Other forms of PRA had connections with Institute of Development Studies (IDS) Sussex.

7   For an insightful review of participation by decades – 1970s, 1980s and 1990s – see Cornwall (2000).

8   USAID is not the only agency to end support abruptly, but it may have been a trend setter. Other bilaterals have recently followed suit in their abandonment of projects (see Chapter 1, pp15–16).

9   Authors increasingly antedate the emergence of PRA, putting it in the mid, instead of late, 1980s. An interesting speculation is whether innovations that spread tend to be thought to have originated earlier than they did.

10   PRA was originally, and still often is, participatory rural appraisal and, occasionally, participatory rapid appraisal. Increasingly, it is now construed as participatory reflection and action. It has been described as a family of approaches, behaviours and methods for enabling people to conduct their own appraisal, analysis, planning, action, monitoring and evaluation. It often includes activities in small groups and showing things visually. For historical detail, see Chambers (1997, pp102–129).

11   For examples of developments and applications of PRA in the UK, see www.devfocus.org.uk.

12   Some sources for these are Kane (2001) for popular education; Reason and Bradbury (2001) for participatory action research; Haverkort, van der Kamp and Waters-Bayer (1991) and Guijt and van Veldhuizen (1998) for Participatory Technology Development; Hammond and Royal (1998), Elliott (1999) and Ashford and Patkar (2001) for Appreciative Inquiry; Gibson (1996) for Planning for Real; and Boal (1979), Mda (1993), McCarthy and Galvão (2004) and Abah (2004) for popular theatre.

13   For a historical review, see Chambers (1997, Chapter 6).

14   In India, the Xavier Institute of Social Service in Ranchi and the Gandhigram Rural Institute (deemed university) were, to the best of my knowledge, during 1990 the first to introduce PRA into their curricula.

15   Sources for methods are numerous and include Jones (1996), Shah, Kambou and Monihan et al (1999), Mukherjee (2001), Kumar (2002) and Jayakaran (2003).

16   The reader wishing more detail is invited to visit www.ids.ac.uk/ids/particip or to write to Participation Group, Institute of Development Studies, University of Sussex, Brighton, BN1 9RE, UK.

17   REFLECT was originally defined as Regenerated Freirian Literacy with Empowering Community Techniques. See the journal *Education Action* in the References, and *PLA Notes*, vol 32 (1998).

18   See, for example, Absalom et al (1995); Pratt (2001); Cornwall, Musyoki and Pratt, 2001); Cornwall and Pratt (2003).

19   For excellent accessible sources on participation and gender, see Guijt and Shah (1998); BRIDGE (2001); Akerkar (2001), Bell and Brambilla (2001); and Kanji (2003). The BRIDGE *Gender and Participation: Cutting Edge Pack* is available on request from BRIDGE, IDS, University of Sussex, Brighton, UK, and from www.ids.ac.uk/bridge.

20   Available at www.ids.ac.uk/ids/particip.

21   In contrast to inexperienced academics, sensitive field facilitators using PRA approaches and methods have been acutely aware of the difficulties many women have in finding undisturbed blocks of time for meetings, and of the need to make deliberate and often inconvenient efforts to offset this disadvantage. See, for example, Bilgi (1998); Guijt and Shah (1998, p15); Murthy (1998, p90); and Sarin (1998, p129).

22   Pearse and Stiefel (1979), cited in Cornwall (2000, p1), cited in Kanji and Greenwood (2001, p8).

23   Other ladders upon which these draw include Pretty (1994, 1995b) and Andrea Cornwall (pers comm) and the sources they acknowledge.

24   They scored these for how common they had been ten years earlier, where they were now, and where they hoped they would be in the future. There was a pronounced transition from command and inform to consult, represent and, most of all, empower. This contrasts with the intention and spirit of the 'conversation' initiated in late 2003 by Tony Blair with the British public, of which he was reported to say: 'The purpose of the conversation is so that people know exactly where we stand' (Simon Carr, in the *Independent* (London), 3 December 2003, who observed that this was not a conversation but a tutorial).

25   A total institution as defined by Goffman (1961, p11) is 'a place of residence and work where a large number of like-situated individuals, cut off from the wider society for an appreciable period of time, together lead an enclosed, formally administered round of life'. PRA approaches and methods have been used to enable institutionalized patients in a mental hospital (Fiona Chambers, pers comm), as well as drug probationers (Josh Levene, pers comm), to analyse and express their needs and realities, and they have also reportedly been used in a prison in South Africa. I know of no published sources.

26   For accounts of these remarkable participatory urban appraisal studies, see Moser and Holland (1997) for Jamaica; and see Moser and McIlwaine (1999, 2000a, 2000b) for Colombia and Guatemala and Moser (2003). Most recently, Moser and McIlwaine (2004) for a synthesis of the Colombia and Guatemala studies together.

27   Over some six years in India, I saw thousands of men defecating in daylight, but can only recollect seeing a woman twice.

28   Community-led total sanitation was a focus of the South Asia Conference on Sanitation (SACOSAN) held in Dhaka on 21–23 October 2003. Major debates took place on eliminating hardware subsidies for latrines that deter self-help and would slow or stop the spread of community-led total sanitation (CLTS).

29   For accounts of some of the earlier PPAs, see Holland with Blackburn (1998). For an overview of PPAs, see Robb (1998, 2002). For an analysis of the findings of World Bank PPAs, see Narayan with Raj Patel et al (2000). For participatory approaches and policy influence, including PRSPs, see McGee with Norton (2000). For an excellent practical overview and analysis including Uganda and Vietnam case studies, see Norton et al (2001), which also has a good list of references and abstracts of selected texts on PPAs.

30   The Oxfam UK Poverty Programme has been among the organizations that have encouraged 'a massive increase' in the use of participatory appraisal in the UK in a wide range of sectors. Other South–North sharing and transfers include participatory budgeting, pioneered in Brazil, being introduced in Manchester (Samuel Musyoki and Peter Taylor, pers comm).

31   A review of participatory numbers (Chambers, 2003) has over 50 sources. For statistical applications, see Barahona and Levy (2003), Levy (2003) and other publications of the SSC (Statistical Services Centre) at the University of Reading. During 2001–2003, an informal group in the UK met every few months in various places (IDS Sussex, International HIV/AIDS Alliance, ODI, Reading University and CDS Swansea) to discuss and share experiences and to evolve a code of conduct. A book of collected papers on party numbers is being edited by Jeremy Holland at the Centre for Development Studies, Swansea, j.d.holland@swansea.ac.uk.

32   This is the translation in Wheelwright (1959, p29).

5

PRA, Participation and Going to Scale

> *The speed with which the use of PRA methods spread around the world was amazing. I wish I could say the same for participatory processes (Meera Kaul Shah, 2003, p192).*

This chapter presents and analyses issues in the spread of participation and participatory methodologies.[1] Part 1, a 1995 article 'Making the best of going to scale', is mainly concerned with PRA (participatory rural appraisal). Part 2 extends to cover a wider range of experience and examples, draws practical lessons and points to ways forward for going to scale with participatory approaches.

Part 1: Making the Best of Going to Scale (1995)[2]

Lenders, donors and governments have demanded and tried to implement PRA training and application on a large scale and in a short time. This has raised problems of quality. Training has often been superficial, focusing on methods and neglecting behaviour and attitudes, and application has often been routinized and one-off. Choices have to be made between working with initiatives and programmes which are small, slow and beautiful, and those which are big, fast and flawed. Cases can be made for both. The best way forward may be slower than the speed demanded by sponsors but faster than the speed advocated by experienced field practitioners, with trade-offs between scale and speed, and quality. Performance can be improved through stress on behaviour and attitudes, longer-term engagement with institutions and programmes, and introducing benign viruses/good memes[3] for quality and spread.

Introduction

Predictably, PRA is being demanded on a large scale. Large donor[4] organizations, Northern NGOs and large NGOs in the South are increasingly coming to use, and encouraging or requiring the use of, PRA approaches and methods in their projects and programmes. The role call is impressive. It includes FAO, IFAD, UNDP, UNICEF, and the World Bank; CIDA, DANIDA, FINNIDA, GTZ, NORAD, ODA, SDC, and SIDA; ACORD, ActionAid, CARE, Christian Aid,

Farm Africa, Ford Foundation, Intercooperation, NOVIB, OXFAM, PLAN International, Redd Barna, SCF, World Vision, World Neighbours and the World Resources Institute. It also includes large Southern NGOs, BRAC, MYRADA and others, as well as thousands of smaller NGOs.[5] And any listing like this, by one person, is bound to leave out other major actors (to whom I apologise). Less well recognized, government departments in the South are increasingly adopting PRA and requiring its use on a wide scale, not least in forestry, poverty programmes, soil and water conservation and watershed management, water and sanitation, and urban programmes.

Scale has already been achieved. To identify the poorest, and select and de-select households in poverty programmes, well-being ranking was used by MYRADA during the early 1990s in hundreds of villages in south India, and later by ActionAid for a population of some 36,000 in Pakistan. Staff of ActionAid, Nepal, in 1991 facilitated participatory evaluation of activities they had supported in some 130 villages (Phuyan, 1992). In Kenya, the Soil and Water Conservation Branch of the Ministry of Agriculture has [1995] for six years been developing and extending a participatory approach to watershed planning and management (Thompson, 1995). In India, Forest Departments have widely adopted JFM (Joint Forest Management) in which PRA approaches and methods are a significant element, by now probably with thousands of communities. In Integrated Pest Management in Indonesia, at least 1500 groups of farmers have made participatory maps which they use to plot the location and prevalence of pests, to plan action, and to monitor changes (Russ Dilts, pers comm).[6] Again in Indonesia, from late 1994 through early 1995, as a component of a poverty alleviation programme, PRA activities were conducted in 285 of the poorest and most remote villages (some requiring a three-day walk to reach) in four months from the first training of trainers. In Vietnam, an IFAD-supported programme has carried out 350 activities described as PRAs (but using questionnaires!) in less than six months. And there are now quite numerous other examples.

Proposals by some government departments to go to scale are now formidable. In Kenya, the Soil and Water Conservation Branch of the Ministry of Agriculture is proposing in the 1995–1996 financial year to launch participatory planning in 809 catchments covering 177,000 hectares and 93,000 farm families (Thompson, 1995). In India, PRA approaches and methods have been incorporated in the guidelines for the national programme for watershed management, intended eventually for some 30,000 villages in 300 districts in 22 states, covering an ultimate 15 million hectares. This began with the training of 336 state-level trainers from 56 training institutions in 14 four-week courses conducted between April and August 1995. The trainings were to have no lectures, and to include a week on PRA, with 3–4 days in villages. A multi-media package has been prepared for the ultimate training of 12,000 field staff. In Indonesia, the use of PRA is being considered for a new anti-poverty programme which is proposed for over 2000 villages with UNICEF support, and for 20,000 villages in another Government programme. And there are other examples from India, Pakistan, South Africa, Sri Lanka, Uganda, Vietnam and elsewhere.

Questions of quality

The trend seems set to continue. Short of massive negative experiences or some freak change of fashion, more and more field departments of government and other large organizations will seek to adopt and apply PRA approaches and methods on a large scale in the months and years to come.

This presents dangers and opportunities. Recent experience and analysis have shed light on the institutional problems presented by participatory approaches, and their implications for strategy (Kar and Backhaus, 1994; Samaranayake, 1994; Backhaus and Wagachchi, 1995; Guijt, 1995; Thompson, 1995). Going to scale raises acute questions of quality assurance. Shortcomings have included:

- neglect of behaviour and attitudes;
- top-down training in classrooms by people without field orientation or experience;
- opportunists claiming to be trainers, or to 'use PRA' when they are not aware of empowerment issues (some university academics have been among the worst offenders);
- reward systems which stress targets for disbursements and for physical achievements (often donor-driven);
- rushing in and out of communities in order to achieve preset targets for villages covered and sums disbursed;
- routine and ritual use of methods;
- one-off extractive appraisal without analysis, planning or action;
- interaction only or mainly with those who are better off and men;
- overriding bottom-up priorities with predetermined top-down packages;
- labelling conventional questionnaires as 'PRA'; and even
- the fabrication of 'outputs'!

Concerns about practices such as these have been repeatedly raised by PRA trainers and others (see e.g. Absalom et al, 1995). These errors have sometimes been recognized and embraced. Approaches, corrections and changes which have had or have promised positive outcomes include:

- increased priority given to behaviour and attitudes in training;
- more time for participation and institution-building in the early stages of programmes and projects, with bigger budgets for training, and less for infrastructure;
- tenacious and persistent internal working groups, as for participation in the World Bank, and as for RRA and PRA in FAO;
- no targets for disbursements or coverage, and provision that unspent budgets can be rolled forward from year to year;
- changes in project procedures to provide for participation and diversity;
- a process approach permitting continuous revisions to on-going projects;
- preceding, not following, LFA (logical framework analysis)[7] (see pp67–72) or ZOPP with PRA activities involving the poor, women, and marginal groups in their own analysis, identifying their own priorities;

- starting on a pilot and experimental basis in part of an organization, or in one geographical area;
- continuity over years with an outside facilitating organization;
- stability in supportive senior management.

Together these contribute to a shift towards more participatory management cultures in organizations.

A moment of choice

The fact that so many organizations are going to scale confronts those of us engaged in the development and spread of participatory approaches and methods with choices and dilemmas. Each of us has to decide for ourselves what it is best to do. What follows is a personal view, and I may be wrong. Reader, please decide for yourself.

A major personal decision is where to act on the continuum between the small and beautiful, and the big and blotchy. This can be expressed as three options.

The first option is to go for the small and secure. Quality can be assured by working on a small scale with a very few communities. This can be both personally satisfying and professionally safe. Intense local engagement can also explore the potentials of PRA and generate innovations at the community level.

The second or middle option is extended engagement with particular organizations at a district or regional level, working over months and years in support of participatory approaches and incremental organizational change. This permits PRA to influence institutional culture, and can generate insights into the means and potentials for institutional change.

The third course is to work with organizations which are going to bigger scale quickly. This involves trade-offs. The principle is that the best should not be the enemy of the good or of the less bad. This course may be risky. There will be abuses and deceptions. Critics will not be few. Compromises will have to be made. Negative academics will find plenty to expose and be wise about. To accept the challenge of scale does, then, require courage.

In my view, all three approaches are needed and are complementary. Each of us will make our own choices, using our own best judgements. As ever, pluralism seems the best way forward, with different people doing different things in different places, some on a small scale, intensively, some with sustained commitment and engagement in the middle range, and others on a large scale, extensively, with all sharing experience and learning from each other.

Given the risks and inevitable defects, the case needs to be put for working with the third option, accepting the challenge of going quite fast to scale. I would argue that becoming involved in an imperfect process, where abuses and errors may at first abound, can be personally and professionally responsible. Two reasons stand out.

First, the benefits to poor people can be greater from doing less well on a wide scale than from doing better on a small scale. The total gain to poor people may be much greater through initiating and supporting small changes in large organizations and programmes than through big gains in small programmes. Real world alternatives and causal chains are complex and uncertain, but the recognition of trade-offs between quality, scale and impact has, I believe, to be part of responsible decisions about where to work and what to do.

Second, in going to scale, even when much goes wrong, there may be benign viruses/good memes in PRA (behaviour and attitudes, handing over the stick, 'they can do it', 'use your own best judgement at all times', and so on), which can gain a foothold in large organizations, and then start to work away and spread. Bureaucratic structure can be exploited. In a large-scale watershed programme, for example, it can be required that the maps used for planning must be made by, and retained by, farmers. This has the potential to force staff to facilitate, to startle staff with what farmers can do, and to empower farmers in the planning, implementing, monitoring and evaluation process. In the longer-term, good memes may contribute to more participatory procedures, management styles and organizational cultures. There will also be some, in every organization, for whom the approach and methods are legitimating and liberating, allowing and enabling them to interact and facilitate in new, empowering ways from which they would otherwise be barred.

Experience to date suggests the importance of long-term engagement between an individual, team or training NGO and any large organization which seeks to adopt a participatory approach. There is no quick fix. The in-out consultancy can sow seeds but most likely they will wither. The watershed programmes in Kenya and India which are going to scale are both building on five to six years of experience and engagement with other organizations which have supported change with training, experiment and learning from experience. Similarly, the SIDA-supported government programme in Northern Vietnam has received sustained support and training from the same joint team over at least four years. Those who become involved with going to scale would do well to reflect on the implications of these similar experiences.

What is happening, and going to happen, demands personal decisions. Things are happening fast. Spread seems to be exponential. The word 'URGENT' is overworked. But both chaos theory and common sense indicate that there are times and places when small shifts have big effects later, moving whole systems into different paths and spaces. I sense this to be one such time. My best judgement is that what is done, and not done, during the next few months and years, will, seen and unseen, have huge effects, in fact or by default, in future decades; and that many of these effects or lack of effects will apply to women, the poor and the marginalised. The question is whether we have the vision, judgement and guts to see and do the right things now.

A programme of action

Let me propose a programme of action:

- *Draw up a personal code of ethics,*[8] either individually, or in small groups of professionals, to guide decisions and actions. This could include 'uncompromisables', sticking points on which we will not yield, for those of us involved in going to scale.

- *Hang in with a big programme over a matter of years*, trying to slow it when it is too fast, establishing footholds, supporting those who wish to change, and helping those in power to shift the steering wheel bit by bit in a more participatory direction.
- *Stress behaviour and attitudes again and again* as centrally important, including self-critical awareness and learning, embracing error, sitting down, listening and learning, not interrupting, facilitating.
- *Develop, innovate, improve, share and apply* behaviour and attitude training modules and materials (URGENTLY).
- *Train other trainers*, with critical learning and improvement through feedback from trainers trained, those trained by them, and the experience of field action.
- *Observe, record and learn* from the experience of participatory research going to scale in big organizations, warts and all, and sharing the insights widely.
- *Encourage self-evaluations* and critical reflection within organizations.
- *Work with the benign virus/good meme effect*: improve these and their insertion and spread.
- *Build alliances and share experiences* with all the above to be sensitive, sustained and efficient between actors at all levels, between organizations, and between countries and continents.

All this demands participatory research, learning, sharing and training. As things are, I do not think we are anywhere near being able to meet the needs of the time. People in the future may look back and wonder how and why we were so slow to act, and acted on such a small scale, when the opportunities were so vast.

The *Book of Common Prayer*[9] begins its confession with errors of omission: 'We have left undone those things which we ought to have done'. Where governments and other large organizations are going to scale, we are faced with a choice: whether to get involved or not. The stakes are high. Scope abounds for errors of omission. Not to act is a choice, itself an action. I have expressed a personal view in this note. Have I got it right, or wrong?

Each of us has to use our own best judgement. What is yours? What is right for you?

Part 2: Experiences, Lessons and Ways Forward (2004)

Since 1995, the spread of PRA/PLA has continued to be versatile in scaling out to many applications and exponential in scaling up by large organizations. PRA spread fast and wide because it was seen to supply a demand for participation, met a need felt by practitioners, and was promoted by networks and enthusiasts. Much practice was bad, with classroom training, routinization, wasting people's time, raising false expectations, rushing and targets, and saturating accessible communities. Proactive warnings throughout the 1990s may have helped but were not enough to prevent much bad practice.

The spread of participatory methodologies can be through a spectrum or combination of modes – mandatory, administered, enabling, facilitating, disseminating and/or self-spreading and spontaneous. Four programmes which have gone to scale with participation are a source of learning and ideas: the NWDP (National Watershed Development Programme) in India, the MRDP (Mountain Rural Development Programme) in Vietnam, IPM (Integrated Pest Management) in Indonesia, and CLTS (community-led total sanitation) in Bangladesh. Two types of programme that seem to work are either grounded, complex and evolutionary, or facilitated, disseminated and self-managing. Key issues, learning and choices concern: single sector or multiple; who gains, and gains what; manual or menu; facilitation, trust and realism; lateral spread; champions and continuity; subsidy or self-reliance; and threats and vulnerability. Stating lessons is not enough. To do well in going to scale with participation requires that institutions transform. For this there are recent experiences, sources and ideas to draw on, with as a common theme, the need for congruence from the bottom up.

Until 1995

Issues of going to scale were not new in 1995. They had been faced, no doubt, in the ancient civilizations. During the 1950s and 1960s, they were prominent in the community development movement, implemented largely through government bureaucracies. They were analysed by David Korten in his seminal 1980 article 'Community organizations and rural development: A learning process approach'.[10] Famously, he identified and named the shift from blueprint to learning process. Korten's analysis included the history of three Asian successes – the Indian National Dairy Development Board, the Bangladesh Rural Advancement Committee, and Thailand's Community-based Family Planning Services. With these he distinguished and described three stages: learning to be effective, learning to be efficient and learning to expand. This expansion was in terms of size, coverage and activities.

Another step forward was the 1992 international workshop at Manchester on 'Scaling-up NGO impacts: Learning from experience'. In the edited papers of the conference, Michael Edwards and David Hulme (1992) identified four strategies for NGOs in order to scale up or have a wider impact: working with government; organizational growth; lobbying; and advocacy. To these, drawing on the experience with RRA (rapid rural appraisal) and PRA, was added generating, spreading and improving approaches and methods.[11]

Korten, and Edwards and Hulme were not primarily concerned with methodology. I use the word *primarily* because how things are done is part of almost any analysis. The difference, here, is starting with methodologies and then examining how they are and can be spread, and what happens as a result.

Since 1995: Versatile and exponential spread

Since 1995, when the article which starts this chapter was written, the spread of PMs (participatory methodologies) has continued fast. Much has been written on going to scale with them.[12] The main focus and source of experience drawn on here is PRA/PLA; but much applies to other PMs and to participation, more generally. The spread of PRA/PLA has extended to various applications, countries, areas within countries and organizations. Today, many networks of organizations and practitioners exist. There are probably few countries in the world (perhaps North Korea, Saudi Arabia, Iraq, Libya, some of the Arab Emirates and some small islands) where PRA/PLA has not been practised or had an influence.[13]

Two forms of spread have been *scaling out*, meaning spread from one application or activity to another, and an increase in the types of participation; and *scaling up*, meaning spread through increasing the scale of an organization or programme and the quantity of participation – for example, the number of participants or of places where it takes place (after Gaventa, 1998, p155).

Versatility in scaling out to applications

In scaling out from appraisal and from rural applications to many others, PRA/PLA and related or similar approaches have continued to spread as they had already by 1995: from appraisal and planning, to implementation and participatory monitoring and evaluation (PM&E); and from rural to urban and many other domains of application, including, for some trainers and practitioners, from development activities to personal and family life. A partial listing of some common domains can indicate the diversity and versatility of applications.[14]

Applications in *natural resources and agriculture* (Borrini-Feyerabend et al, 2004; Pimbert, 2004) include:

* watersheds, and soil and water conservation;
* forestry (especially JFM, Joint Forest Management) and agroforestry;
* fisheries and aquaculture;
* conservation and use of plant genetic resources (Friis-Hansen et al, 2000);
* biodiversity and wildlife reserve management (Roe et al, 2000);
* village and community resource management planning and action;
* Integrated Pest Management (IPM; see pp137–139)
* agriculture, crops and animal husbandry (PRGA, circa 2002; Catley, 2004);
* irrigation (Gosselink and Strosser, 1995);
* marketing; and
* farmer participatory research (FPR) and participatory technology development (PTD).

Applications in *programmes for equity* include:

* understandings of well-being (Narayan et al, 2000; White and Pettit, 2004);
* women's empowerment and gender awareness (Guijt and Shah, 1998; Akerkar, 2001; Cornwall, 2003; Kanji, 2004);
* work with those who are powerless and vulnerable, including children (Chawla and Johnson, 2004), the homeless (AAA, 2002), the disabled, the aged, minorities, refugees, the mentally distressed, and others who are marginalized;
* micro-finance;

- selection: finding, selecting and deselecting people for poverty-oriented programmes;
- income-earning: identification and analysis of non-agricultural income-earning opportunities;
- analysis by poor people of livelihoods and coping, leading to household plans.

Applications in *rights and security* include:

- rights and advocacy (Pettit and Musyoki, 2004);
- REFLECT (Regenerated Freirian Literacy through Empowering Community Techniques) for human rights and literacy (*Education Action*, 1994–2004; Archer and Goreth, 2004);
- emergency assessment and management, including participation by communities and their members in complex political emergencies;
- participatory human rights assessments and monitoring (see pp111–112);
- violence, abuses and physical insecurity (see pp108–109).

Applications in *health and nutrition* include:

- health assessments and monitoring;
- food security and nutrition assessment and monitoring;
- water and sanitation assessment, planning, location and action (rural and urban);
- sexual and reproductive health, including HIV/AIDS awareness and action (see p108; Gordon and Cornwall, 2004; Welbourne, 2004);
- adolescent sexual behaviour.

Applications in *policy and action* include:

- impact on poor people of structural adjustment and other policies;
- community planning and action;
- local government (Gaventa, 2004);
- slum improvement (Patel, 2004);
- land policy;
- participatory poverty assessments (PPAs) (see pp110–112);
- consultations with the poor, in 23 countries (Narayan et al, 2000), as a preliminary for the *World Development Report 2000/2001* (World Bank, 2000) on poverty and development;
- poverty reduction strategy papers (PRSPs) (part of the conditionality for debt relief in heavily indebted countries).

Applications in *institutional and personal change* include:

- organizational analysis;
- participatory learning groups in organizations (Cornwall, Pratt and Scott-Villiers, 2004);

- field experiential learning (see pp177–181);
- reflection and developing self-critical awareness.

In all applications, there have been excellent and inspiring examples; but speed of scaling up has contributed to much bad practice.

Exponential in scaling up

Big organizations in many countries have tried to apply PRA/PLA and participatory methodologies on a large scale. National NGOs such as BRAC and Proshika in Bangladesh, and all or almost all major international NGOs, have used it and often promoted it through encouragement and training. The World Bank's flagship participatory projects, and social funds in many countries, have sought to be participatory. Some national and departmental programmes have gone to scale. In Kenya, early starts were made by the Department of Soil and Water Management facilitated by the International Institute for Environment and Development (IIED). In Indonesia, the government sought to incorporate elements of PRA in a wildly unrealistic nation-wide programme of participatory planning covering 60,000 villages. This was all to be completed within the 1995–1996 budget year (Mukherjee, 1998). Three programmes of the Indian Government – JFM (Joint Forest Management), PIM (Participatory Irrigation Management) (Indian NPIM, 1994) and the NWDP (National Watershed Development Programme) (see pp135–136) were also exceptionally large and used PRA/PLA approaches and methods to varying degrees.

Explaining spread

Three factors help to explain why PRA/PLA spread so fast and so widely.[15]

The first is donors' and lenders' widespread *demand* for participation. As participation became *de rigueur* aid speak, so PRA became the way to get it. Much of its spread can be attributed to the powerful influence of the Participatory Development Learning Group in the World Bank, supported by SIDA and led by Aubrey Williams and Bhuvan Bhatnagar. Initiated in December 1990, it led to the report *The World Bank and Participation* in September 1994 (World Bank, 1994b).[16] For a time during the 1990s, there was also an international aid agency group meeting on participation. Soon after James Wolfensohn became president of the World Bank in June 1995, he began personally to monitor 15 flagship participatory projects. In 1998, Parmesh Shah, a leading innovator of PRA, was appointed with responsibilities for participation in the World Bank. During the second half of the 1990s, staff in multilateral and bilateral agencies, whether personally committed to it or not, realized that they needed to incorporate participation within their projects and programmes. Participation, and often with it PRA, were 'mainstreamed' (Blackburn et al, 2000). The label PRA became a public convenience. 'PRA will be used' appeared in project documents, and consultants parroted back the phrase that they did not understand. Stamped PRA the project passed scrutiny; the participation box got a tick.

Second, PRA met a *need*. It came at a time when many were looking for a better way to relate to and empower people who were poor, weak and marginalized, not least women. Its decentralized ethos reversed normal patterns of hierarchical power with its memes of 'hand over the stick' and 'use your own best judgement at all times'. It provided space for innovation, allowing for the situation-specific reinvention of methods and approaches. Those coming new to it could pioneer in their own right. Moreover, the PRA approaches, behaviours and methods could meet needs because they really did tend to 'work'. In part, this was through the amazing ability of the visual and group methods to enable people to express, analyse and present complexity, and to enjoy, learn and gain confidence from the process. Many around the world, especially in NGOs, saw the opportunity and did not look back.

The third factor was the *promotion* of PRA. In his review of the global spread of PRA, Kamal Singh (2001, p182) remarks on the importance of South–South exchanges and networking.[17] South–South exchanges took two main forms: one was roving international workshops (the first ones occurring in India and then in the Philippines); the other was the many visits made by trainers, especially from India, to other countries. Singh describes an 'energetic and ardent cadre of first generation champions' (ibid, p183), who then contributed to a second generation of champions and trainers. Networks of practitioners were also significant. National and international networks interacted. Ideas, methods and information were shared and disseminated, not least through *PLA Notes*, edited and distributed free by IIED.[18] Local and national networks could access a global family of networks, with open-ended and flexible support from IDS Sussex and IIED, derived, in turn, from the open-ended and flexible funding that they received from donors.[19] Networking was loose and decentralized, without a global institutional form or apex,[20] driven by enthusiasm and with little standardization.

Concerns about quality[21]

What actually spread

With PRA, what actually spread can be thought of as a hierarchy and sequence, as depicted in Figure 5.1.

PRA as label, rhetoric, requirement and methods spread like wildfire. Without the deeper and more difficult changes in behaviour, attitudes, ethics, philosophy and institutions, this meant loss of quality. Unsurprisingly, as PMs, in general, and PRA/PLA in particular, spread, local people were abused as bad practice abounded. The label PRA was all too often used for sloppy, biased, exploitative and uncritical work.

Bad practices

Bad practices took on six main forms:

1 *Training and consultancy* posed dilemmas. For years, the demand for training considerably exceeded the supply of good trainers or trainers who could and

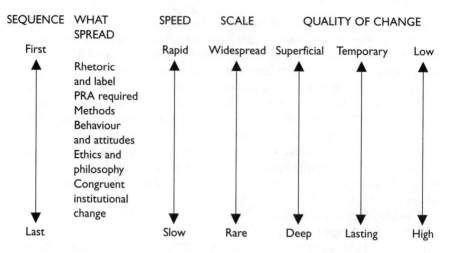

Figure 5.1 *How PRA has spread: sequence, speed, scale and quality of change*

would hold the line by insisting on quality. As a result, consultants identified themselves as PRA trainers when they had little or no field experience, and little or no awareness of the importance of behaviour and attitudes. Much training was classroom based, shoddy, rushed, routinized and superficial, and focused on methods to the neglect of behaviour, attitudes, ethics and philosophy.

2   *Routines and ruts*: there is a tension between routines and flexibility. An argument for routines is that standardization is necessary with going to scale in order to achieve targets. An argument for flexibility is that good participatory processes always differ and cannot proceed by fixed methods or time scales. In some cases, routinization was grotesquely mindless, as in Indonesia when the national programme (Mukherjee, 1998) required one map, one seasonal diagram and one Venn diagram in each village. The verb 'to PRA' came into use, with targets for the numbers of communities 'PRA'd'. A case can be made for some standardization of process for a programme with a thematic focus. But the moment that happens, there is a danger of it digging a rut and becoming an irrelevant ritual performed by rote.

3   *Exploitation*: PRA methods serve well for outsiders' research. Indeed, they serve almost too well because of the overwhelming data and the quality of insights that they can generate in a short time. But they also take people's time and energy. These are far from costless. There have been many cases where local people have been exploited, thinking that there will be benefits from their participation when there will be none. The researchers depart, having extracted local people's 'outputs' – primary resources which they then process elsewhere for their own benefit from the added value.

4   *Expectation*: PRA processes, including group visual methods, facilitated by outsiders, tend to raise expectations. After devoting time, energy and creativity to appraisal, analysis and sometimes planning (and even if great care is exercised and the outsiders are completely transparent and honest), local people may

still expect some follow-up. The ethical problems posed are worrying, but are now better recognized and more often grappled with. Sometimes, facilitators believe that outside support will be forthcoming, and even strive to obtain it, but without result. Reflecting on what I wrote in 1995, I am shocked that I did not stress this problem more. I did mention 'one-off extractive appraisal without analysis, planning or action'; but I did not refer to the tendency for appraisal to run ahead of action, and often to be followed by nothing at all except disillusion and anger among community members who have become involved and given their time. Not only is such behaviour wrong in itself; it also makes later participatory initiatives more difficult.

5   *Targets and rushing:* abuses are, in part, a function of scale and speed. Big programmes usually have targets for numbers of communities or watersheds to be covered, or groups to be formed. But targets misfit, deter and even prevent participation. Lenders, donors and governments who find something that looks good often want to go to scale instantly, in hundreds or thousands of communities. As the World Bank might be supposed to say to successful NGOs:

> *Anything you do well acts as a trigger,*
> *Anything you can do we can do bigger.*
> *Damned with our scaling-up instantly curse,*
> *Anything you can do we can do worse.*

Lack of good trainers, and target-oriented and disbursement-driven bureaucracies, have been major constraints. Almost everywhere, demand for training has exceeded the supply of good trainers. Good PRA/PLA and PM trainers who have really 'got it' must now number hundreds, if not thousands, worldwide. But even now at the time of writing (2004) they are not enough. And many of the best will not work on top-down, target-driven programmes. To wean big field bureaucracies from targets is business that has barely begun.

6   *Saturation:* There are many accounts of assessible communities which have been bombarded with PRA by different agencies and individuals, at different times and for the same or different purposes, and of how each has been unaware of the earlier activities of others, of the community members' time that has been taken, or of the disillusion that has been left behind. Some communities developed defensive strategies. Several villages in Malawi, described as having been 'carpet-bombed' with PRA, were said to have sent out a team to intercept and negotiate with visitors before they were allowed to enter. Yam Malla has told me that when he approached a village in Nepal, a man came out to meet him with a sheet of paper and started drawing a map. 'Have you ever done this before?' 'At least 100 times'.[22]

During the past ten years, behaviour, attitudes, ethics, philosophy and institutional change have been given more and more prominence. Resolute trainers have held out against superficial training, and insisted on longer engagement and organizational commitment to change. Some refuse assignments unless organizations are willing to commit fully at all levels. An early example was IIED in The Gambia. After an initial training for ActionAid

The Gambia, in which its senior staff did not participate, IIED declined an invitation for further training, judging the organization unlikely to make the wider managerial changes necessary for PRA to be successfully absorbed (Howes, 2002, p86).[23] More recently, PRAXIS in India has negotiated with organizations requesting training for a longer-term commitment to institutional change. Trainers have refused commissions that run counter to their principles and good practice. A trainer in Bangladesh was asked by an international agency to conduct PRA training in a hotel in three days. When she insisted on fieldwork and a longer period, they found someone else without the same scruples. She lost the contract. They lost quality.

Much poor practice persists, especially with large programmes in India (A. C. Shah, 2003). But, in many cases the *direction* of change appears to be for the better.

Proactive warnings were not enough

With the spread of any methodology, quality is always of concern. In the evolution and spread of PRA during the early 1990s, dangers were foreseen from early on. The proceedings of the February 1991 PRA trainers' workshop at Bangalore (Mascarenhas et al, 1991, pp42, 44) recorded:

Too popular too soon

> *There is a well-recognized danger that capture by donors or central government agencies, who might issue instructions for the adoption of methods, could result in adopting without the appropriate attitudes. . . Higher-level planning targets disrupt bottom-up demands and desires. . . Senior officials in organizations are obstructive, particularly if they miss the first day before going to the field, and thus have not changed their behaviours or preconceived notions.[24] . . . Institutions say they are doing PRA, when they carry on as before.*

Trainers and practitioners quickly took alarm and began to warn and admonish aid agencies and governments. International networking and exchanges (for an account of which, see Singh, 2001) enabled information and insights to circulate fast and well. A note on PRA written in May 1993 for World Bank staff with advice on how to proceed, and what to do, said:

> *Good PRA cannot be commanded. The head of an organization cannot order staff to 'use PRA'. Good PRA is sensitive to personal behaviour, attitudes, beliefs and commitment. It requires, often, changes in the culture and management of an organization before it can be used widely. This means that any introduction of PRA has to start slowly and proceed incrementally, and needs to be associated with participatory management.*

Other notes to lenders and donors followed. In May 1994, 22 development practitioners, researchers and trainers from the South and North went through a participatory process to produce a consensus statement: 'Sharing our concerns and looking to the future' (Absalom et al, 1995), which expressed alarm at developments and gave a strong message to donors. This was followed by 'Sharing our experience: An appeal to donors and governments' (Adhikari et al, 1996) from a 1996 workshop at Bangalore and Madurai. This was sent to over 50 individuals in multilateral and bilateral agencies and was variously circulated and published by them. Then PRAXIS convened a workshop in Calcutta in 1997. A joint statement, 'Going to scale with PRA: Reflections and recommendations' (Adhikari et al, 1997), was drawn up and signed by the 26 participants, who were mainly PRA trainers from countries in South Asia. The recommendations included that:

- Trainers and training institutes should commit to the long term in working with organizations.
- The behaviour and attitudes of trainers should be considered when they are being selected.
- Training itself should be conducted in a participatory mode, with the trainer's behaviour as a role model.
- Training should emphasize behaviour and attitudes more than methods.

Warning statements from these workshops were published in India as *PRA Reflections from the Field and Practitioners* (PRAXIS, circa 1997) and widely circulated and made available on websites. For several years at IDS Sussex, urged by colleagues in the South, we ran an annual week's workshop for aid agency staff on participatory approaches and their implications. There were numerous other publications and initiatives in other countries in the same direction. An international workshop at IDS in 1996 led to the book *Who Changes? Institutionalizing Participation in Development* (Blackburn with Holland, 1998), which reviews extensive experience gained with scaling up participation and PRA, with implications for policy and practice.[25]

I do not know how much impact these actions, warnings, admonitions and publications had. They fell far short of what was needed. But perhaps they helped; and perhaps, over time, they will be more internalized and acted upon. The questions to ask now are whether there are new insights, and what more should be done.

Options for the spread of PRA

Those seeking to promote participation may see only one or a few approaches for scaling up. Taking a wide view, at least six modes can be identified (see Figure 5.2).

All six modes have many variants, and can be combined and sequenced in many ways.

Experiences with spread: Four programmes compared

One source for ideas is to compare examples of going to scale. This section compares four that are relatively well documented. Two others stand out for the

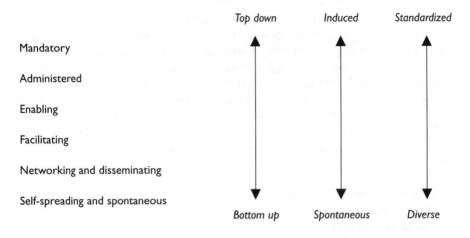

Notes: *Mandatory*: a law or administrative order requires participatory organization and action. Examples are the committees elected under the Andhra Pradesh Farmers Management of Irrigation Systems Act of 1997. Another is the Indian constitutional amendment requiring a third of elected members of *panchayats* (low-level local government bodies) to be women.

Administered: spread is through and with direct administration. Examples include the NWDP in India (pp135–136), the MRDP (Mountain Rural Development Programme) in Vietnam (pp15, 137) and the RIPS (Rural Integrated Project Support Programme) in Tanzania (pp14–15).

Enabling: a law, administrative order or procedure, and/or an outside organization, provides a frame of rules enabling local organizations to form or activities to take place. An example is the Order of the Government of India of 1 June 1990 on Participatory Forest Management (Shah, 1998, p163), which gave rise to JFM reported to have covered 14 million hectares by 2002 (A. C. Shah, 2003).

Facilitating: outsiders have a facilitating, catalytic and supportive role, and local people decide whether or not to organize and act, as with IPM (pp137–139) and CLTS (pp109, 139).

Networking and disseminating: participatory approaches and methods are disseminated and picked up and used by whoever wishes. This was the main approach with PRA, augmented by facilitation and training.

Self-spreading and spontaneous: local people spread and adopt an approach on their own, with or without local facilitators. Organization and spread take place locally without the intervention of an outside organization (such as the government, NGOs or the private sector). Examples are the *mabati* women's groups and *harambee* groups and schools in Kenya shortly before and after independence in 1963 (see pp88–90). Dissemination of crops, which farmers seek and spread on their own, such as the taboran maize on the Perkerra scheme, is also in this category (see p8).

Figure 5.2 *Modes for scaling up participatory practices*

remarkable success of their spread. One is REFLECT (now Reflect), originally Regenerated Freirian Literacy through Empowering Community Techniques, which combines Paulo Freire's theoretical framework on the politics of literacy with PRA approaches and visualisations ((*PLA Notes*, 1998; *Education Action*, 1994–2004). This was developed by David Archer and others through field practice in El Salvador, Uganda and Bangladesh between 1993 and 1995. By 2004, it had spread through the work of at least 350 organizations, including NGOs, CBOs (community-based organizations), governments and social movements, in over 60 countries (Archer and Goreth, 2004). The other example is the Participatory Research and Gender Analysis system-wide programme of the CGIAR (Consultative Group for International Agricultural Research) (www.prgaprogram. org), initially led by Jacqueline Ashby at CIAT in Colombia. This has had four thrusts: methodology development; capacity-building; partnerships and networks; and institutionalization, and has inspired, supported and linked with many initiatives in natural resource management, seed breeding and other agriculturally related research.

There is scope for a book-length comparative study to draw lessons from these and others. The four programmes reviewed here represent three quite distinct types:

1   administered, large-scale, natural resource management, with a preset methodology and targets – for example, the NWDP in India (Joint Forest Management in India is similar).[26]
2   administered and facilitated, medium-scale, multi-sectoral management, with evolutionary methodology – for example, the MRDP in Vietnam (the RIPS programme in Tanzania is similar; see Chapter 1);
3   facilitated, disseminated and self-managing – for example, IPM in Indonesia and CLTS in Bangladesh.

National Watershed Development Programme (NWDP) for Rain-fed Agriculture, India

This enormous programme was inspired, in part, by a few exceptional watershed programmes supported by NGOs. The NWDP did not pilot test its methodology. After guidelines (GOI, 1994) had been drawn up, it was driven to scale with great speed. Its style is top-down standardization with detailed, carefully designed procedures, and a variety of programme implementing agencies (PIAs) implementing the programme in the watersheds. The guidelines (GOI, 1994) were influenced by experienced NGO leaders and pioneers of PRA, including Jimmy Mascarenhas and Anil C. Shah. These guidelines drew on NGO experience (e.g. Fernandez, 1993). They provide for the decentralized control of funds, mandate participatory practices and seek to incorporate some PRA methods. In practice, the programme has been driven by targets, with weak feedback or capacity to innovate. During the late 1990s, it had an annual budget of close to US$500 million (Kolavalli and Kerr, 2002b, p214) and in 2002 was reported to have covered over 16 million hectares.

Islands of good practice have distorted perceptions. One community with exceptional leadership, Ralegaon Siddhi in Maharashtra, has for over a decade been receiving visitors daily. As a watershed Mecca, it misleads the great and good who quote it in their speeches and writing. It was cited, for example, in the foreword to the guidelines (GOI, 1994, pii). One evaluation of the NWDP (Kerr et al, 2002) found that the few successful and innovative projects (40 out of 1000 villages in two districts in Maharashtra) 'may have enjoyed special attention that cannot be replicated on a large scale'. In the NWDP, as a whole, benefits to poor people, such as they were, tended to be temporary wage employment. Other evidence from studies and evaluations (e.g. Kolavalli and Kerr, 2002a, 2002b; Ramakrishnan et al, 2002; Shah, 2003) indicated that overall performance had been disappointing and had fallen far short of that of the NGO precursors of the programme.

The NWDP has attracted much attention and generated a large literature (see, for example, Turton et al, 1998; JRD, 1999). Some of its weaknesses can be attributed to:

- instant cascade training (trainers trained trainers, who trained trainers, who trained trainers): 336 state-level trainers from 56 training institutions were trained over a four-month period between April and August 1995;
- implementation without a pilot phase (Shah, 1999, p617);
- target orientation with pressures to disburse;[27]
- reliance on guidelines while failing to change capabilities, incentives and behaviours in government bureaucracy;
- resistance, distortion and subversion, with funds and resources that could, in practice, be appropriated by officials and local interests.

On the last two points, a study of decentralized natural resource management (the NWDP and JFM) in three states found 'strong resistance to decentralization from established officials within the public administration, and only cursory fulfilment of guidelines that had been written to ensure participatory decentralized processes' (Ramakrishnan et al, 2002). In a telling paragraph, the study authors observed that:

> *The use of administrative programmes for natural resource management to politically allocate state resources has clearly led to a mutation of the Guidelines. It has meant, amongst other things, that criteria for village selection are subverted, that the process of PIA selection has not been transparent and that the actual work undertaken favours the preferences of the politically powerful, as opposed to those it is meant to benefit, and in some cases leads to rent-seeking by line department officials (ibid, piii).*

My interpretation is, then, that this programme went to scale because it was centrally mandated and driven by huge budgets and targets. The good intentions and ingenuity of its original pro-poor guidelines were no match for the complexity of the tasks entailed, the pressures of local political interests or the temptations to rent-seeking officials. Isolated atypical cases were overperceived. The outcomes were generally disappointing. Those who gained most were those with property and power.

Participatory Rural Development, Vietnam

Sweden's continuity of support for Vietnam has borne fruit in a programme that has continuously evolved. It began with the Bai Bang pulp and paper factory during the Vietnam War, when Sweden was the only Western donor. This developed into the Vietnam–Sweden Forestry Cooperation Programme (1991–1996), which then became the MRDP (1996 onwards).[28] This is a government programme with government staff, characterized by interactive learning and innovation. It has grown and changed gradually, with continuous learning and modification of methodology, starting slow and small and then finding participatory ways to expand.

PRA was introduced in 1991. Vietnam had the advantage of an extension staff who had not been disabled and de-motivated by the World Bank-driven top-down training and visit extension system (Benor and Harrison, 1977; Chambers, 1997a, pp71–72). The first two years were spent trying out and modifying the methodology, to which technical assistance from India contributed. PRA was then facilitated by extension staff who became sensitized to the knowledge and capabilities of the farmers. 'As a catalytic influence for jump-starting the development process, PRA proved to be unrivalled' (Paul, 2001, p66).

After four years of the project, only 70 villages had been covered. The search for a strategy for scaling up faster was provoked by the arrival of an IFAD-funded project which sought to use 'PRA' in much less time in many more neighbouring communities. The IFAD approach was subsequently modified but still remained more rapid. Partly in response to this challenge, the Vietnam–Sweden programme developed a system of lateral spread by villagers. In this, villagers carried out PRAs on their own in neighbouring villages to which they then provided follow-up services and back-up support. Subsequently, the MRDP held methods development-review workshops and developed and used a programme management, information and learning system to link village PRA planning to the annual planning of districts and provinces (Shanks and Toai, 2000, pp63–64). The programme has many natural resource-based activities. In 2000, Commune and Village Development Budgets began to be introduced. 'Put simply: A Village Development Budget is money handled by villagers who decide together how, when and on what they want to spend it – for the benefit of everyone involved' (MRDP, 2001, p17). In 2001, MRDP was working in 250 villages in five provinces.

My interpretation is that this programme went to scale relatively slowly because it was confronting issues of professional, institutional and personal orientation in government, and issues of complexity and diversity at the community level. Adequate time to develop methods and approaches, continuity and commitment of Vietnamese and technical cooperation staff, protection from top-down targets, and decentralization of budgets to villages were important elements in providing space for innovation, learning, local diversity and achievements.

Integrated Pest management (IPM), Indonesia[29]

IPM in Indonesia was developed and spread in the 1980s and by the early 2000s had some one million farmer participants.[30] It is used to control brown plant hopper and other pests in rice with sharply reduced applications of pesticide. Farmers are brought together for *in situ* learning through their own observations, mapping, experiments and analysis. They carry out their own monitoring, keep their own records, and coordinate and synchronize their actions. An FAO Technical Support Unit with strong continuity of committed and charismatic leadership played a significant part in developing and spreading the methodology.

IPM was spread through FFSs (Farmer Field Schools). This term began to be heard in Indonesia in 1990. Five years later, FFSs had been conducted in more than 15,000 villages and over one million agro-ecosystem diagrams had been produced by farmers themselves. NGOs played a part in this (Kingsley and Musante, 1996); but the main actors were from the government. The process was facilitated by 'normal' government extension workers who had intensive hands-on training in which they grew a rice crop and themselves conducted IPM field studies. There was also an 'unwritten curriculum' of teaching participants respect for farmers as they experienced growing rice themselves. During the mid 1990s, the programme shifted towards community organization and management of IPM and became known as Community IPM. Farmers themselves became facilitators, and by 1996 over half of all IPM Farmer Field Schools were being run by farmer trainers, with no loss of quality (Dilts and Hate, 1996). According to Dilts (2001, p20), the keys to the success of IPM included:

- Trusting in people as being able and willing to take control.
- Making efforts to push down roles which reside 'at the top' as in the case of strategic planning, which is now done at community level by farmers.
- Tolerating, encouraging and enjoying diversity as the stimulus for learning.

In Indonesia, IPM became a national movement, with federations. A Peasants' Charter (Fakih et al, 2003, pp153–162) was drawn up and presented to the minister of agriculture at a national IPM congress. IPM provided space and legitimacy for groups to come together, organize and make demands. Perhaps most significant was the clear benefits to farmers. They had to use much less pesticide. Huge savings resulted and yields rose. 'The total economic benefit' in Indonesia (up to 1990) was estimated to be over US$1 billion (Kenmore, 1991, cited in Conway, 1997, p215).

IPM has been a staggering success across the globe. In the words of Russ Dilts (2001, p18):

> *A people-centred IPM movement has grown in Asia over the last ten years, and is now spreading to parts of Africa, Latin America, and the Middle East. During this period, many variants have evolved and continue to evolve. . . From the first Farmer Field Schools consisting of 25 farmers each to a people centred IPM movement, which counts several millions of farmers in many countries (e.g. more than one million farmers have been trained in Indonesia alone), the IPM programme has indeed gone to scale.*

My interpretation is that the reasons IPM went to scale so rapidly and well included stable support and leadership; thorough and extended hands-on training of facilitators growing rice and conducting IPM themselves; the initial focus on a single crop; participatory, empowering and enjoyable processes; and, above all, clearly perceived gains by participating farmers.

Community-led total sanitation (CLTS), Bangladesh

The fourth example is at an earlier stage than the previous three (see p109 and VERC, 2002; WSPSA, 2002; Kar, 2003). CLTS is a nascent movement in which communities are facilitated to conduct their own appraisals and come to their own conclusions. Unlike earlier sanitation programmes, there is no hardware subsidy. Communities take matters into their own hands, latrines are dug and shared, landless people are provided places where they can dig theirs, and when coverage is complete and open defecation has ended, notice boards are put up proclaiming total sanitation. The benefits include better health, especially less diarrhoea; convenience, especially for women; increased incomes; less expenditure on treatment for sickness; a clean environment; social solidarity; and pride and self-respect. Except for loss of income to local medical practitioners, all other local people appear to gain.

My interpretation is that CLTS initially spread quite fast and well because some NGOs welcome it (overcoming the problems of slow, ineffective programmes based on subsidy), its facilitation was good, and, above all, it worked, with win–win multiple gains experienced by the whole community.[31]

Many lessons and ideas can be drawn from these four programmes and other sources. In comparing the programmes, it is important to recognize the existence of differences and that lessons may not always be transferable.

What does not work

Drawing lessons from the NWDP about what does not work does not make a judgement on whether it would have been better not to have attempted it. However, there is an obvious question of whether attempting anything so complex, on such a scale, with a bureaucracy and local power elite so likely to capture the benefits was at all sensible. Watershed development as conceived has been complicated by many factors – absentee farmers, conflicting upstream and downstream interests, misfit of administrative, social and watershed boundaries, and local social and power structures – making it at the best of times inherently difficult to take to scale well.

From this and other evidence, what does not work includes:

- devising a process and compiling a manual without evolutionary field testing;
- time-bound, top-down cascade and manual-based training;
- target and disbursement-driven participation, and rushing to scale;
- funds, subsidies and physical works pushed into contexts vulnerable to corruption and elite capture;

Table 5.1 Going to scale: The four programmes compared

Characteristic	1. NWDP, India	2. MRDP, Vietnam	3. IPM, Indonesia	4. CLTS, Bangladesh*
Scale	Vast scale; national programme covering 18 million hectares (2002)	Medium scale; 250 villages in five provinces (2001)	National programme involving some one million farmers	Over 2000 hamlets (2004)
Units of organization	Watersheds	Communities and community groups	Groups of neighbouring rice-growing farmers	Small nucleated rural communities (baras, or hamlets)
Speed and coverage most determined by	Targets, budgets, need to disburse	Process, learning, feedback and quality concerns	Number of trained facilitators supported in the field	Number of trained facilitators supported in the field
Evolution of methodology	Experience and ingenuity in a manual, in part PRA; no pilot phase	Two years evolving and piloting PRA, then a PRA-based learning process	Pilot tested and evolved; found to work; main elements replicated	PRA based; evolved in the field; found to work; adapted and varied as it spreads
Methodology and approach training	Regulated and standardized Initially large-scale cascade training	Adaptive and evolutionary Continuous and incremental	Scope for local creativity Intensive and lengthy facilitators' hands-on induction training	Igniting local creativity Intensive facilitators' hands-on induction training
Who gains most in practice	Bureaucrats, implementing agencies, local elites and irrigators	Poorer people are targeted; but potentially all may gain	All rice farming families and, indirectly, others in communities	All in the community, poor and non-poor, especially women
Main mode of spread	Government selection of watersheds and of agencies to implement	Facilitation by government staff and trained villagers	Facilitation by government staff and trained farmers	Catalysis by NGO staff, including lateral spread by local facilitators
Continuity of champions in supporting roles	Low; frequent transfers of IAS officer champions	High, with support from Sweden–Vietnam programme	High, with support from FAO/government cooperative programme	Too early to say
Subsidies for hardware and works	Substantial	Moderate	Minor support for materials only	None; explicitly excluded
Sustainability judged to be	Low	High	Higher still; groups continue after FAO's withdrawal	High, as for IPM; time will show

Note: * Since CLTS is only recently established, its characteristics are more likely to change than others.

- lack of continuity and commitment of staff; and
- lack of gradualist capacity development at the community level.

The NWDP has also lacked many of the advantages that have favoured the other programmes.

Two types of approach that have worked

In PRA, it is combinations of characteristics that seem to work. Although there are many different approaches,[32] two combinations that stand out are:

1   grounded, complex and evolutionary; and
2   facilitated, disseminated and self-managing.

Grounded, complex and evolutionary

The MRDP and RIPS in Tanzania (see pp14–15) are based on the same impressive model, whose defining characteristics are:

- being grounded in the field, with continual reality checks;
- a decades-long commitment by a donor agency;
- long-term continuity and close collaboration and relationships between national and foreign staff;
- implementation by government staff and organizations;
- PRA-related methodology and training continuously evolving;
- a learning and changing ethos;
- being multi-sectoral;
- decentralization to community groups;
- protection from top-down targets and drivers for disbursement.

Criticisms of lack of sustainability, domination by and reliance upon expatriates, and even some sort of neo-colonialism are, in these contexts, misinformed. Collegial collaboration over a long period between nationals and a few non-nationals has allowed and made for mutual understanding and strong relationships – doing things which neither could have done on their own. In both Tanzania and Vietnam, benefits have spread to the national level, with bottom-up learning grounded in the realities of the field. As always, the personal character of the main actors has been a key factor.

The passing out of fashion of this project or programme model, when we can see better now than ever how well it works for grounded relationships, innovation and learning, is a tragic casualty of the fickle fads of development (see pp14–16). It is to the credit of the Finnish, Swedish, Tanzanian and Vietnamese Governments that they have hung in and continued their collaboration when they could so easily have called it a day. A renaissance of these sorts of sustained and evolutionary programmes would be in the interests of poor people. It has seemed unlikely; but there is hope in a generally favourable evaluation of Sida area-development projects (Farrington et al, 2002) and their potential for both reducing poverty within a geographical area and informing poverty reduction strategy processes.

Facilitated, disseminated and self-managing

IPM and CLTS both began as single-sector activities for pest management and sanitation, respectively. IPM has become a large-scale movement, while CLTS has the potential to become one. They have in common that they are:

- able to bring clear, substantial and quick benefits to all concerned;
- based on participatory appraisal, analysis, planning and action;
- facilitated, not dictated;
- spread to others by local people themselves; and
- collective, with built-in quality assurance; if one or a few defect, all lose (a social ratchet effect assures sustainability and quality).

The question remains whether IPM and CLTS are exceptional, or whether there are other potential movements that could similarly be identified, piloted, evolved and then supported to spread.

Ideas, learning and choices

Single sector or multiple

Some regard single-sector PRA as second best: insensitive to people's priorities, which are often diverse and differ by community. It can be seen as a solution (a water supply, an agroforestry technology, a soil and water conservation method, and so on) in search of a problem. Certainly, the record of top-down transfer of technology approaches is not good. But this is misguided when there is an intervention from which many, if not all, in a community are likely to benefit. A holistic open-ended multi-sectoral approach has its place; but so has the approach focused on a single sector. It is a question of costs, benefits and feasibility. It is striking that Perez and Tschinkel (2003), after studying watershed programmes in ten countries in Latin America, Africa and Asia, conclude that 'although it may seem contradictory to the holistic approach, successful watershed management requires highly focused interventions. The critical challenge is to identify and act upon the points of highest leverage, which are often counter-intuitive and not obvious.' They go on to recommend 'promotion of practices that are locally effective, but are also likely to continue to spread without external assistance'. This is a radical alternative, indeed, to the Indian NWDP.

Who gains? What is gained?

In the NWDP, the main gains have been by those with irrigation. The poorer people and most women gained less or not at all (Amita Shah, 2001). In the other three programmes, gains have been much wider. The MRDP is a community project that stresses livelihood gains by the poorer in the communities. In IPM, all farmers gain through the rise in production, reduced risks and higher incomes. In CLTS, all in the community have access to latrines, and all gain in cleanliness, health, a better environment, reduced health expenditures and self-respect, and the well-being of women is especially enhanced.

With IPM, the multiple gains can be social and intellectual, as well as economic:

> *Farmers throughout the region have responded enthusiastically to IPM FFSs [farmer field schools] wherever they have been organized. Some farmers are primarily motivated by the reduced costs and reduced production risk obtained through application of ecological principles to crop management. Some are intellectually stimulated by the subject matter and excited by the experience of designing and carrying out their own experiments. For others, the main attraction is the group interaction, discussions and debates that are an important part of every FFS. The most striking confirmation of this enthusiasm has been the spontaneous appearance of farmer-to-farmer FFSs, in which field school graduates began to organize season-long FFSs for other local farmers (Pontius et al, 2002, pp14–15).*

Menu, not manual: Avoiding the template trap

The NWDP had, from the start, an elaborate and carefully devised Guidelines (GOI, 1994), providing a detailed template for what should be done. WDTs (watershed development teams) were to be trained and were to use PRA techniques that 'should enable the WDT and the village community to arrive at a common outline of an action plan' (GOI, 1994, p25). Many contingencies are anticipated and provided for. Financial arrangements are specified in detail. Not much is left to chance or discretion. The manual cannot fail to be consulted repeatedly during implementation.

In the MRDP, IPM and CLTS there is a menu, more than a manual. PRA and other methods are treated flexibly. In the MRDP, 'The actual PRA tools and methods were of secondary importance to the more consultative processes of interaction between government staff and villagers' (Shanks and Toai, 2000). In IPM, 'A national IPM programme needs to create a menu of activities that can be used creatively by field trainers to help alumni establish their own IPM programmes' (Pontius et al, 2002, p49). In CLTS, villagers who facilitate in neighbouring villages do things their own way and are often more effective than a trained outside facilitator (Kamal Kar, pers comm).

In IPM, it has been important to avoid 'the template trap':

> *Programmes should avoid the trap of trying to develop a formulaic approach to community IPM. Creating a template that would generate village IPM programmes across a country is a snare and a delusion. Templates are convenient for those who are charged with planning and managing large projects. However, they are a constraint for field workers. Field workers are in the position of actually being able to develop activities that are relevant, feasible and effective (Pontius et al, 2002, p49).*

The manual reflex, though, is deeply embedded. When some ActionAid country programmes were slow to adopt ALPS, the international directors asked for a manual of 'best practice' (David and Mancini, 2004). Nevertheless, as we have seen (see pp69–70), the guidance provided was emphatically 'notes', ideas and experiences, not instructions, as indicated by 'Health warning: Ideas and options only – innovate and learn' at the head of each page. But in some countries the manual reflex and culture was too strong, and Bangladesh, India and Nepal all produce their own manuals.

Manuals are, however, not irreversible. REFLECT initially had a 'Mother Manual'. Feedback soon showed that it was constraining and misfit many conditions in which it was applied. The approach was abandoned and local initiatives and facilitators' inventiveness were encouraged (Gautam, 1998; Phnuyal, 1999). This more flexible approach then allowed a thousand flowers to bloom, with diverse creative practice and a remarkable spread around the world.

Facilitated, not forced; trust, not targets; realism, not rush

The style and pace of MRDP, IPM and CLTS have much in common. In contrast with NWDP, they all had time and space to evolve, test and modify their methodologies. With the MRDP, 'the funding agency SIDA was very tolerant about the time required to develop and test out new methodologies' (Paul, 2001, p65). And they were able to continue to develop and adapt they way they did things.

All have been spared strong top-down drivers in the form of targets[33] and have had more of a culture of trust:

> *Speed is not of the essence in developing community IPM. Building local institutions is more important, and this takes time. National plans tend to generate constraints on flexibility because of the importance that they put on targets, log frames, and budgets in the planning process (Pontius et al, 2002, p49).*

Speed is determined by what local people do. In describing the scaling up of IPM, Dilts (2001, p19) has written: 'The job of outside organizers is to provide tools, methods, skills, experience and opportunity only. It is up to the farmers themselves if they want to organize, for what and how.' Similarly, for CLTS in Bangladesh, outsiders may convene and facilitate appraisal and analysis by community members; but it is the community members to decide whether and how to act (Kar, 2003). There is a bottom-up realism, not top-down rush.

Lateral spread

Lateral spread by villagers themselves is a feature of all three programmes. With the MRDP, 'Using local people and organizations to carry out PRAs in surrounding communities has proven to be a very effective strategy for spreading out and scaling up. Costs are lower and results are more rooted in local realities, resulting in more effective and more efficient use of all resources' (Paul, 2001, p67). With IPM, more than half the facilitators are farmers themselves who have been trained. With CLTS, some community facilitators are working on their own initiative, encouraging neighbouring communities to go for total sanitation. Visits and preaching by Imams and lay preachers, and visits between communities are spreading the idea and raising the possibility of CLTS becoming a laterally self-spreading movement.

Champions and continuity

Champions and continuity have been significant in all three programmes. In Chapter 1 (pp14–20) we saw how significant were continuity and champions in positions of leadership, with examples such as irrigation development in the Philippines and RIPS in Tanzania. Of the four programmes considered here, only the NWDP lacked long-term champions. The IAS (Indian Administrative Service) officers involved in early design and, at later stages, in different Indian states were subject to the normal transfers of their service and moved on. In contrast, in the other three programmes continuity and commitment of champions were key factors in sustained spread: for example, Bardolf Paul, Edwin Shanks and Bui Dinh Tooai in the MRDP; and Peter Kenmore, Russel Dilts and others of United Nations FAU (Food and Agriculture Organization) with IPM. With CLTS, it is early days; but as of 2004, there has been considerable continuity among the champions. In Tanzania, this was the case with Colonel Nsa-Kaisi and Colonel Tarimo, and Tanzanian and Finnish research and technical cooperation staff.

Vulnerability and subsidies versus self-help

Large-scale participatory programmes are vulnerable to changes in their institutional and political environment and to the rules that govern them. Some of the most serious threats can come through financial arrangements. Reviewing the revised guidelines for the India NWDP programme, Anil Shah has pointed out that funds earlier released direct to village institutions are now routed through the intermediate Project Implementing Agency, 'a sure recipe for institutionalizing corruption' (Shah, 2003, p7).

Subsidies for inputs or hardware are a common threat. They inhibit self-help. They induce adoption, which will then not spread on its own and is abandoned when the subsidies are withdrawn, or even before (for example, latrines left derelict, pillaged for materials or used to house chickens or for other purposes).[34] A study of subsidies in the NWDP found that they induced farmers to do things they would not otherwise have done (Kerr et al, 1996). The Forest Cooperation Programme in Vietnam was undermined and threatened when IFAD launched a parallel, larger-scale and more generous, but less participatory, programme in neighbouring communities. The spread of IPM has been impeded by credit and subsidy schemes which, for example, support agrochemicals (Bentley and Andrews, 1996, p2), and also by the efforts of agrochemical companies to market their products and then introduce their own variants of IPM based on their use. In 2003, the spread of CLTS in Bangladesh was slowed when a nationwide survey of latrines led people to expect a subsidy programme.[35]

Learning lessons is not enough

None of the problems in going to scale with participatory programmes in bureaucracies is new. The drive to scale up NWDP repeated the experience of

Community Development during the 1950s. British colonial governments, the US foreign assistance programme, the United Nations and the Ford Foundation were all vigorous and vociferous in promoting community development, especially in India. Pilot projects were precipitously expanded to national scales. By 1960, over 60 nations in Asia, Africa and Latin America had community development programmes. By 1965, most of these had been curtailed or drastically reduced (Holdcroft, 1984).[36] They had fallen foul of generic problems, all of which were manifested again in the NWDP: bureaucratic rivalries, especially with ministries of agriculture; paternalistic behaviour by staff; subsidies for 'aided self-help projects', which induced dependence; top-down targets for disbursements and outputs; and community development workers' biases towards local elites.

Reviewing the experience, David Korten (1984, p177) wrote:

> *Prominent among the barriers to effective participatory programs are pressures on development financing agencies to move too much money too quickly in time-bounded, pre-planned projects in pursuit of short-term results; while the need is for a flexible, sustained, experimental, action-based, capacity-building style of development effort for which both donors and recipient bureaucracies are ill equipped.*

Learning and stating these and other lessons was not enough. During the 1990s, the NWDP in India repeated the mistakes of community development in India during the 1950s. Lender, donor and recipient bureaucracies were 'ill equipped' for learning and changing. Korten was pointing to the complex, opaque and obtuse domain of institutional change. Institutional, here, refers to formal and informal procedures, rules, regulations, norms, incentives and regularities of practice. Unless this challenge of institutional change is met, the same lessons will continue to be 'learnt' as long as organized life as we know it survives.

Transforming institutions

The article with which this chapter opens addressed the personal dilemmas faced by trainers and facilitators when organizations want to go to scale with participation. This has led to the challenge of how to transform organizations and their institutions. The personal dilemmas remain, but the range of actors and options is wider. The actors are all of those who work in or influence development agencies, whether government, aid, civil society or the private sector. The options are a cornucopia of advice from a burgeoning literature on management and development. Out of this, four sources of experience and ideas stand out.

Four sources of ideas for going to scale with PRA[37]

The first source is John Thompson's (1995) article 'Participatory approaches in government bureaucracies: Facilitating the process of institutional change', in which he analysed three cases and indicated elements for transforming public agencies (see Box 5.1). These are amply confirmed by RIPS in Tanzania and by MRDP in Vietnam.

Box 5.1 Ten key elements for transforming public agencies into strategic enabling institutions

Ten key elements comprise the following:

1 a policy framework supportive of a clear role for local people in research and development;
2 strong leadership committed to the task of developing learning organizational systems, capacities and working rules;
3 long-term financial commitments and flexible funding arrangements from key donor agencies;
4 better systems of monitoring and evaluating performance, and new mechanisms for ensuring accountability;
5 careful attention to, and patience in working out the details of, systems and procedures;
6 creative management so that improved policies, procedures and field practices, once developed, can be scaled up and implemented effectively;
7 an open, supportive yet challenging organizational climate in which it is safe to experiment and safe to fail;
8 small interdisciplinary teams or working groups of innovative and committed agency professionals working in collaboration with external resource persons capable of acting as catalysts for change;
9 regular documentation and analysis of lessons for improving practice and building an institutional memory;
10 a flexible, integrated, phased training programme over a sustained period of time, involving key actors at different levels.

Source: Thompson (1995, p1544)

The second source is *Development and the Learning Organization* (Roper, Pettit and Eade, 2003), a goldmine of 24 essays from *Development in Practice* (Pettit and Roper, 2002), in part informed and inspired by Peter Senge's (1990) work on the learning organization.

The third source comprises publications based on the experience of the Organization Learning Forum, a coalition of initiatives coordinated by Patta Scott-Villiers from the Participation Group at IDS Sussex (Pasteur, 2004), which also links with other research. This worked on participatory approaches to institutional learning and change in DFID and Sida, and accompanied ActionAid in its experience with ALPS. Collaboration with DFID in Uganda and Brazil brought out the central significance of relationships in development (Pasteur and Scott-Villiers, 2004), a theme developed by Rosalind Eyben (2004b). Collaboration with Sida in Sweden and Kenya demonstrated the potential for small groups within an organization to conduct their own participatory research and reflection, and share this with others (Cornwall, Pratt and Scott-Villiers, 2004). Collaboration with ActionAid in Brazil, Ethiopia, India and Kenya brought to light the crucial issue of bottom-up congruence (Scott-Villiers, 2002; David and Mancini, 2004).

The fourth source is initiatives for ILAC (Institutional Learning and Change) in the CGIAR. These originate in the challenges of rapid change, a new poverty mandate, a growing complexity of relationships, limitations of the traditional centre-outwards transfer-of-technology approach of agricultural research and of economic impact evaluation, and a funding crisis. ILAC is part of, and supported by, innovative approaches for evaluating agricultural research and development (Horton and Mackay, 2003a, 2003b). It is described as a process of reflection, reframing and use of lessons learned during the research process that results in changed behaviour and improved performance (Watts et al, 2003), and is based upon and requires four sets of activities:

1   developing a supportive external environment;
2   fostering a culture of learning and change;
3   reorienting management systems; and
4   developing and enhancing individual awareness, knowledge and capabilities.

Aspects of ILAC are explored and elaborated upon in the nascent literature (e.g. Douthwaite et al, 2003; Hall et al, 2003; Horton and Mackay 2003a, 2003b; Watts et al, 2003).

Three ideas

The 21st century question is how to transform institutions to become more participatory and to have bigger pro-poor impacts. Learning lessons involves much more than gaining knowledge. The agenda is personal and professional, as well as institutional, change. This can be confusing. If almost everything has to change, it is hard to know what to do or where to start. Three ideas stand out.

The first concerns *values and procedures*. The potentials of expressing values and of devising procedures as a means for transforming organizations is easy to underestimate. A participatory process can lead to a consensual mission statement for which there is wide support and ownership. ActionAid, with its manifesto of values in *Fighting Poverty Together* (ActionAid, 1999) and empowering procedures in its Participatory Review and Reflection Processes (see pp69–70 and David and Mancini, 2004) is a pertinent illustration.

The second concerns *departments of human resources and finance*. Staff continuity and commitment were stressed in Chapter 1. To these were added congruence of institutional culture in Chapter 3. Rewards and incentives are also strong determinants of behaviour. However, in aid agency meetings concerned with participation, the two key departments of human resources (or personnel) and finance rarely turn up.[38] Yet, it is human resources who advertise for, select and train staff, and finance who drive the pressures to disburse. Support from finance was critical in ActionAid's introduction of the radical ALPS system, which had 'far-reaching implications for finance staff' (David and Mancini, 2004, p11). Perhaps the highest and most neglected priority in transforming public agencies is learning and change in these two departments. This extends also to politicians where they pre-empt, overrule or influence what is done. Those concerned have to change their perceptions and priorities, and then adapt recruitment, training, career paths, transfer policies, accounting procedures and incentives. This is not least in order to give programme and front-line staff the freedom and encouragement to pioneer, introduce and spread participatory practices, without disabling pressures or interference from above.

The third concerns change through transformative memes. These are not minor or trivia. Their smallness belies their potency:

- *Words and sayings.* Words can set the scene for change, as with the six power and relationship (PAR) words: partnership; empowerment; ownership; participation; accountability; and transparency. The word comes first, and then the challenge of narrowing the gap between word and action. Similarly, using, repeating and embedding sayings can reorient behaviour and attitudes, as in a PRA/PLA mode: besides 'hand over the stick', 'they can do it' and 'use your own judgement at all times', there is also 'unlearn', 'sit down, listen and learn', 'ask them', 'embrace error', 'fail forwards', 'celebrate diversity', 'doubt' and 'shut up!' Others include 'who gains and who loses?' and 'is your questionnaire (or target, or logframe or reporting requirement) really necessary?'
- *Stories.* Denning (2000) has argued that stories that are good to tell and frequently repeated are a powerful means of changing organizational culture. They can be what Gluckman called 'apt illustrations',[39] telling ways of making a point. They can be personal experiences, such as those of attitude and behaviour change described in *ABC of PRA* (Kumar, 1996, p17–21). For Reeler (2004) in 'Story-telling: Getting to the heart of things', stories can be case studies, fictional tales, personal tales, and various forms of drama and role play. He concludes:

  > . . . story-telling, as part of a developmental practice, may take a different kind of time and timing, less package-able in manuals, less of a warm-up exercise, less prone to a planned outcome, but no less rigorous in getting to where the heart of developmental work lies, and over time more fruitful.

Humour helps. As with the court jesters of mediaeval European monarchs, humour can allow the saying of the unsayable that needs to be said. The act of telling a story embeds it in the mind and memory. And good stories and jokes spread on their own.

- *Non-negotiables.* Non-negotiable principles, behaviours and values belong here (see pp74–76). The process of identifying and articulating them is a process of learning and change. And they, too, may spread by imitation.
- *Methods.* The case for procedural change was made in Chapter 3. The ways in which things are done influence interactions, relationships and learning. Participatory ways of doing things – of holding meetings, arriving at decisions,

and working together more generally – can be introduced gradually. PRA methods, particularly card writing and forms of group-visual synergy, can be democratic, popular, effective and potent.

- *Spaces.* Physical arrangements affect interactions and relationships. One of the first things to examine in seeking to transform an organizational culture is the physical arrangements of offices and meeting rooms: trying to ensure that there are more places than just the toilets where people can meet casually. An accessible tea or coffee place room where people meet informally by chance can seem a trivial matter. It is not.

Congruence from the bottom up

Bottom-up congruence means that the culture, institutions, procedures and relationships at the middle and upper levels of an organization are congruent with and support those needed at the grassroots. For scaling up participatory approaches and methods, this is fundamental. It means being participatory at all levels. For many bureaucracies and administrators, this demands a radical reversal of perceptions, attitudes and behaviour.

The point about support to what is variously known as the frontline, the coalface, the shop floor, the field and the grassroots is nothing new in the business world. In the 1980s, the organization chart of the North American chain store Nordstrom was 'upside down', with sales and sales support people at the top (Peters, 1989, p370). In the words of René McPherson, the managing director of another company:

> We didn't waste time with foolishness. We didn't have procedures; we didn't have lots of staff people. We let everybody do their job on the basis of what they need, what they say they'll do, and what their results are. And we gave them enough time to do it. . . We had better start admitting that the most important people in an organization are those who actually provide a service or make and add value to products, not those who administer the activity (cited in Peters and Waterman, 1982, p250).

For good spread of participation and participatory methodologies, it is not enough simply to support field facilitators. Congruence is also critical. The common pattern of administrative scaling up, as with the NWMP and JFM in India, is a top-down driven approach, with targets, manuals and, then, local distortions occurring in implementation. There is a glaring misfit, an incongruence, between hierarchy, targets, detailed guidelines, budgets and local interests, on the one hand, and behaviours, attitudes and other conditions for good local-level participation, on the other. As Shepherd concluded from his study of an environmental project in the Himalayan foothills, participation 'cannot be bolted onto an existing project concept. . . It has implications for the entire gamut of a scheme's working practices' (Shepherd, 1998, p97). This has been the experience with community IPM, which 'requires a decentralized approach that not only allows local initiative and innovation, but also encourages it. Dynamic field-based decision-making needs to be applied *not only by farmers but also by facilitators and programme managers'* (Pontius et al, 2002, p49; my emphasis).

Quite often the biggest blockage is in middle management. Senior policy-makers may adopt the rhetoric of participation. They may issue instructions enabling and requiring participatory practices. Front-line field staff may be well trained and well motivated. However, middle managers can feel threatened from above and below. Fearing their boss may change, they play it safe, use the language, practice prudent pretence and concealment, and wait for the nuisance to pass. Threatened by practices below which they do not understand or appreciate, their behaviour remains controlling and is inconsistent with local empowerment. They dig in, play for time and behave as before, deterring and diminishing participation.

The practical challenges of institutional change can be formidable. After a decade of experience with the introduction of PRA into government bureaucracy in Vietnam, Bardolf Paul (2001, p69) stressed the importance of the same attitudes and philosophy in other aspects of work that precede and follow what is described as PRA, and how this:

> . . . is by far the biggest challenge to widespread use and scaling-up of the methodology. Allowances have to be built into projects and programmes for the 'conversion' of those who will never experience a PRA. . . We all know how nearly impossible it is to teach PRA without any direct involvement; so what methods can be used to change the attitudes of those who will never be directly involved?

There are many dynamics for reversals to achieve bottom-up congruence. Involving senior and middle managers in immersions and field experiences (see pp177–181) is one means. Much is written about champions, networks, alliances, partnerships and relationships, and their part in spreading participatory methodologies. Personal, professional and institutional elements are intertwined and influence each other, like magnets in a magnetic field. What occurs in a spirit of participation often upends much that is 'normal', and in several senses puts the last first and the first last. Sometimes a critical mass is needed. If one part turns on its head, the other parts may force it back to how it was. If several parts upend, they may support each other in their new orientation, like a magnetic field that has reversed.

The best place to start and continue with is the field reality. Inspiring organizations, as we saw in Chapter 3 (pp78–80), manifest a congruence of commitment, culture, practices and relationships at all levels. Each level empowers the level 'below' it: field staff empower poor women and men; field managers empower field staff; regional managers empower field managers; and so on. The reversals reinforce each other throughout the system: with recruitment, lower levels recruit for the higher levels; with time scales, the lower levels determine the pace of action and change; and with priorities, the concerns of 'lowers' are followed and supported by 'uppers'.

Charles Owusu (2004) observed that 'ActionAid started with the premise that change must begin from within the organization itself. In other words, we decided to act exactly in the same way as we expect others to act.'

The struggle for congruence leads to asking who are Owusu's 'we' and where change should be grounded. The 'we' are individuals in organizations who take responsibility and act. The starting points are personal vision, commitment, energy, action and example, which trigger and support good change. Where participatory methodologies have spread well, there have always been people who combine commitment and realism. Their grounding is not in a headquarters or an office, but in the field. Those who come first are the poor and the marginalized, and those who work with them as facilitators; and the uppers – senior and distant – go to them and learn from and with them. The key for going to scale with participation, then, is more than just institutional transformation. It is, and crucially, bottom-up congruence of personal perceptions, behaviour and attitudes.

Notes

1   For helpful comments on an earlier draft I was (and remain) grateful to Christoph Backhaus, Andrea Cornwall, Irene Guijt, Deb Johnson, Kamal Kar, Mary Ann Kingsley, Robert Leurs, Ben Osuga, Bardolf Paul, Jules Pretty and John Toye. Responsibility for opinions, errors and omissions remain mine.

2   This section is taken from the article 'Making the best of going to scale' that was published in *PLA Notes* (Chambers, 1995), which was addressed primarily to PRA trainers and practitioners faced with the demands of going to scale faster than many considered prudent. I have rephrased some of the language, such as 'benign virus' to 'meme', also substituted in the article itself.

3   When several people objected that a virus could not be benign, I toyed with substituting yeast or 'good gene'. I wanted a word for self-spreading elements that continuously worked away to assure quality and improvement. The word meme, coined by Richard Dawkins (1976), can do this. Good meme is used here for an idea, habit, skill, story or any kind of behaviour or information that spreads with a methodology and enhances its quality (and, therefore, its survival and spread). For PRA, examples of memes are 'ask them' 'sit down, listen and learn' and 'use your own best judgement at all times'.

4   In 1995, I was still using *donor* to include both those who lent and those who gave. Today I prefer *lender and donor*. Lenders put countries into debt, whereas donors do not. More stringent criteria are therefore needed for loans than grants. In practice, as in Chapter 11 of the *World Development Report 2000/2001: Attacking Poverty* (World Bank, 2000), the distinction is fudged with expressions such as *donor funds, aid money, resource flows, concessional funds, concessional financing* and *concessional assistance*. For a critique see Chambers (2001).

5   This is the listing of organizations exactly as in the 1995 article. Not all of these are detailed in the glossary.

6   Through 2000, the number of rice farmer field schools in Indonesia had risen some 25-fold to over 37,000 (Pontius et al, 2002, p15). Over 6000 other non-rice Farmer Field Schools were also reported. IPM evolved before and in parallel with PRA, with overlapping approaches and methods.

7   Logical framework analysis is discussed in Chapter 3, pp67–69, 'Illogical control: The logframe'.

8   In 2003 an informal network of practitioners in the UK drew up a code of conduct for using participatory approaches and methods for generating numbers. See Holland (in preparation).

9   The reference is to the *Book of Common Prayer* of the Church of England.

10 For abbreviated versions, see Korten (1981) and and Korten and Klauss (1984, pp176–188).

11 See my short chapter 'Spreading and self-improving: A strategy for scaling-up' in Edwards and Hulme (1992, pp40–47).

12 For participatory approaches in government bureaucracies, see Thompson (1995), and in projects, see Scherler et al (1998). For PRA, specifically, see Singh (2001); Holmes (2002); and Cornwall and Pratt (2004). Other sources include, in chronological order, PRAXIS (circa 1997); seven chapters on scaling up in Blackburn with Holland (1998, Part 1), including Gaventa's final chapter, 'The scaling-up and institutionalization of PRA: Lessons and challenges'; IIRR (2000): a good source, synthesising a workshop held at IIRR (International Institute of Rural Reconstruction) in the Philippines; Blackburn et al (2000), written for the World Bank; IH/AA (2001a and 2001b); Gonsalvez and Armonia (2001); Gonsalves (2001): a useful summary (this whole volume of *LEISA* is on 'Lessons in scaling up'); Guendel et al (2001); DeJong (2003); Hancock (2002); and Snapp and Heong (2003).

13 PRA/PLA appears to be least widespread or well established in countries at the extremes of power, wealth and/or totalitarianism, such as the US, Saudi Arabia, Libya, Iraq and North Korea. For the record, it is practised and is, in some cases, widespread in China, Iran, Myanmar, Palestine, Syria, Tibet and Yemen.

14 Sources can be accessed with word searches at www.ids.ac.uk/ids/particip. Of the innumerable sources, only a few are cited here either because of their quality or because they are liable not to be widely known.

15 I draw here on accounts by my colleagues Singh (2001) and Cornwall and Pratt (2003), as well as my own experience.

16 Much of the work on the several drafts of *The World Bank and Participation* was done by Jennifer Rietbergen-McCracken, who was one of the early pioneers in the evolution of PRA.

17 In South–South exchanges, PRA practitioners and people interested in PRA, from Asia, Africa and Latin America, spent two to three weeks in communities and in workshop mode, sharing experience and practice. The first three exchanges were in India, and later ones in the Philippines and Zimbabwe. For these exchanges between PRA practitioners and other pathways of spread, see a fascinating diagram from the research of Tim Holmes in 'Rapid spread through many pathways' (Holmes, 2002).

18 The incalculable contribution of *RRA Notes*, later *PLA Notes*, edited from IIED, has been supported with commendable consistency by SIDA, now Sida since its inception in 1988. *RRA Notes/PLA Notes* would not have had such a huge influence had it not been free to subscribers in countries in the South, thanks to this support. The contrast with USAID, which killed off Cornell's excellent *Rural Participatory Development Review* after a few years by withdrawing support, is little short of stark. Sida deserves praise and

recognition for hanging in with what continues to be a highly cost-effective use of aid money.

19   The contribution of IDS Sussex to this process was made possible by flexible funding from a number of donors, none of whom required a logframe. These were, most notably, the Ford foundation, SDC, Sida and ODA (which became DFID). Other flexible support came from the Aga Khan Foundation, Danida, NOVIB and the Paul Hamlyn Foundation. The budgets included a line item, invaluable both substantively and for the encouragement and trust it expressed, entitled 'Unforeseen Opportunities'.

20   IIED took a lead in obtaining funding from Danida for a network of 15 resource centres for participatory learning and action (RCPLAs), of which 13 are in the South and 2 (IIED and IDS Sussex) are in the North. The role of network coordination has passed from the IIED to PRAXIS in India. A nice reflection of democratic relationships between networks came from an international meeting of networks in Nepal in 1996 when the informal and friendly message from IDS was: 'We want to hand over the stick', and the equally informal and friendly response was: 'Who are you to say that you have a stick to hand over? Be yourselves and do your thing.'

21   The reader is referred to fuller and more authoritative treatments of quality issues in Blackburn with Holland (1998).

22   Drawing the map for a visitor could be seen negatively as simply a learned behaviour or protecting others in the village from having their time wasted; it can also be seen positively as an intelligent courtesy, a means of informing and helping the visitor.

23   Clark University in the US was then invited and conducted a more structured training programme (Howes, 2002, pp86–87).

24   This referred to an experience with the first PRA where a group from MYRADA, led by Jimmy Mascarenhas, spent five days in Kalmandargi village in Karnataka. We spent part of the first day discussing how we would behave, not lecturing, not dominating, and so on. A government officer who arrived on the second day inadvertently undermined the process by behaving in the traditional manner of a bureaucrat with villagers. He was, though, a quick learner and had changed by the evening.

25   I recommend the whole book, which is as relevant today as it was when published in 1998, and especially John Gaventa's chapter: 'The scaling-up and institutionalization of PRA: Lessons and challenges' (Blackburn with Holland, 1998, pp153–166) and the IDS Workshop 'Reflections and recommendations on scaling-up and organizational change' (ibid, 1998, pp135–144).

26   Both the NWDP and JFM in India have a voluminous literature. Valuable sources of insight, more nuanced and balanced than presented here, are to be found in the References under Kerr et al (1996; 2002), Kolavalli and Kerr (2002a, 2002b) and Ramakrishnan et al (2002), who report on research on NWDP and JFM conducted in Andhra Pradesh, Madhya Pradesh and Karnataka. This is summarized in Baumann and Farrington (2003).

27 A Secretary of a State Government who had recently been given charge of the watershed programme in his state assured me in conversation that there would be no targets, and that he had cleared this with higher authorities. A year later targets were back in.

28 This section is based on Shanks and Toai (2000), Paul (2001) and materials presented by Edwin Shanks in 1998 at an IDS study workshop for aid agency staff. The first two sources are recommended as fascinating and insightful descriptions of process.

29 Sources for this section include Pretty (1995a, pp97–99); Conway (1997, pp212–218); Dilts (2001); and Fakih et al (2003).

30 For a time line for IPM in Indonesia, see Fakih et al (2003, p6).

31 The successful spread of CLTS is, however, vulnerable to five linked threats: (i) poor facilitation; (ii) large budgets and pressures to disburse; (iii) standardization of designs, raising costs and excluding poorer people; (iv) reintroduction of hardware subsidies; and (v) governments setting targets, using sanctions and counting latrines instead of open-defecation-free communities.

32 There are other types that work. A comparative analysis of the spread of a wider range of participatory methodologies, such as REFLECT, Appreciative Inquiry (AI) and Planning for Real, in more varied modes and contexts, could be very useful and generate more insights, adding to and qualifying what is suggested here.

33 This is not to say that there are no targets. World Vision in Bangladesh has targets for numbers of communities it hopes will be totally sanitized by the end of a planned period. It is more a question of style of facilitation and work, criteria of success, and incentives and rewards to staff. Some administrative cultures combine targets with a self-defeating punitive orientation. That is not the case with the three programmes considered here.

34 One latrine, I was told but did not see, had been converted into a shrine.

35 The movement was also undermined by the last minute insertion into the Dhaka Declaration of a clause that approved hardware subsidies to the poorest of the poor who have no means of helping themselves. This is a case where 'normal' philanthropic and professional reflexes to help the poor are precisely wrong and self-defeating. Subsidies to the poorest of the poor go, in practice, to the less poor; many of the poorest lack land on which to dig a latrine and rely on neighbours to allow them to dig temporary structures; and hope of subsidies deters mutual help and self-help in the community.

36 This paragraph is largely derived from Holdcroft's 1984 review of community development, which is recommended reading for a summary of these lessons.

37 These are chosen for relevance, recentness and accessibility. Some others that are excellent (e.g. Hobley, 2000) are less accessible.

38 For example, with a show of hands it has appeared that finance and human resources dapartments have been totally or almost entirely absent in quite large (50–300 persons) meetings in the Asia Development Bank, DFID, FAO and the World Bank, and in a smaller meeting of New Zealand Aid staff.

39 I thank Caroline Moser for the term and its source.

6

Behaviour, Attitudes and Beyond

The question of attitudes, behaviour and values is fundamental to the successful growth of participatory approaches in all fields (Bardolf Paul, 2003, p139).

Attitudes and behaviour are not one-time events. They are lived day by day as we ask ourselves, how did I behave today? (Rajendra Prasad, 2003, p163).

The 'best' PRA experiences for me have invariably been when the practitioners are able to leave their various 'hats' at home and behave simply as concerned human beings (Tilly Sellers, 2003, p187).

... without changing attitudes and behaviour in our institutions, and without putting our own interests last, participation will be a dream (Mwajuma Saiddy Masaiganah, 2003, p119).

When observing a field school, it should be difficult to identify the fieldworker except that he/she should be the first one into the mud and the last one to talk (Dilts and Hate, 1996, p3).

This chapter presents the case that behaviour and attitudes are a key point of entry for doing better in development. Part 1 argues that scientists' behaviour and attitudes are a missing link in agricultural science. Part 2 explores wider implications for norms and practices for all development professionals.

Part 1: Behaviour and Attitudes: A Missing Link in Agricultural Science (1998)[1]

The argument is that 'our' (professionals', scientists', outsiders') behaviour and attitudes are a key missing link for good agricultural science; and that unless they are confronted and transformed, as part of a new definition of professionalism, the agriculture of small farmers, and the needs of many of the food-insecure of the world will not be met. The argument, set in the context of agricultural science and scientists, has implications also for other development professions concerned with the diversity and complexity of human lives and livelihoods.

Context

For purposes of broad analysis, the agricultural systems of the world can be classified into three types: industrial, green revolution, and CDR (complex, diverse and risk-prone).[2] An estimate published in 1995 (Pretty, 1995a, p2) gave the numbers of people supported by industrial agriculture as some 1.2 billion, by green revolution agriculture as 2.3–2.6 billion, and by CDR agriculture as 1.9–2.2 billion.

Complex and diverse agriculture is now a priority. First, and most important, CDR agriculture must be supporting a majority of the poorest and most vulnerable people in the world, a majority of them females. Second, there is evidence (see, for example, Pretty, 1995a; Pretty et al, 1996; Hazel and Fan, 2000) that the potential and priority of CDR agriculture has been underestimated, and that it often has a potential for two-fold or three-fold increases in production with little or no use of external inputs.[3] Third, industrial and green revolution agriculture are themselves in some cases shifting towards more complex and diverse systems, and can be expected to continue to shift in that direction, towards systems with more enterprises, activities and linkages internal to the farm. These changes can be anticipated as, variously, subsidies are withdrawn, labour and management become more available,[4] biological pest management and organic manure substitute for pesticides and artificial fertilizers, and farming intensifies.

The question then is how agricultural science and scientists can best serve an agriculture which combines increasing complexity and diversity, and especially that of poor CDR farmers.

Whose reality counts?

Scientists and CDR farmers have different mindsets and realities. Some contrasts of realities (ways of thinking, experiences, values, methods, incentives, and especially working environments) can be outlined as in Table 6.1.

The strategies of CDR farmers differ from those of industrial and green revolution farmers. The latter often seek to standardize, simplify, control, and to minimise management, substituting capital for labour. Their reality is closer to that of scientists and their research stations. In contrast, CDR farmers often seek to reduce risk and increase food and income by complicating and diversifying in

Table 6.1 *Contrasting tendencies in the realities and mindsets of scientists and resource-poor CDR farmers*

Scientists' realities	CDR farmers' realities
Universal	Local
Reductionist	Complex
Uniform	Diverse
Stable	Dynamic
Controlled	Uncontrolled

their farming systems, intensifying labour use, adding to their enterprises, and maximizing management. Many are skilful engineers: they build bunds, confine, control and concentrate rainwater flows, flatten fields, and shape land in a myriad of ways. They make, manage and exploit spatial niches such as silt deposition fields, termite mounds, animal pens, and other pockets of fertility which contain, capture and concentrate nutrients, soil and water (Wilken, 1987; Premkumar, 1994; Scoones, 1995; Carter and Murwira, 1995). They multiply the internal links and flows within their farming systems, through creating and exploiting microenvironments, and through aquaculture, composting, cut-and-carry for stallfed livestock, cover crops, manuring, multiple and serial cropping, agroforestry, home gardening, and the use of kitchen waste; and they bring in resources such as fodder, fuel, fibre, nutrients, soil and water from outside the boundary limits of their farms.

For this they need choices of diverse materials, resources and ideas. In normal agricultural science, in contrast, scientists seek to increase productivity and diminish risk through simplifying, standardizing and controlling the environment. The procedures for testing and releasing new seed varieties themselves standardize, limiting diversity (Witcombe et al, 1996). Scientists then pass on to extensionists packages of standard practices. But what CDR farmers often want is not standard packages but baskets of diverse choices among which they can pick and choose the better to exploit local micro variations and microenvironments, to buffer their systems against risk, and to help them adapt and respond to dynamic and unpredictable conditions.

The issue then is whose reality counts? In the traditional transfer of technology (TOT) mode, it is the reality of the scientists. It is their reality which is to be transferred. In the words of Paulo Freire (1974, p95):

> *It appears that the act of extension . . . means that those carrying it out need to go to 'another part of the world' to 'normalize it', according to their way of viewing reality: to make it resemble their world.*

Put crudely, the farm is to be simplified and standardized and made to resemble the research station. To serve CDR agriculture requires a reversal: for scientists to work more closely with farmers in their conditions, and for the research station to generate diversity, to provide farmers with wider ranges of choices of enterprise, variety, practices and principles to try out.

The questions then are not just whose reality counts? but also:

- Whose knowledge counts?
- Whose preferences and criteria?
- Whose needs?
- Whose appraisal?
- Whose planning and implementation?
- Whose experimentation?
- Whose monitoring and evaluation?

And the answers shift in their balance towards those of farmers.

Capabilities: 'They can do it'

Many scientists may accept the thrust of this argument, but consider farmers incapable. There are, though, four bodies of evidence which suggest that farmers, especially CDR farmers, have greater capabilities and knowledge than had been supposed by most professionals.

First, through insights from farming systems research, the complexity and diversity of farming systems, especially in the tropics, is now better understood and appreciated, and the skill and knowledge needed for their management.

Second, new methods have shown farmers' capabilities for complex analysis to be greater than had been supposed. Methods such as participatory farm and resource mapping, matrix scoring and ranking (Drinkwater, 1993), seasonal calendars (Gill, 1991), nutrient flow diagramming (Lightfoot et al, 1994), and trend and change diagramming have often astonished scientists, and farmers themselves, with the detail and complexity of information and assessment they reveal.

Third, farmers' knowledge is now acknowledged to have the edge over that of scientists in domains which concern their own priorities, livelihood strategies, practices and priorities, local conditions and whatever requires continuous observation.

Fourth, farmers are often highly innovative, as well documented in the work of Anil Gupta and the publication *Honey Bee*.[5]

Power, dominance and error

Unfortunately, education and training condition students and professionals to believe that their knowledge is superior in domains where it is not. It is a commonplace that professionals, whether agriculturalists or not, often behave in a superior manner with farmers, lecturing, criticising, and instructing, being impatient and in a hurry, and neither listening well nor showing respect or interest.

This prevents learning and leads to error. Those who are dominant and powerful (or 'uppers') tend to find it difficult to learn from those who are subordinate and weak (or 'lowers').[6] The assumption that 'we know' and 'they are ignorant' prevents 'us' from learning. Our own beliefs are then self-validating. A sobering example is psychoanalysts. For three generations since Freud, they believed that incest was a fantasy. They then imposed that reality on the victims, though the victims knew otherwise. Psychoanalysts may have been more powerful in relation to their clients than agricultural scientist are with theirs; and therefore more vulnerable to their own fantasies, and more disabled from learning. But the warning is there, that all interpersonal power can deceive.[7]

The question then is to what extent this applies in the relations between scientists and extensionists on the one hand, and farmers on the other. A warning comes from recent meticulous research in the forest–savanna transition zone in Guinea. There, Fairhead and Leach (1996) found that all professionals had believed that local people destroyed the forest; and that face-to-face with visitors to their villages, local people confirmed this though they knew it was untrue. They reflected back the false reality of those who were influential: they knew what their visitors believed, wanted benefits from them, and told them what they knew they expected. Moreover, when the benefits are subsidies, farmers' behaviour can mislead because they will adopt practices which are not sustainable without the subsidies (Kerr et al, 1996). Is it, then, quite common, that scientists and extensionists are misled, with the realities they seek to transfer or induce reflected back to them through prudent and rational behaviour?

The behaviour and attitudes of the visitor appear the key. Dominance, age, charisma, and power all make it difficult to learn. Distinguished old men are the most disabled because of the respect with which they are so often treated. I have been on field visits with a renowned extensionist and observed the eagerness with which farmers sought to find out what he wanted them to say. They then said it to back to him, reflecting and reinforcing his version of reality and his (in my view erroneous) beliefs. A single farmer who, in a meeting, protested other priorities, was told to sit down and shut up. It was through the exercise of interpersonal dominance that the distinguished extensionist denied himself the opportunity to learn from that farmer.

Participatory research

The importance of behaviour and attitudes is reinforced by what is required for good collaboration in research between farmers and scientists. As M. S. Swaminathan has said, for sustainable food security:

> *A major challenge will be in integrating the different components of sustainable crop production into synergetic production systems. For this purpose, research on the development of integrated, intensive farming systems will have to be undertaken in the fields of farmers. Sustainable agricultural practices help to substitute market purchased chemical inputs with knowledge and farm grown inputs. They are thus best developed through participatory research with farm families.*

Many scientists have been pioneering participatory research. To take seed-breeding as but one example, D. M. Maurya's early (Maurya et al, 1988) pioneering work on selection of varieties by farmers as part of the breeding process has been followed by further involvement of farmers at almost every stage, including choices for the original crosses (Witcombe et al, 1996).[8]

Participatory research with farm families implies mutual learning. Here is a description of what happens when farmers themselves have made diagrams of farm resource flows:

Farmer–scientist discussions over bioresource flow models not only result in farmers learning new ways to recycle materials, but also inform the extension services, both government and non-government, what kinds of inputs farmers need to develop ecologically sustainable farming systems. Similarly, researchers learn what new experiments are needed from them (Lightfoot et al, 1994, p23).

Participatory research with farm families brings scientists and farmers together. How they then relate and interact, how they present and perceive one another, what sort of people they are as human beings – these are then critical for success. The boundaries of what constitutes good science and good scientific method widen to include not just what is done in the laboratory or on the research station, but also what is done with farmers and on farmers' fields. If agricultural science is to serve its local stakeholders well, then this social dimension becomes a key part of good agricultural science.

A scanning of some of the literature on agricultural extension, farmer participatory research (FPR) and participatory technology development (PTD) however, reveals little on how scientists actually behave when they interact with farmers. Exceptions include Robert Rhoades's classic (1982) *Art of the Informal Agricultural Survey* and Jacqueline Ashby's seminal video *The IPRA Method* (CIAT, undated) from the late 1980s. But elsewhere I have found little. A prestigious and popular textbook on agricultural extension (van den Ban and Hawkins, 1988) concerns itself mainly with changes in attitudes and behaviour among farmers and hardly at all among extensionists (see, for example, van den Ban and Hawkins, 1988, pp46, 134, 154–156). This reflects the interpretation that would have been put on the title to this paper three decades ago. Then it would have been the behaviour and attitudes of farmers, not those of scientists, that was the missing link. Nor are scientists' behaviour and attitudes prominent in the 'Farmer First' literature (see e.g. Chambers et al, 1989; Scoones and Thompson, 1994). Other works directly on farmer participation (e.g. Farrington and Martin, 1988; Okali et al, 1994) cover procedures, case studies, interfaces and interactions but do not stress how scientists and other outsiders behave face-to-face with farmers, let alone what sort of people scientists are as people or how they relate to others.

Yet for good farmer participatory research, the behaviour and attitudes of scientists need to ensure that it is the realities and priorities of farmers that come first. This will be more important the further the research is along Biggs' (1989) continuum of modes of participatory research, from contract to consultative to collaborative to collegial. For what is required is that scientists step down and hand over much of the initiative and decision-making to farmers, entailing a relationship and behaviour which a scientist or extensionist may find uncongenial. The challenge is personal.

Where the debate concerns the personal dimension, it typically stresses confidence, the presentation of the self, skills, and rewards and incentives. A powerfully argued policy paper on improving the effectiveness of agricultural research and extension in India (Farrington et al, 1998, p27) stresses the need for social science *skills* [my emphasis] and notes that a requirement for achieving a well-functioning client-oriented research system is to:

> . . . *enhance the willingness of research staff to identify and respond to clients'*
> *needs. This. . . poses some of the most intractable challenges, including the*
> *introduction of merit-based promotion, the redefinition of staff appraisal and*
> *performance criteria to reflect client orientation more strongly, and the rigorous*
> *implementation of these. . . Only limited progress can be made with all the*
> *other recommendations made in this paper unless these challenges are met first*
> *(Farrington et al, 1998, p27).*

The willingness of research staff to identify and respond to clients' needs can surely be enhanced in these institutional ways. But unless 'skills' are interpreted widely, they may not touch the interpersonal dimension – what sort of people the scientists are, how they relate to farmers, their deeper commitment, how they behave, how they are perceived as people. Behaviour and attitudes remain a missing link.

Good behaviour and attitudes

Appropriate behaviour and attitudes do not always come easily. For some it is second nature. For many, a superiority complex resulting from education and training has to be unlearnt. The practice of participatory rural appraisal (PRA) (Mascarenhas et al, 1991) has identified pillars and linkages as in Figure 6.1:

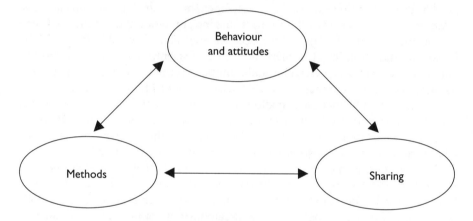

Figure 6.1 *Pillars of PRA and linkages of change*

For analysis by local people, the behaviour and attitudes of the facilitators have been found to be critical. Much PRA training now gives this priority over the methods. The same applies if farmers are to be enabled to their own experimentation and analysis. Thus Lightfoot et al (1994, p23) write of ensuring that all members of a team 'are in listening mode', and urge: 'Remember that it is important to hand over the drawing instrument to the farmer as soon as possible', so that it is the farmer who diagrams, and not the outsider.

These issues were explored in a South–South International Workshop convened in South India in July 1996 by two NGOs ActionAid, and SPEECH. The report (Kumar, 1996) entitled *ABC of PRA: Attitude and Behaviour Change*[9] lists precepts under the two headings of offsetting biases and self-critical awareness. These include how to do the following:

- ensure participation of shy and submissive people;
- be sensitive;

- be humble;
- be nice;
- create mutual trust;
- be transparent;
- learn and share together;
- learn not to interrupt;
- hand over the stick;
- be an active listener;
- avoid leading questions;
- respect innovation;
- learn to unlearn;
- learn not to be judgemental.

Under each of these headings there is an average of nine behavioural suggestions.

Perhaps the most difficult lessons for dominant, energetic, enthusiastic and talkative outsiders are:

- *Learning not to put forward one's own ideas.* This runs counter to the transfer-of-technology ideology, and so presents big problems. Yet it is essential at first if 'lowers' (poor farmers, women. . .) are to gain confidence and feel free and able to express their own realities and conduct their own analysis.
- *Learning not to criticize.* Often farmers' practices appear wrong. The moment these are criticized, the outsider can be seen as a threat or as a person to be deferred to, inhibiting farmers from putting forward their own ideas.
- *Learning to keep quiet and not interrupt.* Some uppers habitually interrupt lowers, putting them even further down. Perhaps the hardest lesson of all is learning to keep quiet. Interruptions of diagramming or of discussions often sabotage a process, and direct attention away from the subject, making participants more conscious of the presence of an outsider.
- *Relaxing, not rushing.* A pervasive defect of uppers' behaviour is being in a hurry. It goes with being important. Field visits are endemically vulnerable to being late and rushing. A relaxed approach with plenty of time makes the difference. (How often good things happen when a vehicle breaks down, an unanticipated night stop is made, and there is suddenly informality and plenty of time, if the visitor has the wit to seize the opportunity).
- *Developing rapport.* The converse of rushing is taking time to gain rapport, being interested, being human, and behaving in the many small ways that make for good relationships.

A principle running through these injunctions is that of putting the first (the upper) last, so that the last (the lower) can be first. When there are initially sharp imbalances in power, prestige, and status, as in many scientist – resource-poor farmer relationships, the upper has to go to special lengths to achieve an equal and mutual sharing. Visual methods provide one means. Farmers can be empowered by making their own model, map or diagram, expressing and analysing their reality. A farm map or model can provide a focus, agenda and vehicle for farmers and researchers to exchange technical ideas about how new flows and new enterprises might be integrated into ongoing farming systems, and how degraded natural resources might be rehabilitated (Lightfoot et al, 1994, p23). Matrix scoring of crop varieties (Drinkwater, 1993; Manoharan et al, 1993) is another powerful method which can astonish both scientists and farmers with the depth and detail of farmers' comparative knowledge.

Nor is this a zero sum game in which the scientist loses so that the farmer can gain. Power is not a commodity, despite the language of 'losing' and 'surrendering' power. Some agricultural scientists, if a minority, have always found it immensely interesting and exciting to learn from and with farmers. The new visual methods make good experiences more accessible. Often all that is needed now is the behaviour and attitudes to go with them.

Potential

The potential from changed behaviour and attitudes appears vast. They could generate and be part of processes which would transform and focus agricultural research to fit the multiple local priorities of CDR and other farmers with complex and diverse systems. These changes could, perhaps, lead to the realization of much of the latent potential of the CDR agriculture, as well as some of that of green revolution and industrial agriculture to the extent that those change towards more sustainable forms.

The resistances are many. Some are professional and institutional: the rigidities and inertias of educational systems; the hierarchies of research and extension bureaucracies; the dominant mode and mental set of the transfer-of-technology ('we know, they are ignorant') model; norms and regulations like those for testing and releasing crop varieties; and reward systems and institutional cultures which discourage or penalise participation and work with farmers.

Other resistances are personal. Long education and training have a tendency to induce a complex of superiority. Ego, a sense of deserving respect, a fear of uncontrollable participatory situations, preferences for the laboratory over the field, and for plants and equipment over people – these are some of the understandable personal conditions which can inhibit or prevent appropriate behaviour. Nor are agricultural scientists and extensionists alone in having these difficulties.

They are, though, and however understandably, facing backwards. Development professionals and professions are in the midstream of a wide and deep shift of paradigm. Much in management literature (e.g. Handy, 1989; Peters, 1989; Senge, 1990) stresses flexible interaction between groups and levels in order to cope with complex and dynamic conditions. This is pushing us towards participation, towards multiple realities, towards decentralization and diversity. And these require new behaviours and new attitudes.

Practical implications

Four implications stand out:

1 *Personal roles and behaviour*: for scientists and extensionists to become less teachers and transferors of technology, and much more facilitators and providers of support to farmers, enabling them to do their analysis and experimentation, find out what they need, and then seeking to supply it.
2 *Professional methods*: for participatory methods, including visual diagrams and maps, to be adopted and further developed.
3 *Institutional change*: for participatory procedures, values and behaviours to become part of the culture of research and extension organizations.
4 *Teaching and training*: for teaching and training to stress and focus on attitude and behaviour change.

In August 1998 the Lal Bahadur Shastri National Academy of Administration at Mussoorie in India hosted a National Workshop on Attitude and Behaviour Change in Participatory Processes (Mathur, 1998). This sought to put together a selection of exercises which could be adopted by training institutions throughout India. In its final sessions the Workshop increasingly focused on the culture and style of training institutions themselves, and of the conduct of training. It recognized the need for these to change from didactic to participatory modes, not least so that those taught or trained can then themselves reproduce the participatory mode of relating and sharing.

The first step towards these changes is to recognize the missing link. For agricultural science truly to serve resource-poor farmers, women and the marginalized, appropriate behaviour and attitudes are crucial. An authoritarian or dominating scientist is a bad scientist. A democratic and sensitive scientist, who knows how to keep quiet and how to hand over the stick, can be a good scientist. Good behaviour and attitudes are a part not only of good agricultural science, but of all science which concerns people, their lives and livelihoods.

Part 2: In Search of Learning and Change (2004)

All development professions, not just agricultural scientists, face these challenges and opportunities. Behaviour and attitudes have been a widespread, almost universal, blind spot in development. In moving forward, changes in behaviour present a widely feasible entry point. As the behaviours and attitudes of teachers, trainers and facilitators change from a top-down mode, they increasingly model the behaviour and relationships for good participation in the field. Training activities for attitude and behaviour awareness and change are best through field experience, action and reflection. Drawing up codes of practice has a part to play, especially for participatory work with those who are more marginalized and powerless. Practitioners of participation increasingly recognize the relevance of ABC (attitude and behaviour change) in the office and home as well as field. Workshops and conferences proliferate, but development organizations rarely give priority to experiential learning and critical reflection for their staff. Two ways forward are bursting with promise: participatory field research on poverty undertaken by development professionals themselves; and immersions where they live with and learn from poor people. Neither is yet common, but both, combined with reflection, have shown their potential for personal and professional transformation.

All professions, not only agricultural scientists, face these challenges and opportunities. Action and change are, however, difficult and slow to occur. Workshops on ABC held in India, with the aim of introducing ABC modules into government training institutions (e.g. Mathur, 1998), may have sown some seeds but have not led to any revolutionary change. Top-down behaviour and attitudes are resiliently buffered against change by personal and professional conditioning, by habits of teaching, and by institutional procedures and cultures.

So it is not surprising that personal behaviour and attitudes have remained a blind spot in much development awareness and practice. As other chapters in this book indicate, development activity could be more effective if only the actors behaved and related differently. As argued above, this applies with force in agriculture. It applies, too, in almost all development contexts. The personal dimension of development is pervasive. It is like the air we breathe, so universal that we rarely notice it. The arguments apply to all professionals whose lives and work affect development, whether they are policy-makers, fieldworkers or local people; in the centre or at the periphery; senior or junior; male or female; in aid agencies, government departments, universities, colleges or training or research institutes; and in NGOs or the private sector, including consulting organizations.

Behaviour and attitudes came to the fore early in the evolution of PRA. They were scarcely a discovery. Many had been deeply aware of their significance earlier, not least those working in the tradition of Training for Transformation (Hope and Timmel, 1984). But with the facilitation of PRA visual methods of analysis, it was quickly evident that talking by the outsider, so natural and necessary in semi-structured interviewing, was often an impediment. Learning to keep quiet was a new and, for some, profoundly challenging skill. What was needed was to start a process, and then hand over the stick, the chalk, the pen (or, later, the camera, the video camera and the editing equipment), and listen and watch or go away while a process continued with its own dynamic.

It is difficult to judge how much over the past decade the behaviour and attitudes of development professionals have shifted from command, control and teach towards empower, enable and co-learn; but small changes do seem to have taken place on quite a wide scale. If progress is scattered and limited, it is also bright with promise. The six PAR (power and relationship) words, for example – partnership, empowerment, ownership, participation, accountability and transparency (Groves and Hinton, 2004) – have been memes, spreading and working away in development discourse and practice.

In the following sections, eight ideas or elements are presented that may have the potential to transform practice and performance in development:

1   behaviour as entry point;
2   behaviour and attitudes of teachers, trainers and facilitators;
3   activities for ABC;
4   codes of practice and respect;
5   the personal impacts of participation;
6   'deeper' training, learning and change;
7   space and time for reflection and change; and
8   experiential learning through research and reflection.

Attitudes, ego and power: Behaviour as entry point

The six PAR words concern power relations, and touch on the ego and the self. Partnership implies equality when power relations are usually unequal. A corollary of empowerment is disempowerment, handing over, and allowing and encouraging others to do what may be beyond one's control and unpredictable. Ownership implies that ownership and credit for successes are not claimed but attributed to others. Participation in its fuller forms means that others claim control and autonomy. Accountability means being beholden for one's behaviour towards others, with downward accountability reversing power relations. And transparency brings with it vulnerability to scrutiny and criticism.

Attitudes, ego and power can be confronted boldly and directly. That will be right for some and may be part of the wave of the future. At the same time, it can be simpler and safer to start with behaviour. Behaviour can be altered more easily than attitudes; attitudes can be changed more easily than values; and values are often less fixed than beliefs. Awareness of, and changes in, behaviour can occur at the level of play, fun and practice. In contrast, changes in beliefs and values require something deeper. Confronted directly, they are the stuff of evangelism. Changes in behaviour, and the experiences and reflection that can follow, are less intrusive, less committing, more open to experiment, and respect each person's right to interpret experience and draw their own conclusions. It is one thing to say to a person: 'You should, like me, be a believer in Buddhism (or Christianity, Confucianism, Hinduism, Islam, Judaism or another faith).' It is quite another to say: 'Try doing this; see what you experience, and reflect; make up your own mind.' Changing behaviour generates new experiences, reflections, learning and relationships, which in turn lead to changes at other levels.

Small changes in behaviour that at first sight appear trivial or tokenistic can prove significant. Changing seats in a vehicle, or sitting quietly on the ground, may seem inconsequential but can help to level relationships and enhance learning (see Box 6.1). Many of the changes in behaviour that make a difference concern power relations – handing over the stick (or pen, or chalk), sitting down, listening, learning, not criticizing, not interrupting and so on. As Box 6.1 illustrates, after 'uppers' change their behaviour, 'lowers' may come out with things they would not otherwise have said.

> ## Box 6.1 How behaviour affects the power balance and what we are told
>
> *On our way to a community review session with a group of partner staff, we decided to change power relations by not sitting in the air-conditioned front seat of the land cruiser. The partners were initially reluctant to sit in front; but when they did, after our insistence, several things happened.*
>
> *We started sweating profusely and our heads started banging the roof of the car. They, however, opened up and gave us details of community activities/problems that they would previously not have told us. Power was immediately levelled and we became colleagues/partners (Lewis Aritho, ActionAid Kenya, cited in Owusu 2001).*
>
> In a workshop in Iran, after I had sat silent for a minute on the ground, lower than the participants, one of them pointed out that at the start of the workshop I had been culturally insensitive: I had told people to write their first names on their name tags. They had followed the instruction, but for many their first name was not the name they were known by. Had I not been quiet, and lower, I doubt whether I would have been told this.

Behaviour and attitudes of teachers, trainers and facilitators

The top-down transfer of knowledge is embedded in most education systems and establishments. It is even fixed in the infrastructure of amphitheatres, lecture halls, seating arrangements and seminar rooms, and in the setting and facilities of flip charts, blackboards, whiteboards, screens, overhead projectors, slide projectors, videos and now power point. Perhaps more important, however, is the socialization and expectations of teachers, trainers and facilitators, who expect to transfer knowledge, and of students, trainees and participants, who expect to receive it. Those who are turned out as finished proto-professionals by traditional top-down teaching systems are then conditioned to behave likewise in the bureaucracies that they join and in their relationships with clients. The top-down cultures, behaviours and attitudes of normal teaching and normal bureaucracy are congruent and mutually reinforcing. All this is well enough known.

The scope for more participatory approaches, and for substituting learning for teaching, is both vast and exhilarating. The literature on participatory learning goes back decades and is continuously being augmented.[10] Unfortunately, much PRA training, especially but not only early on in government institutions, has been in the traditional didactic mode, neglecting behaviour and attitudes. I have seen a syllabus for a ten-day training in PRA at an extension education centre in which behaviour and attitudes were not even mentioned. I have also seen a sequence of six videos of a PRA training that appeared to consist of nothing but a lecturer lecturing about participation. As self-awareness increases, though, such practices should become less common.

One hopeful tendency is the evolution of individual practice. Many, perhaps most, of those who introduce others to PRA have experienced a transition of style and practice from teaching and training to facilitating, and from treating people as students and trainees to recognizing them not just as participants who take part, but as colleagues, contributors and co-learners. In part, this is through a progressive use of 'ask them' and recognition that 'they can do it'. It used to take me 20 minutes to 'teach' the method of matrix scoring; but I have now found that three or four minutes is better, with minimum basics giving space for learning through practice and creativity, 'using your own best judgement'. Box 6.2 illustrates how far this can go: participants are not taught theory, but theorize from their own practice.

Box 6.2 A case study about teaching PRA techniques

Until a year ago, while conducting a PRA training we used to give a long background of PRA to the participants before they go to practice in the field. We would also describe the key features of each PRA technique and tell them the steps for using them. There used to be temptations from both sides . . . especially in TOT training of trainers to 'clarify' everything about the techniques first, only then go to practice in the field.

In a REFLECT training (*training* of local facilitators) conducted in El Salvador in January 1998, just after the introduction of participants and facilitators we directly started mapping the area. The participants had never done mapping and had not read anything about it. They produced a beautiful community map within two hours and also shared experiences and observations about various aspects of the village life.

Later we asked the participants to reflect . . . in small buzz groups, how exactly they could produce such a good map. They then wrote down one or two pages about the steps and process of their work, as well as copied the map from ground to paper. We as trainers benefited more from this experience. We could learn how we can learn by doing and why it is not necessary to give theory first. Participants can theorise from their own practice.

Source: Bimal Phnuyal (pers comm, 1998)

Ideally, then, a trainer or facilitator models the behaviour and attitudes that are appropriate. Most obviously, this can be through providing participants with experiences that act as opportunities to express and analyse their own realities and experience and come to their own conclusions. Going further, a starting point can be making space for participants 'to negotiate what the training will be about, how it will proceed and what it can accomplish' (Norrish, 1994). Curriculum development can then itself be participatory with 'students' (Taylor, 2003). The Asian Health Institute, an NGO in Japan, starts its five-week courses with blank sheets of paper on which participants plan the programme. They say what they hope for and would like. Faculty members say what is on offer and what they can do. The blank sheets are then gradually filled up. Their principles are:

- Each is responsible for own learning.
- Process becomes content.
- Learning is thinking, feeling, acting.
- Equal responsibilities.

A participatory training methodology developed in India is also dynamic: 'whilst participants themselves work towards solutions, they are also continuously helping the facilitators [trainers] to evolve the training design' (Saxena and Pradhan, 2002, p59). A course or workshop becomes a co-production with co-learning.

These are far cries, indeed, from traditional top-down, 'we know best' course planning, lecturing or, for that matter, intrusive evangelism.

Activities for ABC

There are many games, exercises and activities for ABC that can be used in workshops.[11] These have many labels and styles. What the numerous sources show is that there are many ways of helping one another learn and change. If there is a gap, it concerns reflection: how one thinks critically about an experience and internalizes whatever there may be to learn and change. In PRA experience, the most effective experiences are not in workshops, but in the field with members of communities. Four examples can illustrate:

1   The first is where 'uppers' are taught by 'lowers', sometimes known as LAST (lowers as teachers). This reverses relationships and is often fun. Uppers tend to be clumsy. They learn respect for lowers' skills and lowers gain in confidence.
2   The second is awareness and correction of behaviour in field situations. One approach is a contract drawn up together by a team, with dos and don'ts, and with a code of (usually non-verbal) signs to give positive or negative feedback between team members. Another, evolved by Anil Shah in India, is 'shoulder-tapping' (see Box 6.3).
3   A third activity is taking a video of participants (and facilitators!) This works well if participants are helping villagers or slum dwellers in their daily tasks. The videos are later played back to participants and also to the local people. The effects can be variously painful[12] and hilarious, leading to leveling and learning, as well as laughter.
4   A fourth approach is to reverse roles. Sam Joseph (1995) has described what he calls Win–Win Trainings in which villagers are co-trainers and facilitators for outsiders. Agreement is negotiated that villagers will host and manage a field experience in which outsiders stay overnight in the village and the village is paid for the service provided.

Box 6.3 Shoulder-tapping

Anil Shah gave this account of a village visit by a group of district officers in India. He explained that the purpose of a transect was to observe. His account continues:

We do not advise, but ask – ask open-ended questions without implied advice. I told the officers that it was very difficult for educated people, more so for those in authority, not to give advice. Therefore, when I hear anyone giving advice or asking questions with implicit advice, I tap his shoulder and, if necessary, offer my services to rephrase the advice or query to turn it into an open-ended question.

Shah described this exchange concerning earth bunds. One of the visiting officers said to Dudhabai (a villager):

'You should not collect earth.' 'Sir, you are advising', I said. 'What is it you want to say?' I intervened in English.

'Earth should be collected from the upward slope of a bund so that the leveling process is speeded up', he explained.

I then asked on his behalf: 'Why do you collect earth from both sides for constructing a bund?'

Dudhabhai was ready with his explanation. 'Bunding work should result in minimum loss of cultivable land. By taking earth from both sides, the depression formed is shallow and we are able to raise a crop very close to the bund.'

Shah concludes that ' Even if it starts mechanically and artificially, a PRA exercise can, perhaps, contribute to the opening of mind, more so if someone is around to tap the shoulder when one starts to advise instead of listening and learning.'

Source: Shah (1991, pp103–106).

Codes of practice and respect

Codes of behaviour that respect others can be part of good change. These can apply to all relationships, especially those of 'uppers' with 'lowers'. They can be drawn up individually or collectively. They can be private or public, mandatory or advisory. They can encourage hearing what 'others' say and sensing what they feel. Codes of practice can be based on informed consent and respect for others. The more the other person is socially stigmatized, vulnerable and powerless, so the greater the tendency is to treat the other as an object. By the same token, respect becomes all the more important in the relationship.

Debt-bonded sex workers are a case in point. Various combinations of debt, isolation (they are often far from home), illegality, gender (most are women) discrimination and social exclusion make them exceptionally powerless. Ethical guidelines for participatory research with sex workers can be based on the realities and feelings that they express (see Box 6.4). The questions they raise, and the behaviour and attitudes they request, may well apply equally to others who are variously marginalized, powerless, regarded as incapable or considered criminal, disreputable or irresponsible – whether they are physically disabled, mentally ill, drug addicts, street children, prisoners, squatters, refugees, illegal immigrants, or others. The issues and behaviours concern power, ownership, sharing, respect, trustworthiness, transparency and accountability.

Box 6.4 Ethical guidelines for participatory research with sex workers

The principles listed below reflect the voices of debt-bonded sex workers in different countries in Asia. They begin with the premise that all research projects adopt trust and equity as their core values:

- **OWNERSHIP:** 'It's our life, right?' Research projects must be committed to the principle that ownership and control of the project rests with the sex workers.
- **RESPECT FOR SELF-IDENTIFICATION:** 'Let us tell you who we are.' Research must address sex workers as they see themselves, and not as others see them.
- **CONSULTATION:** 'We know many things you do not know. You know many things we do not know. Let's share together.' Projects should be conducted through a consultative process, giving respect to the opinions and choices of sex workers.
- **VOLUNTARY PARTICIPATION:** 'Today, many decisions are made for us. We want to be able to decide for ourselves.' In sex work situations, women may be subtly coerced or unduly influenced to engage in research. Sex workers should be able to enter into research voluntarily and with adequate information.
- **CONFIDENTIALITY:** 'Many people want to harm us with their looks and their words, their laws and their policies. We need to be careful; we need to be private.' Researchers should inform sex workers about plans for confidentiality for each stage of the research.
- **TRANSPARENCY:** 'Tell us again who you are and what you are doing, again and again.' All aspects of the research process should be open to scrutiny and criticism (e.g. which information is being gathered and why, what roles different members of staff play).
- **ACCOUNTABILITY:** 'How can we ever really know what you are doing? You live in another world from us.' Build bridges to ensure accountability (e.g. translate materials, report back continually, allow sex workers to choose a monitoring committee).

Source: Developed by Jackie Pollock, affiliated with EMPOWER, an organization of sex workers in Thailand (Pollock, 2002)

Participation and ownership apply to codes of practice themselves. The codes of others can provide ideas and inspiration. But they are likely to be better, mean more and make more difference if they are drawn up jointly by those who will be affected by the codes (the lowers) and those who are to practice them (the uppers).

Personal impacts of participation

When PRA and participatory approaches, more generally, are adopted in organizations, changes in behaviour are quite often reported. In Vietnam, over a period of years, as a PRA approach in the Vietnam–Sweden Forestry Cooperation Programme was piloted and then spread, extension workers 'became sensitized to the knowledge and capabilities of farmers, and accepted the importance of involving farmers in the planning and development process. . . Over time, there was a noticeable change in the way extension staff approached and worked with problems of local resource management and village development' (Paul, 2001, p66).

Insights into the personal impacts of participation can be found in individual statements. One source is the Pathways to Participation project of IDS Sussex Participation Group.[13] This set out in January 1999 to evaluate experience with PRA. It built on the tradition of critical reflection embedded in many participatory methodologies. PRA trainers, facilitators and practitioners in eight countries were invited to reflect on their experiences. The project went into depth in Kenya, Mexico, Nepal and The Gambia. Another source is the disarmingly frank statements of personal attitude and behaviour made by participants in the 1996 ABC workshop in India (Kumar, 1996, pp17–22). I can also draw on changes I have experienced, how I have seen others react and what they have said. Again and again, those who have taken part in participatory training (especially those who have facilitated, watched and taken part in participatory approaches and methods) have said that the experience led to personal change. This does not always happen. Nonetheless, people repeatedly say that there have been changes not just in their attitudes and how they behave, but in themselves as people and in their values and personal philosophies.

One experience that quite often has a startling impact is the discovery that 'they can do it': that local people who are variously poor, illiterate, female and low status have a greater capacity to map, diagram and present and analyse complexity than most outsider professionals expect. Thus Neela Mukherjee, with a background in economics and applied econometrics, the author of several books on PRA (see, for example, Mukherjee, 1995, 2001), writing about a PRA training in which she took part in 1991:

> *I felt that the methods were not relevant, interesting or rigorous. Then we went to the field and in the village we agreed to have positive attitudes and respect the community. My problem was not in respecting people. I just wanted to know what we would gain from respecting people and using stones and so on. I was invited into the hut of a poor agricultural labourer in the most marginalised part of the village. We asked the old man in the hut to show the village in a sketch map and gave him some chalks. This was the turning point of my life. He started sketching the village, showing the poorest huts – the only ones he knew.*

> *I was amazed to see the professional expertise with which this illiterate man used seeds and chalks. I was also impressed with the wealth of information and how he was enjoying telling people his history. I got many answers from that one day in the field (Mukharjee in Kumar, 1996, p20).*

Not all change is as it seems. Behaviour can be superficial and artificial, laid on for the context or to impress someone, especially someone powerful or influential. Behaviour can also be compartmentalized – participatory in the field, but not in the office or the home. Such inconsistency, dissonance and hypocrisy have been noted by reflective practitioners in Nepal (Pratt, 2001). But for some, participatory behaviour flows from fieldwork to the office, affecting management styles and practices, and to the home, affecting relationships there. One manager in Nepal said that he noticed a trend when doing interviews for management positions:

> *I ask them what kind of management style do they have. All of them, surprisingly, say they use participatory management style. And it seems that even in the organizational culture, in management, this participatory approach is there . . . even in the management practices, people are using it very much . . . in terms of making decisions . . . we encourage people to give their views, consulting with all levels of staff before coming to decisions, allowing them to come together. And even using some of the [PRA] tools, like preference ranking, to solve problems (cited in Pratt, 2001, p56).*

In search of deeper training, learning and change

My horror of evangelism and of being 'got at' to change,[14] has held me back from facilitation that opens up deeper questions. The reader may not endorse my preference to start with behaviour rather than attitudes, values or beliefs. It is a personal thing. For whatever reasons, I have preferred to play it safe on the surface with a focus on fun (see, for example, Chambers, 2002). This weakness need not be imitated by others. One great frontier is to evolve and spread approaches that can help oneself and others to change profound attitudes, as well as behaviours. On this subject there is a mass of experience and literature from psychotherapy, including group psychotherapy. In participatory development, one effective ideology has been Training for Transformation, also known as DELTA (Development Education and Leadership Teams in Action) (Hope and Timmel, 1984),[15] with repeated reflective training in Freirian and Christian traditions. Another approach has been that of the CDRA (Community Development Resource Association) in Cape Town, its inspiring annual reports,[16] and Allan Kaplan's *Development Practitioners and Social Process: Artists of the Invisible* (Kaplan, 2002), most chapters of which conclude with a reflective exercise.

In India, R. S. Saxena and S. K. Pradhan (2002) have been, as they put it, 'in search of a meaningful participatory training methodology'. They find the top-down attitudes of officials reinforced by caste, class and the belief that suffering and poverty in this life are punishments for the ill deeds of the previous incarnation. A complete role reversal is required; but with conventional training they found that attitudes did not change. So they have evolved a participatory workshop process with reflection on attitudes for attaining success, on personal strengths and weaknesses, and on building positive attitudes. Participants construct a personal self-image profile with two columns ('I am' and 'I need to be') for personal attitudes and characteristics, with 'excellent' and 'needs improvement' listed below for behaviours. Fieldwork with communities is stressed, and win–win situations in which participants, communities and the overall project all gain. A participant commented on coming to understand what Gandhi meant when he said: 'You must be the change you wish to see in the world.'

Some of the best experiential learning enables a person to feel what it is like to be another. The learning may not be immediate; rather, it may work itself through over time. An example was a ten-day workshop in Bangladesh of ActionAid staff from around the world, held in 2001. It was billed as a Participatory Methodologies Forum. I was one of those who went expecting to share ideas and methods. A planning team that convened days before the workshop evolved different ideas and facilitated a workshop that was about power (for an excellent account, see *Transforming Power* ActionAid, 2001b). The disappointed expectations and deep frustration some of us felt were themselves a source of learning about how others experience our behaviour. As participants put it:

> *The planning team denied that it had an agenda. We do that all the time in communities – starting apparently open-ended participatory processes when really we do have an agenda all the time. We have objectives and strategies which may be out of synch with communities. How can we become more open and transparent?*

> *Now we know what it is like to be 'participated at'. Participatory processes can disempower people. They risk wasting the time of people who have less time to waste than us. We got impatient with the planning team, and communities get impatient with us*

Space and time for critical reflection and change

One of the most pervasive weaknesses of development agencies is the failure to provide staff with opportunities for experiential learning and time for reflection. Many are caught up in a culture of over-commitment, long hours and intensive work. This is particularly acute in NGOs. Those who are taken as role models work into the night, and start again as soon as they wake up. For them, continuous work is an addictive drug. Staff who go home 'on time' feel guilty. Families suffer, as does personal learning and change. They see no need for courses. What matters is to get on with the urgent jobs to hand.

There are many manifestations of this systemic pathology across development agencies. Though bilaterals and multilaterals often have both funds and opportunities to send their staff for field learning experiences, most of them seem to take them up quite rarely. Of over 700 participants in the seven annual PRA Thematic International Workshops organized in India by PRAXIS (the Institute for Participatory Practices), one could count on two hands the number of individuals who have come from multilateral or bilateral aid agencies.[17] And one bilateral donor staff member had to take leave to come.

Yet, time is needed, without pressures and without rush, to ask the 'big' questions, and to understand others' worldviews and tacit and explicit ideas (Dyck et al, 2001, pp617–618). Many organizations convene annual workshops and retreats, but often with overloaded agendas, too much show and tell, too many meetings on the side, and too little time for reflection. Any time allocated is invaded by other sessions that run on, and by contributors who complain that they have been excluded. Parkinson's Law[18] has a corollary: that retreat workshop presentations prolong and proliferate to overflow the time available.

There is, however, a discernible trend. In writing, more and more authors are prepared to struggle to be honest about their feelings, failures and learning. Tony Vaux in *The Selfish Altruist* (2001) reflects critically and with disarming honesty on his experiences in relief work in famine and war; and several authors describe their experiences as facilitators in *The Art of Facilitating Participation* (White, 1999). Be it noted that the self-critical reflection we are discussing is a far cry from public confessions in totalitarian countries, or declarations of sinfulness in evangelical meetings. It is, rather, a quiet willingness to be reflexive, to share and learn from reflection and to treat mistakes as opportunities for mutual learning.

It is none too soon that the word *reflection* is re-entering the vocabulary of development. The *Pathways to Participation* project (Cornwall and Pratt, 2003) found that PRA practitioners valued critical reflection. PRA itself illustrates the shift. For most of the 1990s, its first decade, it retained its original meaning of 'participatory rural appraisal'. During the later 1990s, the Pakistan PRA network redefined it as 'participation, reflection and action',[19] and this meaning has spread.

The Community Development Resource Association in South Africa, in its report *Measuring Development* (CDRA, 2001, pp10–11) has this to say:

> *There is a peculiar form of self-abasement amongst development workers – donors and practitioners alike. It begins with the fairly righteous stance that we may not spend money intended for the poor on our own development. So we tend not to make time to learn. Yet, this lack of respect for ourselves as our most important 'instruments' in the development project results very quickly in a lack of respect-in-practice for those we claim to serve . . . we value action over learning, often doing things to the poor that are inappropriate, even destructive. The benign and laudable claim that resources should go to those they are intended for quickly becomes a more harmful refusal to learn from experience.*

Mahila Samatha (see pp74–75) sets aside one tenth of staff time for personal development.[20] I know of no other organization that does so. Responsible management in development organizations, one would have thought, would insist on reflective retreats, whether individual or collective, for its staff. Self-critical reflection and respecting the self are still blind spots in development, even though they are a starting point for transforming practice and performance.

There is a danger, though. Things can go too far the other way. Too much time can be taken. Groups themselves can then become addictive, narcissistic and overly inward-looking. Facilitators can become institutions, like psychoanalysts with their patients. Diminishing returns can set in. After a year of an organizational change process, one DFID field office reportedly declared that it had had enough and wanted to be free to get on with the job. Critical reflection, retreats and renewal are to be optimized, not maximized. The Sida participation group that met once a month for a year and a half called itself *Lagom*, which means 'not too much, not too little – just enough' in Swedish, a term reflecting the group's desire to engage optimally with the process, and not spend too much, or too little, time and energy on it (Cornwall, Pratt and Scott-Villiers, 2004, pp6–7).

Direct experiential learning through research, immersions and reflection

Chapter 2 noted the shift of aid agencies from field projects to policy dialogue and sector and direct budget support, and the increasing tendency for their staff to be trapped in capital cities. Before, with field-based projects, there were reasons to travel and some chance of 'ground-truthing'. Today, the more that aid agencies stress pro-poor policies, the more their staff are trapped, willing or unwilling prisoners, corralled and cocooned in offices and meetings in headquarters and in capital cities, and isolated from the poor. In the words of a Sida staff member:

> In the 1970s, there were more chances to work in the field. Now there's virtually no chance to work with reality. Now we have all these policies on rights, democracy, etc; but they're all part of a make-believe world that is so disconnected from what is really going on (Andrea Cornwall, pers comm).

Direct, profound and empathetic experience with poor people seems now largely limited to committed workers in some Southern organizations. In some of these, both fieldworkers and leadership are closely involved, face to face, in the struggles of poor people. There are examples in India. SEWA, the trade union of self-employed women, has adopted and developed the exposure and dialogue approach of immersion, living with poor people, and then reflection as part of its staff induction and management system (SEWA, 2002). The leaders of MKSS (Movement for the Empowerment of Peasants and Workers) in Rajasthan, an NGO that has been dramatically successful in its tenacious and courageous struggle against corruption, have lifestyles and ways of working that are close to those of the poor. The Arthik Anusenda Kendra in the Mirzapur district of Uttar Pradesh is another such NGO, outstanding in its commitment to enabling the victims of endemic discrimination and exploitation to claim their rights and gain a decent livelihood. And Harsh Mander (2001) in *Unheard Voices: Stories of Forgotten Lives*, brings home through the written word the awfulness and inspiration of the lives of poor people whom most of us never encounter, but only see or imagine from a distance. There are also inspiring examples in other countries.

In dissonant contrast with the daily lives of poor people, however, there is a culture of workshops and conferences about development that has its own pathology. How many readers have been invited and gone to a workshop or conference on poverty? And how many workshops or conferences are held in posh hotels? For myself, I am ashamed at the thought. For years I was outraged. Such hotels should not even exist, let alone host comfortable conferences on poverty, with all their attendant hypocrisy. But the privilege of the comfortable bed, the television set, the World Service of the BBC and not just CNN, the almost obscene quantity and choice of food at breakfast – these seep into one's expectations and come to appear as the norm, even a right. We truly are the pigs in George Orwell's *Animal Farm*. But then, the host organizers feel that they need to welcome their guests appropriately and be 'up to international standards'. Well, of course there has to be a business centre or center so that participants can access their emails. And for the organizers there can be a financial dilemma: the hotel offers a special discount that is cheaper than the NGO training centre.[21] The politically correct comes with its price. And so the 'norm' is repeated. Yet, the most memorable workshops I have been to, and where I have learnt most, have been in 'remote' rural places, sleeping on the floor and sharing snoring, cold water and basic amenities. As is so often the case, mild discomfort and congenial conviviality have been directly related. For two of the best of these experiences (both in Nepal), it took hours to walk in.

Two ways forward through experiential learning appear full of promise.

The first is for development professionals, whether in funding agencies, governments or civil society, to undertake field research in PPAs (participatory poverty assessments) themselves. At the end of her review of 'The self in participatory poverty research', McGee (2002, pp14–43) concludes that 'policy-makers knowing poverty through immersion in the unfamiliar terrain of daily deprivation and struggle for survival' can become a new channel through which participatory poverty research can impact upon policy. In 1998, the UNDP PPA in Shinyanga region in Tanzania may have been the first in which government officials were key researchers. In the UPPAP (Uganda Participatory Poverty Appraisal Process) five officials took part in each the nine districts (Yates and Okello, 2002, p76).

A further step forward was an innovation of SDC (the Swiss agency for Development and Cooperation) in Tanzania in late 2002. This showed how a cheap, short research effort can have a big impact on researchers. As part of its country programme formulation, SDC organized a four-week participatory and qualitative study with 26 poor rural and urban households, and a few focus groups. The researchers were SDC and project staff. One activity was to 'blend into' an ordinary day with a very poor family. Poor people drew pictures and used cameras to show significant aspects of their lives and aspirations, receiving albums of photographs as a thank you afterwards. The staff initially felt that they knew about poverty, but were shocked by what they found. There were striking insights – for example, how much more important shelter and quality of housing were to poor people than had been supposed (Jupp et al, 2003). Most striking of all was how personally and professionally transformational this was for the researchers (see Box 6.5). Afterwards, they often referred to this *Views of the Poor* research when making a point (Jupp, 2004, p13). Seeing, hearing, experiencing and learning directly and personally confers confidence and authority, as well as relevance and realism.

Box 6.5 Reflections of participatory poverty researchers, Tanzania

I thought I knew about village life as my roots are in the village and I still visit family in my village from time to time. But I know nothing about what it is like to be poor and how hidden this kind of poverty can be.

I could not believe that the family only had one broken hoe to cultivate with. It was like trying to dig with a teaspoon. I will never forget that.

The image of the baby crying all day with hunger will always be with me.

I've worked in rural villages for more than 20 years; but I have never had an experience like this.

Even village leaders could not tell you what we experienced for ourselves.

We hear the untold stories. It was an eye opener as families shared their problems which would never be aired in group meetings. They treated us like confidantes.

We had no idea what poverty was really like until we were involved in this study.

Source: Jupp (2004, pp4–5) and Dee Jupp, pers comm

Such participatory research requires experienced and sensitive training and facilitation.[22] Subject to that, its potential contribution to personal and professional development, and to pro-poor commitment and grounded realism, would seem almost unbounded.

The second way forward involves immersions in which development professionals experience life with poor people.[23] These immersions are usually for a few days, preceded by preparation and followed by reflection. Common features are accompanying an individual's daily life and helping with daily tasks; staying overnights;[24] learning and writing up life histories; casual encounters through wandering around; and a period of reflection afterwards. Sometimes there is a specific focus of interest or research. The participant may be 'abandoned' (Joseph, 1995), but is more commonly supported by a guide and facilitator, who also acts as interpreter, if necessary.

Immersions are not new. They are integral to social anthropologists' methodology. George Orwell (1933) spent months *Down and Out in London and Paris*. In the late 1930s, Hans Singer lived with unemployed families in the UK as part of the influential Pilgrim Trust study of unemployment. As his biographer records: 'the [research] team was to immerse itself in the lives of the unemployed by living with them in the poor areas of the country' (Shaw, 2002, p21). It is only during the past two decades, however, that immersions have begun, albeit slowly, to spread. In the 1980s, Karl Osner evolved the methodology of the EDP (APNSD, 2002), and with his leadership the NGO Justitia et Pax organized field immersions with poor people. These were taken up by some in GTZ and BMZ, and by some leaders in Germany; as of 2004, such immersions have taken place over 50 times. EDP immersions have been adopted and internalized by the trade union SEWA in India for the induction and orientation of new staff. For its part, the World Bank under James Wolfensohn has encouraged immersions for its senior staff, carried out through GRIP (the Grassroots Immersion Programme) and the VIP (Village Immersion Programme) in the South Asia region, which involves a wide range of staff. Several hundred World Bank staff members have had the experience. The best-known immersion was that of Ravi Kanbur in Gujarat, whose (1999) account was widely circulated and influential, not least for the *World Development Report 2000/2001:Attacking Poverty* (World Bank, 2000). For some NGOs, living and working in communities is their mode of operation. And ActionAid India has required or encouraged its staff to spend up to two weeks a year living in communities.

Strangely, apart from the World Bank, no other multilateral or bilateral agency is known to have yet adopted immersions as official policy.[25] There is more and more talk of experiential learning, critical self-awareness and realism about poverty. Immersions for development professionals are an obvious means of achieving these. Many organizations claim to be serious about the MDGs (Millennium Development Goals), pro-poor policy and practice, and making a difference for the better. But the claim rings hollow while their staff remain isolated and trapped by workshops, meetings and emails. Doctors meet their patients. Psychotherapists listen to their clients. Can policy-makers understand and prescribe well without being with poor people and understanding their lives, livelihoods, conditions and priorities? Furthermore, how well can they be fired by anger, passion and commitment in attacking poverty unless they have been close to it? Unfortunately, intelligent professionals who would gain most are good at finding reasons why they should not go. Some think they do not need to. Others think they have enough field experience already. There is growing testimony that they are wrong; but in the meantime, both they and poor people are the losers.

A staff member of a bilateral reflected:

> *I have asked myself what would have happened if I had spent one week per year in a village somewhere over the past decade. I am quite sure it would have made a difference to me. Ten different contexts, and a number of faces and names, to have in mind when reading, thinking, writing, taking decisions and arguing in our bureaucracy.*

The case is obvious and should be overwhelming. As and when regular immersions become widely accepted and adopted as good practice for development professionals, the gains for poor people (in ways that they value) should be very large indeed.

In late 2003, having been hosted by Kamlaben, a member of SEWA, in an immersion, Judy Edstrom wrote of:

> . . . *feeling that I have learned so much from this courageous woman, that my own sense of adversity pales next to what Kamlaben has confronted and overcome. I feel humbled by this woman and believe that when a challenge confronts me in the future, I can honestly ask myself one of two questions. First, 'would Kamlaben have this option?' to put the query in perspective. Or second, 'what would Kamlaben do in this situation?' Not in the sense of being confronted with the same challenges, but of seeking to find the straightforward answer that keeps close to the Truth – family, health, spirituality and, most of all, a sense of personal dignity.*

It is here that we approach the 'beyond' of 'beyond behaviour and attitudes'. The testimonies of those who have lived, however briefly, with poor and marginalized hosts indicate how this can be a source of deeper change and, some would say, transformation. It is not predictable; it is not assured; it is not even necessary as a justification; but, empirically, it is common. The personal meeting, as a learner and guest with a poor person as teacher and host, the challenge to know how best to behave, and the need to adapt and be natural – the sheer unfamiliarity of it all, with so much to take in, and then afterwards the opportunity to review, reflect and digest the experience – are a powerful combination. The result can be more than new insights and things learnt. It can challenge values and beliefs, and raise questions about the sort of people we are and want to be, and what we do.

Notes

1   This section is based on the later revision (published in Balakrishan, 1998, pp108–121) of a paper of the same title, 'Behaviour and attitudes: A missing link in agricultural science', presented at the Second International Crops Science Congress, New Delhi, and published in V. L.Chopra et al (eds) *Crop Productivity and Sustainability: Shaping the Future* (Chambers, 1998). I hesitated over the assertive arrogance of the paper's title. My own behaviour and attitudes ought to reflect the self-doubt, openness to error and respect for the knowledge of others that I advocate. For the Congress, the editors and transcribers toned it down by transforming 'science' into 'scene', a correction I have re-corrected. Twice I have added and removed a question mark at the end.

2   For an elaboration of this distinction, see the Introduction in Chambers, Pacey and Thrupp (eds) (1989).

3   For a number of striking demonstrations of the potential of CDR agriculture, see a remarkable collection edited by Norman Uphoff, *Agroecological Innovations* (Uphoff, 2002).

4   In 2004 this has to be qualified by noting that especially in parts of Eastern and Southern Africa, disability and death from HIV/AIDS have reduced rural labour availability and may well continue to do so for many years. Rural to urban migration is also a significant factor qualifying the generalization.

5   *Honey Bee*, edited by Anil Gupta, is a periodical that documents farmers' innovations, mainly but not only from India. For information, contact Professor Anil Gupta, Indian Institute of Management, Vastrapur, Ahmedabad.

6   For more on uppers and lowers see *Whose Reality Counts?* (Chambers, 1997a, pp58–60, 206–208).

7   For a fuller account and references, see *Whose Reality Counts?* (Chambers, 1997a, Chapter 5, 'All power deceives').

8   Farmers' participation with scientists in breeding has since become more widely accepted and practised, not least in the CGIAR (Consultative Group for International Agricultural Research) system.

9   *ABC of PRA* (Kumar, 1996) is available from PRAXIS (Institute for Participatory Practices, C – 75, South Extension Part II, New Delhi – 100 049, India) and also at www.praxisindia.org.

10   See, for example, Chambers and Stevens (2002) for an annotated list (updated in a 2003 reprint) of 21 sources for ideas and activities for participatory workshops and how to obtain them, and Peter Taylor and Jude Fransman (2003, 2004) for numerous recent sources on learning and teaching participation in higher-education institutions.

11   See Chambers (2002, pp165–179) for some ABC exercises.

12   A video that showed me messing up with an overhead projector, trying and failing to find a transparency, was so embarrassing that I could not bring myself to see it again. But the memory is there, and the lesson indelibly etched.

13   See Cornwall and Pratt (2003)and Cornwall, Musyoki and Pratt (2001) for Kenya; Pratt (2001) for Nepal; and Holmes (2001) for The Gambia.

14   A horror of evangelism is itself an attitude. I recognize some of its origin in myself in the boarding school experience of being asked repeatedly by one of the masters whether I had yet 'taken the step' of 'bringing Jesus into my life'. I was damned if I was going to take the step. I am still damned, and still abhor missionary intrusiveness.

15   In Shinyanga region in Tanzania, in 1998, there was a one-week workshop for district-level staff from eight districts. Those from one district stood out from the rest for their attitudes and behaviour: sitting down, showing respect, listening, facilitating, not dominating. I asked them what made them different. They said they had had PRA training a few years earlier. I was surprised and impressed. But when I probed, they revealed that before the PRA they had had three DELTA trainings. Almost certainly, I concluded, the DELTA, not the PRA, training would explain most of the difference.

16   The CDRA annual reports are really annual reflections. I warmly recommend them. They can be accessed at www.cdra.org.za.

17   CARE is the closest to a bilateral or multilateral agency that has sent a number of staff.

18   Parkinson's Law, proposed by C. Northcote Parkinson in a book of that name, is that work expands to fill the time available for its completion.

19   'Participation, action and reflection' would have been better; but the acronym PAR already stood for 'participatory action research', and confusion would have resulted. Reflection and action interact; but reflection is best when grounded in the experience of action.

20   Organizations with dangerous tasks and plenty of time in between them, such as fire fighters, may spend quite a lot of time *training*; but that is not the same as action-reflection and critical self-awareness.

21   This was said to be the case in Amman, when some queried why a regional PRA workshop was held in a central hotel when it could have been in a less central NGO training centre. I have also been rebuked for the relative luxury of the hotel in Brighton, where we once put workshop participants for reasons of economy (a special deal) and convenience.

22   Much valuable experience and advice is to be found in Jupp (2004).

23   For some of the history, see Ledesma and Osner (1988); Osner (1999, 2002); Osner and Kraus (2000); and McGee (2002, pp34–35), whose chapter 'The self in participatory poverty research' is full of relevant insights. Staff of GTZ and BMZ, and German parliamentarians, have over the years taken part in EDPs (Exposure and Dialogue Programmes); but EDPs are not required as a matter of internal policy in those organizations. For a review of immersions, see Eyben (2004c) and Irvine et al (2004), which has references to various sources. For an overview of EDP and for its use for dialogue on key issues, see Osner (2004).

24   In a workshop on immersions held at IDS Sussex in December 2003, staying overnight was considered a non-negotiable, with three nights a good minimum.

25   However, among the multilaterals, IFAD (International Fund for Agricultural Development) is considering it, in conjunction with SEWA, and there is interest in several bilaterals.

7

For Our Future

Responsible Well-being: A personal agenda for development[1]

It is not that we should simply seek new and better ways for managing society, the economy and the world. The point is that we should fundamentally change how we behave (Havel, 1992).

What we need is an impassioned, intellectually honest, and, above all, open-ended debate about how each person should best conduct his or her life (Forsyth, 1991, p269).

The theme of this chapter is personal reflection and responsibility. Part 1 is an editorial written for *World Development*, and concerns realities, power and personal agendas for development. Part 2 expands and extends the analysis and proposes concepts and actions to transform development.

Part 1: Responsible Well-being: A Personal Agenda for Development (1995)

If development means good change, questions arise about what is good, and what sorts of change matter. Answers can be personally defined and redefined. The changing words, meanings and concepts of development discourse both reflect and influence what is done. The realities of the powerful tend to dominate. Drawing on experience with participatory approaches and methods which enable poor and marginalized people to express their realities, responsible well-being is proposed as a central concept for a development agenda. This links with capabilities and livelihoods, and is based on equity and sustainability as principles. The primacy of personal actions and non-actions in 'development' points to the need for a pedagogy for the non-oppressed. This includes self-critical awareness, thinking through the effects of actions, and enabling those with power and wealth to experience being better off with less. Others are invited and encouraged to reflect, improve on this analysis, and write their own agenda.

Introduction

To write about a development agenda is rash and perhaps arrogant. There are multiple realities – ecological, economic, social, political, and personal. Change accelerates and uncontrolled global forces make prediction ever harder. Any development agenda is value-laden, and some academics abhor anything that smacks of moralizing. Yet not to ask questions about values is value-laden by default, and not to consider good things to do is a tacit surrender to professional conditioning, personal reflexes, and fatalism. Perhaps the right course is for each of us to reflect, articulate and share our own ideas about values, problems, potentials and priorities, accepting these as provisional and fallible. Paraphrasing Heraclitus, we can then recognize that concerning what we think and what we should do, nothing will be permanent but change. Right behaviour then includes trying to understand ourselves and changing what we do. Doubt, self-awareness and embracing error are virtues. This means that while thinking and acting, we also question how we think, what we think, and the rightness of what we do. It is in that tentative and self-doubting spirit that this editorial is written.

What is development?

The eternal challenge of development is to do better. Usually this is tackled by identifying policies, programmes and projects. Both the *Human Development Report 1997* (UNDP, 1997) and the *World Development Report 1997* (World Bank, 1997) follow in a long tradition by listing policies and actions to make the world a better place, especially for the poor. The argument of this editorial is that this does not go far enough. There is a crucial missing link. We need to add the personal dimension. This implies stepping back and engaging in critical self-examination. To do better, we have to examine not just the normally defined agenda of development 'out there;' but ourselves, how our ideas are formed, how we think, how we change, and what we do and do not do.

Words are a starting point. Fritjof Capra (1996, p282) has put it that:

> The uniqueness of being human lies in our ability to continually weave the linguistic network in which we are embedded. To be human is to exist in language. In language we coordinate our behaviour, and together in language we bring forth our world.

For professionals committed to development, the world we wish to bring forth is linked to what we mean by development.

On the cover *of The Development Dictionary* (Sachs, 1992), a sentence by Wolfgang Sachs proclaims, 'The idea of Development stands today like a ruin in the intellectual landscape. Its shadow obscures our vision.' In an editorial in the *Forest Trees and People Newsletter* (1995, pp26–27) Daphne Thuvesson has written 'As the existing system crumbles around us, new and exciting alternatives are sprouting up in the rubble.'

Sachs's pessimism and Thuvesson's optimism are both needed.[2] The record of 'development' is mixed. Those who damn the errors, failures and deficits tend to ignore the counterfactual, how much worse things could have been if nothing had been done. Those who laud achievements and successes tend to overlook how much better things might have been even than they were. A balanced view has to recognize renewals and continuities in the landscape as well as ruins and rubble, and older trees as well as new sprouts.

To explore the terrain, let us start, as *The Development Dictionary* does, by examining words and concepts that are common currency in contemporary development discourse and with which we seek to 'bring forth our world'.

Development has been taken to mean different things at different times, in different places, and by different people in different professions and organizations. The dominant meanings have been those attributed by economists and used in economics.

Development has thus often been equated with economic development, and economic development in turn with economic growth, often abbreviated simply to growth. But the meanings given to development have also evolved,[3] not least through the concept of human development in the *Human Development Reports* of UNDP. In all cases, though, however clinical the analysis or disparate the definitions, the word seems to have had two aspects: it has been normative; and it has involved change. So the underlying meaning of development has been good change. That is the sense in which it is used here. Views have differed, and perhaps always should and will differ, about what is good and what sorts of change are significant.

Change is continuous in what changes and how it changes, and in what we see as good. All this is reflected in words and meanings. These are both formative and adaptive: they both influence and express conditions, ideologies, perceptions, practices and priorities. That vocabularies and meanings evolve is then itself necessary and good, and both cause and effect of other changes.

A changing vocabulary

So it has been that new words are continuously introduced and spread. Additions to the common lexicon of development have been prolific. New words have been added faster than old have fallen into disuse. Some such as integrated, coordinated, planning and socialism have peaked and passed into decline. Others in the eclectic and perhaps ephemeral language of post-modernism, such as deconstruction, narrative and meta-narrative, text and subtext, have largely languished in academic and literary backwaters. Others, such as equity and poverty, have been robust and resilient. Yet others, some old, some new, which have come close to the mainstream of much development discourse during the past two decades include:

accountability, capabilities, civil society, consumer, decentralization, democracy, deprivation. diversity, empowerment, entitlement, environment, gender, globalization, governance, human rights, livelihood, market, ownership, participation, partnership, pluralism, process, stakeholder, sustainability, transparency, vulnerability, well-being.

Of these, only three – environment, market and participation – receive chapters in *The Development Dictionary*.

The power of language

The power of vocabulary to change how we think and what we do is easy to underestimate. It influences the course of development in many ways: through changing the agenda; through modifying mindsets; through legitimating new actions; and through stimulating and focusing research and learning.

New language is easily dismissed as rhetoric or jargon. Seasoned sceptics can see changes in words and meanings as transient, superficial and insignificant. Those impelled by authority or prudence to use new words signal their cynicism by dubbing them 'buzz words', 'flavour of the month' and 'politically correct'. So consultants, bureaucrats, and those seeking contracts, support, security or promotion tap out and parrot[4] the latest vocabulary.

Language is, however, about much more than rhetoric and opportunism. It shapes and interacts with the ways we think and behave. An obvious case is gender syntax. Reversing 'he or she' to 'she or he', or using 'she' as the pronoun for 'the African farmer,' have not come easily to many, but their capacity to challenge and shock, and their gradual acceptance, have been a small but significant bridgehead into male-biased thinking and patriarchy. So in our development context, we can see that language has helped to bring forth and change the world of development professionals. This has happened in three ways: introducing, stressing and defining words; combining them in new ways; and listing and disaggregating.

Introducing, emphasizing and defining words

How the thinking and actions of development professionals may have been affected over the past two decades can be assessed by reflecting on the contexts of the words listed above. Table 7.1 shows how they can be separated.

A personal impression is that 20 years ago none of these, except equity and poverty, was as prominent as today. Increasingly, these words are embedded in the mindsets of development professionals, and increasingly used by them

Table 7.1 *Development vocabulary*

The human condition	Capabilities, deprivation, entitlement, livelihood, poverty, vulnerability, well-being
Organization, power and relationships	Accountability, consumer, decentralization, empowerment, ownership, participation, partnership, process, stakeholder, transparency
Domains and dimensions	Civil society, environment, globalization, governance, market
Values	Democracy, diversity, equity, gender, human rights, pluralism, sustainability

unreflectively, that is to say, without forcing, and without feeling insecure or self-conscious or a need to justify or explain their use. In this process they change how development realities are constructed and seen. An example is the new and specialized meanings of capabilities and of entitlements as progressively elaborated by Amartya Sen (1981, 1985). New words can also confront old. Livelihood has been put forward as a challenge to the reductionism and specificity of employment. Deprivation has been put forward as a challenge to the narrowness of poverty.

Combining words

Combinations of words have been influential in three ways.

First, they have been used to focus and present radical concepts in a technical guise. *Primary stakeholders* as proposed in the World Bank,[5] is a technical phrase which implies a priority for poor people affected positively or negatively by a policy, project or programme. The term was widely welcomed and applauded but reportedly had to be put in cold storage by the Bank because of political pressures from governments in the South. But by then it had escaped and had a life of its own. *Social development* was not much used 20 years ago, but now there are many social development advisers, and the Social Development Summit was held in Copenhagen in 1995.

Second, combining words can expand disciplinary views and provide bridges between disciplines. Put negatively 'Like blinkers, the terms we adopt to express ourselves limit the range of our view' (Capra, 1996, p268). Put positively, we can expand and alter our view and what we do by combining terms. This can be illustrated by the shift in priorities and thinking that has been taking place from things and infrastructure to people and capabilities. As the importance of people has risen in the development agenda, the practical question has been how to help the professions, notably engineering and economics, that have dominated donor agencies especially the World Bank, to accommodate the new priorities. The transition has been eased linguistically by applying to people the familiar language and concepts of things and numbers. So we have learned to speak of *human capital, human infrastructure, human resource development, social infrastructure, social investment,* and now *social capital.* On the negative side, these may standardize, depersonalize, and miss much that matters to people, and may purport to measure what cannot meaningfully be measured. On the positive side, they make it easier for economists to incorporate people and social institutions in their mental and mathematical models.

Third, combinations of words can be formative, starting largely undefined and presenting a challenge and opportunity to provide a meaning, as this editorial does below with *responsible well-being. Sustainable livelihoods* was embodied in the title of a conference (Conroy and Litvinoff, 1988), caught on as a phrase, and then was progressively explored and elaborated for meanings of sustainable, of livelihood, and of the two words taken together (e.g. Bernstein et al, 1992; Chambers and Conway, 1992). *Social exclusion* opens up a new perspective on deprivation. Most recently, *state capability* (World Bank, 1997) draws attention to what a state can and should do in relation to its ability to act.

Listing and disaggregating

Listing and disaggregating are means of qualifying the reductionism of much development thinking. Listing adds diversity and complexity. Disaggregating unpacks concepts. Thus the reductionism of poverty defined for professional convenience by a single measure of income or consumption has been qualified in three ways: by listing and examining other dimensions of deprivation, such as vulnerability, physical weakness, powerlessness, discrimination, humiliation and social exclusion; by separating out aspects of poverty itself, and using the terms income-poverty (as in UNDP, 1997) or consumption poverty for that subset which is normally measured and used for comparisons; and by enabling poor people themselves to use their own words and concepts to express, list and analyse their realities – local, complex, diverse, dynamic and uncontrollable as they so often are (Chambers, 1997a, Chapter 8).

Whose language counts?

If vocabulary can make so much difference, we must ask: who changes the words we use? Whose language brings forth our world and guides our actions? Who defines what words mean?

The world brought forth is usually constructed by the powerful in central places or by those well placed to influence them. The words and concepts of development both express and form the mindsets and values of dominant linguistic groups, disciplines and professions, and organizations. Among linguistic groups, the English language is, irreversibly it seems, the most influential. Other transnational languages such as Arabic, Chinese, French, Portuguese, Russian and Spanish – can dominate national and other vernaculars. Among disciplines and professions, the words and concepts of engineering preoccupied with things, and applied economics preoccupied with quantification, still set the agenda and vocabulary of much development discourse. The procedures which fit and reinforce their paradigms, such as the logical framework and social cost-benefit analysis, are authoritatively taught and required. Among organizations, those clustered in the Eastern United States are pervasively influential, including the World Bank and the IMF (International Monetary Fund), with the greatest concentration of development professionals, power and intellectual capability in the world; UNDP increasingly through the *Human Development Report*; and the US government. These are major sources of new vocabulary and ideas which gain currency. The President of the World Bank, in particular, exercises enormous power over development thinking and action through the words he,[6] or his speech-writers, choose to use. Robert McNamara's 1973 Nairobi speech on poverty is an example, followed now by James Wolfensohn's promotion of participation.

Personal values and concepts

All, though, need not be determined by the powerful, from the central cores and from above. Richard Forsyth (1991) has presented a challenge for each person to devise her or his own religion. Similarly, development professionals, in a spirit of self-doubting pluralism, can help one another by drawing up and sharing personal lists and patterns of values and concepts, and seeing where and how these differ and cohere. There is space here for reflection on how one's personal realities and values have been formed, and to choose, change and give meaning to a personal list of words and concepts. There is scope here too to give priority to the values and preferences of the weak.

For all development professionals, there are many sources of values, vision and concepts. The great religions will always be sources of inspiration to explore for values and vision. For analytical concepts and insights there are now numerous new sources. The theories of chaos, edge of chaos and complexity (Gleick, 1988; Resnick, 1994; Waldrop, 1994) contribute insights and analogies: how complex self-organizing systems can be based on few rules, with parallels in decentralized, democratic and diverse human organization; how small actions at certain times can have huge effects later, pointing to the power of individual choice and responsibility; and how there can be zones of stability in turbulence, suggesting reassertions of continuities even in chaotic conditions. The new ecology contributes understandings of local heterogeneity, networks, dynamism, sequences, transitions and synergies, with continuous change and adaptation: in Capra's (1996, p295) words, some of the basic principles are 'interdependence, recycling, partnership, flexibility, diversity and, as a consequence of all those, sustainability'. Other sources include soft systems theory (Checkland, 1981) and management theory and practice (e.g. Handy, 1989; Peters, 1989; Senge, 1990). Sources such as these present vocabularies, concepts and ways of thinking to be tapped and more can be expected.

Another source is the experience with PRA (participatory rural appraisal). This has influenced my own view. Others will judge for themselves whether for them too it may help. PRA[7] is a family of continuously evolving approaches, methods, values and behaviours which has turned much that is conventional on its head. It seeks to enable local and marginalized people to share, enhance and analyse their knowledge of life and conditions, and to plan, act, monitor and evaluate. In its philosophy, practice and vocabulary it has come to stress:

- the question 'whose reality counts?' raising issues of equity and empowerment, and of enabling women, poor people and others who are marginalized to express their realities and make them count;
- the primacy of the personal, especially behaviour and attitudes, and exercising personal judgement and responsibility.

Let us examine these in turn.

Whose reality counts?

In our world of global communication, those who are connected electronically are a new exclusive elite. Those who are not connected to internet, email and fax are a new group of the excluded. At the same time, the realities of professionals and of poor people are notoriously disparate. Again and again the realities of those who are poor and marginalized are ignored or misread. The challenge is how to give voice to those who are left out and to make their reality count.

Participatory methodologies, perhaps most notably PRA, have shown both power and popularity in enabling those who are subordinate to express their realities.[8] Insights and priorities have included, for example, the importance of all-weather roads for access to medical treatment and markets during the rains, the need to reschedule the timing of school fees away from the most difficult time of year, and training health staff to be friendly and respectful to poor people seeking treatment. In Bangladesh, where the focus of analysis by poor people was on 'doables,' differences in priorities between women and men, and between urban and rural, were highlighted (UNDP, 1996). The first doable priority of urban women was drinking water, and the second private places for washing. A widespread desire of poor people was enforcement of the anti-dowry laws. Elsewhere, a better understanding of sectoral priorities, for example between health and education, has also resulted.

Thematic investigations using PRA approaches and methods have also illuminated local realities in a range of contexts, for example:

- area stigma – how living in an area with a bad reputation for violence makes it difficult to get jobs (from Jamaica – Moser and Holland, 1997);
- how a quarter of girls of school age were 'invisible' to the official system (from The Gambia – Kane et al, 1998);
- how the problems and priorities of women differ not only from those of men but also between women depending on their access to basic services and infrastructures, and their social background (from Morocco – Shah and Bourarach, 1995);
- how an official belief that indigenous tenure systems no longer existed was wrong, and how diverse and crucial they were (from Guinea – Freudenberger, 1998);
- the ability of local people to define sustainable management and conservation practices for themselves (from India and Pakistan – Gujja et al, 1998).

Strikingly, through PRA processes local people have again and again presented values and preferences which differ from those of outsiders or those supposed for local people by outsiders. When asked to card sort households in what was originally wealth ranking (Grandin, 1988) local people have so consistently sorted not by wealth but by some composite concept close to well-being, that the process has been renamed well-being ranking. In well-being, income has often had a surprisingly low priority compared with health, family life, respect and social values.[9] Empirically, well-being and its close equivalents seem to express a widespread human value open to diverse local and individual definitions.

PPAs and PRA approaches and methods are not panaceas. They do, though, present new opportunities for policy influence on behalf of those normally excluded. They can bring poor people and policy-makers together in new ways. They can present realities in visual diagrams with a new credibility. To the question

'Whose voice counts?' they have shown that the answer can be, more than before, the voices of those previously unheard.

Personal behaviour and attitudes

The experience of PRA has been expressed in, or leads to, words and concepts which have not been prominent in mainstream development thinking. Some of these are commitment, disempowerment, doubt, fulfillment, fun,[10] generosity,[11] responsibility, self-critical awareness, sharing, and trust.

These have had little place in the headlines of the literature of development. None features as a chapter heading in the *Development Dictionary* (Sachs, 1992).[12] In addition, PRA has adopted and evolved a number of injunctions:

* Ask them
* Be nice to people.
* Don't rush.
* Embrace error.
* Facilitate.
* Hand over the stick.
* Have fun.
* Relax.
* They can do it (i.e. have confidence that people are capable).

Strikingly, these words, phrases and injunctions point to personal behaviour and attitudes. The three original pillars of PRA (Mascarenhas et al, 1991) were:

1 methods (many involving visualizations through diagramming, mapping, scoring and so on);
2 sharing;
3 behaviour and attitudes.

There is a growing consensus that of these, by far the most important are behaviour and attitudes (see, e.g. Absalom et al, 1995; Kumar, 1996; Blackburn with Holland, 1998). Yet these have been absent from most professional training and from most agendas of development. Taken together with the one-sentence manual: 'Use your own best judgement at all times', the experience and ethics of PRA stress not just personal behaviour and attitudes, but personal responsibility.

Responsible well-being

The two themes generated by the PRA experience – locally defined concepts of well-being, and personal responsibility – can be combined as responsible well-being, a two-word concept to explore. The challenge is to see what this might mean for all people, in their relations with themselves, with others, and with the environment. Two basic principles on which there is wide agreement are equity and sustainability. Two elements which are both ends and means in development thinking are livelihood and capabilities.[13] These can be linked with each other as in Figure 7.1.

The overarching end is well-being, supported by capabilities and livelihood. Equity and sustainability as principles qualify livelihood to become livelihood *security*, and well-being to become *responsible* well-being.

Each word can be presented in a statement:

* *The objective of development is well-being for all.* Well-being can be described as the experience of good quality of life. Well-being and its opposite, ill-being, differ from wealth and poverty. Well-being and ill-being are words with equivalents in many languages. Unlike wealth, well-being is open to the whole range of human experience, social, psychological and spiritual as well as material. It has many elements. Each person can define it for herself or himself. Perhaps most people would agree to including living standards, access to basic services, security and freedom from fear, health, good relations with others, friendship, love, peace of mind, choice, creativity, fulfillment and fun. Extreme poverty and ill-being go together, but the link between wealth and well-being is weak or even negative: reducing poverty usually diminishes ill-being; amassing wealth does not assure well-being and may diminish it.
* *Livelihood security is basic to well-being.* Livelihood can be defined as adequate stocks and flows of food and cash to meet basic needs and to support well-being. Security refers to secure rights, physical safety and reliable access to resources, food and income, and basic services. It includes tangible and intangible assets to offset risk, ease shocks and meet contingencies.[14] Sustainable livelihoods maintain or enhance resource productivity on a long-term basis, and equitable livelihoods maintain or enhance the livelihoods and well-being of others.
* *Capabilities are a means to livelihood and well-being.* Capabilities refers to what people are capable of doing and being. They are a means to livelihood and fulfilment, and their enlargement through learning, practice, training and education are a means to better living and to well-being.
* *Equity: the poor, weak, vulnerable and exploited should come first.* Equity qualifies all initiatives in development. Equity includes human rights, intergenerational and gender equity, and the reversals of putting the last first and the first last, to be considered in all contexts. The reversals are not absolute, but to balance and level.
* *Sustainability: to be good, conditions and change must be sustainable – economically, socially, institutionally and environmentally.* Sustainability means that long-term perspectives should apply to all policies and actions, with sustainable well-being and sustainable livelihood as objectives for present and future generations.

When well-being is qualified by equity and sustainability it becomes responsible well-being, as the overarching end, to which all else is means. Well-being is then not at the cost of equity and sustainability, but is enhanced when it contributes to them. Responsible well-being recognizes obligations to others, both those alive

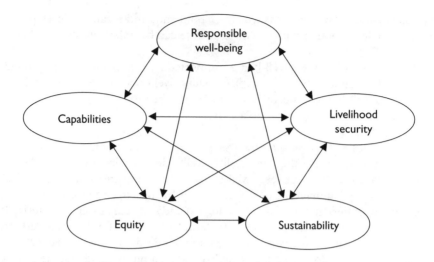

Note: The overarching end is well-being, with capabilities and livelihood as a means. Equity and sustainability are principles that qualify livelihood to become livelihood *security*, and well-being to become *responsible* well-being.

Figure 7.1 *The web of responsible well-being*

and future generations, and to their quality of life. In general, the word 'responsible' has moral force in proportion to wealth and power: the wealthier and more powerful people are, the greater the actual or potential impact of their actions or inactions, and so the greater the scope and need for their well-being to be responsible. Responsible well-being refers thus to doing as well as being; it is 'by' as well as 'for'. The objective of development then becomes responsible well-being by all and for all.

The primacy of the personal

Because the responsible of responsible well-being applies to all human beings, it points to the personal dimension.

The neglect of the personal dimension in development at first sight seems bizarre. It is self-evident to the point of embarrassment that most of what happens is the result of what sort of people we are, how we perceive realities, and what we do and do not do. Whether change is good or bad is largely determined by personal actions, whether by political leaders, officials, professionals or local people, by international currency speculators, executives of transnational corporations, non-NGO workers, or researchers, by mothers, fathers or children, or by soldiers, secret agents, journalists, lawyers, police, or protesters. Especially, what happens depends on those who are powerful and wealthy. One might have supposed then that trying to understand and change their perceptions, motivations and behaviours would have been at the centre of development and development studies, and a major concern for the IMF, the World Bank, other donor agencies, governments and NGOs. Yet there have been few studies of individual officials as leaders.[15] Studies of greed and generosity are few.[16] There are quite a number of institutes devoted to development studies but there is, to my knowledge, no institute devoted to the study of greed or power.

Part of the neglect stems from academic culture with its anathema of evangelism, its value of objectivity, and its search for general rather than individual explanations. More potently, perhaps, the neglect is a defence. It can disturb profoundly to reflect on what one does and does not do. It embarrasses to be confronted by poverty and suffering compared with one's own condition. When a poor farmer in India asked me my income I could not reply. To put the personal to the fore in this editorial is to expose my own hypocrisy and to make it difficult to continue. But hypocrisy is no excuse for silence.

The enormity of this missing link is illustrated by the most recent *Human Development* and *World Development Reports* (UNDP, 1997; World Bank, 1997). The *Human Development Report* 1997 is concerned with poverty. It recommends six essential actions – empowering individuals, households and communities; strengthening gender equality; accelerating pro-poor growth; improving the management of globalization; ensuring an active state; and taking special actions for special situations. All of these require action by those who are powerful and relatively wealthy. For its part, the *World Development Report 1997* is devoted to The State in a Changing World. It presents many recommendations for action. In recognizing the importance of leadership and vision (e.g. pp14, 123, 154–155, 166), noting political constraints and vested interests, and lamenting the 'unbridled pursuit of riches or power' (p159) it gets closer to the personal. But it does not go the whole way. It does not come to terms with the need for personal change. Where the moving force is to come from is not clear. Incentives are recommended, but the question remains who determines and pushes through the incentives? Neither report confronts the personal dimension.

In contrast, the concept of responsible well-being puts the personal in the centre. Responsible well-being is an individual condition. The major issue is how to encourage and enable the powerful and wealthy accept this ideal, or something close to it, and to define it for themselves in ways which make things better for those who are weak and poor.

A pedagogy for the non-oppressed[17]

For responsible well-being, it is then especially individuals who are powerful and wealthy who have to change. This entails confronting and transforming abuses of power and wealth. For this, one need is for a pedagogy for the non-oppressed (including ourselves, the sort of people who read *World Development*), to enable us to think and act differently. There are many disparate domains for analysis and action, among them: how we treat and bring up children; how to achieve reconciliation after conflict; how donor agency staff behave on mission (as noted by Taylor, 1997, pp151–152); how to rehabilitate those who have suffered a PhD.

Besides these and others, and relating directly to responsible well-being, three areas stand out for methodological innovation and application.

(a) How to facilitate personal change and self-critical epistemological awareness

Methodologies exist, and more are needed, to facilitate personal awareness, including epistemological awareness – meaning being self-critically aware of how we learn and mislearn and how we construct our realities. It is difficult to exaggerate the central importance of this subject. The degree to which economists have been found to disagree (see, e.g. Frey et al, 1984, pp986–989) is, to a non-economist, alarming when they exercise so much power. It is also striking how dramatically their dominant views change, as illustrated in Hans Singer's (Singer, 1997) earlier editorial on 'The Golden Age of the Keynesian Consensus – The Pendulum Swings Back'. Part of the way to resolve differences between economists, and to enable them to be more in touch and less wrong, is through self-aware introspection; it is through reflection to understand how their views, like those of others, have been formed, and to be open to doubt and embracing error.

Similarly, reflection and awareness of interpersonal behaviour and power relations is critical. On the behaviour and perceptions of donor staff on mission and of host government staff who deal with them, depends the well-being of millions of poor people. Because of their power, such missions are vulnerable to being misled. Yet to my knowledge they have never been studied or documented beyond the level of personal anecdote.

The implication is programmes for self-critical awareness, and attitude and behaviour change, which, in turn, have implications for bureaucratic recruitment, procedures, incentives and cultures. The World Bank, under the leadership of James Wolfensohn, is attempting to grasp this nettle. Senior staff are not only to receive exposure to management practices in institutions such as Harvard, but are also to have a week of immersion in a village or slum. This may seem a small innovation. It is, though, a major departure from past practice, and if it lasts and spreads, may prove a defining watershed of change.

(b) How to enable those with power and wealth to think through and recognize the effects of their actions and non-actions

The truism of 'out of sight, out of mind' has awesome implications for those with power to make a difference. A little reflection on causal chains will suggest that a decision in a meeting in Washington to hold a poor African country to debt repayments will kill children; but those who make the decision will never see this, and never be called to account. Indeed, they deserve sympathy and understanding for the responsibility they shoulder, though those they harm deserve an altogether different level of compassion.

A mechanism is needed for such meetings, and for individual decisions and actions, for thinking through the implications. Lessons could be learned from therapeutic jurisprudence where attempts are made to identify the effects of proposed laws. With development decisions two advocates could be appointed to argue, one on behalf of women, children, the poor and the excluded, and one on behalf of future generations, in each case analysing and presenting likely effects of alternatives. The causal and linkage diagramming which has proved effective in PRA could be part of the analysis.

Many of the key decisions that affect the poor are made by those who work for transnational corporations. Nothing said here should weaken the normal means of trying to influence them through ethical investments and consumption, through organized pressure and through governments. But in addition, they too can be invited to define responsible well-being for themselves; they too are human and capable of good actions. At the launch of the *Human Development Report* 1997, the Nobel Peace Prize laureate Oscar Arias asked whether aerospace executives who sold arms to countries with bad human rights records would read the diaries of those in prison. Perhaps those executives should be invited and encouraged, again and again, to read those diaries, and to analyse, in a participatory way, the causal links between their arms sales and the repression and imprisonment of others. Perhaps all of us could and should do the same for our actions and inactions, using visual diagramming as a tool. Perhaps companies should be shamed who do not include advocates of the poor and of future generations in their deliberations. If some would show leadership in these directions, others might follow.

(c) How to enable those with more wealth and power to welcome having less

For well-being to be responsible, in a sustainable global eco-social system, those with more have to accept having less. This applies to both wealth and power. The biggest challenge for development as good change in the long term, is to find more ways in which those with more wealth and power will not just accept having less, but will welcome it as a means to well-being, to a better quality of life.

Much normal thinking about wealth and power is zero-sum. In this thinking, for those with less to gain, those with more must have less, and so lose. If all are assumed to be selfish, zero-sum conflict can appear inevitable. But as Norman Uphoff (1992) has argued, there is scope for positive sum thinking and action. In conflict resolution there are often gains for all. Generosity brings its own non-material rewards. Empowering others can be deeply satisfying. The PRA experience of changing dominating behaviour, sitting down, handing over the stick, and enabling others to conduct their own analysis and explore their own realities, has often been a source of excitement, fun, fulfillment and learning for all those concerned. The needs and opportunities here have barely begun to be recognized. The methodological challenge is to find more ways for reversing the normal view: for those with wealth and power to find and feel themselves better off with less; for having less in material terms to be experienced as a gain; and for disempowering oneself to empower others to be experienced as positive.

Overview

In a context of accelerating change, words and concepts will continue to succeed one another. The question is whether in the volatile and transient vocabulary of development, some stable continuity of core concepts, continuously redefined, can or should be sought. An analogy from chaos theory is a strange attractor, a pattern continuously reaffirmed in turbulence, like the Red Spot on Jupiter. The same words or concepts might then be used, in the same relations with each other, as in the web of responsible well-being, while being constantly reexamined and redefined both collectively and individually.

Responsible well-being, interlinked with capabilities and livelihood, and with foundations in principles of equity and sustainability, is simply one set of concepts inviting exploration. Whether it can serve a common purpose others can judge. Whether concepts such as these can go further and be drivers for good change is for trial. In the spirit of the one sentence manual adopted in PRA – 'Use your own best judgement at all times' – each development professional can critically reflect, and draw up and use a personal list of ends and means. Perhaps what we should seek, then, is not consensus but pluralism, not a conclusion but a process, and not permanence but change in evolving concepts. For that we need an ethic of action, self-critical reflection, search and sharing.

In that spirit, let me conclude by inviting and encouraging others to reflect, to think out their own concepts and definitions, and to write and share their own editorials, improving on what has been presented here.

Part 2: To Transform Development (2004)

Since 1997 the polarization of power and wealth in the world has become even more extreme. The personal dimension is central in mediating every big issue but continues to be relatively neglected. Words and concepts used in development have remained potent. Social capital and sustainable livelihoods have met needs in powerful organizations and have been widely adopted and influential. Responsible well-being, pointing to individual agency, has languished at the same time as the scope for action and impact has been enhanced by growing interconnectedness. The methodologies proposed earlier are needed more than ever. So are new lines of thinking: to complement rights of the poorer and weaker with obligations of the richer and more powerful, worldwide and between all levels; to recognize power and relationships as central issues; to integrate institutional and personal change; to ground pro-poor policies and practice in realism; to think for oneself and take responsibility; to choose words and identify priorities for oneself; and to seek guidance by reflecting on what a poor person would wish one to do.

Between 1997 – when the editorial that is the first part of this chapter was written – and today, much has happened. Polarization has been galloping ahead. Wealth and power have become more blatantly unequal and inequitable than ever. In world politics, pathologies of power, greed, misinformation, ignorance and aggression have manifested themselves repeatedly, most recently in the invasion of Iraq and its sequel. In much development aid, the big shifts have been away from earlier, more project-oriented, approaches towards policy influence and direct budget support. The diversity and complexity of poverty, and of the livelihoods and aspirations of poor people, have become better recognized. International campaigns like Jubilee 2000 for debt relief have had some successes. In development studies and practices, though, despite all these changes, there is still a sense of treading water, or swimming in treacle, or running up a downward-moving escalator. Much energy is expended; but the structures remain little changed. Institutions reproduce themselves. People are socialized into behaving much the same as their predecessors. It is as though we need something new – a key, or springboard, or launching pad, or point of departure. It is alarming that so little changes. Something is missing. There has to be a better way of going about things.

I may not have answers; but let us at least revisit some of the analysis in the 1997 editorial. The main points made earlier apply now with more force than ever.

Evolving ideas, words and concepts

With the continuing rapid evolution, adoption and relegation of ideas, policies and practices in development, words have continued to change. Since 1997, there have been newcomers to the list. These are words and concerns most of which were around before, but which have become more central. Poverty reduction strategy papers (PRSPs) and the Millennium Development Goals (MDGs) have become prominent in development policy. The MDGs, in particular, have become both mantra and focus in the official development discourse. Almost every document performs an obeisance in their direction. *Human rights*, too, are now a more accepted concern, and for many NGOs *rights-based approaches* (RBAs) have increasingly been espoused, overlaying earlier approaches based on needs. *Citizenship* has also come in, with attention to democratic processes, accountability, and civic and political rights and activism. *Corruption* is more openly raised and discussed, ironically at the same time as it has increased in the most powerful nation. *Multidimensional* as a word used to qualify poverty and deprivation was not in the 1997 list, and came in strongly with the *World Development Report 2000/ 2001:Attacking Poverty* (World Bank, 2000). It flags and expresses the departure from the reductionism of concepts of poverty based on only income or consumption. *Multi-stakeholder* has also made an appearance. *Congruence,* referring to consistency of behaviour, attitudes and relationships between actors, and between levels, organizations and locations, is increasingly used and if widely adopted would highlight the contradictions between centralizing, standardizing and autocratic organizational cultures, and personal styles and the rhetoric of participation, partnership, decentralization, diversity and democracy. *Relationships,* with the insight that these mediate all development processes (Eyben, 2004a), are more and more part of development discourse. Most significantly, *power* (see pp66ff), once almost a taboo word outside academic circles unless referring to local elites, is now freely spoken about and more honestly recognized, not just by radicals, but also by more of the powerful actors themselves.

Responsible well-being, though, has not been adopted and has not spread. If not stillborn, it has shown little sign of life. Apart from a moving personal account by Patta Scott-Villiers (2004), and an email from Richard Bawden using the term 'responsible, sustainable and inclusive well-being', I know of no case where it has been used. This is in spite of the wide circulation of *World Development*, in which the 1997 editorial was published, and some elaboration of the term in *Whose Reality Counts?* (Chambers, 1997a, pp9–12). In contrast, the concepts expressed by two other pairs of words – *social capital* and *sustainable livelihoods* – which were already current in 1997, have continued to spread and have become part of the common currency of development. Since my argument is that new words and concepts can make a difference, we can ask whether lessons can be learnt from why these have taken off and responsible well-being has not.

Social capital was used several times during the 20th century,[18] and after a long gestation in academia, rapidly spread to become common in development discourse during the late 1990s. Since about 1995, its rise has been meteoric and controversial (see, for example, Fine, 2001; Harriss, 2002; Eade, 2003). It is used as a portmanteau for 'relations of trust, reciprocity, common rules, norms and sanctions, and connectedness in institutions' (Pretty and Ward, 2001). It can also variously include friendship, mutual support, networks, respect, solidarity and social cohesion, and even 'the glue that binds society together'.[19] Its explosive adoption and spread has its recent origins in Robert Putnam's 20 years of research and statistical analysis in Italy, which found a correlation between 'civic engagement' and economic development (Putnam, 1993) and provoked considerable academic criticism.

The concept of social capital met needs in the World Bank (Bebbington et al, 2004).[20] First, it gave non-economist social scientists a credible means of persuading economists of the significance of social factors in development – for example, a study of social capital (Narayan and Pritchett, 1997), econometric in focus, produced correlations that suggested that lack of social capital was a powerful determinant of household poverty. Second, and as persuasively argued by John Harriss (2002), it was a means of depoliticizing development, evading questions of inequalities of power and wealth. Third, it justified working with civil society rather than with local government. Though the concept and its applications were much disputed in academia, it was vigorously adopted, researched and spread in and by the World Bank, where it could be seen as the 'missing link' in development.[21]

Practitioners vary in their judgements of the practical utility of social capital. Not all would go as far as an observer of Jamaican experience who concluded: 'Understanding social capital means investing in the potential strengths of individuals, groups, and communities. It is the only path to development' (Wint, 2003, p413). But notwithstanding the critiques of why it has been so widely adopted, what *social capital* names and covers is important, and its very generality and inclusiveness is an asset as well as a liability.

Sustainable livelihoods has had a more steady but also extensive spread. The two words were used together in the May 1985 discussions of the Advisory Panel on Food Security, Agriculture, Forestry and Environment of the World Commission on Environment and Development and included in the Brundtland Report

(WCED, 1987b), which had a huge circulation and influence.[22] Then there was a large international conference, and the term was put in the title of the book that followed: *The Greening of Aid: Sustainable Livelihoods in Practice* (Conroy and Litvinoff, 1988). A big step was when analytical content was given in a diagram (Scoones, 1998), which included not only different forms of capital such as natural, human, financial and social,[23] but also institutions, providing a realistic and quite comprehensive checklist for practical analysis. Organizations, including Oxfam during the early 1990s and later DFID, adopted, developed and disseminated sustainable livelihood approaches. DFID set up a Sustainable Livelihoods Support Office as part of its Rural Livelihoods Department. IDS Sussex manages a website –'Livelihoods connect' (www.livelihoods.org) – for learning lessons and sharing experiences from practical applications of a sustainable livelihoods approach. And a prolific literature has been generated (see, for example, Carney, 1998, 2002; Carney et al, 1999; Hussein, 2002; Solesbury, 2003).

Besides meeting institutional needs, sustainable livelihoods had a lot else going for it. 'Sustainable' is a deeply significant and accepted environmental word that resonates with environmentalists and natural scientists, as well as with others. During the 1990s, livelihood largely replaced employment to make space for the actual complexity and diversity of how most poor people gain a living. It is also not difficult to see how sustainable qualifies livelihood and adds the dimension of security. Further, 'sustainable livelihoods' belongs to no one discipline and provides a common neutral ground on which all can meet. Nor in the way it is applied does it have moral, personal overtones. Although it could be used to point a critical finger at 'us' and the unsustainability of our livelihoods, it is used for 'them' and 'their' context, not for 'us' and 'ours'.

Responsible well-being shares with *social capital* and *sustainable livelihoods* the asset, seen by some academic critics as a liability, of a *portmanteau* character of commodious imprecision. This has the advantage of inviting many interpreters to give their own meanings, and provides space for many definitions and dimensions. Also, well-being, as an antonym to poverty, has a certain universality, with equivalents in different languages and cultures, and is widely accepted and used in development discourse.[24]

On other counts, though, *responsible well-being* has lacked the advantages of the other two. It does not lend itself to be the theme of an international conference. It has not, to my knowledge, been part of any international report.[25] It has virtually no literature. It has no institutional champion. It does not serve the interests of any organization. It has no internal political, persuasive and practical function, as social capital had for social scientists in the World Bank, and as sustainable livelihoods had for natural and social scientists in the DFID and elsewhere. It is difficult to see how it could be operationalized in a programme. It does not lend itself to research and is not based upon or supported by research, as social capital was seen to be with the work of Robert Putnam (1993), and as sustainable livelihoods has come to be. Its moral overtones do not commend it to academics or hard-nosed development professionals. Nor is it politically neutral. Social capital and sustainable livelihoods divert attention from inequalities in power relations and property rights; responsible well-being directs attention towards them.

Perhaps most of all, in pointing to personal responsibility, especially of the rich and powerful, *responsible well-being* discomforts and exposes those of us who are 'haves' for what we do and what we leave undone. It shares this with precisely that aspect of sustainable livelihoods, as described earlier (Chambers and Conway, 1992), which never took off. This was the idea that a sustainable livelihood should not damage but enhance the livelihoods of others (whether through claims, access, international trade, environmental effects or in other ways) now and/or in the future. This, of course, applies most to the rich and powerful, to their lifestyles, and to their impacts both on the livelihoods of others and on the environment through pollution, climate change and resource depletion. A worldwide campaign for awareness and abstinence was implied, one part of which could be personal-livelihood environmental balance sheets for the rich (ibid, p31). The concept of sustainable livelihoods has, however, been applied selectively only to the poor. As with so much of development research, discourse and action, the searchlight is not directed at 'us'. 'We' do not have to look at ourselves, only at 'them': those whom we seek to do good to, help and empower.

And yet, there is a universality to both sustainable livelihoods and responsible well-being. They both concern physical, social, political and ethical aspects of the human condition. Both raise questions of rights and obligations. They apply to all of us: we all need livelihoods; we all augment or weaken sustainability; our acts and omissions all affect the livelihoods of others; we all carry social and political responsibilities. However we see and express it, we all seek well-being. The sticking point, the barrier, is looking critically at *and changing* our own behaviour, that of the 'haves'. This demands something stronger, deeper and more explicit than words, and less easy to evade. Words may help; but they can never be enough.

Agency and responsibility

With the realities and narrow self-interest of the powerful dominating the world stage to a degree that few could have foreseen in 1997, responsible well-being, stressing responsible on the part of the 'haves' (those with power and wealth), is needed more now than ever. *Pro-poor* is stamped on every development document and repeated in every speech. But to my knowledge, not much progress has been made with the development or spread of the three pro-poor methodologies proposed in the 1997 editorial (see Part 1):

1 *personal change.* To be sure, there are immersions (see pp177–181); but they have not yet taken off, let alone become part of normal, expected professional practice. They are still a tiny side show, not mainstream priorities on the development agenda.
2 *thinking through effects of actions and non-actions.* An initiative in Zambia may, though, be a straw in the wind. This is an attempt to analyse what would be likely to happen with a proposed land reform. It includes a repeat, a decade later, in the same communities and by the same team, of the earlier PPA (Norton et al, 1994; Milimo et al, undated) focused this time on land reform issues, and combined with separate stakeholder and institutional analysis of organizations that would be involved (Anis Dani, pers comm).

3   *enabling those with more wealth and power to welcome having less.* There are efforts
like the Hunger Project which give the very rich psycho-social rewards for
parting with some of their money, and the Rockefeller Foundation sponsors
workshops for young heirs of fortunes. There are inspirations in great religions
and in the lives some people have led. But otherwise, is there anything that
could be called a pedagogy for the non-oppressed? Or more sharply, a pedagogy
for the oppressors? If so, where and what is it? And if not, why not? What is
wrong with us?

We have agency, the ability to act and change the world, and this brings with it
responsibility for the effects of actions and inactions. Responsibility is an unsmiling
word, often used critically: 'That is your responsibility', 'Who is responsible for
this?' and 'Who can we pin responsibility on?' – meaning, who can we blame? A
dictionary (Collins, 1998) gives these definitions:

> *Responsible: 1 . . . having control or authority (over). 2 . . . being accountable*
> *for one's actions and decisions . . . 3 (of position, duty, etc) involving decision*
> *and accountability. 4 being agent or cause (of some action) . . . 5 able to take*
> *rational decisions without supervision: accountable for one's actions . . . 6 able*
> *to meet financial obligations: of sound credit.*

All of us have agency and responsibility, and these vary with wealth and power
and rise or fall with socio-economic, political and technological change.

Recent years have seen a daunting, though largely un-remarked, rise in agency
and, with it, responsibility. Several factors have contributed to this. There is more
wealth in the world, and its distribution is more polarized and concentrated. The
same is true of power. At the same time, we are all more connected and more able
to exert influence than before. For those with money and access, the revolutions
in transport and communications have multiplied the number of activities that
are open. Mobile phones and email have transformed communications. Over the
past decade, for those with access to the internet and with money for travel, the
range of things to do that make a difference has risen exponentially, almost beyond
the reach of the imagination. It is easier than ever, and with a broader choice than
ever, for a middle-income person in an OECD country to choose to give money,
to team up with others who are like minded or to campaign for causes. The
responsibility of those with more power is even more awesome. The scope they
have, through their actions and inactions, to make a difference to those who are
marginalized, deprived and powerless simply blows the mind. A few, like George
Soros, seize their chances; but most do not.

One consequence of this heightened interconnectedness is that small actions
can be more significant. Two examples stand out. First, there is vulnerability to
small events that make a big difference. The so-called 'butterfly effect', where a
butterfly flapping its wings in one part of the world could lead to a storm in
another, was illustrated in the flawed Florida election, where a handful of votes
and chads tipped the balance to Bush, not Gore, with impacts which have touched
billions of people and will touch billions more in future generations.[26] The lesson
here is vigilance, commitment and the ever-increasing responsibility that American

citizens have towards their fellow human beings. The second example is collective action. As is amply illustrated in *Global Citizen Action* (Edwards and Gaventa, 2001), international action by citizens and civil society can be coordinated in ways that were almost unimaginable before the 1990s. The effective clout that can be mustered and applied is indicated by the degrees of success achieved by the protest that led to the World Bank's withdrawal from the Narmada Project in India, the landmines campaign, Jubilee 2000, and other international movements for human rights, social justice and the environment. Small actions have always been able to combine to become big movements; but now they can add up and be transmitted in ways we did not have earlier, and do this faster and on a global scale. It follows that since our scope for action is greater, so, too, is our responsibility.

The limits of responsibility are for debate. Questions are easy; answers are difficult, as two representative questions can show. The first is a question of commission, of something done: a campaign to promote bottled milk for babies in a poor country is successful. Thousands of mothers buy baby milk. As a result, thousands of children have diarrhoeal episodes, the termination of breast-feeding shortens birth intervals, families are poorer and children die who would not have died without the campaign. Who is responsible?

Similar questions can be asked about unsuccessful development projects;[27] about loans and debts incurred with the World Bank, the IMF, the regional development banks and commercial banks; about structural adjustment policies; about agricultural subsidies in North America and Europe; about the dumping of agricultural surpluses; and about quotas and tariffs erected by industrialized countries.

With questions of commission, there are problems of attribution. Many actors are involved, with many degrees of awareness or ignorance, wilful or otherwise. It is easy to deny the reality, to say that there were many other causes, to plead ignorance, or to blame others or the system: 'I was only doing my job.'

The second is a question of omission, of something not done. While writing a draft of this chapter, I saw an Oxfam Afghan crisis appeal in the newspaper, which stated in bold print: '**Just £25 from you could provide enough to feed two people for the winter.**' But I did not rush for my cheque book. Instead, I went back to my laptop to record this example. So, if people in Afghanistan go hungry, who is responsible? Am I?

The same question can be asked about other charities we do not support, about things we spend money on, about issues we do not raise in meetings, about corruption we do not confront, about human rights abuses we do not tackle, and about campaigns in which we do not take part.

With questions of omission, there are problems of awareness, linkages and choice. There is no shortage of excuses and evasions: the money would go on other things; other people will take care of this; this is something the government should do with the taxes I pay; I am already contributing to other causes; charity begins closer to home in my family and community; I would never know where the money went or whether it really made any difference; and I can't do everything.

There may be no simple answers. What matters is to puzzle again and again, to be alert and sensitive, and to keep on trying to see what best to do. And to rejoice that for many of us the choice is wider than before and continues to become wider still.

Readers will have their own sources of guidance and inspiration. Many are linked with the great religions and with cultures. Many are political, through movements and activism. For some, there is a primacy in politics, as Colin Leys (1970) argued so forcefully. Nothing here should detract from these. But in looking for ways forward, six lines of thinking look promising. Like responsible well-being, they invite exploration and application:

1   Adopting obligations-based approaches.
2   Transforming power and relationships.
3   Grounding pro-poor realism.
4   Congruence in personal and institutional change.
5   Reflexive responsibility and thinking for oneself.
6   'Ask them' for guidance on the way.

From rights to obligations

Rights-based approaches to development have been advocated and widely adopted. They have been pursued with most vigour by certain NGOs, with more caution by bilateral agencies, and not openly by the World Bank on the grounds that its charter constrains it to be non-political. The *Human Development Report 2000: Human Rights and Human Development* (UNDP, 2000) put rights high on the international agenda. DFID's (2000) paper *Realising Human Rights for Poor People* is another landmark, providing a framework and laying out an agenda with three cross-cutting principles: participation, inclusion and 'fulfilling obligation'. Also remarkable are the *Draft Guidelines:A Human Rights Approach to Poverty Reduction Strategies* (OHCHR, 2002) of the Office of the High Commissioner for Human Rights.

The scope of human rights as defined and ratified by many states in the International Bill of Rights[28] has been interpreted and extended beyond more strictly legal into more general social dimensions (see, for example, UNDP, 2000). To illustrate this breadth, these have included livelihood security (Moser and Norton, 2001) and the right to appear in public without shame (OHCHR, 2002, pp42–43).

Rights are one side of the coin. Whether they are considered socially constructed or (more usually) inherent in being human, they can be claimed by right-holders. Those who need to claim them most are those who enjoy them least. Obligations or duties[29] are the other side of the coin and apply most to those with wealth and power and who already more fully enjoy their rights. The Universal Declaration of Human Rights is applied mainly to the poor. There is no Universal Declaration of Human Obligations applied primarily to the rich. Why ever not?

Obligations to uphold and fulfil rights are normally construed to rest primarily with the state for its citizens. In practice, fulfilling the state's obligation proves quite weak, since many actors besides the state are implicated in whether or how much people, especially poor people, can enjoy their rights. This is the more so when rights extend beyond the political and legal spheres into those which are economic and social. In economic and social spheres the neo-liberal state is expected to do less – and there are, anyway, practical limits to what states can do. As Brian Pratt (2003) has observed: 'Proclamations at international conferences of economic, social and cultural rights, such as livelihoods, education, health and shelter, are barely worth the paper they are written on as they are not enforceable in the absence of a credible duty bearer.'

This turns our attention to other potential duty-bearers besides the state. One view is that the duty to avoid depriving others 'must be universal and therefore applies to every individual and institution, including corporations' (Shue, 1980, p112, cited in Stammers, 1995, p496).

To what extent *non-state institutional* actors – for example, transnational corporations (TNCs) – have legal or moral obligations relating to human rights is a matter of debate and definition (see DFID, 2000, p27; Nyamu-Musembi, 2002, pp15–17). There is a tendency to see the regulation of TNCs as a role for the state: the Office of the High Commissioner for Human Rights (OHCHR) guidelines argue that developing states should enhance their negotiating capacity in international fora, as well as for dealing with TNCs. In this view, the burden of responsibility falls on the state to regulate the TNCs, rather than on the TNCs to regulate themselves.

For their part, questions of *individual* duties or obligations have received relatively little attention. The first article of the Universal Declaration of Human Rights (UN, 1948) declares that 'All human beings ... should act towards one another in a spirit of brotherhood'. Apart from that, only one part of 1 of the 30 Articles of the Declaration touches on duties: Article 29 (1) reads: 'Everyone has duties to the community in which alone the free and full development of his [sic] personality is possible.' The African Charter on Human and People's Rights (OAU, 1981) goes further, stating that every individual shall have the duty 'to respect and consider his fellow beings without discrimination, and to maintain relations aimed at promoting, safeguarding and reinforcing mutual respect and tolerance' (ibid, Article 28), 'To preserve the harmonious development of the family and to work for the cohesion and respect of the family; to respect his [sic] parents at all times, to maintain them in case of need', and 'To preserve and strengthen positive African cultural values in his relations with other members of the society, in the spirit of tolerance, dialogue and consultation and, in general, to contribute to the promotion of the well-being of society' (OAU, 1981, Article 29).[30]

These statements are limited. They apply in 'the community' with the Universal Declaration, and in the family, community, state and Africa in the African Charter. They are also out of date. In an age of globalization and excesses of power and wealth, they are not specific about global duties, do not cover non-state actors like TNCs, and do not deal with the duties of the wealthy and powerful people who are those most able to make a difference for the better.

There is, then, a case for a much more even balancing of rights with duties or obligations, and for complementing RBAs (rights-based approaches) with OBAs (obligation-based approaches). Taking obligations to apply more to the haves than the have-nots, two levels stand out for remark.

The first is the developed or OECD state. The OHCHR guidelines (2002, p55) affirm that 'A developed state should not only formulate a PRS [poverty reduction strategy] in relation to poverty within its domestic jurisdiction; it should also have a strategy for poverty reduction beyond its borders.' This includes indicators of tariff- and quota-free access for developing states, one of which is domestic and export subsidies for agriculture in OECD states. This recognizes the obligations of developed states not just to their own citizens, but to poor people in developing states. Their obligations are global.

The second level is individual. All human beings, rich and poor, powerful and weak, have obligations as well as rights. These vary with power and wealth. For those who are powerless and poor, the balance for equity and justice is realizing more of their rights: the more these are realized, the more their obligations rise, for there is more they can do. For those with power and wealth, the balance for equity and justice is the other way round: it is meeting more of their obligations, their rights having largely been met. The implication is that the rights-based approach, focusing on 'them', must be complemented and balanced by an obligation-based approach, focusing on 'us'. It is a reflection of our self-serving mindsets that this is not already more a part of development thinking and action. There are complementary reversals here for the haves who are relatively rich and powerful: turning the gaze back on themselves to scrutinize their actions and non-actions and the effects that these have; supporting and empowering the poor ('putting the last first'); changing power relations ('putting the first last'); and seeking guidance on what to do ('ask them').

Obligation-based approaches can be put into perspective by comparing them with three other approaches (see Table 7.2).

Transforming power and relationships

Power and relationships have emerged as a recurrent theme in this book: in Chapter 2, concerning how language and demands for information can be instruments of power and of disempowerment; in Chapter 3, on how procedures, rules and principles can be used to reverse and balance power; in Chapter 4, in seeing how participation is about power relations; in Chapter 5, on congruence from the bottom up; and in Chapter 6, regarding attitudes, behaviour, ego and power. There is also a considerable literature on power and relationships.[31] Even so, it has not been central, or even, until recently, much mentioned, in the mainstream development discourse of, for example, the multinational banks, the bilateral aid agencies, INGOs or governments in developing countries. As a word, *power* has been almost taboo. Yet, power is everywhere. Considering development without power and relationships is like analysing irrigation without considering water and its distribution. The evidence and arguments of this book converge on the conclusion that power and relationships are at the core of development. Yet they have been almost pathologically repressed and neglected.

In order to discuss this, we need, first, to clarify types of power. The word is often used to describe *power over*, implying control; but there are other more positive forms: *power to*, referring to 'the unique potential of every person to shape his or

Table 7.2 *Four approaches to development* *

Approach	Benevolent for welfare	'Participatory' for 'partnership'	Rights-based for empowerment	Obligation based for responsibility
Core concept or value	Doing good	Effectiveness, efficiency	Rights of 'have-nots'	Obligations of 'haves'
Dominant basis and mode	Technical	Social	Political	Ethical, behavioural
Process	Blueprinted	Consultative	Transformative	Reflective
Relationships of aid providers to recipients	Paternal, providing funds, assistance	Instrumental to programmes and projects	Influencing governments; empowering people	Reciprocal, learning and being guided
Primary stakeholders perceived as	Beneficiaries	Implementers	Citizens	Guides, teachers, sources of insight, inspiration and commitment
Accountability	Upward to aid agency, taxpayers, INGO supporters	Upward with some downward	Multiple**: upwards, downwards, horizontal, etc	Personal: internal, values, and then mainly downward
Procedures	Bureaucratic conformity	More acceptance of diversity	Negotiated, evolutionary process	Critical reflection, immersions, experiential learning
Organizational drivers	Pressure to disburse	Balance between pressure to disburse and results	Pressure for results and impact assessment	Space for agency; expectations of responsible use of discretion

Note: * The four approaches are not comprehensive; there are others – notably, variants of participation. Nor are they mutually exclusive. They are delineated in order to sharpen and clarify characteristics. In practice, they coexist and overlap. The challenge is to get the mix and balance right for each person, group, context and time.
** Multiple accountabilities include international human rights monitors and international non-governmental organizations (INGOs), as well as intra-community and intra-group accountabilities
Source: first four columns adapted from Groves and Hinton (2004) with the fifth column added

her life and the world' (VeneKlasen and Miller, 2002, p55); *power with* through collaboration, solidarity, collective action and so on; and *power within* through self-worth and confidence. Power is often thought and spoken of in an undifferentiated way as a good thing to have. Power is 'gained', 'seized' or 'captured', and 'lost', 'abandoned' or 'surrendered'. It is as though it were a commodity subject to a zero-sum game where more for one person means less for another. In practice, there are many power relationships in which all gain. Uppers with power can change their behaviour towards lowers. By convening, catalysing, facilitating, coaching and supporting lowers, uppers' *power over* can be turned into *power to empower*. This can give the satisfactions of enhancing the agency and fulfilment of lowers who gain in their *power to*. Part of this can be fostering *power with* in many ways such as decentralization, alliances, networks, social movements and communities of practice, and *power within* through capacity-building and development. Lowers then gain through the synergy of *power with, power within* and *power to*. Uppers too can gain not just by diminishing the stresses of a *power over* control orientation, but also from the satisfaction and fulfilment of doing what is right. Using one's own *power over* to empower others can often be effective, liberating, fulfilling and fun: a gain in well-being, not a loss. [32]

Power over, especially when exercised crudely, brings many disadvantages. It misleads ('all power deceives') through deference, lies and concealment.[33] It inhibits or destroys trust. It deters initiative, creativity and local diversity. It prevents

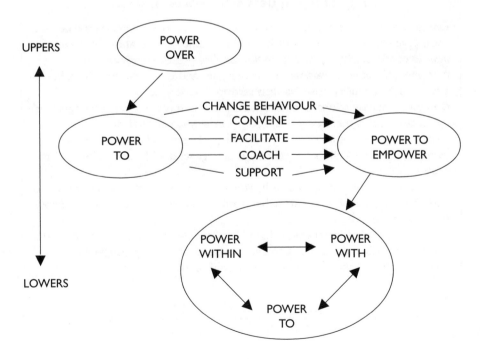

Figure 7.2 *Transforming power*

relationships of learning together. It generates resentment. It weakens or prevents actions that are pro-poor through orders, controls and sanctions from the top, which prevent responsiveness to the priorities and needs of poor people below. The list could be longer, but the point is made.

Power and relationships are intimately interwoven. The problems with the exercise of *power over* are implicit in the recent and emerging vocabulary of development. Six of the words most used in current development speak – empowerment, accountability, ownership, partnership, participation and transparency – are about power and relationships; and with all six there are chasms between what the rhetoric implies and actual behaviours and relationships (see Box 7.1). Development professionals asked to score these for their relative importance, and then for the degree of hypocrisy with which they are used, have given different answers. For Associate Programme Officers of DFID, partnership was top on both counts; for forest officers and NGOs working on foresty in India, it was transparency. Most commonly, though, it is empowerment that is considered the most important word and the one with the biggest gap between rhetoric and behaviour. Changes in relationships are also implied in emergent terms that are gaining currency: congruence; consistency; reciprocity; colleague and collegiality; ally and alliances; networking; sharing; and trust.

Box 7.1 The gap between words and actions

Empowerment implies power to those who are subordinate and weak; but the usual practice between levels of hierarchy is control from above. Aid agencies impose conditionalities at the same time as they preach empowerment.

Accountability between partners is two-way up and down the aid chain; but in practice accountability downwards is rare and weak.

Ownership implies national and local autonomy; but this is limited by aid agencies' influence on policy, human rights and governance, whether this influence is exerted directly on governments or indirectly through citizens and civil society.

Partnership implies collegial equality; but aid agencies with funds often call the shots.

Participation is considered a means by some and an end by others, and is used to describe a range of practices stretching from compulsory labour to spontaneous self-organization.

Transparency implies information shared between partners, and accessible in the public domain; but aid agencies and governments often keep budget details and other information about decision-making confidential.

Source: IDS (2001)

The importance of power and relationships is the central theme of *Inclusive Aid: Power and Relationships in International Development* (2004, edited by Leslie Groves and Rachel Hinton), which brings together many illustrations. In her paper *Relationships Matter for Supporting Change in Favour of Poor People*, Rosalind Eyben (2004a) makes the case that although many officials in aid agencies, especially those with big budgets, see aid as about instruments, it is really always about relationships. The shift to budget support and policy influence has made this clearer. For lenders and donors to strive for *power over* is counterproductive. Influence requires *power with* through collegiality, mutual trust, joint learning and collaboration. Aid is then about investing in relationships.

Grounding pro-poor realism

Meeting the responsibilities that obligations bring demands realism. Development policies, programmes and practices are now more than ever proclaimed to be pro-poor. Few would dispute that responsibility is to be sought in finding the right things to do and doing them. Yet, the record, for all its successes, remains dismal. It is no good recognizing obligations and 'meaning well' if what is done does not fit the priorities and aspirations of those who are poor and marginalized or, as so often occurs, does them harm.

Solutions can be sought in a grounded realism, based on sensitive insights into the life experiences, conditions, needs, aspirations and capabilities of poor and marginalized people, matched by a realistic understanding of what is possible. A pre-condition for such grounded pro-poor realism and understanding is for 'uppers' to be sensitive in their behaviour and to use empowering approaches and methods. These have been a feature of good participatory poverty assessments (PPAs). Since 1997, many more PPAs have been carried out, increasingly on sub-national levels, and linked with poverty reduction strategy paper (PRSP) processes. The *Voices of the Poor* study (Narayan et al, 2000) was a breakthrough on an international level, enabling many poor people, in 23 countries, to express their realities and how these had changed, their ideas of good and bad life, and their aspirations. Crucial to the success of that study was the training of facilitators in how they should behave and relate to those whose views and analysis they were eliciting. Non-dominating, friendly and empathic behaviour and attitudes were the key.

Congruence in personal and institutional change

Pro-poor realism requires, however, much more than good PPAs and insights. It is difficult to achieve unless institutional and personal change go together in organizations, whether government, civil society or aid agency. As in Table 7.3, the shift is from a paradigm of things to one or people. Institutional change and personal change interact, interlock and reinforce each other. They can move together in the same direction: towards hierarchy, control and standardization, or towards participation, empowerment and diversity. From a hierarchical starting point, if development organizations are to reorient towards learning, change and

Table 7.3 *Professional, institutional and personal conditions, values, norms and roles: Shifts for a grounded pro-poor realism*

	From	Towards
Paradigm of and for	Things	People
Orientation	Top down	Bottom up
Valued achievements	Targets and disbursements	Empowerment
Modes/approaches	Standardized	Diverse
Roles and behaviour	Teacher, supervisor; controlling	Facilitator; coach; enabling
Accountability stressed, and directly mainly	To donors and taxpayers	To all stakeholders, especially poor
	Upwards	Downwards
Sources of understanding poor people's realities	Bookish; workshops	Direct; immersions
Learning and change	Didactic; instructions	Experiential learning

Note: the shifts in Table 7.3 are not absolute, but involve a change of balance in order to give more weight to the people side

responsiveness, so, too, must those who work in them. And if those who work in them are to reorient, so, too, must their organizations. On the personal side, this means that those in 'upper' roles, to whom 'lowers' are accountable, have to transform their behaviour, attitudes and roles from dominators to enablers, from controllers to coaches, and from instructors to facilitators. Only then can reversals of power relations enable upward flows of realistic insights. On the institutional side, this means that procedures, incentives, expectations and organized experience are needed to encourage and support individuals in their trajectories of personal development, learning and change.

Such change does not come easily. Targets for outputs and disbursements can overwhelm and reorient those who support participation back again into upper–lower behaviours and relationships. It is arguable that in the World Bank the drivers and incentives to lend and spend large sums fast are so strong that they override inclinations to behave and relate differently. The World Bank immersions are a bold and necessary initiative; but the long-term test will be whether they make a difference in what the World Bank does and how it does it. In other development organizations, the MDGs, whatever their merits, also threaten with a self-defeating top-down orientation. To resist this propensity requires insight, courage and commitment on the part of many actors, not least those furthest removed from the action – in the headquarters of the World Bank, the UNDP, the regional banks, the bilateral agencies, and in national governments. It will depend, once again, on powerful individuals who are willing and able to resist reflexes and to argue and act in ways that are informed by a pro-poor realism.

Commitment by individuals to pro-poor realism is one thing. Commitment of organizations, with change in relationships and cultures, is then another. Individuals and organizations can show synergy; but neither can guarantee the other. In practical terms, this is more than a question of congruence between levels. It entails transformations of whole organizations by individuals and groups, and of individuals and groups by organizations. It is walking on both legs, not hopping on either, with varied sequences and mixes of divergence, debate, disagreement, conflict, convergence and congruence.

The hope has to be that those who are serious about poverty can combine and work as allies, catalysts and co-learners; that they will gain understanding and authority through experiential learning directly from and with poor people; and that this will help them to transform their organizations. How many will do this, and how many organizations will encourage or let them, remains to be seen. But there are encouraging signs.

Reflexive responsibility

The themes in this book, chapter by chapter, bring us to the personal dimension in development: personal commitment and continuity in Chapter 1; how individual champions make a difference in Chapter 2; how procedures affect relationships in Chapter 3; ethics and personal responsibility for the quality of process in Chapter 4; how people have to come first in order to go to scale well in Chapter 5; and seeing behaviour and attitudes as central to good change in Chapter 6. All of these elements point towards the primacy of the personal in this last chapter.

This personal dimension in development is now more discussed and more widely recognized. Michael Edwards concludes *Future Positive* (1999) with a section on personal accountability and a final chapter 'How can I help?'. Tony Vaux, in *The Selfish Altruist* (2001) has given us an honest, self-aware and self-critical review of the personal and ethical dilemmas he encountered in relief work in famine and in war, and which many of us never have to face directly, even though they are there for us in our interconnected world. For all its terrible side, the HIV/AIDS pandemic has led many health professionals to a more sensitive and humane approach, showing the way in the importance of relationships. A main theme stressed at a conference of government staff from the Department of Social Development, held in Port Elizabeth, South Africa, in March 2004, was personal transformation.

It is more acceptable now to try to be insightful about oneself, not in self-abasement, but in wishing to be more open and honest. This is not easy. Gandhi believed that the way to tell whether something was right or wrong is whether you feel you have to hide it. We are all fallible and most of us have things we want to keep to ourselves. But the direction is clear: it is towards shining a light on, and diminishing, more of our inconsistencies and hypocrisies, and opening the blind eyes we habitually turn on what we do not want to see. It is, in Rosalind Eyben's words, reflecting on ourselves and on our relations with others (Eyben, 2004a, p21):

- Who are we and why do we understand the world in a certain way as a result of who we are?
- How does that understanding have an impact on our behaviour and our relations with others?

Enjoying thinking for oneself

Moving in this direction does not have to mean an overload of guilt-ridden moralizing. Reflexive responsibility means being self-aware while working out our own ideas and priorities. This makes it easier to exercise agency. It is something to enjoy.

It can be fun, for example, to puzzle and produce personal lists of words and priorities that we would like to be used in development. There is no one right answer, no one way, no single concept. Pluralism, diversity and debate can be celebrated and enjoyed. The reader may wish to think through a personal list of words and priorities before seeing mine. With words, there is a double practical challenge – to gain currency for the word and what it implies, and then to narrow the gap between the meaning and the reality. Redistribution of wealth, for example, is an obvious and effective way of simultaneously enhancing the well-being of those who are poor and the responsible well-being of the non-poor (if only they or we can recognize and feel this), making responsible well-being a win–win for all.

Another way forward is Richard Forsyth's idea from 'Towards a grounded morality' (Forsyth, 1991). It is that each of us can form and evolve our own 'religion', mindset, way of making sense of the world and ethics. This can be part of education: not dictating or implanting, but sowing and nurturing, allowing and encouraging diversity. 'A basic concept of learning and teaching participation is that individuals participate in generating their own personal theories which are relevant to their own context' (Taylor and Fransman, 2003, p8). Experiential learning and reflection lead naturally to seeing and interpreting things in new ways, to evolving personal practice, and to a grounded confidence on which further learning can grow.

'Ask them' for guidance

On the development journey, there will always be far to go and always new ideas. As we travel, we will continually be looking for new steps ahead and will constantly be learning. We have been learning ways to enable those who are poor and marginalized to analyse their realities, to identify and express their priorities, to know and realize their rights, and to gain for themselves and their families more of what they need and deserve. We are learning the value of experiential learning from direct exposure and interaction in immersions, and from the reflections that can follow. The deep and troubling questions that these raise can only be asked and answered by each of us for ourselves. For myself, the answers are inconsistent with how I live. The gap of hypocrisy is broad, embarrassing and papered over with comfortable evasions.

Box 7.2 A personal list of words and priorities for development

Word, focus or activity

Dimension

Conceptual:	Reversal
Wealth:	Redistribution
Power:	(Power), obligation, obligation-based approaches
Relationships:	(Relationships), respect, understanding, trust, reciprocity, congruence
Personal:	Reflection, passion, outrage, commitment, self-awareness, humour, fun, creativity, right living, love

Methodological   Learn how to:

- Feel better with less wealth.
- Feel good empowering others.
- Think through the effects of actions and non-actions.
- Bring up children.
- Improve gender relations.
- Conduct across-group encounters, learning and immersions.
- Transform institutions for bottom-up congruence.
- Replace formal teaching with experiential learning.
- Become self-aware without taking oneself too seriously.
- Provide positive, creative expression for male aggression and energy, especially for youth.
- See another person's point of view.
- Prevent and resolve conflict.

One thought is that diversity is fundamentally good. This includes differences in ethics and codes, as long as these are open to question and debate. We are all irreducibly different individuals, with idiosyncratic histories, feelings and consciousness. What matters most and works for one may not matter so much or may not work for another. In seeking to know what best to do, there are many choices. There are the values and practices shared by the great religions. Some pray. Some seek the guidance of their God, gods or sacred texts. Some meditate. Some, agnostics and humanists, question and reflect. It is to be celebrated that the paths are many and diverse as long as they tolerate and rejoice in the diversity of others.

Is this a point at which a concept of responsible well-being can help? That, too, demands personal answers. In Patta Scott-Villiers's (2004) words:

> *Responsible well-being based on self-awareness is a desirable end for development. It implies mental and material wellness nursed by taking a responsible part. It applies to all of us, rich and poor, the providers and recipients of development, and it turns the idea of giver and taker into a spiral of reciprocity. It is achieved through individual learning. This is not a call for an idealized approach to development only applicable to residents in ivory towers. This is about each individual within their sphere using the space around them to consider both the without and the within, and in so doing making their work and its relationships a little more enjoyable and congruent, a touch more energized and spiced with an edge of questioning and creativity.*

Responsible well-being remains a phrase in search of a meaning and a methodology. It invites further definition. But who defines responsibility? And who defines well-being? It has been becoming more accepted in development that the poor, weak and marginalized should analyse and express what matters to them; what for them is ill-being and what is well-being; and what for them would make a difference. The challenge is to make space for them to do this, to amplify their voices, to listen, hear, understand and then act. Harsh Mander's riveting book *Unheard Voices* horrifies, shocks, distresses and tells us what we do not want to know (Mander, 2001). It also inspires through the tenacity and guts that many poor people show. They are capable of so much more than the professional classes have supposed. In many matters touching their lives, they know most and best; and we know that we should ask them what their aspirations are for well-being for themselves. Can we go beyond that and ask them what they would regard as responsible well-being, as a good and responsible life for us – for those who are better off than they are? Might we then not want to listen so much? Or might their answers show us the best ways forward?

At the end of an earlier book, *To the Hands of the Poor* (Chambers et al, 1989), N. C. Saxena, Tushaar Shah and I quoted the words of Mahatma Gandhi:

> *I will give you a talisman. Whenever you are in doubt, or when the self becomes too much with you, apply the following test. Recall the face of the poorest and the weakest man whom you may have seen, and ask yourself, if the step you contemplate is going to be of any use to him. Will he gain anything by it? Will it restore him to a control over his own life and destiny? In other words, will it lead to Swaraj[34] for the hungry and spiritually starving millions? Then you will find your doubts and your self melting away.*

The questions we then asked was – how often, and in what circumstances, with what learning and understanding, are the poor man, and more, the poor woman and child, met, listened to, and understood; and how often are the distant effects of decisions and actions, and of indecisions and non-actions, reflected upon?

From those questions one final idea can follow. This is open to all, whoever we are and whatever we believe. It is, as with Gandhi's talisman, when in doubt, to recall a poor person we have known. It is then to ask what she would have us do. It is to ask what she would wish, advise, encourage and allow. This goes further than just putting the last first, or the first last. It demands imagination, reflecting upon the realities of the poor person, her aspirations and ideas of the good life, the example she sets, and our own recognition of causality and how our own decisions and actions are connected with her and others like her. And she can also be he. The question then is whether, when faced with daily and strategic dilemmas and decisions, asking what that poor person would have us do can be a guide, putting some of the *responsible* into *well-being* as a part of right and good living. Can it make it easier to see what to do? Can it stiffen commitment and courage? Can it show how those who are poor, powerless and deprived can gain more of what they need and deserve? Can it point to ways of transforming power and seeking social justice? Can it ease anxiety and be a source of peace of mind?[35] Above all, can it inspire good action grounded in realism?

These are personal questions. In seeking answers, experiential learning, critical self-awareness and reflection all help. And it matters who we are and what we become. But in the end it is action that counts most, and good effects from what we do.

Notes

1   The first part of this chapter is an invited editorial published in *World Development* (Chambers, 1997b). I am grateful to Geoff Barnard, Jenny Chambers and Janet Craswell for helpful comments on a draft.

2   For a classical and entertaining discussion of the need for the interaction of both poles of a range of development dichotomies, see Streeten (1983).

3   See, for example, *Development* (1997) for a useful overview.

4   Or, to change the zoological metaphor:

> *Consultants with contracts to win*
> *use language they know to be in.*
> *Chameleons, they*
> *fake a fashion display:*
> *camouflaging for cash is no sin.*

5   The term 'primary stakeholders', defined as 'those expected to benefit from or be adversely affected by [World] Bank-supported operations, particularly the poor and marginalized' had a chequered history. It was included in early drafts of *The World Bank and Participation: Report of the Learning Group on Participatory Development*, and applauded by many Bank watchers. But it was dropped from the final version (World Bank, 1994b), reportedly because some Bank directors from countries of the South objected that it constituted interference with internal political affairs.

6   All presidents of the World Bank have, so far, been men.

7   For introductory sources, see Mascarenhas et al (1991) and Chambers (1997a). For recent sources and concerns, see *RRA Notes* (1988–present) (now *PLA Notes*), Absalom et al (1995), Kumar (1996) and Mallik et al (1996).

8   Participatory poverty assessments (PPAs) using PRA approaches and methods have been pioneered in Ghana (Norton et al, 1995; Dogbe, 1998), Zambia

(Norton et al, 1994; Norton and Owen, 1996; Milimo et al, undated, Shilito and Brock, eds), South Africa (Murphy, 1995; Teixeira and Chambers, 1995; Attwood, 1996; May, 1996) and in Bangladesh (UNDP, 1996) using a variety of processes. For reviews of PPAs, see Norton and Stephens (1995); Robb (1998, 2002); Chambers and Blackburn (1996); Holland with Blackburn (1998); Norton (1998a, 1998b); and Norton with others (2001).

9   For fuller presentations of the evidence about wealth and well-being as criteria see *RRA Notes*, no 15 and Chambers (1997a, pp176–179).

10 In this list, fun is an apple among oranges. The other words are serious and moral. Fun looks frivolous. The fact that fun is out of reach for so many – the desperately sick, suffering and poor; those who are abused and trapped; victims of violence; those fleeing in terror from war – may make it seem obscene in a development vocabulary. But it is as important as the others. With play and fun come creativity, laughter, the breakdown of barriers, the expression of realities, new insights, and the weakening of defences and of structures of power. That it is out of reach for so many is an outrage.

11 In an earlier draft I used 'altruism'. But altruism is an austere, unsmiling word with overtones of 'do-gooding.' I am grateful to Norman Uphoff (1992, p341) for pointing out that altruism and generosity can be used interchangeably. His Chapter 12 is exciting and essential reading on this.

12 There is, however, a chapter by Marianne Gronemeyer on 'Helping', which is close to altruism or generosity. But the chapter has a negative orientation. Gronemeyer analyses the modernizing of the idea of help. Help, she argues, has evolved from spontaneous response to a cry of need, to an instrument for the sophisticated exercise of power, in which neediness is determined not by the cry of the afflicted, but by the diagnosis of the development establishment.

13 Parts of this section are derived from Chambers (1997a, Chapter 1), with minor modifications.

14 For further discussion of livelihoods, including sustainable livelihoods, see Chambers (1987); Conroy and Litvinoff (1988); Bernstein et al (1992); Chambers and Conway (1992); and Davies (1996).

15 David Leonard's (1991) study *African Successes: Four Public Managers in Kenyan Rural Development* is a notable exception.

16 One study (Frank et al, 1993) found, alarmingly, that economists were more likely than non-economists to act in a non-trusting, non-cooperative, self-interested manner. The median gift to big charities by economists among 1245 randomly selected college professors was substantially lower than for non-economists; and about 9 per cent of economists gave nothing, against a range of 1–4 per cent for other disciplines. In a prisoners' dilemma game, economics students defected 60 per cent of the time compared with 39 per cent for non-economists.

17 A sharper antithesis to *Pedagogy of the Oppressed* (Freire, 1970) would be 'pedagogy for the oppressors'; but this would unnecessarily alienate some and not apply to others who might also benefit from a pedagogy for the non-oppressed.

18   This discussion draws heavily upon John Harriss's delightful and piercing polemic *Depoliticizing Development:The World Bank and Social Capital* (Harriss, 2002).The term social capital was evidently adopted independently by several authors, including Meyer Fortes (a source identified by Caroline Moser) in 1958 and Bourdieu in 1980.

19   This phrase, also in inverted commas, is from Deborah Eade's editorial in *Development in Practice* (Eade, 2003), which gives a balanced overview.

20   Anthony Bebbington, Scott Guggenheim, Elizabeth Olson and Michael Woolcock have written a fascinating study (Bebbington et al, 2004) of the history of concepts of social capital in the World Bank. This work gains authority and credibility by analysing the agency of individual actors, and how the concept was debated and has evolved through the interplay of professional and institutional commitments and interests.

21   Grootaert (1997), cited in Harriss (2002).

22   See *Food 2000* (WCED 1987a), the report of the Advisory Panel on Food, Agriculture, Forestry and Environment convened by the World Commission on Environment and Development, and the Brundtland Report (WCED, 1987b, pp129,138).

23   Interestingly, Scoones (1998, pp4–5, 17) proposed four capitals – natural, economic/financial, human and social – noting that other forms of capital could be identified (for example, political capital and symbolic capital) and that DFID had separated out physical capital as a fifth form.The five capitals – physical, natural, human, financial and social – have since become standard.

24   See, for example, Sen (1993, 1999); Narayan et al (2000, Chapter 2); and Alcamo et al (2003).

25   As one of the 51 authors of *Ecosystems and Human Well-being* (Alcamo et al, 2003), the conceptual framework for the Millenium Ecosystem Assessment, I tried to introduce the concept of responsible well-being. I did not articulate it well, and it was met with polite scepticism. It was rejected in part because it was seen as normative (but so were other concepts, though less obviously so). Missing this opportunity diminished the responsible dimension of my own well-being. Had I been more confident and more of a fighter, it might have got in as more than an aside. It is centrally relevant to that book and to the spirit of the assessment.

26   An 'olde' English version of the butterfly effect runs:

> *For want of a nail, the shoe was lost.*
> *For want of a shoe the horse was lost.*
> *For want of a horse the rider was lost.*
> *For want of a rider the battle was lost*
> *For loss of the battle the kingdom was lost.*

A 21st century version might be:

> *For want of oil, the chads were lost.*
> *For want of chads, the state was lost.*
> *For want of the state, the election was lost.*

> *For want of the election, Kyoto was lost.*
> *For want of Kyoto, the Earth was lost.*

There was lack of drops of oil at one end of the causal chain, and billions of barrels at the other.

27   I include myself here among those who bear responsibility for an unsuccessful development project, in my case for a pastoral grazing scheme in Samburu District in Kenya. With hindsight it is not difficult to see much that was done that should not have been done, and much that should have been done that was not done. What matters now is to learn the lessons and pass them on.

28   The International Bill of Rights includes the Universal Declaration of Human Rights, the International Covenant in Civil and Political Rights and the International Covenant in Economic, Social and Cultural Rights.

29   For definitions and discussion of duties and obligations, see UNDP (2000, pp16, 24–26).

30   The other duties concern serving and supporting the state, including paying taxes and contributing to African unity.

31   For sources on power, see, for example, Lukes (1974); ActionAid (2001b); VeneKlasen with Miller (2002); and Gaventa (2003).

32   For more on gains from personal disempowerment, see *Whose Reality Counts?* (Chambers, 1997a, pp235–236).

33   In *Whose Reality Counts?* (Chambers, 1997a), Chapter 5 on 'All power deceives' explores and elaborates this theme. I therefore do not expand upon it here.

34   *Swaraj* means self-determination. I have given the quotation in full, including this sentence with its reference to spiritual starvation. Arguably, it is precisely those who are not hungry, and who are wealthy and powerful, who are more prone to spiritual lack.

35   As an agnostic, I am out of my depth here. Readers of different faiths will have different ways of seeking to know what to do. I recollect a phrase from my nominally Christian upbringing: 'whose service is perfect freedom'. The thought, here, is that it lifts a burden of anxiety to know that you have a source of guidance when needed.

References

AAA (Aashray Adhikar Abhiyan) (2002) *Basere ki Kahani (Story of Shelter):A Study of the Problems in the Night Shelters in Delhi Using Participatory Research*, Aashray Adhikar Abhiyan, Delhi, January

Abah, O. S. (2004) 'Voices aloud: Making communication and change together', *Participatory Learning and Action*, no 50, pp45–52

Absalom, E. et al (1995) 'Participatory approaches and methods: Sharing our concerns and looking to the future', *PLA Notes*, vol 22: 5–10

Abugre, C. (2000) Still Sapping the Poor? A Critique of IMF Poverty Reduction Strategies, World Development Movement and ISODEC, London (available at www.wdm.org.uk/cambriefs/Debt/sappoor.pdf)

Acharya, A., A. Fuzzo de Lima and M. Moore (2004) *Aid Proliferation: How Responsible Are the Donors?*, Working Paper 214, IDS, Sussex, January

ActionAid (1999) *Fighting Poverty Together: ActionAid's Strategy* 1999–2003, ActionAid, London

ActionAid (2000) *ALPS:Accountability, Learning and Planning System*, ActionAid, London, July (available at www.actionaid.org/resources/pdfs/alps.pdf)

ActionAid (2001a) *Notes to Accompany ALPS*, ActionAid, London, April (available at www.actionaid.org/resources/pdfs/alps_notes.pdf)

ActionAid (2001b) *Transforming Power*, Participatory Methodologies Forum, February 2001, ActionAid, London

ActionAid (2002) 'Lessons from ActionAid's annual review and reflection process', *IA Exchanges Special*, ActionAid, London, October

Ademoloku, L., N. Kulemeka and M. Laleye (1997) 'Political transition, economic liberalisation and civil service reform in Malawi', *Public Administration and Development*, vol 17(2), pp209–222

Adhikari, G. B. et al (1996) 'Sharing our experience: An appeal to donors and governments', *PRA Reflections*, PRAXIS, pp19–26

Adhikari, G. B. et al (1997) 'Going to scale with PRA: Reflections and recommendations', *PRA Reflections*, pp27–32

AduGyamfi, J. (2003) 'New approaches to addressing complex trauma and psychological challenges in Africa', *Education Action*, vol 17, pp15–16, May

Agyarko, R. de Graft (1997) *'In Spite of the Rains the Ground is still Dry': The Ghana Participatory Poverty Assessment Studies – Impact, Implications and Lessons for the Future*, unpublished paper, Participation Group, IDS, Sussex

Ahmed, I. I. with M. Lipton (1997) *Impact of Structural Adjustment on Sustainable Rural Livelihoods:A Review of the Literature*, Working Paper 62, IDS, Sussex, December

Akerkar, S. (2001) 'Gender and participation: Overview report', in BRIDGE (ed) *Gender and Participation: Cutting Edge Pack*, BRIDGE, IDS, Sussex, www.ids.ac.uk/ids/bridge

Akumu, W. (2002) 'Farmers want a more efficient irrigation board', *The Nation* (Nairobi), 13 December, drawing upon a report of the Kenya Institute of Public Policy Analysis and Research

Alcamo, J. et al (2003) *Ecosystems and Human Wellbeing: A Framework for Assessment*, Report of the Conceptual Framework Working Group of the Millennium Ecosystem Assessment, Island Press, Washington, DC, and Covelo, London

Alcorn, J. B. (2000) *Borders, Rules and Governance: Mapping to Catalyse Changes in Policy and Management*, Gatekeeper Series No 91, Sustainable Agriculture and Rural Livelihoods Programme, IIED, London

Almy, S. W. and P. M. Mbithi (1972) 'Local involvement in the Special Rural Development Programme' in *An Overall Evaluation of the Special Rural Development Programme 1972*, IDS Evaluation Team Report for the Ministry of Finance and Planning, Institute for Development Studies, University of Nairobi, Nairobi

Anderson, J. (1971) 'Self help and independency: The political implications of a continuing tradition in African education in Kenya', *African Affairs*, vol 70 (278), January

APMSS (Andhra Pradesh Mahila Samatha Society) (1994–2004) *Andhra Pradesh Mahila Samatha Society Report 1993–1994* and subsequent years

APMSS (circa 1998) *Mana Jaaga (Our Space)*, Andhra Pradesh Mahila Samata Society, Hyderabad, India (text by V. Lokesh Kumar and P. Purandhar)

APNSD (Association for the Promotion of North–South Dialogue) (2002) *Development Has Got a Face: The EDP of the Association for the Promotion of North–South Dialogue: A Brief Profile*, APNSD, Bonn, www.exposure–nsd.de

Apthorne, R. (1966) 'A survey of land settlement schemes and rural development in East Africa', *East African Institute of Social Research Conference Papers*, January, no 352

Apthorpe, R. (1972) *Rural Co-operatives and Planned Change in Africa: An Analytical Overview*, Rural Institutions and Planned Change, vol 5, UNRISD, Geneva

Archer, D. and N. M Goreth (2004) 'Participation, literacy and empowerment: The continuing evolution of Reflect', *Participatory Learning and Action*, October, pp35–44

Arnstein, S. R. (1969) 'A ladder of citizen's participation', *Journal of American Institute of Planners*, vol 35, July, pp216–224

Ashby, J. (1989) *The IPRA Method*, video, CIAT, Cali, Colombia

Ashford, G. and S. Patkar (2001) *The Positive Path: Using Appreciative Inquiry in Rural Indian Communities*, DFID, IISD and MYRADA, Denmark

Ashley, C. and D. Carney (1999) *Sustainable Livelihoods: Lessons from Early Experience*, DFID, London

Ashley, C. and S. Maxwell (eds) (2001) *Rethinking Rural Development: Development Policy Review, Theme Issue*, vol 19(4), December

Attwood, H. (1996) 'South African participatory poverty assessment process: Were the voices of the poor heard?' Paper for the PRA and Policy Workshop, IDS Sussex, 13–14 May (see also Attwood and May, 1998)

Attwood, H. and J. May (1998) 'Kicking down doors and lighting fires: The South African PPA' in Holland with Blackburn (eds) *Whose Voice?*, IT Publications, London, pp119–130

Backhaus, C. and R. Wagachchi (1995) 'Only playing with beans?' Attempting to introduce a participatory approach into a large-scale government rural development programme in Sri Lanka' in Kievelitz and Scherler (eds) *Participatory Learning Approaches*, GTZ, Eschborn, Bonn, Germany.

Bagadion, B. and F. Korten (eds) (1989) *Transforming a Bureaucracy: The Experience of the Philippine National Irrigation Administration*, Kumarian Press, West Hartford, Connecticut

Balakrishnan, R. (ed) (1998) *Participatory Pathways*, Special issue of Social Change (Journal of the Council for Social Development, Delhi), vol 28, nos 2 and 3, June–September

Banerjee, D. and R. Muggah (2002) *Small Arms and Human Security: Reviewing Participatory Research in South Asia*, Regional Centre for Strategic Studies, Colombo

Barahona, C. and S. Levy (2003) *How to Generate Statistics and Influence Policy Using Participatory Methods in Research: Reflections on Work in Malawi 1999–2002*, IDS Working Paper, IDS, Sussex

Baumann, P. and J. Farrington (2003) Decentralising Natural Resource Management: Lessons from Local Government Reform in India, ODI Natural Resource Perspectives 86, London, June

Baumann, P. and S. Sinha (2001) *Linking Development with Democratic Processes in India: Political Capital and Sustainable Livelihoods Analysis*, Natural Resource Perspectives 68, ODI, London, June

Bayer, W. and A. Waters-Bayer (2002) *Participatory Monitoring and Evaluation (PM&E) with Pastoralists: A Review of Experiences and an Annotated Bbibliography*, Participation Kiosk, GTZ, Eschborn, www.eldis.org/fulltext/PDFWatersmain.pdf

Bebbington, A., S. Guggenheim, E. Olson and M. Woolcock (2004) 'Exploring social capital debates at the World Bank', *Journal of Development Studies*, vol 40, pp33–64

Beecher, H. W. (1887) 'Proverbs from the Plymouth Pulpit', cited in R. Thomas Tripp (ed) *The International Thesaurus of Quotations*, Penguin Reference Books, London (1976)

Begg, D., S. Fischer and R. Dornbusch (2003) *Economics*, seventh edition, McGraw-Hill, London

Bell, B., J. Gaventa and J. Peters (eds) (1990) *Myles Horton and Paulo Freire We Make the Road by Walking – Conversations on Education and Social Change*, Temple University Press, Philadelphia (republished by IT Publications, London)

Bell, E. and P. Brambilla (2001) 'Gender and participation: Supporting resources collection', in BRIDGE (ed) *Gender and Participation*, IDS, Sussex, www.ids.ac.uk/ids/bridge

Belshaw, D. G. R. (1968) 'Agricultural extension, education and research', in G. K. Helleimer (ed), *Agricultural Planning in East Africa*, East African Publishing House, Nairobi, pp57–80

Bennett, B. (2002) 'Market scoping: Methods to help people understand their marketing environment', *PLA Notes*, vol 45, October pp71–75

Bennett, F. with M. Roberts (2004) *From Input to Influence: Participatory Approaches to Research and Inquiry into Poverty*, Joseph Rowntree Foundation, York (available at www.jr.org.uk/bookshop)

Benor, D. and J. Q. Harrison (1977) *Agricultural Extension: The Training and Visit System*, World Bank, Washington, DC, May

Bentley, J. and K. Andrews (1996) *Through the Roadblocks: IPM and Central American Smallholders*, Gatekeeper Series 56, IIED, London

Bernstein, H., B. Crow and H. Johnson (eds) (1992) *Rural Livelihoods: Crises and Responses*, Oxford University Press in association with the Open University, Oxford, UK

Bhatnagar, B. and A. C. Williams (eds) (1992) *Participatory Development and the World Bank: Potential Directions for Change*, World Bank Discussion Papers 183, World Bank, Washington, DC

Bhattarcharjee, P. (2001) *Participatory Review and Reflection Process: Workshop Report*, 24–25 January 2001, Bangalore Regional Office, ActionAid India

Biggs, S. D. (1989) *Resource-poor Farmer Participation in Research: A Synthesis of Experiences from Nine Agricultural Research Systems*, OFCOR Comparative Study Paper No 3, ISNAR, The Hague, The Netherlands

Biggs, S. and A. Neame (1995) 'Negotiating room for manoeuvre: reflections concerning NGO autonomy and accountability within the new policy agenda' in Edwards and Hulme (eds) *Beyond the Magic Bullet: NGO Performance and Accountability in the Post-Cold War World*, Kumarian Press, Bloomfield, CT, pp31–40

Bilgi, M. (1998) 'Entering women's world through men's eyes', in Guijt and Shah (eds) *The Myth of Community: Gender Issues in Participatory Development*, IT Publications, London

bint Talal, B. (2003) *Rethinking an NGO: Development, Donors and Civil Society in Jordan*, I.B. Taurus, London, New York

Bird, B. and M. Kakande (2001) 'The Uganda Participatory Poverty Assessment Process', in Norton et al (eds) *A Rough Guide to PPAs: Participatory Poverty Assessment – An Introduction to Theory and Practice*, ODI, London, pp43–56

Black, R. and H. White (eds) (2004) *Targeting Development: Critical Perspectives on the Millennium Development Goals*, Routledge, London and New York

Blackburn, J., R. Chambers and J. Gaventa (2000) *Mainstreaming Participation in Development*, OED Working Paper Series No 10, World Bank, Washington, DC, (also in Hanna and Picciotto (eds) *Making Development Work*, pp61–82)

Blackburn, J. with J. Holland (eds) (1998) *Who Changes? Institutionalizing Participation in Development*, IT Publications, London

Blackmore, S. (2003) 'Consciousness in meme machines', *Journal of Consciousness Studies*, vol 10(4–5), pp19–30

Boal, A. (1979) *Theatre of the Oppressed*, Pluto Press, London

Booth, D., J Holland, J. Hentschel, P. Landjouw and A. Herbert (1998) *Participation and Combined Methods in African Poverty Assessment: Renewing the Agenda*, Social Development Division, Africa Division, DFID, London, February

Borrini-Feyeraband, G., M. Pimbert, M. T. Farvar, A. Kothari and Y. Renard (2004) *Sharing Power: Learning by doing in Co-management of Natural Resources Throughout the World*, IIED, London and IUCN/CEESP/CMWG, Cenesta, Tehran

Bourdieu, P. (1980) 'Le capital sociale: notes provisoires', *Actes de la Recherche en Sciences Sociales*, vol 31, pp 2–3 (cited in Harriss, 2002, p4)

Box, L. (1999) 'Sectoral incapacity? An alternative view point' in *Linking Sector-wide Approaches with Capacity*, A Gateway on Capacity Development Issue 3, www.capacity.org, December

BRIDGE (2001) *Gender and Participation: Cutting Edge Pack*, BRIDGE, IDS, Sussex www.ids.ac.uk/ids/bridge

Brock, K. and R. McGee (eds) (2002) *Knowing Poverty: Critical Reflections on Participatory Research and Policy*, Earthscan, London

Brown, D. D. (1971) *Agricultural Development in India's Districts*, Harvard University Press, Cambridge, Massachusetts

Brown, D., M. Howes, K. Hussein, C. Longley and K. Swindell (eds) (2002) *Participation in Practice: Case Studies from The Gambia*, ODI, London

Brown, L. D. and J. Fox (2001) 'Transnational civil society coalitions and the World Bank: Lessons from project and policy influence campaigns' in Edwards and Gaventa (eds) *Global Citizen Action*, Lynne Rienner Publishers, Boulder, Colorado, pp43–58

Buhler, W., S. Morse, E. Arthur, S. Bolton and J. Mann (2002) *Science, Agriculture and Research: A Compromised Participation?*, Earthscan, London

Bunting, A.H. (ed) (1970) *Change in Agriculture*, Duckworth, London

Campilan, D. (2002) 'From capacity development to participatory research performance: What have we learned?' in CIP-UPWARD (ed) *Capacity Development for Participatory Research*, CIP-UPWARD, Los Banos, Laguna, the Philippines, pp77–84

Capra, F. (1996) *The Web of Being: A New Synthesis of Mind and Matter*, Harper Collins, London

Capra, F. (2002) *The Hidden Connections*, HarperCollins, London

Carney, D. (1998) *Sustainable Rural Livelihoods: What Contribution Can We Make?* Papers presented at the Department for International Development's Natural Resources Advisers' Conference, July 1998, DFID, London

Carney, D. (2002) *Sustainable Livelihoods Approaches: Progress and Possibilities for Change*, DFID, London

Carney, D. with M. Drinkwater and T. Rusinow (CARE), K. Neefjes (OXFAM), S. Wanmali and N. Singh (UNDP) (1999) *Livelihoods Approaches Compared*, Brief comparison of the livelihoods approaches of the UK Department for International Development (DFID), CARE, Oxfam and the United National Development Programme (UNDP), DFID, London, November

Carswell, G. (1997) *Agricultural Intensification and Rural Sustainable Livelihoods: A 'Think Piece'*, Working Paper 64, IDS, Sussex, December

Carter, S. E. and H. K. Murwira (1995) 'Spatial variability in soil fertility management and crop response in Mutoko Communal Area, Zimbabwe', *Ambio*, vol 24 no 2, March, pp77–84

CDRA (Community Development Resource Association) (2000) *The High Road – Practice at the Centre*, Annual Report 1999/2000, CDRA, South Africa, www.cdra.org.za

CDRA (2001) *Measuring Development – Holding Infinity*, Annual Report 2000/2001, CDRA, South Africa, www.cdra.org.za

CDS (Centre for Development Studies) et al (2002) *PRAMs: Linking Participation and Institutional Change*, Background working paper on the Participatory Rights Assessment Methodologies (PRAMs) Project (draft 2), CDS, Swansea and Associates Edinburgh Resource Centre Ltd, 31 October, Trivandrum, Kerala, India

Cernea, M. (1997) 'The Risks and Reconstruction Model for Resettling Displaced Populations', *World Development*, vol 25(10), pp1569–1587

Cernea, M. (ed) (1999) *The Economics of Involuntary Resettlement: Questions and Challenges*, The World Bank, Washington, DC

Chabala, H. A., D. H. Kiiru, S. W. Mukuma and D. K. Leonard (1973) 'An evaluation of the Programming and Implementation Management System', Working Paper No 89, Institute for Development Studies, University of Nairobi, Nairobi, March

Chambers, R. (1969) *Settlement Schemes in Tropical Africa: A Study of Organizations and Development*, Routledge and Kegan Paul, London

Chambers, R. (ed) (1970) *The Volta Resettlement Experience*, Pall Mall Press, London

Chambers, R. (1971) 'Creating and expanding organisations for rural development' mimeo, published 1977 in J. S. Coleman, L. Cliffe and M. Doornbos (eds) *Government and Rural Development in East Africa: Essays on Political Penetration*, Martinus Nijhoff, The Hague, pp119–138

Chambers, R. (1974) *Managing Rural Development: Ideas and Experience from East Africa*, The Scandinavian Institute of African Studies, Uppsala

Chambers, R. (1983) *Rural Development: Putting the Last First*, Longman, Harlow, UK

Chambers, R. (1987) *Sustainable Livelihoods, Environment and Development: Putting Poor Rural People First*, Discussion Paper 240, IDS, University of Sussex, Sussex, December

Chambers, R. (1990) 'Complexity, diversity and competence: Towards sustainable livelihoods from farming systems in the 21st century', Paper presented to the 1990 Asian Farming Systems Research and Extension Symposium, Bangkok, November

Chambers, R. (1992) 'Spreading and self-improving: A strategy for scaling up', in M. Edwards and D. Hulme (eds) (1992) *Making a Difference: NGOs and Development in a Changing World*, Earthscan Publications, London

Chambers, R. (1993a) 'Methods for analysis by farmers: The professional challenge', *Journal of Farming Systems Research–Extension*, vol 4(1), pp87–101

Chambers, R. (1993b) *Challenging the Professions: Frontiers for Rural Development*, Intermediate Technology Publications, London

Chambers, R. (1995) 'Making the best of going to scale', *PLA Notes*, vol 24, pp57–61

Chambers, R. (1997a) *Whose Reality Counts? Putting the First Last*, Intermediate Technology Publications, London

Chambers, R. (1997b) 'Editorial: Responsible wellbeing – A personal agenda for development', *World Development*, vol 25(11), pp1743–1754

Chambers, R. (1998a) 'Public management: towards a radical agenda' in M. Minogue, C. Polidano and D. Hulme (eds) (1998) *Beyond the New Public Management: Changing Ideas and Practices in Governance*, Edward Elgar, Cheltenham, UK, and Northampton, Massachusetts, pp117–131

Chambers, R. (1998b) 'Behaviour and attitudes: A missing link in agricultural science?' in V. S. Chopra et al (eds) *Crop Productivity and Sustainability: Shaping the Future*, Oxford and IBH Publishing Co, New Delhi and Calcutta

Chambers, R. (2001) 'The World Development Report: Concepts, content and a Chapter 11', *Journal of International Development*, vol 13, pp299–306

Chambers, R. (2002) *Participatory Workshops: A Sourcebook of 21 Sets of Ideas and Activities*, Earthscan, London

Chambers, R. (2003) 'Participation and numbers', *PLA Notes*, no 47, pp6–12

Chambers, R. and J. Blackburn (1996) *The Power of Participation: PRA and Policy*, Briefing Paper, IDS, Sussex, UK

Chambers, R. and G. Conway (1992) *Sustainable Rural Livelihoods: Practical Concepts for the 21st Century*, IDS Discussion Paper 296, IDS Sussex, UK

Chambers, R. and I. Guijt (1995) 'PRA – five years later. Where are we now?' *Forests, Trees and People Newsletter*, vol 26/27, pp4–14

Chambers, R. and J. Moris (eds) (1973) *Mwea: An Irrigated Rice Settlement in Kenya*, Weltforum Verlag, Munchen

Chambers, R., A. Pacey and L. Thrupp (eds) (1989) *Farmer First: Farmer Innovation and Agricultural Research*, Intermediate Technology Publications, London

Chambers, R. and J. Pettit (2004) 'Shifting power: To make a difference' in L. Groves and R. Hinton (eds) (2004) *Inclusive Aid: Power and Relationships in International Development*, Earthscan, London, pp137–162

Chambers, R., J. Pettit and P. Scott-Villiers (2001) *The New Dynamics of Aid: Power, Procedures and Relationships*, IDS Policy Briefing, no 15

Chambers, R., T. Shah and N. C. Saxena (1989) *To the Hands of the Poor: Water and Trees*, Oxford and IBH Publishing, New Delhi, Bombay, Calcutta

Chambers, R. and J. Stevens (2002) '21 Sources of ideas for trainers and facilitators' in R. Chambers (ed) *Participatory Workshops: A Sourcebook of 21 Sets of Ideas and Activities*, Earthscan, London

Chambers, R. and B. W. E. Wickremanayake (1977) 'Agricultural extension: Myth, reality and challenge' in B. H. Farmer (ed) (1977) *Green Revolution? Technology and Change in Rice-growing Areas of Tamil Nadu and Sri Lanka*, Macmillan, London and Basingstoke, pp155–167

Chawla, L. and V. Johnson (2004) 'Not for children only: Lessons learnt from young people's participation', *Participatory Learning and Action*, no 50, pp63–72

Checkland, P. (1981) *Systems Thinking, Systems Practice*, John Wiley and Sons, Chichester, UK

Chopra, V.L., R. B. Singh and A. Varma (eds) (1998) *Crop Productivity and Sustainability: Shaping the Future, Proceedings of the 2nd International Crop Science Congress*, Oxford and IBH Publishing Co, New Delhi and Calcutta

CIAT (late 1980s) *The IPRA Method*, video, Cuitio Internacional de Agricultura Tropical, Cali, Colombia

CIP–UPWARD (International Potato Center – Users' Perspectives with Agricultural Research and Development) (2002) *Capacity Development for Participatory Research*, CIP–UPWARD, Los Banos, Laguna, the Philippines

Cliffe, L. and J. Saul (eds) (1972) *Socialism in Tanzania: An Interdisciplinary Reader, volume 2 – Policies*, East African Publishing House, Dar es Salaam

Coleman, J. S., L. Cliffe and M. Doornbos (eds) (1977) *Government and Rural Development in East Africa: Essays on Political Penetration*, Martinus Nijhoff, The Hague

Collins (1998) *Collins English Dictionary, Millennium Edition*, HarperCollins, Glasgow

Conroy, C. and M. Litvinoff (eds) (1988) *The Greening of Aid: Sustainable Livelihoods in Practice*, Earthscan Publications Ltd in association with the International Institute for Environment and Development, London

Conway, G. (1985) 'Agro-ecosystem analysis', *Agricultural Administration*, vol 20, pp31–55

Conway, G. R. (1987) 'The properties of agroecosystems', *Agricultural Systems*, vol 24, pp95–117

Conway, G. (1997) *The Doubly Green Revolutiuon: Food for All in the 21st Century*, Penguin Books, London

Conway, G., P. Sajise and W. Knowland (1989) 'Lake Buhi: Resolving conflicts in a Philippines development project', *Ambio*, vol 18(2), pp128–135

Cooke, B. and Uma K. (eds) (2001) Participation: The New Tyranny?, Zed Books, London

Coote, A. (1997) *Citizens' Juries: Theory into Practice*, Institute for Public Policy Research, London

Corcoran-Tindill, M. (2002) *Encouraging Congruent Practice in Irish Development Organisations: Turning the Gaze Back on Ourselves and Asking: What's Really Going On?*, MA dissertation, Development Studies Centre, Holy Ghost College, Kimmage Manor, Dublin

Cornwall, A. (1997) *Roundshaw Participatory Well-being Needs Assessment, Final Report*, Merton, Sutton and Wandswoth Specialist Health Promotion Service, UK

Cornwall, A. (2000) *Beneficiary, Consumer, Citizen: Perspectives for Participation for Poverty Reduction*, Sida Studies No 2, Sida, Stockholm

Cornwall, A. (2003) 'Whose voices? Whose choices? Reflections on gender and participatory development', *World Development*, vol 31(8), pp1325–1342

Cornwall, A. and I. Guijt (2004) 'Shifting perceptions: From infinite innovation to the quest for quality', *Participatory Learning and Action*, no 50, pp160–167

Cornwall, A., S. Musyoki and G. Pratt (2001) *In Search of a New Impetus: Practitioners' Reflections on PRA and Participation in Kenya*, Pathways to Participation, IDS Working Paper 131, IDS, Sussex, September

Cornwall, A. and G. Pratt (eds) (2003) *Pathways to Participation: Reflections on PRA*, Intermediate Technology Publications, London

Cornwall, A. and G. Pratt (2004) *Ideals in Practice: Enquiring into Participation in Sida*, Lessons for Change Series No 12, IDS, Sussex

Cornwall, A., G. Pratt and P. Scott-Villiers (2004) *Participatory Learning Groups in an Aid Bureaucracy*, Lessons for Change Series No 11, IDS, Sussex

Cornwall, A., V. Schattan and P. Coelho (eds) (2004) *New Democratic Spaces? IDS Bulletin*, vol 35(2), IDS, Sussex, April

Cornwall, A. and A. Welbourn (eds) (2002) *Realizing Rights: Transforming Approaches to Sexual and Reproductive Well-being*, Zed Books, London

Cowie, W. (2000) (ed) *Participatory Development/Developpement Participatif, Canadian Journal of Development Studies*, Special issue, vol XXI

Cox, S. and A. Robinson-Pant with B. Elliott, D. Jarvis, S. Lawes, E. Millner and T. Taylor (2003) *Empowering Children through Visual Communication*, School of Education and Professional Development, University of East Anglia, Norwich

Cracknell, B. E. (2000) *Evaluating Development Aid: Issues, Problems and Solutions*, Sage Publications, New Delhi, Thousand Oaks, London

David, R. and A. Mancini (2004) *Going Against the Flow: The Struggle To Make Organisational Systems Part of the Solution rather than Part of the Problem – The Case of ActionAid's Accountability, Learning and Planning System*, Lessons for Change Series No 8, IDS, Sussex

Davies, S. (1996) *Adaptable Livelihoods: Coping with Food Insecurity in the Malian Sahel*, Macmillan Press, Basingstoke, UK, and St Martin's Press, New York

Dawkins, R. (1976) *The Selfish Gene*, Oxford University Press, Oxford (new edition with additional material published in 1989)

DeJong, J. (2003) *Making an Impact in HIV and AIDS: NGO Experiences of Scaling Up*, ITDG Publishing, London

Denning, S. (2000) *The Springboard: How Storytelling Ignites Action in Knowledge-era Organizations*, Butterworth and Heinemann, Boston, Oxford, Auckland, Johannesburg, Melbourne, New Delhi

Development (1997) *Forty Years in Development: The Search for Social Justice, Development*, vol 40(1)

Devereux, S. (2001) 'Livelihood insecurity and social protection: A re-emerging issue in rural development' in C. Ashley and S. Maxwell (eds) (2001) *Rethinking Rural Development: Development Policy Review, Theme Issue*, vol 19(4), December, pp507–519

de Waal, D. (2000) 'The development of participatory media in southern Tanzania', *Forests, Trees and People Newsletter*, vol 40/41, pp14–18

DFID (Department for International Development) (1997) *Eliminating World Poverty: A Challenge for the 21st Century*, White Paper on International Development, Cm 3789, HMSO, London

DFID (1999) *Sustainable Livelihoods Guidance Sheets*, DFID, London , April

DFID (2000) *Realising Human Rights for Poor People*, DFID, London, October

Dilts, R. (2001) 'From farmers' field schools to community IPM', *LEISA*, vol 17(3), October, pp18–21

Dilts, R. and S. Hate (1996) *IPM Farmer Field Schools: Changing Paradigms and Scaling-up*, Agricultural Research and Extension Network Paper No 596, ODI, London January, pp1–4

Dogbe, T. (1998) '"The one who rides the donkey does not know the ground is hot": CEDEP's involvement in the Ghana PPA' in J. Holland with J. Blackburn (eds) *Whose Voice? Participatory Research and Policy Change*, IT Publications, London, pp97–111

Douthwaite, B., T. Kuby, E. van de Fliert and S. Schulz (2003) 'Impact pathway evaluation: An approach for achieving and attributing impact in complex systems', *Agricultural Systems*, vol 78(2), pp243–265, November

Drinkwater, M. (1993) 'Sorting fact from opinion: The use of a direct matrix to evaluate finger millet varieties', *RRA Notes*, vol 17, pp24–28

Dubash, N. K., M. Dupar, S. Kothari and T. Lissue (2001) *A Watershed in Governance? An Independent Assessment of the World Commission on Dams*, World Resources Institute, Lokayan and Lawyers' Environmental Action Team, Washington, DC

Dyck, B., J. Buckland, H. Harder and D. Wiens (2000) 'Community development as organizational learning: The importance of agent–client reciprocity', *Canadian Journal of Development Studies*, vol 21, Special Issue: Participatory Development, pp605–620

Eade, D. (1997) *Capacity-Building: An Approach to People-centred Development*, Oxfam, Oxford, UK

Eade, D. (2003) 'Editorial', *Development in Practice*, vol 13(4), August, pp307–309

Edington, J. (2001) 'Logical? Monitoring against logical frameworks', IA Exchanges, ActionAid UK, March, p9

Education Action (1994–2004) nos 1–18, continuing, ActionAid, London, www.reflect-action.org

Edward, C. G. (1969) 'Understanding the role of community development officer in Embu District, Kenya', Third-year dissertation, Department of Political Science, University College, Dar es Salaam, March

Edwards, M. (1999) *Future Positive: International Cooperation in the 21st Century*, Earthscan, London

Edwards, M. and J. Gaventa (eds) (2001) *Global Citizen Action*, Lynne Rienner Publishers, Boulder, Colorado

Edwards, M. and D. Hulme (eds) (1992) *Making a Difference: NGOs and Development in a Changing World*, Earthscan Publications, London

Edwards, M. and D. Hulme (eds) (1995) *Beyond the Magic Bullet: NGO Performance and Accountability in the Post-Cold War World*, Kumarian Press, West Hartford, Connecticut

Eicher, C. K. and J. M. Staatz (eds) (1984) *Agricultural Development in the Third World*, The Johns Hopkins University Press, Baltimore and London

Ellis, F. (1999) *Rural Livelihood Diversity in Developing Countries: Evidence and Policy Implications*, Natural Resource Perspectives Number 40, ODI, London, April

Elliott, C. (1999) *Locating the Energy for Change: An Introduction to Appreciative Inquiry*, International Institute for Sustainable Development, Winnipeg, Canada

Estrella, M. with J. Blauert, D. Campilan, J. Gaventa, J. Gonsalves, I. Guijt, D. Johnson and R. Ricafort (2000) *Learning from Change: Issues and Experiences in Participatory Monitoring and Evaluation*, IT Publications, London

Eyben, R. (2003) *Donors as Political Actors: Fighting the Thirty Years War in Bolivia*, Working Paper 183, IDS, Sussex, April

Eyben, R. (2004a) *Relationships Matter for Supporting Change in Favour of Poor People*, Lessons for Change Series, No 8, IDS, Sussex

Eyben, R. (2004b) 'Who owns a poverty reduction strategy? A case study of power, instruments and relationships in Bolivia' in L. Groves and R. Hinton (eds) (2004) *Inclusive Aid: Power and Relationships in International Development*, Earthscan, London, pp57–75

Eyben, R. (2004c) *Immersions for Policy and Personal Change*, Policy Briefing, IDS, Sussex

Eyben, R., S. Lister et al (2004) *Why and How to Aid Middle-Income Countries*, IDS Working Paper, IDS, Sussex

Fairhead, J. and M. Leach (1996) *Misreading the African Landscape: Society and Ecology in a Forest–Savanna Mosaic*, Cambridge University Press, UK

Fakih, M., T. Rahardjo and M. Pimbert with A. Sutoko, D. Wulandari and T. Prasetyo (2003) *Community Integrated Pest Management in Indonesia: Institutionalising Participation and People-centred Approaches*, Institutionalising Participation Series, IIED London and IDS, Sussex

Farmer, B. H. (ed) (1977) *Green Revolution? Technology and Change in Rice-growing Areas of Tamil Nadu and Sri Lanka*, Macmillan, London and Basingstoke

Farmer, P. (2003) *Pathologies of Power: Health, Human Rights and the New War on the Poor*, University of California Press, Berkeley, Los Angeles, London

Farrington, J. (2001) *Sustainable Livelihoods, Rights and the New Architecture of Aid*, Natural Resource Perspectives Number 69, ODI, London, June

Farrington, J., R. Blench, I. Christoplos, K. Ralsgård and A. Rudqvist (2002) *Do Area Development Projects Have a Future? Natural Resource Perspectives*, 82, ODI, London, December

Farrington, J. and A. Martin (1988) *Farmer Participation in Agricultural Research: A Review of Concepts and Practices*, Agricultural Administration Unit Occasional Paper 9, Overseas Development Institute, London

Faucheux, S. and G. Froger (1995) 'Decision-making under environmental uncertainty', *Ecological Economics*, vol 15, pp29–42

Faucheux, S. and C. Hue (2001) 'From irreversibility to participation: towards a participatory foresight for the governance of collective environmental risks', *Journal of Hazardous Materials*, vol 86, pp223–243

Fernandez, A. P. (1993) *The MYRADA Experience: The Interventions of a Voluntary Agency in the Emergence and Growth of People's Institutions for Sustained and Equitable Management of Micro-watersheds*, MYRADA, Bangalore, July

Fine, B. (2001) *Social Capital versus Social Theory: Political Economy and Social Science at the Turn of the Millennium*, Routledge, London and New York

Flower, C. and V. Johnson (2004) 'Completing the globe: tackling poverty and injustice in the North', *Participatory Learning and Action*, no 50, pp107–116

Food 2000 (1987) *Food 2000: Global Policies for Sustainable Agriculture – A Report of the Advisory Panel on Food Security, Agriculture, Forestry and Environment of the World Commission on Environment and Development*, Zed Books, London and New Jersey

Forests, Trees and People Newsletter, International Rural Development Centre, Swedish University of Agricultural Sciences, Box 7005, 750 07 Uppsala, Sweden

Forster, R. (ed) (1996) *ZOPP Marries PRA? Participatory Learning and Action – A Challenge for our Services and Institutions*, Workshop documentation, GTZ, Eschborn, Germany

Forsyth, R. S (1991) 'Towards a grounded morality', *Changes*, vol 9(4), pp264–276

Fowler, A. (1997) *Striking a Balance: A Guide To Enhancing the Effectiveness of Non-governmental Organisations in International Development*, Earthscan, London

Fowler, A. (ed) (2000) *Questioning Partnership: The Reality of Aid and NGO Relations*, IDS Bulletin, vol 31(3), July

Francke, M. (2003) 'Including the poor excluded people of Ayacucho in the construction of the "truth": Reflections on methods and processes for the realization of rights', Unpublished paper available from mfrancke@pucp.edu.pe

Frank, R., T. Gilovich and D. Regan (1993) 'Does studying economics inhibit cooperation?' *Journal of Economic Perspectives*, vol 7, pp159–171

Fraser, E., A. Thirkell and A. McKay (2003a) *Tapping into Existing Social Capital: Rich Networks, Poor connections: User Guide*, (Social Development Direct, London; Sinani Durban; IPID Colombo) DFID, London

Fraser, E., A. Thirkell and A. McKay (2003b) *Tapping into Existing Social Capital: Rich Networks, Poor connections: Research Findings*, (Social Development Direct, London; Sinani Durban; IPID Colombo) DFID, London

Freire, P. (1970) *Pedagogy of the Oppressed*, The Seabury Press, New York

Freire, P. (1974) *Education for Critical Consciousness*, Sheed and Ward, London (original edition, Editora Paz e Terra, Rio de Janeiro, 1967)

Freling, D. (ed) (1998) *Paths for Change: Experiences in Participation and Democratisation in Lindi and Mtwara Regions, Tanzania*, Oy Finnagro Ab, Finland

Freudenberger, K. S. (1998) 'The use of RRA to inform policy: tenure issues in Madagascar and Guinea' in J. Holland with J. Blackburn (eds) (1998) *Whose Voice? Participatory Research and Policy Change*, IT Publications, London, pp67–79

Frey, B., W. W. Pommerehne and G. Gilbert (1984) 'Consensus and dissension among economists: An empirical enquiry', *American Economic Review*, vol 74(5), pp986–994

Friis-Hansen, E. and B. Sthapit (eds) (2000) *Participatory Approaches to the Conservation and Use of Plant Genetic Resources*, International Plant Genetic Resources Institute, Rome

Gasper, D. (1997) 'Logical frameworks: A critical assessment of management theory, pluralistic practice', *Working Paper* 264, Institute of Social Studies, The Hague, December

Gasper, D. (2000) 'Evaluating the "logical framework approach" – towards learning-oriented development evaluation', *Public Administration and Development*, vol 20(1), pp17–28

Gautam, K. (1998) 'An encounter with a 17th century manual', *PLA Notes*, vol 32, June, pp40–42

Gaventa, J. (1980) *Power and Powerlessness: Rebellion and Quiescence in an Appalachian Valley*, University of Illinois Press, Chicago

Gaventa, J. (1998) 'The scaling-up and institutionalization of PRA: Lessons and challenges' in J. Blackburn with J. Holland (eds) (1998) *Who Changes? Institutionalizing Participation in Development*, IT Publications, London, pp153–166

Gaventa, J. (2003) 'Power after Lukes: An overview of theories of power since Lukes and their application to development', Unpublished paper, Participation Group, IDS, Sussex, August

Gaventa, J. and J. Blauert (2000) 'Learning to change by learning from change: Going to scale with participatory monitoring and evaluation' in Estrella et al (eds) *Learning from Change: Issues and Experiences in Participatory Monitoring and Evaluation*, IT Publications, London, pp229–243

Ghimire, K. B. and M. P. Pimbert (eds) (1997) Social Change and Conservation: Environmental Politics and Impacts of National Parks and Protected Areas, Earthscan, London

Gibson, T. (1996) *The Power in Our Hands: Neighbourhood Based – World Shaking*, Jon Carpenter, Carlbury, Oxfordshire, UK

Giglioli, E. G. (1973) 'The national organisation of irrigation' in R. Chambers and J. Moris (eds) (1973) *Mwea: An Irrigated Rice Settlement in Kenya*, Weltforum Verlag, Munchen, pp163–183

Gill, G. J. (1991b) 'But how does it compare with the REAL data?' *RRA Notes*, vol 14, pp5–13

Gleick, J. (1988) *Chaos: Making a New Science*, Sphere Books, London

Glover, J. (1999) *Humanity: A Moral History of the Twentieth Century*, Jonathan Cape, London (Pimlico, London, 2001)

Godfrey, E. M. and G. C. M. Mutiso (1973) *The Political Economy of Self–Help: Kenya's Harambee Institutes of Technology*, Working Paper No 107, Institute for Development Studies, University of Nairobi, Nairobi, June

Goetz, A.-M. and R. Jenkins (2001) 'Hybrid forms of accountability: Citizen engagement in institutions of public-sector oversight in India', *Public Management Review*, vol 3(3), pp363–383

Goffman, I. (1961) *Asylums: Essays on the Social Situation of Mental Patients and Other Inmates*, Anchor Books, Doubleday, London (republished by Penguin Books, Harmondsworth, UK, 1968)

GOI (Government of India) (1994) *Guidelines for Watershed Development*, Ministry of Rural Development, Government of India, Delhi

GOI (2002) *Joint Forest Management: A Decade of Partnership*, Joint Forest Management Monitoring Cell, Ministry of Environment and Forests, GOI, Delhi (cited in VIKSAT (ed) *Joint Forest Management in Gujarat*, pp9–10)

GOK (Government of Kenya) (1962) *African Land Development in Kenya 1946–1962*, Ministry of Agriculture, Animal Husbandry and Water Resources, Government of Kenya, Nairobi

Gonsalves, J. (2001) 'Going to scale: what we have garnered from recent workshops', *LEISA*, vol 17(3), pp6–10

Gonsalves, J. F. and R. Armonia (2001) 'Scaling up local successes' in IFAD et al (eds) *Enhancing Ownership and Sustainability*, IFAD, Rome, ANGOC and IIRR, The Philippines, pp242–247

Gordon, G and A. Cornwall (2004) 'Participation in sexual and reproductive well-being and rights' *Participatory Learning and Action*, no 50, pp73–80

Gosselink, P. and P. Strosser (1995) *Participatory Rural Appraisal for Irrigation Management Research: Lessons from IIMI's Experience*, Working Paper No 38, International Irrigation Management Institute, Colombo

Grandin, B. (1988) *Wealth Ranking in Smallholder Communities: A Field Manual*, IT Publications, London

Gray, C. S. (1966) 'Development planning in East Africa: A review article', *The East African Economic Review*, vol 2 (2), pp1–16

Grootaert, C. (1997) 'Social capital: "The Missing Link"' in World Bank (ed) *Expanding the Measure of Wealth: Indicators of Environmentally Sustainable Development*, World Bank, Washington, DC

Groves, L. (2004) 'Questioning, learning and "cutting edge" agendas: Some thoughts from Tanzania' in L. Groves and R. Hinton (eds) (2004) *Inclusive Aid: Power and Relationships in International Development*, Earthscan, London

Groves, L. and R. Hinton (eds) (2004) *Inclusive Aid: Power and Relationships in International Development*, Earthscan, London, pp76–86

GTZ (Deutsche Gesellschaft für Technische Zusammenarbeit) (1988) *ZOPP: An Introduction to the Method*, GTZ, Eschborn, Germany

Guendel, S., J. Hancock and S. Anderson (2001) *Scaling-up Strategies for Research in Natural Resources Management: A Comparative Review*, Natural Resources Institute, University of Greenwich, UK (available from NRI Catalogue Services, CAB International, Wallingford, OX10 8DE, UK – quote ECN17)

Guijt, I. (1995) *Moving Slowly and Reaching Far: Institutionalising Participatory Planning for Child-centred Development*, An interim analysis, IIED/Redd Barna, Uganda

Guijt, I. (1998) *Participatory Monitoring and Impact: Assessment of Sustainable Agricultural Initiatives – An Introduction to the Key Elements*, SARL Discussion Paper no 1, IIED Sustainable Agriculture and Rural Livelihoods Programme, IIED, London

Guijt, I. (forthcoming) *Seeking Surprise: The role of Monitoring to Trigger Learning in Collective Rural Resource Management*, PhD thesis, Wageningen University and Research Centre, Wageningen

Guijt, I. and J. Gaventa (1998) *Participatory Monitoring and Evaluation: Learning from Change*, IDS Policy Briefing 12, IDS, Sussex

Guijt, I. and M. K. Shah (1998) *The Myth of Community: Gender Issues in Participatory Development*, IT Publications, London

Guijt, I. and L. van Veldhuizen (1998) *What Tools? Which Steps? Comparing PRA and PTD*, IIED Issue Paper no 79, December, IIED, London

Gujja, B., M. Pimbert and M. Shah (1998) 'Village voices challenging wetland management policies: PRA experiences from Pakistan and India', in J. Holland with J. Blackburn (eds) (1998) *Whose Voice? Participatory Research and Policy change*, IT Publications, London

Hall, A., V. R. Sulaiman, N. Clark and B. Yoganand (2003) 'From measuring impact to learning institutional lessons: An innovation systems perspective on improving the management of international agricultural research', *Agricultural Systems*, vol 78(2), pp213–241, November

Hammond, S. A. and C. Royal (eds) (1998) *Lessons from the Field: Applying Appreciative Inquiry*, Practical Press Inc, Plano, Texas

Hancock, J. (2002) *Scaling-up Issues and Options: Supporting the World Bank Rural Development Strategy on Implementation of Good Practice and Innovation*, Draft report, 12 August, available from jim.hancock@fao.org

Handy, C. (1989) *The Age of Unreason*, Business Books Limited, Arrow Books, UK

Hanna, N. and R. Picciotto (eds) (2002) *Making Development Work: Development Learning in a World of Poverty and Wealth*, World Bank Series on Evaluation and Development volume 4, Transaction Publishers, New Brunswick, US and London

Harremoës, P., D. Gee, M. MacGarvin, A. Stirling, J. Keys, B. Wynne and S. Guedes Vaz, (eds) (2002) *The Precautionary Principle in the 20th Century: Late Lessons from Early Warnings*, Earthscan, London

Harriss, J. (2002) *Depoliticizing Development: The World Bank and Social Capital*, Anthem Press, London

Hartley, S. (ed) (2002) *CBR: A Participatory Strategy in Africa*, University College London, Centre for International Child Health, London

Havel, V. (1992) Condensation of a speech to the Davos Development Conference, reported in the *New York Times*, 1 March 1992

Haverkort, B., J. van der Kamp and A. Waters-Bayer (1991) *Joining Farmers' Experiments: Experiences in Participatory Technology Development*, Intermediate Technology Publications, London

Hazel, P. and S. Fan (2000) 'Balancing regional development priorities to achieve sustainable and equitable agricultural growth' in D. R. Lee, and C. B. Barrett (eds) *Tradeoffs or Synergies? Agricultural Intensification, Economic Development and the Environment*, CAB International, Wallingford, UK, Chapter 9

HelpAge International (2002) *Participatory Research with Older People: A Sourcebook*, HelpAge International, London, March

Hirschman, A. O. (1967) *Development Projects Observed*, The Brookings Institution, Washington, DC

Hirschmann, D. (2003) 'Keeping "the last" in mind: Incorporating Chambers in consulting', *Development in Practice*, vol 13(5), November, pp487–500

Hobley, M. (2000) *Transformation of Organisations for Poverty Eradication: The Implications of Sustainable Livelihoods Approaches*, Sustainable Livelihoods Support Office, DFID and Hobley Shields Associates, Somerset, UK

Holdcroft, L. E. (1984) 'The rise and fall of community development 1950–1965: A critical assessment' in C. K. Eicher and J. M. Staatz (eds) (1984) *Agricultural Development in the Third World*, The Johns Hopkins University Press, Baltimore and London, pp46–58

Holland, J. with J. Blackburn (eds) (1998) *Whose Voice? Participatory Research and Policy Change*, IT Publications, London

Holmes, T. (1998) *How to Democratise NGOs? Assessing the Role of Participatory Mechanisms for Increasing Downward Accountability*, Unpublished report, IDS, Sussex, August

Holmes, T. (2001) *A Participatory Approach in Practice: Understanding Fieldworkers' Use of Participatory Rural Appraisal in ActionAid The Gambia*, IDS Working paper 123, June, IDS, Sussex

Holmes, T. (2002) 'Rapid spread through many pathways' in PG IDS (ed) *Pathways to Participation: Critical Reflections on PRA*, Participation Group, IDS, Sussex, pp4–5

Holmquist, F. (1970) 'Implementing development projects' in G. Hyden, R. Jackson and J. Okumu (eds) (1970) *Development Administration: The Kenyan Experience*, Oxford University Press, Nairobi

Hope, A. and S. Timmel (1984) *Training for Transformation: A Handbook for Community Workers*, (set of 3 books), Mambo Press, Gweru, Harare (republished IT Publications, London, 1996)

Horton, D. et al (2003) *Evaluating Capacity Development: Experiences from Research and Development Organizations around the World*, ISNAR, The Hague, IDRC, Ottawa, and CTA, The Hague

Horton, D. and R. Mackay (eds) (2003a) *Special Issue. Learning for the Future: Innovative Approaches for Evaluating Agricultural Research and Development, Agricultural Systems*, vol 78(2), November

Horton, D. and R. Mackay (2003b) 'Using evaluation to enhance institutional learning and change: Recent experiences with agricultural research and development', *Agricultural Systems*, vol 78(2), pp127–142, November

Horton, M. and P. Freire (1990) in B. Bell, J. Gaventa and J. Peters (eds) *We Make the Road by Walking – Conversations on Education and Social Change*, Temple University Press, Philadelphia (republished by IT Publications, London)

Howes, M. (2002) 'ActionAid The Gambia' in D. Brown, M. Howes, K. Hussein, C. Longley and K. Swindell (eds) *Participation in Practice: Case Studies from the Gambia*, ODI, London, pp75—121

Hunter, G. (1967) 'Development administration in East Africa', *Journal of Administration Overseas*, vol 6 (1), pp6–12

Hunter, G. (1970) 'Agricultural change and social development' in A. H. Bunting (ed) *Change in Agriculture*, Duckworth, London

Hussein, K. (2002) *Livelihoods Approaches Compared: A Multi-agency Review of Current Practice*, DFID/ODI, London

Hussein, K. and J. Nelson (1998) *Sustainable Livelihoods and Livelihood Diversification*, IDS Working Paper 69, IDS, Sussex, May

Hyden, G., R. Jackson and J. Okumu (eds) (1970) *Development Administration: The Kenyan Experience*, Oxford University Press, Nairobi

IA Exchanges (2002) *Lessons from ActionAid's Annual Review and Reflection Process, IA Exchanges Special*, ActionAid, October

IDS (Institute of Development Studies) (2001) *The New Dynamics of Aid: Power, Procedures and Relationships*, Policy Briefing 15, IDS, Sussex, August

IFAD (International Fund for Agricultural Development), ANGOC (Asian NGO Coalition for Agrarian Reform and Rural Development) and IIRR (International Institute of Rural Reconstruction) (2001) *Enhancing Ownership and Sustainability: A Resource Book on Participation*, IFAD, Rome, ANGOC and IIRR, The Philippines

IH/AA (International HIV/AIDS Alliance) (2001a) *Expanding Community Action on HIV/ AIDS: NGO/CBO Strategies for Scaling-up*, IH/AA, Brighton, UK, June

IH/AA (2001b) *Scaling-up Training for HIV/AIDS Community Initiatives in Eastern and Southern Africa*, IH/AA, Brighton, UK, December

IndiaNPIM (Indian Network on Participatory Irrigation Management) (1999) *Proceedings of the Fourth National Conference on Participatory Irrigation Management (PIM)*,

Hyderabad, 19–23 January 1999, IndiaNPIM, Central Soil and Materials Research Stations, New Delhi

IIRR (International Institute of Rural Reconstruction) (2000) *Going to Scale: CanWe Bring More Benefits to More People More Quickly?*, IIRR, Y. C. James Yen Center, Silang, Cavite, The Philippines, December

Imhof, A., S. Wong and P. Bosshard (2002) *Citizens' Guide to the World Commission on Dams*, International Rivers Network, Berkeley, CA, US

IMM (Integrated Marine Management), ICM (Integrated Coastal Management) and FIRM (Foundation Integrated Rural Management) (2000) *Sustainable Coastal Livelihoods Newsletter*, vol 1(1), IMM, University of Exeter, UK, ICM, Kakinada, Andhra Pradesh, and FIRM, U Kothapalli Mandal, East Godavari District, Andhra Pradesh

International HIV/AIDS Alliance (2003) *Developing HIV/AIDS Work with Drug Users: A Guide to Participatory Assessment and Response*, International HIV/AIDS Alliance, Brighton, UK, August

Irvine, R., R. Chambers and R. Eyben (2004) 'Learning from poor people's experience: Immersions', *Lessons for Change in Policy and Organisations*, no 13, IDS, Sussex

Iyengar, S. and I. Hirway (eds) (2001) *In the Hands of the People: Selected Papers of Anil C. Shah*, Gujarat Institute of Development Research, Ahmedabad, Centre for Development Alternatives, Gujarat, Development Support Centre, Gujarat

James, R. and D. Mullins (2002) 'Supporting NGO partners affected by AIDS in Malawi', *Informed: NGO Funding and Policy Bulletin*, vol 7, INTRAC, pp10–17, November

Jayakaran, R. (2003) *Participatory Poverty Alleviation and Development: A Comprehensive Manual for Development Professionals*, World Vision, China

Jeanrenaud, S. (2002) 'Changing people/nature representations in international conservation discourses', *IDS Bulletin*, vol 33 (1), January, pp11–122

Jenkins, R. and A. Marie Goetz (1999) 'Accounts and accountability: Theoretical implications of the right-to-information movement in India', *Third World Quarterly*, vol 20(3), pp603–622

Johansson, L. (1995) 'Reforming donor driven projects and state bureaucracies through PRA', *Forests, Trees and People Newsletter*, vol 26/27, April, pp59–63

Johansson, L. (2000) 'Participatory video and PRA: Acknowledging the politics of empowerment', *Forests, Trees and People Newsletter*, vol 40/41, pp21–23

Johnson, V. and J. Webster (2000) *Reaching the Parts; Community Mapping: Working Together To Tackle Social Exclusion and Food Poverty*, Sustain and Oxfam, Oxford

Johnson, V., E. Ivan-Smith, G. Gordon, P. Pridmore and P. Scott (eds) (1998) *Stepping Forward: Children and Young People's Participation in the Development Process*, Intermediate Technology Publications, London

Jones, C. (1996) *PRA Methods*, Topic Pack, Participation Group, IDS, Sussex

Joseph, S. (1995) 'Win–Win trainings' and 'Three-way Win–Win', *Participation in Action*, vol 5, ActionAid India, August

JRD (*Journal of Rural Development*) (1999) *Journal of Rural Development, Special Issue on Watershed Development Part II*, vol 18(4), October–December, National Institute of Rural Development, Rajendranagar, Hyderabad

Jupp, D. et al (2003) *Views of the Poor: The Perspectives of Rural and Urban Poor in Tanzania as Recounted through Their Stories and Pictures*, Swiss Agency for Development and Cooperation, Berne, May

Jupp, D. (2004) *Views of the Poor: Some Thoughts on How To Involve Your Own Staff To Conduct Quick, Low Cost But Insightful Research into Poor People's Perspectives*, Draft handbook, DIPM, UK, available from djupp@tiscali.co.uk

Kakande, M. (2004) 'The donor–government–citizen frame as seen by a government participant' in L. Groves and R. Hinton (eds) *Inclusive Aid: Power and Relationships in International Development*, Earthscan, London, pp87–96

Kanbur, R. (1999) 'Basrabai, Meeraiben and the Master of Mohadi: Back-to-office report' (Annex 2) *Approach and Outline:World Development Report 2000/2001, Attacking Poverty*, www.worldbank.org/poverty/newsl/oct99b.htm

Kanbur, R. (ed) (2003) *Q-Squared: Combining Qualitative and Quantitative Methods Poverty Appraisal: Complementarities, Tensions and the Way Forward*, Permanent Black, Delhi

Kane, E., L. Bruce and M. O'Reilly de Brun (1998) 'Designing the future together: PRA and education policy in The Gambia' in J. Holland with J. Blackburn (eds) *Whose Voice? Participatory Research and Policy Change*, IT Publications, London, pp31–43

Kane, L. (2001) *Popular Education and Social Change in Latin America*, Latin America Bureau, London

Kanji, N. (2003) *Mind the Gap: Mainstreaming Gender and Participation in Development*, Institutionalising Participation Series, IIED, London, and IDS, Sussex

Kanji, N. (2004) 'Reflections on gender and participatory development' *Participatory Learning and Action*, no 50, pp53–62

Kanji, N. and L. Greenwood (2001) *Participatory Approaches to Research and Development in IIED: Learning from Experience*, IIED, London, October

Kaplan, A. (2002) *Development Practitioners and Social Process:Artists of the Invisible*, Pluto Press, London and Sterling, Virginia

Kaplan, A. (2003) 'The taking of the horizon (eradicating poverty together?)', Part II in T. Wallace and A. Kaplan (2003) *The Taking of the Horizon: Lessons from ActionAid Uganda's Experience of Changes in Development Practice*, Working Paper No 4, ActionAid, UK (available from iau@actionaid.org.uk)

Kapoor, I. (2002) 'The devil's in the theory: a critical assessment of Robert Chambers' work on participatory development', *Third World Quarterly*, vol 23(1), pp101–117

Kar, K. (2003) *Subsidy or Self-respect? Participatory Total Community Sanitation in Bangladesh*, Working Paper 184, IDS, Sussex, September

Kar, K., J. Adkins and T. Lundstrom (1998) 'Institutionalisation of participation' in D. Freling (ed) *Paths for Change: Experiences in Participation and Democratisation in Lindi and Mtwara Regions, Tanzania*, Oy Finnagro Ab, Finland

Kar, K. and Backhaus, C. (1994) *Old Wine in New Bottles? Experiences with the Application of PRA and Participatory Approaches in a Large-scale, Foreign-funded Government Development Programme in Sri Lanka*, Draft typescript, 13 June (available from PRA, IDS, Brighton, BN1 9RE, UK)

Kenya Human Rights Commission (2000) *Dying to be Free:The Struggle for Rights in Mwea*, Kenya Human Rights Commission, Nairobi

Kerr, J. in collaboration with G. Pangare and V. Lukur Pangare (2002) *Watershed Development Projects in India:An Evaluation*, IFPRI Research Report 127, IFPRI, Washington, DC

Kerr, J. M., N. K. Sanghi and G. Sriramappa (1996) Subsidies in Watershed Development Projects, Gatekeeper Series 61, International Institute for Environment and Development, London

Kievelitz, U. and Scherler, C. (eds) (1995) *Participatory Learning Approaches in Multisectoral Projects: Experiences from Rural and Urban Development Cooperation in Africa, Asia and Latin America*, GTZ, Eschborn, Bonn, Germany

Kimana, G. (2001) 'Sharing our finances', *Review and Reflection, IA Exchanges Special*, ActionAid, London, September, pp4–5

Kingsley, M. A. and P. Musante (1996) *Activities for Developing Linkages and Coooperative Exchange among Farmers' Organisations, NGOs, Gos and Researchers – Case Study of an*

NGO-coordinated Integrated Pest Management Project in Indonesia, AGREN Paper 59b, January, pp 5–13

KKU (Khon Kaen University) (1987) *Proceedings of the 1985 International Conference on Rapid Rural Appraisal*, Rural Systems Research and Farming systems Research Projects, Khon Kaen University, Thailand

Kolavalli, S. and J. Kerr (2002a) 'Mainstreaming participatory watershed development', *Economic and Political Weekly*, 19 January, pp225–242

Kolavalli, S. and J. Kerr (2002b) 'Scaling up Participatory Watershed Development in India', *Development and Change*, vol 33(2), pp213–235

Korten, D. (1980) 'Community organization and rural development: A learning process approach', *Public Administration Review*, vol 40, September–October, pp480–510

Korten, D. (1981) in *Rural Development Participation Review*, winter, Rural Development Committee, Cornell, Ithaca, NY, pp1–8

Korten, D. (1984) 'Rural development programming: The learning process approach' in D. C. Korten and R. Klauss (eds) (1984) *People-centered Development: Contributions Toward Theory and Planning Frameworks*, Kumarian Press, West Hartford, Connecticut, pp176–188

Korten, D. (1990) *Getting to the 21st Century: Voluntary Action and the Global Agenda*, Kumarian Press, West Hartford

Korten, D. C. and R. Klauss (eds) (1984) *People-centered Development: Contributions Toward Theory and Planning Frameworks*, Kumarian Press, West Hartford, Connecticut

Korten, F. F. and R. Y. Siy (eds) (1989) *Transforming a Bureaucracy: The Experience of the Philippine National Irrigation Administration*, Kumarian Press, West Hartford, and Ateneo de Manila University Press, Quezon City, The Philippines

Kulp, E. (1970) *Rural Development Planning: Systems Analysis and Working Method*, Praeger, New York

Kumar, S. (ed) (1996) *ABC of PRA: Attitude Behaviour Change*, A Report on a South–South Workshop on PRA: Attitudes and Behaviour, organised by ActionAid India and SPEECH (available from PRAXIS, 12 Patliputra Colony, Patna 800013, Bihar, India), www.praxisindia.org

Kumar, S. (2002) *Methods for Community Participation: A Complete Guide for Practitioners*, Vistaar Publications, New Delhi

Kumaran, R. (2004) *Listening as a Radical Act*, ActionAid India Working Paper Series

Laframboise, H. L. (1971) 'Administrative reform in the federal public service: Signs of a saturation psychosis', *Canadian Public Administration*, vol 14(3), pp303–325

Ledesma, A. L. and K. Osner (eds) (1988) *Ways and Steps Towards Solidarity: Experiences and Impetus from a German–Philippines Exposure and Dialogue Program*, The German Commission Justitia et Pax, Bonn, and the Centre for the Development of Human Resources in Rural Asia, Manila

Lee, D. R. and C. B. Barrett (eds) (2000) *Tradeoffs or Synergies? Agricultural Intensification, Economic Development and the Environment*, CAB International, Wallingford, UK

LEISA (*Low External Input and Sustainable Agriculture*) (2001) *Lessons in Scaling Up*, LEISA, vol 17(3), October, ILEIA, Leusden, The Netherlands

Leonard, D. K. (ed) (1973) *Rural Administration in Kenya*, East African Literature Bureau, Nairobi

Leonard, D. K. (1991) *African Successes: Four Public Managers in Kenyan Rural Development*, University of California Press, Berkeley, Los Angeles, Oxford

Levy, H. (ed) (1996) *They Cry 'Respect': Urban Violence and Poverty in Jamaica*, Centre for Population, Community and Social Change, University of the West Indies, Mona, Kingston, Jamaica

Levy, S. (2003) 'Are we targeting the poor? Lessons from Malawi', *PLA Notes*, vol 47, August, pp19–24

Lewis, J. and P. Walker (eds) (1998) *Participation Works! 21 Techniques of Community Participation for the 21st Century*, New Economics Foundation, London, www.new economics.org

Leys, C. (1970) 'The primacy of politics' in D. Seers and L. Joy (eds), *Development in a Divided World*, Penguin, Harmondsworth

Lightfoot, C., M. Prein and T. Lopez (1994) 'Bioresource flow modeling with farmers', *ILEIA Newsletter*, October, pp22–23

Lister, S. and W. Nyamugasira (2003) 'Design contradictions in the 'new architecture of aid'? Reflections from Uganda on the roles of civil society organisations', *Development Policy Review*, vol 21 (1), pp93–106

Lobo, C. and G. Kochendörfer-Lucius (1995) *The Rain Decided to Help Us: Participatory Watershed Management in the State of Mhahrashtra, India*, EDI Learning Resources Series, The World Bank, Washington, DC

Lukes, S. (1974) *Power: A Radical View*, Macmillan, Basingstoke

Mallik, A. H. (1996) 'Sharing our experiences: An appeal to donors and governments', *PLA Notes*, vol 27, October, pp74–76

Mander, H. (2001) *Unheard Voices: Stories of Forgotten Lives*, Penguin Books, New Delhi, London, New York, Victoria, Toronto and Auckland

Mander, H. (2004) *The Ripped Chest: Public Policy and the Poor in India*, Books for Change, Bangalore, bfc@actionaidindia.org

Manoharan, M. K., K. Velayudham and N. Shunmugavalli (1993) 'PRA: An approach to find felt needs of crop varieties', *RRA Notes*, vol 18, pp66–68

Marsden, R. (2001) 'ALPS: Some key challenges', *IA Exchanges*, ActionAid UK, March, pp7–8

Marsden, R. (2004) 'Exploring power and relationships: a perspective from Nepal' in L. Groves and R. Hinton (eds) (2004) *Inclusive Aid: Power and Relationships in International Development*, Earthscan, London, pp97–107

Masaiganah, M. S. (2003) 'Reflecting on the past: My journey to participation', in A. Cornwall and G. Pratt (eds), *Pathways to Participation: Reflections on PRA*, ITDG Publishing, Rugby

Mascarenhas, J., P. Shah, S. Joseph, R. Jayakaran, J. Devavaram, V. Ramachandran, A. Fernandez, R. Chambers and J. Pretty (eds) (1991) *Proceedings of the February 1991 Bangalore PRA Workshop*, RRA Notes vol 13, August

Mathur, Y. (1998) *Proceedings of the Workshop on Attitude and Behaviour Change in Participatory Processes* 24–28 August 1998, Lal Bahadur Shastri National Academy of Administration, Mussoorie, India

Maurya, D.M., A. Bottrall and J. Farrington (1988) 'Improved livelihoods, genetic diversity and farmer participation: a strategy for rice-breeding in rainfed areas of India', *Experimental Agriculture*, vol 24(3), pp311–320

May, J. (1996) 'Kicking down doors and lighting fires: Participating in policy', Paper for the PRA and Policy Workshop, 13–14 May, IDS, Sussex, UK (see also Attwood and May, 1998)

Mayoux, L. (2003a) *Participatory Action Learning System: An Empowering Approach to Monitoring, Evaluation and Impact Assessment*, Draft manual, June, www.enterprise–impact.org.uk

Mayoux, L. (2003b) *Thinking It Through: Using Diagrams in Impact Assessment*, www.enterprise–impact.org.uk

Mayoux, L. (2003c) *Grassrooots Action Learning: Impact Assessment for Downward Accountability and Civil Society Development*, www.enterprise–impact.org.uk

McCarthy, J. and K. Galvão (2004) *Enacting Participatory Development: Theatre-based Techniques*, Earthscan, London

McGee, R. (2002) 'The self in participatory poverty research', in K. Brock and R. McGee (eds) *Knowing Poverty: Critical Reflections on Participatory Research and Policy*, Earthscan, London, pp14–39

McGee, R. with J. Levene and A. Hughes (2002) *Assessing Participation in Poverty Reducation Strategy Papers: A Desk-based Synthesis of Experience in Sub-Saharan Africa*, Research Report 52, IDS, Sussex, February

McGee, R. with A. Norton (2000) *Participation in Poverty Reduction Strategies: A Synthesis of Experience with Participatory Approaches to Policy Design, Implementation and Monitoring*, IDS Working Paper 109, May, www.ids/ac/ids/publicat

Mda, Z. (1993) *When People Play People: Development Communication through Theatre*, Zed Books, London and Witwatersrand University Press, Johannesburg

Mehta, L. (2002a) 'The World Commission on Dams + eighteen months', *Science and Public Affairs*, June, pp24–25

Mehta, L. (2002b) 'Displaced by development: Gender, rights and "risks of impoverishment"' in IDS (eds) *Insights: Responding to Development*, IDS, Sussex, December

Mehta, L. and K. Cockburn (2003) *Tales of the Unexpected*, IDS Policy Briefing 16, IDS, Sussex, May

Milimo, J., T. Shillito and K. Brock (undated) *The Poor of Zambia Speak: Who Would Ever Listen to the Poor?*, D Poverty 4337 in Participation Resource Centre, IDS, Sussex

Milimo, J., A. Norton and D. Owen (1998) 'The impact of PRA approaches and methods on policy and practice: The Zambia PPA', in J. Holland with J. Blackburn (eds) *Whose Voice? Participatory Research and Policy Change*, IT Publications, London, pp103–111

Minogue, M., C. Polidano and D. Hulme (eds) (1998) *Beyond the New Public Management: Changing Ideas and Practices in Governance*, Edward Elgar, Cheltenham, UK, and Northampton, MA, US

Molander, C. F. (1972) 'Management by objectives in perspective', *Journal of Management Studies* vol 9(1), February, pp74–81

Moore, M. and A. Teresa Lima (2004) *Aid Proliferation: How Responsible Are the Donors?* Working Paper 214, IDS, Sussex

Moris, J. (1972) 'Administrative authority and the problem of effective agricultural administration in East Africa', *The African Review*, vol 2(1), June

Morse, B. and T. Berger (1992) *Sardar Sarovar, Report of the Independent Review*, Resource Futures International (RFI) Inc, Ottawa, Canada

Morss, E. R. (1984) 'Institutional destruction resulting from donor and project proliferation in sub-Saharan African countries', *World Development*, vol 12(4), pp465–70

Moser, C. (2003) '"Apt illustration" or "anecdotal information"? Can qualitative data be representative or robust?' in R. Kanbur (ed) *Q-squared: Qualitative and Quantitative Methods of Poverty Appraisal*, Permanent Black, Delhi, pp79–89

Moser, C. and J. Holland (1997) *Urban Poverty and Violence in Jamaica*, World Bank Latin American and Caribbean Studies Viewpoints, World Bank, Washington, DC

Moser, C. and C. McIlwaine (1999) 'Participatory urban appraisal and its application for research on violence', *Environment and Urbanization*, vol 11(2), October, pp203–226

Moser, C. and C. McIlwaine (2000a) *Urban Poor Perceptions of Violence and Exclusion in Colombia*, Latin American and Caribbean Region, Environmentally and Socially Sustainable Development Sector Management Unit, World Bank, Washington, DC

Moser, C. and C. McIlwaine (2000b) *Violence in a Post-conflict World: Urban Poor Perceptions from Guatemala*, Latin America and Caribbean Region, Environmentally and Socially Sustainable Development Sector Management Unit, World Bank, Washington, DC

Moser, C. and C. McIlwaine (2004) *Encounters with Violence in Latin America: Urban Poor Perceptions from Colombia and Guatemala*, Routledge, New York and London

Moser, C. and A. Norton with T. Conway, C. Ferguson and P. Vizard (2001) *To Claim Our Rights: Livelihood Security, Human Rights and Sustainable Development*, ODI, London

Mosse, D. (2003) 'The making and marketing of participatory development' in P. van Ufford and A. Kumar Giri (eds) *A Moral Critique of Development: In Search of Global Responsibilities*, Routledge, London, pp 43–75

Mosse, D. (2005) *Cultivating Development: An Ethnography of Aid Policy and Practice*, Pluto Press, London and Sterling, VA

Moya, X. and S.-A. Way (2004) 'Winning spaces: Participatory methodologies in rural processes in Mexico', *IDS Working Paper*, IDS, Sussex

MRALG (Ministry of Regional Administration and Local Government), Tanzania (1999) *Whose Priorities in Policy Making? Reflections from the Permanent Secretaries' Retreat on Pparticipation in Tanzania*, Tarangire, Arusha, 10–11 February 1999, MRALG, Tanzania

MRDP (Mountain Rural Development Programme) (2001) *Looking at MRDP*, Vietnam–Sweden Mountain Rural Development Programme (MRDP), Hanoi

Mukherjee, N. (1995) *Participatory Rural Appraisal and Questionnaire Survey: Comparative Field Experience and Methodological Innovations*, Concept Publishing Company, New Delhi

Mukherjee, N. (1998) 'The rush to scale: Lessons being learnt in Indonesia', in Blackburn, J. with J. Holland (eds) (1998) *Who Changes? Institutionalizing Participation in Development*, IT Publications, London, pp 23–29

Mukherjee, N. (2001) *Participatory Learning and Action, with 100 Field Methods*, Concept Publishing Company, New Delhi

Mukherjee, N. and B. Jena (eds) (2001) *Learning to Share: Experiences and Reflections on PRA and Other Participatory Approaches, volume 2*, Concept Publishing Company, New Delhi

Mukherjee, N. and C. van Wijk (eds) (2003) *Sustainability Planning and Monitoring in Community Water Supply and Sanitation: A Guide on the Methodology for Participatory Assessment (MPA) for Community-driven Development Programs*, Water and Sanitation Program, World Bank and IRC, The Netherlands

Murphy, C. (1995) *Implications of Poverty for Black Rural Women in Kwazulu/Natal*, Report for the South African Participatory Poverty Assessment, Institute of Natural Resources, Scottsville, South Africa

Murthy, R. K. (1998) 'Learning about participation from gender relations of female infanticide' in Guijt, I. and M. K. Shah (1998) *The Myth of Community: Gender Issues in Participatory Development*, IT Publications, London, pp78–92

Musyoki, S. (2003) 'Can bilateral programmes become learning organisations?' in L. Roper, J. Pettit and D. Eade (eds) (2003) *Development and the Learning Organisation: Essays from Development in Practice*, Oxfam GB, Oxford, UK, pp152–168

Narayan, D., R. Chambers, M. K. Shah and P. Petesch (2000) *Crying Out for Change: Voices of the Poor*, Oxford University Press for the World Bank, Oxford

Narayan, D. with R. Patel, K. Schafft, A. Rademacher and S. Koch-Schulte (2000) *Voices of the Poor: Can Anyone Hear Us?*, Oxford University Press for the World Bank, Oxford

Narayan, D. and L. Prichett (1997) 'Cents and sociability: Household income and social capital in rural Tanzania', Development Research Group, Policy Research Working Paper

1796, World Bank, Washington, DC (see also *Economic Development and Cultural Change*, vol 47(4), pp871–897)

Neefjes, K. (2000) *Environments and Livelihoods: Strategies for Sustainability*, Oxfam, Oxford

Nelson, N. and S. Wright (eds) (1995) *Power and Participatory Development: Theory and Practice*, Intermediate Technology Publications, London

NES (National Environment Secretariat) (1990) *Participatory Rural Appraisal Handbook*, National Environment Secretariat, Kenya; Clark University, Egerton University and the Centre for International Development and Environment at WRI, February

Nierras, R. M. (2002) *Generating Numbers with Local Governments in the Philippines*, Draft manuel, IDS, Sussex

Njeru, M. (2003) 'Baringo cries out as famine bites', *Daily Nation* on the web, www.nationmedia.com, 25 February

Norrish, P. (1994) 'Space to negotiate: How a critical requirement of participatory training is too often ignored', *The Rural Extension Bulletin* 6 December, p16

Norton, A. (1998a) 'Some reflections on the PPA processes and lessons learned', in J. Holland with J. Blackburn (eds) (1998) *Whose Voice? Participatory Research and Policy Change*, IT Publications, London, pp143–146

Norton, A. (1998b) 'Analysing participatory research for policy change' in J. Holland with J. Blackburn (eds) (1998) *Whose Voice? Participatory Research and Policy Change*, IT Publications, London, pp179–191

Norton, A. with B. Bird, K. Brock, M. Kakande and C. Turk (eds) (2001) *A Rough Guide to PPAs: Participatory Poverty Assessment – An Introduction to Theory and Practice*, ODI, London

Norton, A. and D. Elson (2002) *What's Behind the Budget? Politics, Rights and Accountability in the Budget Process*, Overseas Development Institute, London, June

Norton, A., D. Kroboe, E. Bortei-Dorku and D. K. T. Dogbe (1995) *Ghana Participatory Poverty Assessment: Consolidated Report on Poverty Assessment in Ghana Using Qualitative and Participatory Research Methods*, Draft report. AFTHR, World Bank, Washington, DC

Norton, A., D. Owen and J. Milimo (1994) *Zambia Poverty Assessment: volume 5: Participatory Poverty Assessment*, Report no 12985-ZA, Washington, DC, November

Norton, A. and D. Owen (1996) *The Zambia Participatory Poverty Assessment: Notes on the Process and Lessons Learned*, Paper for the PRA and Policy Workshop, IDS, Sussex, Brighton, UK

Norton, A. and T. Stephens (1995) *Participation in Poverty Assessments*, Social Policy and Resettlement Division Discussion Paper, World Bank, Washington, DC, www.worldbank.org/wbi/sourcebook/sba202.htm

Nussbaum, M. C. and A. Sen (eds) (1993) *The Quality of Life*, Oxford University Press, Oxford

Nyamachumbe, F. (2000) '*Utambie wananchi* – Tell the people! Participatory evaluation and video, the case of the Kilwa fish market in Southern Tanzania', interview with Venera Knippel, *Forests, Trees and People Newsletter*, vol 40/41, pp19–20

Nyamu-Musembi, C. (2002) *Towards an Actor-oriented Perspective on Human Rights*, IDS Working Paper 169, IDS, Sussex

Nyangira, N. (1970) 'Chiefs' *barazas* as agents of administrative and political penetration', *Staff Paper*, no 80, Institute for Development Studies, University of Nairobi, July

Oakley, P. et al (1991) *Projects with People: The Practice of Participation in Rural Development*, ILO, Geneva

Oakley, P. and D. Marsden (1984) *Approaches to Participation in Rural Development*, ILO, Geneva

OAU (Organization for African Unity) (1981) *African Charter on Human and Peoples' Rights ('Banjul Charter')*, OAU Doc CAB/LEG/67/3 Rev 5, reprinted in 21 I.L.M. 59 (1982), OAU, Addis Ababa

OECD (Organisation for Economic Co-operation and Development) (2003) *Harmonising Donor Practices for Effective Aid Delivery: Good Practice Papers*, DAC Guidelines and References Series, OECD, Paris

OHCHR (Office of the High Commissioner for Human Rights) (2002) *Draft Guidelines: A Human Rights Approach to Poverty Reduction Strategies*, OHCHR, Geneva

Okali, C., J. Sumberg and J. Farrington (1994) *Farmer Participatory Research: Rhetoric and Reality*, Intermediate Technology Publications on behalf of the Overseas Development Institute, London

Orr, A. (2003) 'Integrated pest management for resource-poor African farmers: Is the emperor naked?', *World Development*, vol 31(5), pp831–845

Orwell, G. (1933) *Down and Out in Paris and London*, Gollancz, London (republished by Penguin Books, Harmondsworth, UK, 1940)

Osner, K. (1999) *The Exposure and Dialogue Programme 'Empowerment through Organising': Brief Report and Initial Evaluation*, Unpublished report, Association for the Promotion of North–South Dialogue, Bonn

Osner, K. (2002) *Exposure, Reflection and Dialog: Empowerment for Shaping Pro-poor Policy*, Presentation of the EDP methodology at the World Bank, Washington, DC, 31 October

Osner, K. (2004) 'Using exposure methodology for dialogue on key issues' in *Reality and Analysis – Personal and Technical Reflections on the Working Lives of Six Women*, Cornell–SEWA–WIEGO Exposure and Dialogue Program, Gujarat, 10–15 January 2004, Working Paper WP 2004–06 Department of Applied Economics and Management, Cornell University, Ithaca, New York. www.arts.cornell.edu/poverty/kanbur/EDPCompendium.pdf

Osner, K. and A. Krauss (2000) *Exposure and Dialogue as a Powerful Instrument for Shaping Policy-making*, Presentation at the Second Annual Meeting of WIEGO (Women in the Informal Economy, Globalizing and Organizing), Cambridge, MA, May

Owusu, C. (2001) 'Facing up to the challenges', *IA Exchanges Special: Review and Reflection*, ActionAid, September, pp13–14

Owusu, C. (2004) 'An international NGO's staff reflections on power, procedures and relationships' in L. Groves and R. Hinton (eds) (2004) *Inclusive Aid: Power and Relationships in International Development*, Earthscan, London, pp108–122

Oyugi, W. O. (1973) ' Participation in development planning at the local level', in D. K. Leonard (ed) *Rural Administration in Kenya*, East African Literature Bureau, Nairobi, pp53–75

Papanek, G. F. (1968) 'Changes in aid strategy' in *Confrontation: The First Development Decade – A Review; The Second Development Decade – A Preview*, Mimeo, Vienna Institute for Development, Vienna, June

Parasuraman, S., G. K. Raj and B. Fernandez (2004) *Listening to People Living in Poverty*, Books for Change, Bangalore

Participation Group, IDS (2002) *Pathways to Participation: Critical Reflections on PRA*, IDS, Sussex

Participatory Learning and Action (formerly PLA Notes) (2004) no 50, Reflections and Directions, October, www.planotes.org

Pasteur, K. (2002) *Changing Organisations for Watershed Management in India: From Policy to Practice*, IDS, Sussex

Pasteur, K. (2004) *Learning for Development: A Literature Review*, Lessons for Change Series No 6, IDS, Sussex

Pasteur, K. and P. Scott-Villiers (2004) *If Relationships Matter, How Can They Be Improved? Learning about Relationships in Development*, Lessons for Change Series No 9, IDS, Sussex

Patel, S. (2004) 'Tools and methods for empowerment developed by slum and pavement dwellers' federations in India', *Participatory Learning and Action*, no 50, pp117–130

Paul, B. (2001) 'Scaling up participatory rural appraisal: Lessons from Vietnam' in IFAD, ANGOC and IIRR, *Enhancing Ownership and Sustainability: A Resource Book on Participation*, IFAD, Rome, ANGOC and IIRR, The Philippines, pp64–69

Paul, B. (2003) 'PRA values: How to become a true believer' in A. Cornwall and G. Pratt (eds), *Pathways to Participation: Reflections on PRA*, ITDG Publishing, Rugby, pp135–139

Paul, S. (2002) *Holding the State to Account: Citizen Monitoring in Action*, Books for Change, Bangalore

Pavignani, E. and V. Hauck (2002) *Pooling of Technical Assistance in Mozambique: Innovative Practices and Challenges*, Discussion Paper No 39, ECDPM, Maastricht, The Netherlands

Perez, C. and H. Tschinkel (2003) *Improving Watershed Management in Developing Countries: A Framework for Prioritising Sites and Practices*, Network Paper 129, AgRen Network, ODI, July

Peters, T. (1989) *Thriving on Chaos: Handbook for a Management Revolution*, Pan Books, London

Peters, T. J. and R. H. Waterman (1982) *In Search of Excellence: Lessons from America's Best-run Companies*, Harper and Row Publishers, New York

Pettit, J. (2000) 'Strengthening local organisation "where the rubber hits the road"', in A. Fowler (ed) *Questioning Partnership*, pp57–67

Pettit, J. and S. Musyoki (2004) 'Rights, advocacy and participation – what's working?' *Participatory Learning and Action*, no 50, pp97–106

Pettit, J. and L. Roper (eds) (2002) *Development in Practice*, vol 12 (nos 3 and 4), August

PG IDS (Institute of Development Studies) (2002) *Pathways to Participation: Critical Reflections on PRA*, Participation Group, IDS, Sussex

Phnuyal, B. K. (1999) 'Rejecting "the manual" for more critical and participatory analysis: REFLECT's experience in El Salvador', *PLA Notes*, vol 34, February, pp68–72

Phuyan, B. (1992) *Participatory Rural Appraisal: Utilization Survey Report Part 1. Rural Development Area Sindhupalchowk, Nepal*, ActionAid, Nepal, Kathmandu, July (available from PRA, Institute of Development Studies, University of Sussex, Brighton BN1 9RE, UK)

Picciotto, R., W. van Wicklin and E. Rice (eds) (2001) *Involuntary Resettlement: Comparative Perspectives*, Transaction Publishers, New Brunswick, US, and London, UK

PID (Program for International Development) and NES (National Environment Secretariat) (1989) *An Introduction to Participatory Appraisal for Rural Resources Management*, PID, Clark University, Worcester, Massachusetts, and NES, Ministry of Environment and Natural Resources, Nairobi, November

Pimbert, M. (2004) 'Natural resources, people and participation' *Participatory Learning and Action*, no 50, pp131–139

Pimbert, M. P. and T. Wakeford (2002) *Prajateerpu: A Citizen's Jury/Scenario Workshop on Food and Farming Futures for Andhra Pradesh, India*, IIED, London, and IDS, Sussex

PLA Notes (1998) *Participation, Literacy and Empowerment*, no 32, June

PLA Notes (2000) *Participatory Processes in the North*, no 38, June

PLA Notes (2003) *Participatory Processes for Policy Change*, no 46, IIED, London, February

Pollock, J. (2002) 'Ethical guidelines for participatory research with sex workers' in *Horizons Report, HIV/AIDS Operations Research*, Population Council/Horizons Program, Washington, DC, May, p10

Pontius, J., R. Dilts and A. Bartlett (eds) (2002) *From Farmer Field School to Community IPM: Ten Years of IPM Training in Asia*, FAO Regional Office for Asia and the Pacific, Bangkok (copies from meetings and publications officer, FAO Regional Office, Phra Athit Road, Bangkok 10200, Thailand)

Pound, B., S. Snapp, C. McDougall and A. Braun (eds) (2003) *Managing Natural Resources for Sustainable Livelihoods: Uniting Science and Participation*, Earthscan, London

Prasad, R. (2003) 'PRA as learning and empowerment – for children too', in A. Cornwall and G. Pratt (eds), *Pathways to Participation: Reflections on PRA*, ITDG Publishing, Rugby, pp156–163

Pratt, B. (2003) 'Rights or values?', *ONTRAC*, no 23, January, INTRAC, Oxford

Pratt, G. (2001) *Practitioners' Critical Reflections on PRA and Participation in Nepal*, Pathways to Participation, IDS Working Paper 122, January

PRAXIS (Institute for Participatory Practices) (circa 1997) *PRA Reflections from the Field and Practitioners*, PRAXIS, Patna, India

Premkumar, P. D. (1994) *Farmers are Engineers: Indigenous Soil and Water Conservation Practices in a Participatory Watershed Development Programme*, Kamalapura, Gulbarga, Karnataka, India

Pretty, J. (1994) 'Alternative systems of inquiry for a sustainable agriculture', *IDS Bulletin*, vol 25(2), pp37–48

Pretty, J. (1995a) *Regenerating Agriculture: Policies and Practice for Sustainability and Self-reliance*, Earthscan, London, and Vikas Publishers and ActionAid, Bangalore

Pretty, J. (1995b) 'Participatory learning for sustainable agriculture', *World Development*, vol 23(8), pp1247–1263

Pretty, J., M. Griffin, M. Sellens and C. Pretty (2003) *Green Exercise: Complementary Roles of Nature, Exercise and Diet in Physical and Emotional Well-being and Implications for Public Health Policy*, Centre for Environment and Society Occasional Paper 2003–1, University of Essex, UK

Pretty, J. and I. Scoones (1995) 'Institutionalizing adaptive planning and local-level concerns: Looking to the future', N. Nelson and S. Wright (eds) *Power and Participatory Development: Theory and Practice*, Intermediate Technology Publications, London, pp157–169

Pretty, J., J. Thompson and F. Hinchcliffe (1996) *Sustainable Agriculture: Impacts on Food Production and Food Security*, Gatekeeper Series 60, International Institute for Environment and Development, London

Pretty, J. and H. Ward (2001) 'Social capital and the environment', *World Development*, vol 29(2), February, pp209–227

PRGA (Program on Participatory Research and Gender Analysis) (circa 2002) *PRGA Program: Synthesis of Phase I (1997–2002)*, CGIAR, www.prgdprogramme.org

Princeton Survey Associates (2002) *The Global Poll: Multinational Survey of Opinion Leaders 2002*, Princeton Survey Associates, Princeton (summarized in Bretton Woods Project e-communication 4 August 2003)

Probst, K. and J. Hagmann with M. Fernandez and J. A. Ashby (2003) *Understanding Participatory Research in the Context of Natural Resource Management – Paradigms, Approaches and Typologies*, Network Paper No 130, AgRen Network, ODI, July

Putnam, R. (1993) *Making Democracy Work: Civic Traditions in Modern Italy*, Princeton University Press, Princeton, New Jersey

Ragavan, J. V. (1967) 'Administrative aspect of improved seed programme', *The Indian Journal of Public Administration*, vol 3 (3), pp511–521

Ramakrishnan, R., M. Dubey, R. K Raman, P. Baumann and J. Farrington (2002) *Panchayati Raj and Natural Resource Management: National-level Synthesis Report*, Ford Foundation, New Delhi (available from www.odi.org.uk and www.panchayats.org)

Rambaldi, G., S. Bugna, A. Tiangco and D. de Vera (2002) 'Bringing the vertical dimension to the negotiating table', Paper to sixth seminar on GIS and Developing Countries, 15–18 May 2002, International Institute for Aerospace Survey and Earth Sciences, ITC, The Netherlands

Reason, P. and H. Bradbury (eds) (2001) *Handbook of Action Research: Participative Inquiry and Practice*, Sage Publications, London, Thousand Oaks, California, and New Delhi

Reeler, D. (2004) *Story-telling: Getting to the Heart of Things*, CDRA Nugget, CDRA, Woodstock, South Africa, www.cdra.org.za

Reij, C., I. Scoones and C. Toulmin (eds) (1996) *Sustaining the Soil: Indigenous Soil and Water Conservation in Africa*, Earthscan Publications, London

Republic of Kenya (1972) *1972/1973 Estimates of Recurrent Expenditure of the Government of Kenya for the year ending 30 June 1975*, Government Printer, Nairobi

Republic of Rwanda (2001a) *Ubudehe mu kurwanya ubukene: Ubudehe to Fight Poverty*, National Poverty Reduction Programme and Ministry of Local Government and Social Affairs, Rwanda

Republic of Rwanda (2001b) *Development of the final Poverty Reduction Strategy Paper (PSP) – May 2001*, Ministry of finance and Economic Planning, Rwanda

Republic of Zambia (1971) *Second National Development Plan, January 1972–December 1976*, Ministry of Development Planning and National Guidance, Lusaka, December

Resnick, M. (1994) *Turtles, Termites and Traffic Jams: Explorations in Massively Parallel Microworlds*, MIT Press, Cambridge, Massachusetts

Rhoades, R. (1982) *The Art of the Informal Agricultural Survey*, International Potato Centre, Lima

Robb, C. (1998) 'PPAs: A review of the World Bank's experience' in J. Holland with J. Blackburn (eds) (1998) *Whose Voice? Participatory Research and Policy Change*, IT Publications, London, pp131–142

Robb, C. (2002) *Can the Poor Influence Policy? Participatory Poverty Assessments in the Developing World*, second edition, World Bank 'Directions in Development', World Bank, Washington, DC

Roche, C. (1992) 'It's not size that matters: ACORD's experience in Africa' in M. Edwards and D. Hulme (eds) *Making a Difference: NGOs and Development in a Changing World*, Earthscan Publications, London, pp180–190

Roche, C. (1997) 'Preface' in D. Eade (ed) *Capacity Building: An Approach to People-centred Development*, Oxfam, Oxford, UK

Roe, D., J. Mayers, M. Grieg-Gran, A. Kothari, C. Fabricius and R. Hughes (2000) *Evaluating Eden: Exploring the Myths and Realities of Community-based Wildlife Management*, Series Overview, IIED, London

Roe, E. (1993) 'Public service, rural development and careers in public management: A case study of expatriate advising and African land reform', *World Development*, vol 21(3), pp349–365

Roper, L., J. Pettit and D. Eade (eds) (2003) *Development and the Learning Organisation: Essays from* Development in Practice, Oxfam GB, Oxford, UK

Roy, A. (2002) *The Algebra of Infinite Justice*, Flamingo, London

RRA Notes/PLA Notes (1988–continuing) Nos 1–49 (from issue 50 renamed *Participatory Learning and Action*, www.planotes.org and (for orders) iied@earthprint.com), IIED, London

Rural Development Participation Review (1979–1982) Cornell University, Ithaca, NY

Sachs, W. (ed) (1992) *The Development Dictionary: A Guide to Knowledge as Power*, Zed Books, London

Samaranayake, M. (1994) 'Institutionalizing participatory approaches', Paper presented at the Dare to Share Fair, GTZ, Eschborn, Germany, 20–21 September

Samaranayake, M. (2001) 'Participatory learning approaches' in IFAD, ANGOC and IIRR (2001) *Enhancing Ownership and Sustainability: A Resource Book on Participation*, IFAD, Rome, ANGOC and IIRR, The Philippines, pp51–55

Samhungu, F. and A. Masendeke (1997) 'Scaling up: Growing up with development', *Appropriate Technology*, vol 24(3), December, pp1–3

Sarin, M. (1998) 'Community forest management: Whose participation?' in I. Guijt, I and M. K. Shah (1998) *The Myth of Community: Gender Issues in Participatory Development*, IT Publications, London, pp121–130

Saul, J. S (1973) 'Marketing co-operatives in a developing country: The Tanzania case' in L. Cliffe and J. Saul (eds) (1972) *Socialism in Tanzania: An Interdisciplinary Reader, volume 2 – Policies*, East African Publishing House, Dar es Salaam

Saxena, R. S. and S. K. Pradhan (2002) 'In search of a meaningful participatory training methodology', *PLA Notes*, vol 44, pp56–59

Scherler, C., R. Forster, O. Karkoschka and M. Kitz (eds) (1998) *Beyond the Toolkit: Experiences with Institutionalising Participatory Approaches of GTZ-supported Projects in Rural Areas*, GTZ, Eschborn, Germany, January

Schneider, A. and B. Goldfrank (2002) *Budgets and Ballots in Brazil: Participatory Budgeting from the City to the State*, IDS Working Paper 149, IDS, Sussex

Scoones, I. (1995) *Hazards and Opportunities: Farming Livelihoods in Dryland Africa – Lessons from Zimbabwe*, Zed Books, London

Scoones, I. (1997) 'Replicating islands of success', *Appropriate Technology*, vol 24(3), December, pp5–9

Scoones, I. (1998) *Sustainable Rural Livelihoods: A Framework for Analysis*, Working Paper 72, IDS, Sussex, June

Scoones, I. and J. Thompson (eds) (1994) *Beyond Farmer First: Rural People's Knowledge, Agricultural Research and Extension Practice*, Intermediate Technology Publications, London

Scott-Villiers, P. (2002) 'How the ActionAid Accountability, Learning and Planning System emerged – The struggle for organisational change', *Development in Practice*, vol 12(3), August, pp424–435; republished in L. Roper, J. Pettit and D. Eade (eds) (2003) *Development and the Learning Organisation: Essays from Development in Practice*, Oxfam GB, Oxford, UK, pp 225–241

Scott-Villiers, P. (2004) 'Personal change and responsible wellbeing' in L. Groves, L. and R. Hinton (eds) (2004) *Inclusive Aid: Power and Relationships in International Development*, Earthscan, London, pp199–209

Sellers, T. (1995) *Participatory Appraisal Workshop Proceedings*, Department of Public Health Medicine, University of Hull and East Riding, Hull, UK

Sen, A. (1981) *Poverty and Famines: An Essay on Entitlement and Deprivation*, Clarendon Press, Oxford

Sen A. (1985) *Commodities and Capabilities*, North Holland, Amsterdam

Sen A. (1993) 'Capability and well-being', in M. C. Nussbaum and A. Sen (eds) *The Quality of Life*, Oxford University Press, Oxford, pp30–53

Sen, A. (1999) *Development as Freedom*, Oxford University Press, Oxford

Senge, P. (1990) *The Fifth Discipline: The Art and Practice of the Learning Organisation*, Doubleday, New York

Seppälä, P. (1998) *Diversification and Accumulation in Rural Tanzania: Anthropological Perspectives on Village Economics*, Nordiska Afrikainstitutet, Uppsala, Sweden SEWA (Self-employed Women's Association) Academy and APNSD (Association for the

Promotion of North–South Dialogue) (2002) *'TanaVana':Warp andWeft of Life*, SEWA Academy, Ahmedabad, and APNSD, Bonn, January

Shah, A. (2001) *Who Benefits from Watershed Development? Lessons from Gujarat, India*, Gatekeeper Series 97, IIED, London

Shah, A. C. (1991) 'Shoulder tapping: A technique for training in participatory rural appraisal', *Forests. Trees and People Newsletter*, vol 14, pp14–15 (also in Iyengar and Hirway, 2001, *In the Hands of the People*, pp 103–106)

Shah, A. C. (1998) 'Challenges in influencing public policy: An NGO perspective' in J. Holland, J. with J. Blackburn (eds) (1998) *WhoseVoice? Participatory Research and Policy Change*, IT Publications, London, pp163–166

Shah, A. C. (1999) 'Unique strengths and mutilating flaws in watershed development', *Journal of Rural Development*, vol 18(4), pp613–620

Shah, A. C. (2001a) 'Clothing the naked emperor through attitude and behaviour change' in S. Iyengar and I. Hirway (eds) (2001) *In the Hands of the People: Selected Papers of Anil C. Shah*, Gujarat Institute of Development Research, Ahmedabad, Centre for Development Alternatives, Gujarat, Development Support Centre, Gujarat, pp95 –102

Shah, A. C. (2001b) 'More or less' in S. Iyengar and I. Hirway (eds) (2001) *In the Hands of the People: Selected Papers of Anil C. Shah*, Gujarat Institute of Development Research, Ahmedabad, Centre for Development Alternatives, Gujarat, Development Support Centre, Gujarat, pp237–241

Shah, A. C. (2003) *Fading Shine of Golden Decade: The Establishment Strikes Back*, Unpublished typescript, DSC, Ahmedabad

Shah, M. K. (2003) 'The road from Lathodaia: Some reflections on PRA' in A. Cornwall and G. Pratt (eds), *Pathways to Participation: Reflections on PRA*, ITDG Publishing, Rugby

Shah, M. K. and K. Bourarach (1995) *Participatory Assessment of Women's Problems and Concerns in Morocco*, Report submitted to the World Bank, Washington, DC

Shah, M. K., S. Degnan Kambou and B. Monihan (1999) *Embracing Participation in Development: Worldwide Experience from CARE's Reproductive Health Programs with a Step-by-Step Field Guide to Participatory Tools and Techniques*, CARE, Atlanta, October

Shah, P., G. Bharadwaj and R. Ambastha (1991) 'Participatory impact monitoring of a soil and water conservation programme by farmers, extension volunteer and AKRSP', *RRA Notes*, vol 13, pp127–131

Shah, P. and M. K. Shah (1995) 'Participatory methods for increased NGO accountability: A case study from India' in M. Edwards and D. Hulme (eds) (1992) *Making a Difference: NGOs and Development in a Changing World*, Earthscan Publications, London, pp183–191

Shankland, A. (2000) *Analysing Policy for Sustainable Livelihoods*, IDS Research Report 49, IDS, Sussex, September

Shanks, E. and B. Dinh Toai (2000) *Field Based Learning and Training in Participatory Approaches to Rural Development: A Decade of Experience in PRA from theVietnam Sweden Cooperation Programme and the Challenge for Formal Education, Research and Donor Organisations*, Resource paper for the Workshop on Changing Learning and Education in Forestry, Vietnam

Shaw, D. J. (2002) *Sir Hans Singer: The Life andWork of a Development Economist*, Palgrave Macmillan, Basingstoke, UK

Shepherd, A. (1998) 'Participatory environmental management: Contradiction of process, project and bureaucracy in the Himalayan foothills' in J. Blackburn with J. Holland (eds) (1998) *Who Changes? Institutionalizing Participation in Development*, IT Publications, London, pp88–99

Shetty, S. (2000) 'Why ALPS?' in ActionAid (2000) *ALPS: Accountability, Learning and Planning System*, ActionAid, London, July (available at www.actionaid.org/resources/pdfs/alps.pdf)

Shue, H. (1980) *Basic Rights – Subsistence, Affluence and US foreign Policy*, cited in Stammers, N. (1995) 'A critique of social approaches to human rights', *Human Rights Quarterly*, vol 17, pp488–508

Singer, H. (1997) 'Editorial: The golden age of the Keynsian consensus – the pendulum swings back', *World Development*, vol 25(3), pp293–295

Singh, K. (2001) 'Handing over the stick: The global spread of participatory approaches to development' in M. Edwards, M. and J. Gaventa (eds) (2001) *Global Citizen Action*, Lynne Rienner Publishers, Boulder, Colorado, pp175–187

Smith, D. R. with A. Sutherland (2002) *Institutionalizing Impact Orientation: Building a Performance Management Approach that Enhances the Impact Orientation of Research Organizations*, Natural Resources Institute, Chatham, UK

Snapp, S. and K. L. Heong (2003) 'Scaling up and out', in B. Pound, S. Snapp, C. McDougall and A. Braun (eds) (2003) *Managing Natural Resources for Sustainable Livelihoods: Uniting Science and Participation*, Earthscan, London, pp67–87

Solem, R.R (1987) *The Logical Framework Approach to Project Design, Review and Evaluation in AID: Genesis, Impact, Problems, and Opportunities*, Working Paper 99, AID, Washington, DC

Solesbury, W. (2003) *Sustainable Livelihoods: A Case Study of the Evolution of DFID Policy*, ODI Working Paper 217, ODI, London

Sones. K. R., D. Duvescog and B. Minjauw (eds) (2003) *Farmer Field Schools: The Kenyan Experience*, Report of the Farmer Field School Stakeholders' Forum, 27 March 2003, ILRI, Nairobi, FAO/KARI/ILRI, Nairobi

Stammers, N. (1995) 'A critique of social approaches to human rights', *Human Rights Quarterly*, vol 17, pp488–508

Stewart, F. and M. Wang (2003) *Do PRSPs Empower Poor Countries and Disempower the World Bank or is it the Other Way Round?*, Working Paper Number 108, Queen Elizabeth House, Oxford, UK, May

Streeten, P. (1983) 'Development dichotomies', *World Development*, vol 11(10), pp875–889

Sutherland, A. and F. Sakala (2002) 'Using visual techniques to initiate discussions on gender violence in Zambia' in A. Cornwall and A. Welbourn (eds) (2002) *Realizing Rights: Transforming Approaches to Sexual and Reproductive Well-being*, Zed Books, London, pp84–95

Swaminathan, M. S. (1996) *Challenges for Sustainable Food Security*, Plenary Address to the Second International Crops Science Congress, New Delhi

Swantz, M.-L. (1995) 'Embracing economies of women: paths to sustainable livelihoods', *Development*, vol 3, pp27–29

Swantz, M.-L. (1998) 'PRA requires change in the bureaucratic system', in D. Freling (ed) (1998) *Paths for Change: Experiences in Participation and Democratisation in Lindi and Mtwara Regions, Tanzania*, Oy Finnagro Ab, Finland, pp108–109

Swantz, M.-L., E. Ndedya and M. S. Masaiganah (2001) 'Participatory action research in southern Tanzania, with special reference to women' in P. Reason and H. Bradbury (eds) (2001) *Handbook of Action Research: Participative Inquiry and Practice*, Sage Publications, London, Thousand Oaks, California, and New Delhi, pp386–395

Swift, J. (1935, first published 1726) *Gulliver's Travels*, Oxford University Press, Oxford

Taylor, L. (1997) 'Editorial: The revival of the liberal creed – The IMF and the World Bank in a globalized economy', *World Development*, vol 25(2), pp145–152

Taylor, P. (2003) *How To Design a Training Course: A Guide to Participatory Curriculum Development*, Continuum, London and VSO, London

Taylor, P. and J. Fransman (2003) 'Learning and teaching participation in institutions of higher learning: overview', *PLA Notes: Learning and Teaching Participation*, vol 48, 5–9 December

Taylor, P. and J. Fransman (2004) *Learning and Teaching Participation in Higher Education, IDS Working Paper*, IDS, Sussex

Texeira, L. and F. Chambers (1995) *Child Support in Small Towns in the Eastern Cape*, Black Sash Advice Office, Port Elizabeth, South Africa

Thompson, J. (1995) 'Participatory approaches in government bureaucracies: Facilitating the process of institutional change', *World Development*, vol 23(9), pp1521–1554

Todaro, M. P. and S. C. Smith (2003) *Economic Development*, eighth edition, Addison Wesley, Boston

Turk, C. (2001) 'Linking participatory poverty assessments to policy and policymaking: Experience from Vietnam' in A. Norton with B. Bird, K. Brock, M. Kakande and C. Turk (eds) (2001) *A Rough Guide to PPAs: Participatory Poverty Assessment – An Introduction to Theory and Practice*, ODI, London, pp57–73

Turton, C. with M. Warner and B. Groom (1998) *Scaling Up Participatory Watershed Development in India: A Review of the Literature*, Network Paper 86, Agricultural Research and Extension Network, ODI, July

UNDP (United Nations Development Programme) (1996) *UNDP's 1996 Report on Human Development in Bangladesh: A Pro-poor Agenda, volume 3. Poor People's Perspectives*, UNDP Dhaka, Bangladesh

UNDP (1997) *Human Development Report*, Oxford University Press, New York

UNDP (2000) *Human Development Report 2000: Human Rights and Human Development*, Oxford University Press, Oxford and New York, for the United Nations Development Programme, New York

UNHCR (Office of the UN High Commissioner for Refugees) (2003) *Global Appeal 2000*, Office of the UN High Commissioner for Refugees, Geneva

UN (United Nations) (1948) *Universal Declaration of Human Rights*, adopted by the UN General Assembly, 10 December 1948, UN Doc A/810, New York

UN (1971) *Integrated Approach to Rural Development in Africa*, Social Welfare Services to Africa No 8, United Nations, New York, July

UN (1992) *The Rio Declaration on Environment and Development*, United Nations, New York

Uphoff, N. (1992) *Learning from Gal Oya: Possibilities for Participatory Development and Post–Newtonian Social Science*, Cornell University Press, Ithaca and London (paperback edition, Intermediate Technology Publications, London 1996)

Uphoff, N. (ed) (2002) *Agroecological Innovations: Increasing Food Production with Participatory Development*, Earthscan Publications, London and Sterling, VA

Vadera, M. (2003) 'Foreword' in T. Wallace and A. Kaplan (eds) *The Taking of the Horizon: Lessons from ActionAid Uganda's Experience of Changes in Development Practice*, Working Paper No 4, ActionAid, UK, pp5–7 (available from iau@actionaid.org.uk)

van den Ban, A.W. and H. S.Hawkins (1988) *Agricultural Extension*, Longman Scientific and Technical, Harlow, UK

Van Koppen, B., R. Parthasarathy and C. Safiliou (2002) *Poverty Dimensions of Irrigation Management Transfer in Large-scale Irrigation in Andra Pradesh and Gujarat*, India, Research Report 61, IWMI, Colombo

van Ufford, P. and A. K. Giri (eds) (2003) *A Moral Critique of Development: In Search of Global Responsibilities*, Routledge, London

Vaux, T. (2001) *The Selfish Altruist: Relief Work in Famine and War*, Earthscan Publications, London

Veen, J. J. (1973) 'The production system' in R. Chambers and J. Moris (eds) (1973) *Mwea: An Irrigated Rice Settlement in Kenya*, Weltforum Verlag, Munchen, pp99–131

VeneKlasen, L. with V. Miller (2002) *A New Weave of Power, People and Politics: The Action Guide for Advocacy and Citizen Participation*, World Neighbours, Oklahoma City

VERC (Village Education Resource Centre) (2002) *Shifting Millions from Open Defecation to Hygienic Latrines*, VERC, Anandapur, Savar, Dhaka, Bangladesh, verc@bangla.net, February

VIKSAT (Vikram Sarabhai Centre for Development Interaction) (2002) *Joint Forest Management in Gujarat*, VIKSAT, Ahmedabad 380-054, India

Waddington, C. H. (1977) *Tools for Thought*, Paladin, St Albans, UK

Wade, R. (2001) *The US Role in the Malaise4 at the World Bank: Get Up, Gulliver!*, Prepared for the G24 Technical Group meeting, Washington, DC, 17–18 April

Waldrop, M. M. (1994) *Complexity: The Emerging Science at the Edge of Order and Chaos*, Penguin Books, London

Wallace, T. (2003) 'Promoting change in the development work of ActionAid Uganda, Part 1' in Wallace, T. and A. Kaplan (eds) *The Taking of the Horizon: Lessons from ActionAid Uganda's Experience of Changes in Development Practice*, Working Paper No 4, ActionAid, UK, pp9–40, available from iau@actionaid.org.uk

Wallace, T. and A. Kaplan (eds) (2003) *The Taking of the Horizon: Lessons from ActionAid Uganda's Experience of Changes in Development Practice*, Working Paper No 4, ActionAid, UK (available from iau@actionaid.org.uk)

Waterston, A. (1965) *Development Planning: Lessons of Experience*, Johns Hopkins Press, Baltimore, Maryland

Watts, J., D. Horton, A. Hall, B. Douthwaite, R. Chambers and A. Costa (2003) *Institutional Learning and Change: An Introduction*, Discussion Paper 03–10, ISNAR, October

WCD (World Commission on Dams) (2000) *Dams and Development: A New Framework for Decision-making*, Report of the World Commission on Dams, Earthscan, London, and Sterling, VA, November

WCED (World Commission on Environment and Development) (1987a) *Food 2000: Global Policies for Sustainable Agriculture*, Report of the Advisory Panel on Food Security, Agriculture, Forestry and the Environment to the World Commission on Environment and Development, Zed Books, London and New Jersey

WCED (1987b) *Our Common Future: Report of the World Commission on Environment and Development*, the Brundtland Report, Oxford University Press, Oxford and New York

Welbourne, A. (1995) *Stepping Stones: A Training Package on Gender, HIV, Communication and Relationship Skills*, Manual and video, Strategies for Hope, ActionAid, London

Welbourne, A. (2002) 'Gender, sex and HIV: How to address issues that no one wants to hear about' in Cornwall, A. and A. Welbourn (eds) (2002) *Realizing Rights: Transforming Approaches to Sexual and Reproductive Well-being*, Zed Books, London, pp99–112

Welbourn, A. (2004) 'Gender, participation, health and positive thinking: A personal perspective', *Participatory Learning and Action*, no 50, pp81–87

Wheelwright, P. (1959) *Heraclitus*, Princeton University Press, Princeton, NJ

White, S. (ed) (1999) *The Art of Facilitating Participation: Releasing the Power of Grassroots Communication*, Sage, New Delhi, Thousand Oaks, London

White, S. and J. Pettit (2004) 'Participatory methods and the measurement of well-being', *Participatory Learning and Action*, no 50, pp88–96

Whyte, M. A. (1987) *Crisis and Recentralisation: 'Indigenous Development' in Eastern Uganda*, Working Paper 1987/1, Centre for African Studies, University of Copenhagen, Denmark

Widstrand, C. G. (ed) (1970) *Co-operatives and Rural Development in East Africa*, Scandinavian Institute of African Studies, Uppsala

Widstrand, C. G. (ed) (1972) *African Co-operatives and Efficiency*, Scandinavian Institute of African Studies, Uppsala

Wilken, G. C. (1987) *Good Farmers:Traditional Agricultural Resource Management in Mexico and Central America*, University of California Press, Berkeley, Los Angeles, London

Wilks, A. and F. Lefrançois (2002) *Blinding with Science or Encouraging Debate? How World Bank Analysis Determines PRSP Policies*, Bretton Woods Project, London and World Vision International, Monrovia, California

Win, E. (2004) '"If it doesn't fit on the blue square it's out!" An open letter to my donor friend' in L. Groves and R. Hinton (eds) (2004) *Inclusive Aid: Power and Relationships in International Development*, Earthscan, London, pp123–127

Wint, E. (2003) 'Social capital: red herring or right on? The Jamaican perspective', *Development in Practice*, vol 13(4), August, pp409–413

Witcombe, J. R., A. Joshi and B. R. Stharpit (1996) 'Farmer participatory crop improvement 1. Varietal selection and breeding methods and their impact on biodiversity', *Experimental Agriculture*, vol 32, pp445–460

World Bank (1988) *Rural Development:The World Bank Experience 1965–1986*, Operations Evaluation Department, World Bank, Washington, DC

World Bank (1994a) *Resettlement and Development:The Bankwide Review of Projects Involving Involuntary Resettlement*, 1986–1993, Environment Department, World Bank, Washington, DC

World Bank (1994b) *The World Bank and Participation*, Operations Policy Department, World Bank, Washington, DC, September

World Bank (1997) *World Development Report 1997:The State in a Changing World*, Oxford University Press, New York

World Bank (1998) *AIDS Assessment Study 10: Malawi*, World Bank, Washington, DC

World Bank (2000) *World Development Report 2000/2001: Attacking Poverty*, Oxford University Press for the World Bank, New York

Worsley, P. (ed) (1971) *Two Blades of Grass:Rural Cooperatives in Agricultural Modernisation*, Manchester University Press, Manchester, UK

WSPSA (Water and Sanitation Program – South Asia) (2002) *Jal Manthan:A Rural Think Tank – Igniting Change; Tackling the Sanitation Challenge*, India Country Team, Water and Sanitation Program – South Asia, 55 New Delhi, April, www.wsp.org

Yates, J. and L. Okello (2002) 'Learning from Uganda's efforts to learn from the poor: Reflections and lessons from the Uganda Participatory Poverty Assessment Project' in K. Brock and R. McGee (eds) (2002) *Knowing Poverty: Critical Reflections on Participatory Research and Policy*, Earthscan, London, pp69–98

Zhao, J. and D. Zilberman (1999) 'Irreversibility and restoration in natural resource development', *Oxford Economic Papers*, vol 51, pp559–573

Index